ALSO BY C. K. WILLIAMS

POETRY
A Day for Anne Frank
Lies
I Am the Bitter Name
The Lark. The Thrush. The Starling. (Poems from Issa)
With Ignorance
Tar
Flesh and Blood
Poems 1963–1983
Helen
A Dream of Mind
Selected Poems
The Vigil
Repair
Love About Love
The Singing

ESSAYS
Poetry and Consciousness

MEMOIR
Misgivings

TRANSLATIONS
Sophocles' Women of Trachis (with Gregory Dickerson)
The Bacchae of Euripides
Canvas, by Adam Zagajewski (translated with Renata Gorczynski and
 Benjamin Ivry)
Selected Poems of Francis Ponge (with John Montague and Margaret
 Guiton)

COLLECTED POEMS

C. K. Williams

COLLECTED

POEMS

Farrar, Straus and Giroux / *New York*

Farrar, Straus and Giroux
19 Union Square West, New York 10003

Some of the new poems in this volume originally appeared, in slightly different form, in the
following publications: *Agni Review*, *The Atlantic Monthly*, *Bat City*, *Faultline*, *The New
Yorker*, *Nightsun*, *Ontario Review*, *Poetry*, *Poetry Now* (UK), *Slate*, *The Threepenny Review*,
Tikken, and *VanGogh's Ear*. All of the new poems appeared in a limited-edition chapbook,
Creatures (Haverford, PA: Green Shade, 2006).

Library of Congress Cataloging-in-Publication Data
Williams, C. K. (Charles Kenneth), 1936–
    Collected poems / C. K. Williams.— 1st ed.
        p.   cm.
    Includes index.
    ISBN-13: 978-0-374-12652-0 (alk. paper)
    ISBN-10: 0-374-12652-6 (alk. paper)
    I. Title.

PS3573.I4483 A17 2006
811'.54—dc22

                            2005051867

www.fsgbooks.com

10 9 8 7 6 5 4 3 2 1

for
Owen and Sully and Turner

Contents

I AM THE BITTER NAME [1972]

THE LARK. THE THRUSH. THE STARLING. (POEMS FROM ISSA) [1983]

WITH IGNORANCE [1977]

TAR [1983]

FLESH AND BLOOD [1987]

I

III

A DREAM OF MIND [1992]

I

II SOME OF THE FORMS OF JEALOUSY

II

III

REPAIR [1999]

THE SINGING [2003]

I

Although the chapbook of poems from Issa, *The Lark. The Thrush. The Starling.*, was published in 1983, the group of which they are a selection was composed from 1973 to 1976, so they have been placed here before *With Ignorance*.

xx

LIES

[1969]

A Day for Anne Frank

God hates you!
                    —*St. John Chrysostom*

1.

I look onto an alley here
where, though tough weeds and flowers thrust up
through cracks and strain
toward the dulled sunlight,
there is the usual filth spilling from cans,
the heavy soot shifting in the gutters.
People come by mostly
to walk their dogs or take the shortcut
between the roaring main streets,
or just to walk
and stare up at the smoky windows,
but this morning when I looked out
children were there running back and forth
between the houses toward me.
They were playing with turtles—
skimming them down the street
like pennies or flat stones,
and bolting, shouting, after the broken corpses.
One had a harmonica, and as he ran,
his cheeks bloating and collapsing like a heart,
I could hear its bleat, and then the girls' screams
suspended behind them with their hair,
and all of them: their hard, young breath,
their feet pounding wildly on the pavement to the corner.

2.

I thought of you at that age.
Little Sister, I thought of you,

thin as a door,
and of how your thighs would have swelled
and softened like cake,
your breasts have bleached
and the new hair growing on you like song
would have stiffened and gone dark.
There was rain for a while, and then not.
Because no one came, I slept again,
and dreamed that you were here with me,
snarled on me like wire,
tangled so closely to me that we were vines
or underbrush together,
or hands clenched.

3.

They are cutting babies in half on bets.
The beautiful sergeant has enough money to drink
for a week.
The beautiful lieutenant can't stop betting.
The little boy whimpers
he'll be good.
The beautiful cook is gathering up meat
for the dogs.
The beautiful dogs
love it all.
Their flanks glisten.
They curl up in their warm kennels
and breathe.
They breathe.

4.

Little Sister,
you are a clot
in the snow,

blackened,
a chunk of phlegm
or puke
and there are men with faces
leaning over you with watercans

watering you!
in the snow, as though flowers would sprout
from your armpits
and genitals.

Little Sister,
I am afraid of the flowers sprouting from you

I am afraid of the silver petals
that crackle
of the stems darting
in the wind
of the roots

5.

The twilight rots.
Over the greasy bridges and factories,
it dissolves
and the clouds swamp in its rose
to nothing.
I think sometimes the slag heaps by the river
should be bodies
and that the pods of moral terror
men make of their flesh should split
and foam their cold, sterile seeds into the tides
like snow
or ash.

6.

Stacks of hair were there
little mountains
the gestapo children must have played in
and made love in and loved
the way children love haystacks or mountains

O God the stink
of hair oil and dandruff

their mothers must have thrown them into their tubs
like puppies and sent them to bed

coming home so filthy stinking

of jew's hair

of gold fillings, of eyelids

7.

Under me on a roof
a sparrow little by little
is being blown away.
A cage of bone is left,
part of its wings,
a stain.

8.

And in Germany the streetcar conductors go to work
in their stiff hats,
depositing workers and housewives
where they belong,
pulling the bell chains,
moving drive levers forward or back.

9.

I am saying goodbye to you before our death. Dear Father:
I am saying goodbye to you before my death. We are so
anxious to live, but all is lost—we are not allowed! I am
so afraid of this death, because little children are thrown
into graves alive. Goodbye forever.

I kiss you.

10.

Come with me, Anne.
Come,
it is awful not to be anywhere at all,
to have no one
like an old whore,
a general.

Come sit with me here
kiss me; my heart too is wounded
with forgiveness.

There is an end now.
Stay.
Your foot hooked through mine
your hand against my hand
your hip touching me lightly

it will end now
it will not begin again

Stay
they will pass
and not know us

the cold brute earth
is asleep

there is no danger

there is nothing

Anne

there is nothing

Even If I Could

Except for the little girl
making faces behind me, and the rainbow
behind her, and the school and the truck,
the only thing between you
and infinity
is me. Which is why you cover your ears
when I speak and why
you're always oozing around the edges,
clinging, trying
to go by me.

And except for my eyes and the back
of my skull, and then my hair,
the wall, the concrete
and the fire-cloud, except for them
you would see
God. And that's why rage howls in your arms
like a baby and why I can't move —
because of the thunder and the shadows
merging like oil and the smile gleaming
through the petals.

Let me tell you how sick with loneliness
I am. What can I do while the distance
throbs on my back like a hump,
or say, with stars stinging me
through the wheel? You are before me,
behind me things rattle their deaths out
like paper. The angels ride
in their soft saddles:
except for them, I would come closer
and go.

Saint Sex

there are people whose sex
keeps growing even when they're old whose
genitals swell like tumors endlessly
until they are all sex and nothing else nothing
that moves or thinks nothing
but great inward and outward handfuls of gristle

think of them men
who ooze their penises out like snail
feet whose testicles clang in their scrotums women
are like anvils to them the world an
anvil they want to take whole buildings
in their arms they want
to come in the windows to run antennas
through their ducts like ramrods and women
these poor women who dream and dream of
the flower they can't sniff it sends buds
into their brain they feel their neural
river clot with moist fingers the ganglia
hardening like ant eggs the ends
burning off

pity them these people there are no wars
for them there is no news no
summer no reason they are so humble they want
nothing they have no hands or faces
pity them at night whispering I love
you to themselves and during the day how they
walk along smiling and suffering pity
them love them they are
angels

The Long Naked Walk of the Dead

for Arthur Atkins

As long as they trample the sad smiles of guitars
the world won't burn. The mother speaks to her daughter
and explains: it is the breath of money in the trees
that drives angels; it is the stillness from morning
to morning when the horses of life have fallen
under their traces in the street and shudder and vanish.

It is the man who meets no one who will touch us
with sharp hands that shake over the concrete
like branches. Or the songs muttering on the paths
crisscrossing the grasses. A bench leaning back.
The sweet arms of gardeners. An enemy passing
with sons and grandsons, all just soldiers.

In flesh that only moves and speaks, the players
slide out like empty trailers to the temple country.
Six hundred thousand on the mountain when it opened.
Every word of the scream, six hundred thousand faces.
The dark metal man gleaming in the talons of silence.
Halfway down in the house of suffering, it is starting.

In There

Here I am, walking along your eyelid again
toward your tear duct. Here are your eyelashes
like elephant grass and one tear
blocking the way like a boulder.

It probably takes me a long time
to figure it out, chatting with neighbors,
trying penicillin, steam baths, meditation
on the Shekinah and sonnet cycles

and then six more months blasting
with my jackhammer before I get in there
and can wander through your face, meeting you
on the sly, kissing you from this side.

I am your own personal verb now. Here I come,
"dancing," "loving," "making poems."
I find a telescope
and an old astronomer

to study my own face with,
and then, well, I am dreaming behind your cheekbone
about Bolivia and tangerines and the country
and here I come again, along your eyelid, walking.

Loss

In this day and age Lord
you are like one of those poor farmers
who burns the forests off
and murders his land and then
can't leave and goes sullen and lean
among the rusting yard junk, the scrub
and the famished stock.

Lord I have felt myself raked
into the earth like manure,
harrowed and plowed under,
but I am still enough like you
to stand on the porch
chewing a stalk or drinking
while tall weeds come up dead
and the house dogs, snapping
their chains like moths, howl
and point towards the withering
meadows at nothing.

The Hard Part

Do you remember when we dreamed about the owl
and the skeleton, and the shoe
opened and there was the angel
with his finger in the book, his smile like chocolate?

And remember? Everything that had been crushed
or burned, we changed back.
We turned the heart around
in the beginning, we closed the blossom, we let the drum go.

But you're missing now. Every night I feel us crying
together, but it's late—
the white bear and the lawyer
are locking the house up and where are you?

The wind walking, the rock turning over with worms
stuck to its haunches—
how will I know what loves me now
and what doesn't? How will I forgive you?

The World's Greatest Tricycle-Rider

The world's greatest tricycle-rider
is in my heart, riding like a wildman,
no hands, almost upside down along
the walls and over the high curbs
and stoops, his bell rapid firing,
the sun spinning in his spokes like a flame.

But he is growing older. His feet
overshoot the pedals. His teeth set
too hard against the jolts, and I am afraid
that what I've kept from him is what
tightens his fingers on the rubber grips
and drives him again and again on the same block.

The Sorrow

with huge jowls that wobble with sad o
horribly sad eyes with bristles with
clothes torn tie a rag hands trembling this
burnt man in my arms won't listen he
struggles pulls loose and is going
and I am crying again Poppa Poppa it's me Poppa
but it's not it's not me I am not
someone who with these long years will
so easily retreat I am not someone after
these torments who simply cries so
I am not so unquestionably a son or
even daughter or have I face or voice
bear with me perhaps it was me who
went away perhaps I did dream it and give
birth again it doesn't matter now I stay
in my truck now I am loaded with
fruit with cold bottles with documents
of arrest and execution Father do you
remember me? how I hid and cried to you?
how my lovely genitals were bound up?
I am too small again my voice thins my
small wrists won't hold the weight again
what is forgiven? am I forgiven again?

The Man Who Owns Sleep

The man who owns sleep
is watching the prisoners being beaten
behind the fence.
His eye pressed to the knothole,
he sees the leather curling into smiles
and snapping, he sees the intricate geography
of ruined backs,
the faces propped
open like suitcases
in the sunlight.

Who is this man
who's cornered the market
on sleeping?
He's not quite finished.
He bends over with a hand on his knee
to balance him
and from the other side they see
that clear eye in the wall
watching unblinking.
They see it has slept,

prisoners and guards: it drives them
to frenzies. The whips hiccup
and shriek. Those dead already roll over
and rub their retinas into the pebbles.
The man who owns sleep has had it.
He's tired.
Taking an ice-cream cone
from the little wagon
he yawns and licks it.
Walking away, he yawns, licking it.

Before This

we got rid of the big people
finally we took grandpa and put half
on the mack truck and half on
the bottom grandma
we locked in with her watches
mommy and daddy had to be cut apart but they
are in separate icebergs you can't
see them under
the red lid

one place or another they are all gone
and it's hard to remember
cars? furcoats? the office?
now all there are
are roomfuls of children sleeping as far
as you can see little mattresses and
between them socks balled up and
underwear and scuffed shoes
with their mouths open.

but how am I here? I feel
my lips move I count breaths I hear somebody
cry out MOTHER HELP ME somebody's hand
touches me peacefully across boundaries
kiss? hit? die? the blankets
harden with urine the fuzz
thins holes come
HOW AM I HERE? MOTHER
HOW AM I HERE?

Dimensions

There is a world somewhere else that is unendurable.
Those who live in it are helpless in the hands of elements,
they are like branches in the deep woods in wind
that whip their leaves off and slice the heart of the night
and sob. They are like boats bleating wearily in fog.

But here, no matter what, we know where we stand.
We know more or less what comes next. We hold out.
Sometimes a dream will shake us like little dogs, a fever
hang on so we're not ourselves or love wring us out,
but we prevail, we certify and make sure, we go on.

There is a world that uses its soldiers and widows
for flour, its orphans for building stone, its legs for pens.
In that place, eyes are softened and harmless like God's
and all blend in the traffic of their tragedy and pass by
like people. And sometimes one of us, losing the way,
will drift over the border and see them there, dying,
laughing, being revived. When we come home, we are half way.
Our screams heal the torn silence. We are the scars.

To Market

suppose I move a factory
in here in my head in my
breast in my left hand I'm moving
dark machines in with gear boxes
and floaters and steel cams
that turn over and start things
I'm moving in fibers through
my left nostril and trucks
under my nipples and the union
has its bathroom where I think
and the stockbroker his desk
where I love

and then if I started turning
out goods and opening
shops with glass counters and rugs
what if I said
to you this is how men live and I
want to would you believe me
and love me I have my little
lunch box and my thermos and
I walk along like one leg
on the way to work swearing
I love you and we have lunch
behind the boiler and I promise
I love you and meanwhile the oil
flowing switches steam wrenches
metal I love
you and things finish get shined
up packed in streamers
mailed and I love you
meanwhile all this while I love
you and I'm being bought pieces
of me at five dollars

and parts at ten cents and
here I am still saying I love
you under the stacks under
the windows with wires the smoke
going up I love
you I love you

What Is and Is Not

I'm a long way from that place,
but I can still hear
the impatient stamp of its hoof
near the fire, and the green clicking
of its voices and its body flowing.

At my window, the usual spirits,
the same silence. A child would see it
as my clothes hanging like killers
on the door, but I don't, and it
doesn't creak in the hallway for me.

It's not death. In your face
I glimpse it. You are reaching
a hand out comfortingly
though it snarls, plunges,
and you know that the baby

won't look up from its game
of beauty. It isn't love or hate
or passion. It doesn't touch us,
dream us, speak, sing or
come closer, yet we consume it.

Hood

Remember me? I was the one
in high school you were always afraid of.
I kept cigarettes in my sleeve, wore
engineer's boots, long hair, my collar
up in back and there were always
girls with me in the hallways.

You were nothing. I had it in for you—
when I peeled rubber at the lights
you cringed like a teacher.
And when I crashed and broke both lungs
on the wheel, you were so relieved
that you stroked the hard Ford paint
like a breast and your hands shook.

On the Roof

The trouble with me is that whether I get love or not
I suffer from it. My heart always seems to be prowling
a mile ahead of me, and, by the time I get there to surround it,
it's chewing fences in the next county, clawing
the bank-vault wall down or smashing in the window
I'd just started etching my name on with my diamond.

And that's how come I end up on the roof. Because even if I talk
into my fist everyone still hears my voice like the ocean
in theirs, and so they solace me and I have to keep
breaking toes with my gun-boots and coming up here
to live—by myself, like an aerial, with a hand on the ledge,
one eye glued to the tin door and one to the skylight.

It Is This Way with Men

They are pounded into the earth
like nails; move an inch,
they are driven down again.
The earth is sore with them.
It is a spiny fruit
that has lost hope
of being raised and eaten.
It can only ripen and ripen.
And men, they too are wounded.
They too are sifted from their loss
and are without hope. The core
softens. The pure flesh softens
and melts. There are thorns, there
are the dark seeds, and they end.

Sleeping Over

for Dave and Mark Rothstein

There hasn't been any rain
since I arrived. The lawns
are bleached and tonight goldenrod
and burnt grass reflect
across my walls like ponds.
After all these days
the textures and scents of my room
are still strange and comforting.
The pines outside, immobile
as chessmen, fume turps
that blend with the soap taste
of the sheets and with the rot
of camphor and old newspapers
in the bare bureau drawers.
Jarred by a headlight's glare
from the country road, the crumbling
plaster swarms with shadows.
The bulb in the barn, dull
and eternal, sways and flickers
as though its long drool
of cobwebs had been touched,
and the house loosens, unmoors,
and, distending and shuddering, rocks
me until I fall asleep.

In December the mare
I learned to ride on died.
On the frozen paddock hill,
down, she moaned all night
before the mink farmers
came in their pickup
truck, sat on her dark
head and cut her throat.

I dream winter. Shutters
slamming apart. Bags
crammed with beer bottles
tipping against clapboard.
Owls in chimneys.
Drafts; thieves; snow.
Over the crusty fields
scraps of blue loveletters
mill wildly like children,
and a fat woman, her rough
stockings tattered away
at a knee, sprints in high,
lumbering bounds among
the skating papers. Out
to the road—red hydrant,
bus bench, asphalt—
a wasp twirling at her feet,
she is running back.

My first kiss was here.
I can remember the spot—
next to a path, to
a cabin, a garden patch—
but not how it happened
or what I felt, except
amazement that a kiss
could be soundless. Now,
propped on an elbow,
I smoke through the dawn, smudging
the gritty sheets with ash.

Day finally. The trees
and fences clarify, unsnarl.
Flagstones, coins, splash
across the driveway crowns
and the stark underbrush
animals go away.
A rickety screen door bangs,

slaps its own echo
twice. No footsteps
but someone is out sifting
ashes in the garbage pit.
Suddenly dishes jangle
the bright middle distances
and the heat begins again:
by now the ground must be
hard and untillable as ice.
Far off from the house,
the lake, jellied with umber
weed scum, tilts toward
the light like a tin tray.
Dead rowboats clog
the parched timber dam
and along the low banks
the mounds of water rubble
I gathered yesterday
have dried and shrunk down
to a weak path wobbling
back and forth from the edge.

The Other Side

Across the way hands
move nervously on curtains,
and behind them, radiated
with arc light, silver,
there is almost no face.
Almost no eyes look at me through this air.
Almost no mouth twists
and repeats, following my mouth, the shrill ciphers
that cross like swallows.

Tonight the breeze from the distillery
stinks of death. Do you think men have died
in the vats tonight? Everyone waits,
sick with the stench of mash
and spirits, and the tubs lick
their own sides with little splashes,
little bubbles that pop, clearing themselves.

In this breeze, it is strange to be telling myself,
Life, what are you saying?
In this breeze, almost like hands, words
climb on the thin gauze of curtains
and drop. Men float
from corner to corner, and, almost like hands,
birds put their sore wings under the eaves
and sleep.

Of What Is Past

I hook my fingers into the old tennis court fence
and kneel down in an overgrowth of sharp weeds
to watch the troopers in their spare compound drill.

Do you remember when this was a park? When girls
swung their rackets here in the hot summer mornings
and came at night to open their bodies to us?

Now gun-butts stamp the pale clay like hooves.
Hard boots gleam.
And still, children play tag and hide-and-seek

beyond the barriers. Lovers sag in the brush.
It's not them, it's us: we know too much.
Soon only the past will know what we know.

Ashes Ashes We All Fall Down

how come when grandpa is teaching the little boy
to sing he can't no matter what remember even
though he taps time hard with his teeth like a cricket even
though he digs in hard with his fingers how come?

and when he grows tall he will name everyone
he meets father or mother but will still have no songs
he leans back among the cold pages he falls down
in the palace of no sleep where the king cries and

in the new country the musical soldiers will
beat him he will sell silver consonants out
of his car the lady will cup his dry testicles
in the drone the soldiers beat him again

I miss you now can you
remember the words at least? and the
new name? when pain comes
you must kill it when beauty comes

with her smiles you must kill them I
miss you again I miss you white
bug I miss you sorrow rain radio I miss
you old woman in my bible in the dream

Trappers

In the dark with an old song
I sit, in the silence,
and it knows me
by heart and comes faltering
gently through me
like a girl in love,
in a room, evening,
feeling her way.

When mountain men
were snowed in for months
in the Rockies, sleet
hissing over the sharp crust
to hollow places, branches
groaning through the night,
they must have done what I do
now, and been as terrified.

I let a word out,
and what comes, an awful drone,
a scab, bubbles up
and drills away unfadingly.
Later, in a place far
from here, feeling softly on her neck
like a fly, she will gaze
into the sunlight, and not see me.

Being Alone

Never on one single pore Eternity
have I been touched by your snows

or felt your shy mouth tremble,
your breath break on me

like the white wave. I have not felt
your nakedness tear me

with hunger or your silver hands
betray me but today I promise

whatever flower of your house
should bloom I will stay

locked to its breast.
Like little fish who live

harmlessly under the bellies of sharks,
I will go where you go,

drift inconspicuously
in the raw dredge of your power

like a leaf, a bubble of carrion,
a man who has understood and does not.

Trash

I am your garbage man. What you leave,
I keep for myself, burn or throw
on the dump or from scows in the delicious river.
Your old brown underpants are mine now,
I can tell from them
what your dreams were. I remember
how once in a closet with shoes
whispering and mothballs, you held on
and cried like a woman. Your nights stink
of putrid lampshades, of inkwells and silk
because my men and I with our trails
of urine and soft eggs and our long brooms
hissing, came close.

What do they do with kidneys and toes
in hospitals? And where did your old dog go
who peed on the rug and growled?
They are at my house now, and what grinds
in your wife's teeth while she sleeps
is mine. She is chewing
on embryos, on the eyes of your lover,
on your phone book and the empty glass
you left in the kitchen. And in your body,
the one who died there and rots
secretly in the fingers of your spirit,
she is hauling his genitals out, basket
after basket
and mangling all of it in the crusher.

Giving It Up

It is an age
of such bestial death
that even before we die
our ghosts go.
I have felt mine while I slept
send shoots over my face,
probing some future char
there, tasting the flesh
and the sweat
as though for the last time.

And I have felt him
extricate himself and go,
crying, softening himself
and matching his shape
to new bodies; merging,
sliding into souls,
into motors, buildings,
stop signs, policemen—
anything.

By morning, he is back.
Diminished, shorn
of his light, he lies crumpled
in my palm, shivering
under my breath like cellophane.
And every day
there is nothing to do
but swallow him like a cold
tear
and get on with it.

For Gail, When I Was Five

My soul is out back eating your soul.
I have you tied in threads like a spider
and I am drinking down your laughter
in huge spoonfuls. It is like tinsel.
It sprays over the crusty peach baskets
and the spades hung on pegs. It is like air
and you are screaming, or I am, and we are
in different places with wild animal faces.

What does God do to children who touch
in the darkness of their bodies and laugh?
What does he think of little underpants
that drift down on the hose like flowers?
God eats your soul, like me. He drinks
your laughter. It is God in the history
of my body who melts your laughter
and spits it in the wounds of my life like tears.

Don't

I have been saying what I have to say
for years now, backwards and forwards
and upside down and you haven't heard
it yet, so from now on
I'm going to start unsaying it:
I'm going to unsay what I've said already
and what everyone else has said
and what hasn't even been said yet.

I'm going to unsay
the northern hemisphere
and the southern,
east and west, up
and down, the good
and the bad. I'm going to unsay
what floats just over my skin
and just under: the leaves
and the roots, the worm
in the river and the whole river
and the ocean and the ocean
under the ocean. Space
and light are going,
silence, sound, flags,
photographs, dollar bills:
the sewer people and the junk people,
the money people and the concrete people
who ride out of town on dreams
and love it, and the dreams,
even the one pounding
under the floor like a drum—
I'm going to run them all down
again the other way
and end at the bottom.

Do you see? Caesar is unsaid
now. Christ
is unsaid. They trade toys
but it's too late.
The doctor is unsaid, cured;
the rubber sheet grows
leaves, luscious and dark,
and the patient feels them
gathering at the base
of his spine like a tail.
It is unsaid
that we have no tails—
an old lady twirls hers
and lifts
like a helicopter.

Time turns
backwards in its womb and floats out
in its unsaying.
It won't start again.
The sad physicist
throws switches but all
the bomb does is sigh inwardly
and hatch like an egg,
and little void-creatures
come, who live
in the tones between notes,
innocent and unstruck.

A baby fighting for air
through her mother's breast
won't anymore: the air is unsaid.
The skeleton I lost in France
won't matter. No picnics,
no flattened grass,
no bulls.

Everything washes up,
clean as morning.
My wife's wet underwear in the sink—
I unsay them,
they swallow me
like a Valentine.
The icebox is growing baby green
lima beans for Malcolm Lowry.
The house fills with love.
I chew perfume
and my neighbor kissing me good morning
melts and goes out
like a light.

There is bare rock
between here and the end.
There is a burnt place
in the silence.

Along my ribs, dying of old age,
the last atom dances
like a little girl. I unsay
her yellow dress, her hair,
her slippers
but she keeps dancing,
jumping back and forth
from my face to my funny bone
until I burst out laughing.

And then I unsay
the end.

Just Right

the way we get under cars and in
motors you'd think we were made for them our hands
slotting in the carbs our feet
on the pedals and how everything
even flowers even the horns of cattle fits
just right it is like nail and hole
even apples even hand grenades with indentations
for our fingers and the detonations patterns finding us
all this given and how ungrateful we are
dreaming that someday we won't touch anything
that all this space will close on us
the fire sprout through us and blossom and
the tides

dear father of the fire save me enough room please
and dear water-mother I'd like two clear drops
to float in brothers and sisters I'll need
your engines and computers I'll need four tall buildings
and heaters and strong-bulldozers with
thick treads and switches and there must be
uniforms
there must be maps and hoses and
tiled rooms to drain the blood off
and will your voices
come telling me you love me? and your mouths
and hands? and your cold
music? every inch of me? every
hour of me?

After That

Do you know how much pain is left
in the world? One tiny bit of pain is left,
braised on one cell like a toothmark.
And how many sorrows there still are? Three sorrows:
the last, the next to the last and this one.

And there is one promise left, feeling
its way through the poison, and one house
and one gun and one shout of agony
that wanders in the lost cities and the lost mountains.
And so this morning, suffering the third sorrow

from the last, feeling pain in my last gene,
cracks in the struts, bubbles in the nitro,
this morning for someone I'm not even sure exists
I waste tears. I count down by fractions
through the ash. I howl. I use everything up.

Ten Below

It is bad enough crying for children
suffering neglect and starvation in our world
without having on a day like this
to see an old cart horse covered with foam,
quivering so hard that when he stops
the wheels still rock slowly in place
like gears in an engine.
A man will do that, shiver where he stands,
frozen with false starts,
just staring,
but with a man you can take his arm,
talk him out of it, lead him away.

What do you do when both hands
and your voice are simply goads?
When the eyes you solace see space,
the wall behind you, the wisp of grass
pushing up through the curb at your feet?
I have thought that all the animals
we kill and maim, if they wanted to
could stare us down, wither us
and turn us to smoke with their glances—
they forbear because they pity us,
like angels, and love of something else
is why they suffer us and submit.

But this is Pine Street, Philadelphia, 1965.
You don't believe
in anything divine being here.
There is an old plug with a worn blanket
thrown on its haunches. There is a wagon
full of junk—pipes and rotted sinks,
the grates from furnaces—and there
is a child walking beside the horse

with sugar, and the mammoth head lowering,
delicately nibbling from those vulnerable
fingers. You can't cut your heart out.
Sometimes, just what is, is enough.

Tails

there was this lady once she used to grow
snakes in her lap

they came up like tulips
from her underpants and the tops
of her stockings and she'd get us
with candy and have us pet
the damned things

god they were horrible skinned
snakes all dead
it turned out she'd catch
them in the garden and skin
them and drive
knitting needles up along the spines
and sew them on
it stank
the skins rotting in the corner heads
scattered all over the floor

it turned out she loved
children she wanted
to do something
for us we ate
the candy of course we touched
the snakes we
hung around god
we hated her she was
terrible

Sky, Water

for Bruce and Fox McGrew

They can be fists punching the water—
muskrats, their whole bodies plunging
through weak reeds from the bank,
or the heads of black and white ducks
that usually flicker in quietly
and come up pointing heavenwards.

A man can lie off the brown scum of a slough
and watch how they'll go in like blades,
deeply, to the bottom,
and in his pale silence
with the long field furrows strumming
like distant music,
he will wonder at and pity
the creatures hooked together like flowers on the water,
who will die flashing in the air,
shaken in the beak of sunlight.

The surface tainted with small blood,
there can be bees and water hydra,
sea-grasses and blown seed,
and before a man's eyes life and death,
silence and the dim scream of love
can rise and furl up
from the bottom like smoke
and thin away.

Downwards

This is the last day of the world. On the river docks
I watch for the last time the tide get higher
and chop in under the stinking pilings. How the small creatures
who drift dreaming of hands and lungs must sting,
rotting alive in the waste spill, coming up dead
with puffy stomachs paler than the sky or faces.
There is deep fire fuming ash to the surface.
It is the last tide and the last evening and from now
things will strive back downwards.
A fish thrown up will gasp in the flare
and flop back hopelessly through the mud flats to the water.
The last man, an empty bottle with no message, is here, is me,
and I am rolling, fragile as a bubble in the upstream spin,
battered by carcasses, drawn down by the lips of weeds
to the terrible womb of torn tires and children's plastic shoes
and pennies and urine. I am no more, and what is left,
baled softly with wire, floating
like a dark pillow in the hold of the brown ship, is nothing.
It dreams. Touching fangs delicately with cranes
and forklifts, it rests silently in its heavy ripening.
It stands still on the water, rocking, blinking.

Shells

It's horrible, being run over by a bus
when all you are is a little box turtle.
You burst. Your head blasts out like a cork
and soars miles
to where the boy sprawls on the grass strip
beside the sidewalk. In mid-air
you are him. Your face touches his face,
you stutter, and you will go all your life
holding your breath,
wondering what you meant.

                    He forgets now
but he knew it in his cheek scorched
by the sweet blades and in his wild groin.
In his mother's arms, screaming,
he knew it: that he was crossing
under the laughter and there was the other voice
sobbing, It's not far, It's not far.

Beyond

Some people,
they just don't hate enough yet.
They back up, snarl, grab guns
but they're like children,
they overreach themselves;
they end up standing there feeling stupid,
wondering if it's worth it.

Some people, they don't have a cause yet.
They just throw their hate here and there
and sooner or later it's hollow
and they say, What is this?
and after that it's too late.
After that you can barely
button your sleeve in the morning—
you just take breaths.

Some people are too tired to hate
and so they think, Why live?
They read the papers, wince,
but they're hardly there anymore.
You go by them in the street
and they don't spit or mutter—
they look at themselves in store windows,
they touch their faces.

Some people, you give up
on them. You let them go,
you lose them.
They were like children, they hardly
knew what they meant. You think to yourself,
Good Riddance.

Patience Is When You Stop Waiting

I stand on the first step under the torn mouths of hours
in a new suit. Terrified of the arched webs and the dust,
of my speech, my own hair slicked with its thin pride,
I jut like a thorn; I turn, my pain turns and closes.

Tell me again about silence. Tell me I won't,
not ever, hear the cold men whispering in my pores
or the mothers and fathers who scream in the bedroom
and throw boxes of money between them and kiss.

At the window, faces hover against the soft glow
like names. If I cry out, it will forget me and go;
if I don't, nothing begins again. Tell me
about mercy again, how she rides in eternity's arms

in the drifts and the dreams come. The night is dying.
Wisely it thinks of death as a thing born of desire.
Gently it opens its sharp ribs and bites through
and holds me. Tell me about my life again, where it is now.

Faint Praise

for Jim Moss, 1935–1961

Whatever last slump of flesh
rolls like a tongue in the mouth of your grave,
whatever thin rags of your underwear
are melting in slow, tiny stomachs,
I am still here; I have survived.

I thought when you died that your angels,
stern, dangerous bats with cameras and laws,
would swarm like bees
and that the silences flaming from you
would fuse me like stone.

There were no new landscapes I could prepare for you.
I let you go.
And tonight, again, I will eat, read,
and my wife and I will move into love
in the swells of each other like ships.
The loose aerial outside will snap,
the traffic lights blink and change,
the dried lives of autumn crackle like cellophane.

And I will have my life still.
In the darkness, it will lie over against me,
it will whisper, and somehow,
after everything, open to me again.

Halves

I am going to rip myself down the middle into two pieces
because there is something in me that is neither
the right half nor the left half nor between them.
It is what I see when I close my eyes, and what I see.

As in this room there is something neither ceiling
nor floor, not space, light, heat or even
the deep skies of pictures, but something that beats softly
against others when they're here and others not here,

that leans on me like a woman,
curls up in my lap and walks
with me to the kitchen or out of the house altogether
to the street—I don't feel it, but it beats and beats;

so my life: there is this, neither before me
nor after, not up, down, backwards nor forwards from me.
It is like the dense, sensory petals in a breast
that sway and touch back. It is like the mouth of a season,

the cool speculations bricks murmur, the shriek in orange,
and though it is neither true nor false, it tells me
that it is quietly here, and, like a creature, is in pain;
that when I ripen it will crack open the locks, it will love me.

Penance

I only regret the days wasted in no pain.
I am sorry for having touched bottom
and loved again.
I am sorry for the torn sidewalks
and the ecstasy underneath, for the cars,
the old flower-lady watching her fingers,
my one shoe in the morning
with death on its tongue.

In the next yard a dog whines
and whines for his lost master
and for the children who have gone
without him. I am sorry
because his teeth click on my neck,
because my chest shudders and the owl cries
in the tug of its fierce sacrament.

I repent God and children,
the white talons of peace and my jubilance.
Everything wheels
in the iron rain, smiling and lying.
Forgive me, please.

It Is Teeming

In rain like this what you want is an open barn door
to look out from. You want to see the deep hoofprints
in the yard fill and overflow, to smell the hay and hear
the stock chewing and stamping and their droppings pattering.

Of course the messengers would come away. A wet mutt,
his underlip still crisp with last night's chicken blood,
will drift through the gate and whine and nuzzle
your knee with a bad look like a secret drinker,

and you will wish for the lions, the claws that erected
and slashed back, because you are tired of lording it,
of caving ribs in, of swinging axes and firing.
Where are the angels with trucks who pulled the trees down?

Now it is pure muck, half cowshit, half mud and blood, seething.
You have to go out back, dragging it, of course. No one
sees you with it. The rain—you throw wakes up like a giant.
The way you wanted it, the way it would be, of course.

From Now On

for Murray Dessner

this knowledge so innocently it goes this sin
it dies without looking back it ripens
and dissolves and behind it behind
january behind bread and trenches there
are rooms with no gods in them there are breasts
with no deaths anymore and no promises
I knew mercy would leave me and turn
back I knew things in their small nests would
want me and say Come and things blossoming
say Go Downwards but still am I no bigger
than one man? not a pint more? a
watt? a filament of pity or sweetness? I turn
over first one side heads and then tails
I love life first then death first I
close I open I split down like an amoeba
into bricks and sunrise and longing
but we are suffering seven directions at once
the mouths in our mouths don't tell us
the sorrowful faces in our tears not
touch us nothing holds us nothing reaps
us we are not lived we are not suffered
the dreams come for us but they fail

I AM THE BITTER NAME

[1972]

I Am the Bitter Name

And Abraham said to him, "And art thou, indeed, he that is called Death?"
He answered, and said, "I am the Bitter Name."

the little children have been fighting
a long long time for their beloved country
their faces are hardening like meat
left out their bodies squashed flat
like flowers in lawbooks don't fit
with the keys to eternal sorrow anymore
is the best toy always death? everyone
crying in the sleepy hair inexhaustible
agony in the dark cups of the skull
unquenchable agony your hands shriek
on my spine like locked brakes in
the torn nostrils tendrils in the mouth
vines the little soldiers play
wounding the little generals play hurt
forever they sharpen things they put
things in things they pull them out
will you make freedom for me? in
the cheekbone fire in the lips my
justice is to forget being here my liberty
wanting to hate them how they are shipped
home in ice-cream bags and being able to

Keep It

the lonely people are marching
on the capital everyone's yelling not
to give them anything but just
buying dinner together was fun
wasn't it? don't give them a thing
the boss said the boss
is dreaming of beautiful nurses
the lonely people are taking
all their little dogs to washington
back home the channels change
by themselves the soap changes
to perfume perfume to cereal the boss
dreams of the moon landing on
spruce street nobody is lonely
on locust nobody is left
at all the sun comes by himself
the buses go along by themselves
and wonder have I told you about
my disease? the lonely people
hold tight at night
on the coast they are tucked
in under the twilight
together the boss walks
across them it was fun it was
so much fun wasn't it?

The Spirit the Triumph

do you remember learning to tie your shoes?
astonishing! the loops you had to make the delicate
adjustments the pulling-through tightening impossible!
the things we learn!
putting a bridle on a horse when he's head-shy
getting your hands under a girl's sweater
no wonder we are the crown of all that exists
we can do anything how we climb chimneys
how we put one foot on the gas one on the clutch
and make the car go nothing too difficult nothing!

crutches artificial arms have you seen that?
how they pick their cups up and use razors? amazing!
and the wives shine it for them at night
they're sleeping the wives take it out of the room
and polish it with its own special rag
it's late they hold it against their bellies
the leather laces dangle into their laps
the mechanisms slip noiselessly
lowering the hook softly onto their breasts
we men! aren't we something? I mean
we are worth thinking about aren't we?
we are the end we are the living end

Madder

"People can screw dead bodies, but they never feed them."

the nations have used up their desire
the cunts of the mothers the cunts
of the bad daughters stinking
of police stations of the sisters
and generations of men saying
look cunt what about me saying look
cunt how I'm bleeding saying cunt cunt
where is forgiveness? what bullshit

you can kiss me goodbye but first put
your hands up let me search you
first goodbye I'll check your rectum
for poison and recite how we spoiled
from the inside like lettuce I'll tell
about freedom vomited on our foreheads
I'll say LOOK WHAT YOU DID and men
reading money aloud laughing aloud

I'm fed up with the sugars of raw
human flesh cursing I gallop over her
with my nicked tongue head to toe
I plow in with my notched cock cursing
the suffering of labels the
suffering of elegant canned goods of
mercy vengeance witness borne
for no end the governments are silent

or I'm dying of grief and loving both
ends of it or of solace and mixing
up whether we're here at all and revenge
or peace and who did it first dear
husbands dear wives tighter they're
washing my mouth out with soap I promise
not to accuse you but this time you
be the secret this time you comfort me

Poor Hope

which is worse the lieutenant raising his rifle
toward the astonished women and children jammed
into the bomb crater raising it not even aiming just carelessly
beginning to do it the way you'd rake a lawn you start
anywhere that or when I saw a boy in a department store
with his mother he was skipping along going toot toot toot
when the mother saw me I could see her flinch about something
and when I passed them she cracked him him! not me
across the mouth stunning him terribly hissing
don't you know where you are? which is worse
to be in the world with that or with that? or is it
that there's god and you think they've killed him?
then the dread god did you really say hit them! kill them!
then to the children then the mothers forgive me then myself then
nothing no sacrament for the people forgotten
in mid-sentence gone except in fuck you! where they cry god
I have thought two ways up the first
is when I felt the boy's spirit become pain because of me
I should have apologized not to him or even the mother
but to YOU! I'm sorry and the other is for the others
in the ditch in their torn clothes just as the bullets go into them
I would go mad and have you seen how men in toilets
at stadiums or the movies stare into the wall
so we won't covet each other's cocks? I would stare
into you like that and never move again never let you die
again never let you be anywhere else staring watching
you boil helplessly back and forth on the ceiling
don't move! trying to electrocute yourself on the wires
stay where you are! trying to slice your body
to pieces on the fluttering cobwebs don't die on me!

Bringing It Home

a room all the way across america
and a girl in the room and the plastic fattening her breasts
starting to sag o god
she thinks they're going o god o god
I would do anything to help her
I would take all of her secret pain onto myself if she'd let me
my best darling
it is your soul melting it
it is the fire in you

I remember fire
everywhere in the world
boys scratching two sticks together so proud of themselves
houses going up in spontaneous combustion or somebody using his
        lighter
and the girl locked in in back still touching her fearful body
(you too my best darling)
and furnaces men with sweat stung out of them
faces cooked broiled smoked while they make things for us

and in america
in her breasts the two fires
like gods the two fires without flame
and her voice this flame rising out of my throat
it says FUCK YOU I DON'T CARE
it says UP YOUR ASS TOO YOU WEIRD FAGGOTS
my best darling my best darling

The Little Shirt

what we need is one of those gods
who comes howling down streets
like a police car into the houses into
the television sets the refrigerators
comes oozing through everything and eats
everything everything the whole box
the darkness the dust
under the stairs the roaches and then us
and then makes us up again
out of her wonderful mouth earth
so that we look into our friends suddenly understanding
flesh how it tightens and lets go
to have this pass through
to be able to blink so that it goes through
to be able to get back from this
so mother death will be happy
so we won't hurt her she
keeps her big hand on us her thighs over our heads
she jumps we fall out like apples
and having to own her
and having to have war for her and fucking
and thankfulness so she won't stink in her people
we believe her
cloudlife airlife scent the
flavors to lick off
going up firing back at ourselves
make me sergeant! get me a hard-on!
to kill
never to go from this

Clay out of Silence

chances are we will sink quietly back
into oblivion without a ripple
we will go back into the face
down through the mortars as though it hadn't happened

earth: I'll remember you
you were the mother you made pain
I'll grind my thorax against you for the last time
and put my hand on you again to comfort you

sky: could we forget?
we were the same as you were
we couldn't wait to get back sleeping
we'd have done anything to be sleeping

and trees angels for being thrust up here
and stones for cracking in my bare hands
because you foreknew
there was no vengeance for being here

when we were flesh we were eaten
when we were metal we were burned back
there was no death anywhere but now
when we were men when we became it

Innings

somebody keeps track of how many times
I make love don't you god don't you?
and how good it is telling me
it's marked down where I can't see
right underneath me so the next time
something unreal happens in the papers
I don't understand it it doesn't touch
me I start thinking
everyone's heart might be pure
after all because what the hell
they don't kill me just each other
they don't actually try making me sad
just do things make things happen
suffer things I erupt
into the feminine like a lion don't
I god? among doves? so even being with me
is like beauty? I move under this god
like a whore I gurgle I roll
like a toy boat what's the score
now god? am I winning?

Becoming Somebody Else

your lists of victims dear
god like rows of sharp little teeth
have made me crazy look
I have crushed my poor balls
for you I have kissed the blank
pages drunk the pissy chalice
water and thrown up dear god your
rabbits dear god your big
whistle do you know how awful
it is trying to plug the holy wound
in my bowels with wrong addresses?
listen let us have death back
when we need him the lost mother
of bliss will sing in the back
seat for you let us come back
with our SS and our own banks
this time and for the corpses
compilers to start out dear concerned
chosen esteemed sufferer warm
gloves god our bodies ladders
lovely look we smile too this
way look our blood too touch us is
it horrible? touch us

Hounding Mercy

our poor angel how sick
he must be of burying his face
in our hot mouths breathing
in maggots and fruity lung tissue
puffing us up when all we do
is empty again the prayers
to the forbidden father stinking
on us like exhaust fumes the candles
stuck guttering in our backsides
suppose though we took your gun in one
hand your excellent scalpel behind
it and kept saying kiss kiss kiss kiss
and before they screamed we'd cut
them before they begged us blast
them and cannibalize them all legs
from one ethics from another somebody's
skull we'd suture until there was
one whole one and who'd need war
or politics would the mothers kill
their beautiful children from sheer
boredom the fathers fight
over the fucked carcasses like sharks?
here is my magic briefcase
which roars here the branch
of my life to beat it with my
handcuffs what will I want now? give
me love give me snow oceans don't speak

What Did the Man Do with the Clouds?

the grandmas are all coming down like f-101's like gulls
screaming HAPPIER! HAPPIER! the grandmas
loom along the parapets like old wars their
grooved bellies grenades the lines kissed
into their faces like barbed wire
grandmas I've got the wings you brought me but they won't work
for me they don't fit anywhere on me
except in my mouth I keep sticking them
onto me like matchbooks but brother adam moses the pope
I don't see anyone the grandmas are all laughing
on the back fence like cold soup grandmas
if I could I'd wind myself onto you like a ribbon
and flow out behind you and be wind be sunrise
the grandmas bagpipe out of their soft wombs like apples
and go up like autumn in long rows like pearls like pearls
goodbye grandmas goodbye again thanks
for my present I swallowed them they're flapping
around inside me like uncle sol in the last chair
maybe someday they'll lift me like you
by the top of my guts out of here goodbye
charlie! go to sleep! eat! you're skin and bones! goodbye! goodbye!

The Matter

there's no no like money's
money makes big holes behind its eyes
when it says no and death
is the next teller
counting you money arches
and peeks down at the caseworker in the spirit drawer
money comes takes your picture without cameras
digs inside without shovels
smiles puts its head in the tube
like a robber
like the anchorite in the cave
like ten dollars
inside money is no candy but her
inside money no rate but just him
the prostitute without her vagina the brother
who wants you to money says no
and the last dollar
which is our friend dog
our history like a condom
lion
king
speaker
is dragged under and riveted
to the bone
like old age

Refuge, Serpent-Riders

a man decided once to go steal truth
all day he would tie himself to his bed
and not listen
at night the ropes would come off
he would go out and open his mouth
tasting what leaked through the moon from the next sky
rolling the stars around in his teeth
like little pits
finally darkness got tired of hanging there
it said how much will you give me? give me
something
the man started getting younger when he heard that
soon he was crawling the rocks
cut his knees he was really sorry
everybody else screamed BEAST FIEND MURDERER!
they pissed up into his maw
they named their lips death
so when they cried it would break in two pieces
then darkness went back
the stories still hid inside him it was morning
nobody had him
he still knew everything

Flat

the pillows are going insane
they are like shells the skulls have risen out of them like locusts
leaving faces in them but cold vacant immobile
heavy with tears
they are like clouds and are so sick of us
so furious with us they swear next time
when we come back if they can they will spring up and our faces will empty
next time they will soar like clouds and dissolve
and not touch us it is morning
our heads thrown back in agony

the pillows are going insane
from the grief of being laid down
and having to stare unquestioningly like flowers
and be in all places like flowers each man one in his house
one in his barracks in his jail cell
they swear if they weren't going insane they would call to each other
like flowers and spring up and come closer
but they must stay quietly
they must have faces like men and wait like men
the dead casings the filling and emptying going insane

A Poem for the Governments

this poem is an onion
it's the same one miguel hernandez's
wife wrote him about in jail
before he died that there was nothing
else for her and the baby to eat
except onions so he wrote
a lullaby for the child about onions
"I awoke from being a child:
don't you awake . . . don't even know
what happens or what goes on"

this poem is an onion
for you mr old men because
I want tears from you now
and can't see how else to get them
I want tears for miguel now
for the poor people and their children
and for the kids you hate going
around cunt-frontwards full of carrying on
and bad shit like mercy and despair
I offer this

because everything else with life
and tenderness in it you've eaten
everything good in the world eaten
everything in my heart eaten
the poor eaten the babies eaten miguel
eaten
now eat this: this is one onion
your history and legacy
it is all there is in our lives
this and tears: eat this

Another Dollar

I dreamed of an instrument of political torture
so that the person thinks he's breathing into a great space
that flows like a river beyond men
into infinity the ethical disconnects like a phone
and what he says everything comes back to him WE ARE NOT DOING THIS
angels skulls prisoners WE ARE NOT DOING THIS
the children scouring themselves like genitals NOT DOING THIS

mother am I the enemy or the little brother?
they threw ropes around me I ran I covered myself
but they touched me the invalids licked me the poor kissed me
afterwards there is a bed afterwards a woman is there
her breasts she is a cloud how she envelops you
the coils shimmer nobody talks anymore nobody dreams this
WE ARE NOT DOING THIS

The Beginning of April

I feel terribly strong today
it's like the time I arm-wrestled a friend
and beat him so badly I sprained his wrist
or when I made a woman who was really beautiful
love me when she didn't want to
it must be the warm weather
I think
I could smash bricks with my bare hands
or screw
until I was half out of my mind

the only trouble
jesus the only trouble
is I keep thinking about a kid I saw starving on television
last night from biafra he was unbearably fragile
his stomach puffed up arms and legs sticks eyes distorted
what if I touched somebody like that when I was this way?
I can feel him going stiff under my hands
I can feel his belly bulging ready to pop
his pale hair disengaging from its roots like something awful and alive
please

I won't hurt you I want you in my arms
I want to make something for you to eat like warm soup
look I'll chew the meat for you first
in case your teeth ache
I'll keep everybody away if you're sleeping
and hold you next to me like a little brother when we go out
I'm so cold now
what are we going to do with all this?
I promise I won't feel myself like this ever again
it's just the spring it doesn't mean anything please

This Is a Sin

right off we started inflicting history
on each other day after day first thing this
is historical and we gave dollars for it
and this and we gave movies and sad poems
and obviously newspapers and a little less
valentines and sometimes it got right
up against us and into us we would squeeze
it out like a worm it would come back
by itself through the pancreas through
the eye or womb and with great tenderness
on the faces of wives and babies we
would reinflict it until there was
such beauty it was unbearable because
it was too much history too much suffering
and also birds suffering their leaps
from branches dogs
lifting their dark mouths the paths
of mantises cows plopping were we afraid
of what would be left of us? sometimes
a person was erased entirely
and children dead of shame stuck
upright in the snow like pipes the wind
screaming over them or I would forget
you darling your breasts the wind
over them our lips
moving darling the child the wind breasts
our lips over them

The Undead

the only way it makes sense
is that we have terrible wounds inside us like mouths hard
metallic made in america
they swing fatly open like wallets and gorge
in strict vaginal contractions what touches us
what comes to us living wants us

how many times the one we kiss with affirms LIFE! LIFE!
but the other when the saints said
they heard thunder it was just it closing and
this time when it opens corpses soar in it officers
at attention shells
this time not enough pain in all asia for it

I want you not comforting me
the soles of our feet beaten until worms of flesh erupt from them
our genitals dialed like wrong numbers don't
put your tongue in me don't give me anything heart
soul laughter anything children turning the light on and off
on and off MA! don't feed me! don't feed me!

Then the Brother of the Wind

there's no such thing as death everybody
knows that also
nothing in the world that can batter you
and hang you on a fencepost like a towel

and no such thing as love that stays inside
getting thicker and heavier falling
into the middle one seed
that weighs more than the universe

and no angels either
and even if there were even if we hadn't laughed
the second heart out and made the second brain
have whole wars happening inside it like bacteria

and if they were made out of tin cans like shacks
in rio and rubber tires like crete sandals
and were all the same place rags in ratholes
in harlem rags sticking to burned faces in bengal

we'd still break like motors
and slip out of them anyway like penises
onto the damp thigh
and have to begin over

The Next to the Last Poem about God

when jessie's fever went up god got farther away so he could see better
he wanted to know everything that happened
when I hit tex my brother in the face with a cap gun
when I ran away from my mother and had a bad fight
with my sister lynn about being different
when I dreamed of being a fighter pilot and shooting my father down
god was there in my dream too think how big he had to be
to get in where I was sailing around in my flying tiger
and the deaf kid he was in his ears somebody told me so it was all right
and jimmy moss when he died it was autumn there were leaves
outside the window just hardening I thought
he must be in the leaves too how big he is how far away
he must be to cover everything like a blanket
you crawl in with a fever and hide and wake up
during the night all better and crawl out again
but maybe when he has to get that far he thins out a little
you know? like rubber? maybe sometimes people punch
their fingers through him by accident or maybe on purpose
the bad people because they wanted to see everything too
because seeing everything would be like owning everything
so they go through and there they were bouncing around
saying everything's good everything figures it all works
you could see them walking across the sky
at night rippling the cover making the stars bend
they said come up here look you can see EVERYTHING! EVERYTHING!
tex I'm sorry I hit you in the face
mom I didn't mean to grow up you should have told me lynn
dad forgive me for getting stronger
sally you for so much and jessie
when you were playing on the bed last night
letting yourself fall backwards onto me with such happy trust
thinking "stand up" meant "let yourself fall any way you want to
I'll catch you" jessie you were almost well your fever
was almost gone and I thought there must be something important

for you like that I still can't think of it but god must know it
because god doesn't forget anything ever
and someday I'll get that far too and find out
and drop messages about what it was and it'll be all right
god told me he said tell jessie I said it'll be all right

Acids

for Jeff Marks

something to dip myself into
like sheep when they're driven through
and the ticks and fleas float off in the trough
the animals struggling to keep their heads out of it
the men dunking them for their own good they get fatter the wool thicker
I would come up
crying
but pure again fingerprints kissmarks the places
I crossed my arms and dug into my back invisible
scales imperceptible bony emotional excrescences
gone a caul
gleaming flushing the surfaces innocence
I would make rivers of it
that would flood at their mouths
and the swimmers
would be done too
and in the city in the tap water
enough scum left to get into us all
we would fall into great laughing heaps of ourselves
can you imagine laughter
shining
and the sounds of lovemaking
etched like printing plates
so you would pull pictures of being young and knowing
what you know now
the first sky the first clouds
like young angels
bumping each other seeing your mother coming shrieking
joyfully so she'll hear you
and come running arms open face open baby!
baby!
and you
flowing being flowed through

like the blood
over the skull then
the veil and before that in your arms
in all of you

They Warned Him Then They Threw Him Away

there's somebody who's dying
to eat god
when the name happens
the juices leap from the bottom of his mouth like waves
he almost falls over with lightheadedness
nobody has ever been this hungry before
you might know people who've never had anything
but teaspoons of rice or shreds
from the shin of an ape well that's nothing
you should know what this person would do
he'd pull handfuls of hair out of his children
and shove them down
he'd squeeze the docile bud in his wife
until it screamed
if you told him god lived in his own penis
he'd bite into it
and tear like a carnivore
this is how men renounce
this is how we obliterate
one morning near the end he'll climb into the fire
and look back at himself
what was dark will be light
what was song will be roaring
and the worst thing is you'll still want this
beyond measure you'll still want this
believe me
you should know this

Ribbons

the goddamned animals might know more than we do about some things
like looking away when somebody they know is hurting them
and the other has to let go and not tear his throat out like us
but we're still more than them about love
a girl so shy she couldn't look at me without crying
so I turned the other way too and you could feel how close we were
as though we'd circled the whole world
and met and fallen in love her legs smoothed
I was stronger there were mists we walked in them

now when does that happen with pigs or horses?
the stallion all he's after is tearing the fence down
the mare gets her tail going like a pump handle
and in the paddock the gelding old sergeant
buries his face in the creaky feed bin and keeps it there
remembering iwo jima remembering the bulge seoul my lai
his wound his two thighs like medals his two thighs
rising into the dark like searchlights only animals would keep quiet then
grind their broad teeth on the grain and shut up not us

The Rampage

a baby got here once who before
he was all the way out and could already feel the hindu
pain inside him and the hebrew and the iliad
decided he was never going to stop crying no matter what
until they did something he wasn't going
to turn the horror
off in their fat sentences
and in the light bulb how much murder to get light
and in the walls agony agony for the bricks for the glaze
he was going to keep screaming
until they made death little like he was
and loved him too and sent
him back to undo all this
and it happened
he kept screaming he scared them he saw them
filling with womblight again like stadiums
he saw the tears sucked back into the story the smiles
opening like sandwiches
so he stopped
and looked up and said all right
it's better now
I'm hungry now I want just to sleep
and they let him

The Nut

a man hammers viciously
viciously like fucking
a bad whore who won't get
undressed even remember?
like trying to crush
the life from the corpse who
sprays blood who won't
die or stop screaming
until the mouth is gone
utterly the last thread
crawling tenderly down
the backbone tenderly
to the tail the legs men
what are we thinking
hammering? the poor whore
smashing her fists on
the wall the carpenter his
sensitive tools suffering
men the terrible claws
men the hammering not
sleeping the hammering
going on to eternity
what is this so much
like pulse like murdering?
the corpse screams the
woman screams men what
is this?

Yours

I'd like every girl in the world to have a poem of her own
I've written for her I don't even want to make love to them all anymore
just write things your body makes me delirious your face enchants me
you are a wonder of soul spirit intelligence one for every one
and then the men I don't care whether I can still beat them all
them too a poem for them how many?
seeing you go through woods like part of the woods seeing you play piano
seeing you hold your child in your tender devastating hands
and of course the children too little poems they could sing or dance to
this is our jumping game this our seeing game our holding each other
even the presidents with all their death the congressmen and judges
I'd give them something
they would hold awed to their chests as their proudest life thing
somebody walking along a road where there's no city would look up
and see his poem coming down like a feather out of nowhere
or on the assembly line new instructions a voice sweet as lunch-time
or she would turn over a stone by the fire and if she couldn't read
it would sing to her in her body
listen! everyone! you have your own poem now
it's yours as much as your heart as much as your own life is
you can do things to it shine it up iron it dress it in doll clothes
o men! o people! please stop how it's happening now please
I'm working as fast as I can I can't stop to use periods
sometimes I draw straight lines on the page because the words
are too slow
I can only do one at a time don't die first please
don't give up and start crying or hating each other they're coming
I'm hurrying be patient there's still time isn't there? isn't there?

The Nickname of Hell

the president of my country his face flushed
horribly like a penis is walking through
the schoolyard toward my daughter I tell him
mr president I will make it all right but
under his hand his penis is lined with many
buttons I tell him the orders are changing
but commanders deep in his penis prime it
I tell him about love I tell him there
is a new god who believes anything I
cringe alongside him I dance like a daughter
it is the schoolyard the daughters play
on the dangerous fences I tell him I love
him I tell him the daughters aren't here
even he is holding me now his arms hold
me his lips you are my bliss he tells me
these are my arms these my lips you
are my penis he tells me his face stings
into mine like a penis you are my joy you
my daughter hold me my daughter my daughter

Bad Mouth

for W. S. Merwin

not bad mouth
in bad mouth
you know how to beat women so they love you afterwards
and come crawling
how to torture whole races and next time they fight
on the same side as you the lamb out of you
bad mouth lives in three houses with scabbards
bad mouth has hurt since the dinosaurs
even his sperm hurts
like napalm
bad mouth thinking
who do I kill?
who lock up in my arms for the last moment? pity
me pity me

good mouth I want to be vile enough for us both
so we'll love more
I want scorpion ladies I want beautiful pain ladies
and wolf brothers to lick their clear breasts with
good mouth worshipping
good mouth wreathing his genes like fuses
good mouth
I want being able to say help me
help me good mouth
the ones down to the raisin like my tongue
are my tongue the last ones before peace
are inside me
good mouth whoever I let live murdered me whoever I pitied burned
please stop me

This Day

probably death fits all right in the world
but every time somebody dies his mother
botches it suddenly she thinks there's not
enough room in her breasts the nipples
are clogged she says the ducts jammed rifles even
so old they sag like laundry she grabs
them and hangs on she doesn't understand she
says she can't understand it mother what
I'm doing is truth mother understand
me at least freedom but o god she can't find
space for an atom her glands burst her
pores swell like bad fruit mother when
we were wolves remember? she doesn't
understand the inside of bodies the voids
wasted the patient holes used up
like planets when I count three she says
everything was a dream everything before
now was really dead was I really dead?

The Rabbit Fights for His Life
The Leopard Eats Lunch

for Harvey Finkle

what if the revolution comes and I'm in it and my job
is to murder a child accidentally
or afterwards to get rid of the policemen?
I had a milkshake last week with a policeman
we talked about his pay raise it eats shit
he told me what if I have that one? SAVAGE
the baby was easy
the baby went up in thin air
I remembered in dostoevsky where they talked
about whether it would all be worth the death of one child
and you decided yes or no according to your character
my character
is how he got back in his car
like a tired businessman and listened to the radio
for a few minutes
and waved
is having to lug him everywhere
I go because I can't take him to his wife crying like this
the children have learned to throw their arms around you
without meaning it to kiss you without feeling it
to know there is something marvelous
and not pay attention
in order to say any of this at all to you
I have made myself up like somebody
in a novel
in order not
to go out of my mind I make it I can only do two things
hold you
bury you

Cellophane

if only we weren't so small next to the stars
we could refuse absolutely to be alive in this eon
to be alive now you can't understand one thing without pain
you can't feel your own face in the morning
without wanting to blow up
if we were bigger
we wouldn't keep happening over and over
like truth that hurts worse than anything
with NO big as the mint
and DO IT filling the air like soot from the incinerator
we'd be as easy as the game war
the wingspan from one death to another
and the centuries the unending centuries
taken away from us in cattle cars
would wail harmlessly
like ghosts

Inches

it would be wonderful to be quiet now
to creak down through the fossils making my last speech
into the blind rocks
or to hang from the bars by my belt
and not speak of us our bellows of helplessness our disgust
to be as silent as planets
even the wind has been burned out
hospitals jails the places learning to be hard like men
something where we would be taken and dispirited
of all things like god to godhead love
in peace
not to have "of" to our deaths anymore
the political would go into the back
it would bury itself in itself
and cry for us
I remember you you were my friend I loved you
very much of it was not for words

The Sting

the not want
jesus
I didn't know this the not want
for woman country daughter the man
hit rocked back crying holding him
the not want
for wounding myself for your mouth
for what my hand is opening getting sleepy
the not want
to ride hooked in you like a thistle
for long grass the earth broken to take breaths
in you
jesus
not want
for dreaming
to be president
to take the whole nation and kiss it
awake being born being desired
not new minds not even not
this grown into the big
and fuller
not want
for being able to not want
for trees taking me underneath clouds
taking me fury
exaltation
why? why baby? why dog? why wife?
why
not want president?
why not want friend with no anguish?
why
angel I love you god I love you why
not want heart in my body in each hand
picture guitar

holy
leave this
let this be here
let me
not want this not

The Last

when I was sleeping this morning one of my feet
fell out of the covers and my daughter
came in and covered it up with her little dolly blanket

I was dreaming right then that flames were shooting out of my cock
and when I woke up with her patting the soft cloth down on me
I believed I understood the end of eternity for the first time

don't ever make me explain this

In the Heart of the Beast

May 1970: Cambodia, Kent State, Jackson State

1.

this is fresh meat right mr nixon?

this is even sweeter than mickey schwerner or fred hampton right?
even more tender than the cherokee nation or guatemala or greece
having their asses straightened for them isn't it?

this is none of your oriental imitation
this is iowa corn grown
this is jersey tomato grown
washington salmon maryland crab
this is from children
who'd barely begun ingesting corruption
the bodies floating belly up like polluted fish in cambodia
barely tainting them
the black kids blown up in their churches
hardly souring them
their torments were so meager
they still thought about life
still struggled with urgency
and compassion
so
tender

2.

I'm sorry

I don't want to hear anymore that the innocent farmer in ohio on guard
    duty means well but is fucked up by his politicians and raises his
    rifle out of some primal fear for his own life and his family's and
    that he hates niggers hates them hates them because he is warped
    and deceived by events

and pulls the trigger

I'm sorry I don't want to forgive him anymore
I don't want to say he didn't know what he was doing
because he knew what he was doing
because he didn't pull the trigger once and run away screaming
they kept shooting the kids said
we thought they were blanks but they kept shooting and shooting
we were so scared

I don't want to forgive the bricklayer from akron who might or might not
        hate his mother I don't care or the lawyer or gas station attendant
        from cleveland who may or may not have had a bad childhood
I don't care
I don't want to know
I don't want to hear anything about it

another kid said the rocks weren't even reaching them!

I don't want to understand why they did it

how could you?
just that

everything else is pure shit

3.

on the front page of the times a girl is screaming
she will be screaming forever
and her friend will lie there forever you wouldn't know she wasn't just
        sleeping in the sun except for the other screaming
and on the editorial page
"the tragic nature of the division of the country . . . the provocation un-
        doubtedly was great and was also unpardonable . . ."

o my god
my god

if there was a way to purify the world who would be left?
there is a list
and it says
this person for doing this
and that person for doing nothing
and this person for not howling in rage
and that for desperately hanging on to the reasons the reasons
and
there is an avenger
who would be left?
who is there now who isn't completely insane from all this?
who didn't dream with me last night
of burning everything destroying everyone
of tearing pieces of your own body off
of coughing your language up and spitting it away like vomit
of wanting to start at the bottom of your house
breaking everything floor by floor
burning the pictures
tearing the mattresses up
smashing windows and chairs until nothing is left
and then the cars with a sledgehammer
the markets
the stores that sell things
the buses
the bridges into the city
the airports
the international harbors
the tall buildings crumpling like corpses
the theaters torn down to the bare stage
the galleries naked the bookstores like mouths open

there should be funerals in front of the white house
bones in the capitol

where do you stop?

how can we be like this?

4.

I remember what it was to come downstairs
and my daughter would be there crawling toward me as fast as she could
crying HI DADDA HI DADDA

and what it was to bury my face in my wife's breasts and forget

to touch a friend's shoulder
to laugh
to take walks

5.

I don't want to call anyone pig

meeting people who tell you they want war they hate communists
or somebody who'll say they hate niggers spics kikes
and you still don't believe they're beyond knowing
because you feel comfortable with them even drawn to them
and know somehow that they have salvageable hearts
you try to keep hope
for a community that could contain both of you
so that you'd both be generous and loving
and find ways that didn't need hatred and killing
to burn off the inarticulate human rage at having to die

I thought if I could take somebody like that in my arms
I could convince them that everyone was alone before death
but love saved us from living our lives reflexively with death

that it could happen
we would be naked now
we'd change now little by little
we'd be better
we would just be here
in this life

but it could be a delusion couldn't it?
it could be like thinking those soldiers were shooting blanks
up until the last second standing there scared shitless
but inside
thinking americans don't shoot innocent people!
I know it!
I learned it in school in the movies!
it doesn't happen like this
and hearing a bullet slam into the ground next to you and the flesh
and every voice in your body saying o no no
and seeing your friend go down
half her head blown away
and the image of kennedy in back of the car
and of king
and the other kennedy
and wanting to explode o no no no no no

6.

not to be loaded up under the flopping bladewash the tubes sucking to
      be thrown out turning to flame burning on trees on grass on skin
      burning lips away breasts away genitals arms legs buttocks
not to be torn out of the pack jammed in the chamber belched out laid
      over the ground like a live fence of despair
not to fog down into the river where the fish die into the rice where the
      frogs die into the trees where the fruit dies the grain dies the
      leaves into the genes

into the generations
more black children
more red children
and yellow

not to be screaming

THE LARK. THE THRUSH. THE STARLING. (POEMS FROM ISSA)

[1983]

In the next life,
butterfly,
a thousand years from now,

we'll sit like this
again
under the tree

in the dust,
hearing it, this
great thing.

❧

I sit in my room.

Outside, haze.

The whole world
is haze

and I can't figure out
one room.

❧

So
mucked up with
kneading
dough she is

she has to use
her wrist to
push her hair back
from her eyes.

That the world
is going
to end someday
does not concern
the wren:

it's time to
build your nest,
you build
your nest.

Spring: another

joke.

This run-down
house: me.

Go ahead, ask,
how's
spring?

Average, just
average.

You're two, that's great.
Go ahead, laugh, crawl
around.

You'll find
out,
you'll see.

❧

Winter,
damn,
again.

Same
frost, same
fire.

❧

Listen carefully.

I'm meditating.
The only thing in my mind
right now
is the wind.

No, wait . . . the autumn
wind, that's right,
the *autumn* wind!

❧

The hail goes
dancing
into the fire.
The coal flares.

I watch the embers
going out, one
by
one.

❧

What a sound his
shell made, that

big cockroach! *Crack!*
like a church bell:
Crack!
Crack!
Crack!

❧

They wash you
when
you're born, then,
when you're finished,
if you're very lucky,
you get washed
again.

❧

A holiday:
every
yard or
two, in
the grass,
among
the flowers,
along
the rushing
stream,
picnickers
sprawled.

❧

What we are
given:
resignation.

What is
taken from us:
resignation.

It is ours that
we can see, do
see, must see

our own bones
bleaching
under the warm moon.

≋

Baby, I don't want
to tell you
again: you can't go out
in weather like this.

Can't you teach
yourself to play
checkers or
something?

≋

The most excruciating
thing
I could imagine: to see,
the way
I am now,

the place I
was born
with all its
mist
blown away.

≋

In the middle
of a bite of
grass,
the turtle stops
to listen for,
oh, an
hour, two
hours,
three hours . . .

≋

When
you were small, I
put you
in
a swing, you
held
a flower.

Next thing
I
knew . . .

≋

This is what,
at last, it is
to be
a human being.

Leaving nothing
out, not
one star, one
wren, one tear
out.

❧

I'd forgotten and
how could I ever
have
my mother, peeling
the apple, giving me
the heart-
flesh.

❧

That night,
winter,
rain,
the mountains.

No guilt. No
not-guilt.
Winter,
rain,
mountains.

❧

I know
nothing anymore
of roads.

Winter
is a road,
I know,

but the body,
the beloved
body,

is it, too,
only a kind
of road?

❧

The fleas, too,
have fled
my burned-down
house. Oh,

there you are,
old friend, and
oh, you, too,
old,
old friend.

❧

It's over now. I watch
the fire. I watch the firelight
wash
the wall. I watch
the shadow on
it of the woman.

I don't
understand it, but
I watch, I
watch.

❧

Did I write this
as I was
dying?

Did I really
write
this?

That I wanted to thank
the snow
fallen on my blanket?

Could I
have written
this?

WITH IGNORANCE

[1977]

The Sanctity

for Nick and Arlene de Credico

The men working on the building going up here have got these great,
little motorized wheelbarrows that're supposed to be for lugging bricks
        and mortar
but that they seem to spend most of their time barrel-assing up the street
        in,
racing each other or trying to con the local secretaries into taking rides
        in the bucket.
I used to work on jobs like that and now when I pass by the skeleton of
        the girders
and the tangled heaps of translucent brick wrappings, I remember the
        guys I was with then
and how hard they were to know. Some of them would be so good to be
        with at work,
slamming things around, playing practical jokes, laughing all the time,
        but they could be miserable,
touchy and sullen, always ready to imagine an insult or get into a fight
        anywhere else.
If something went wrong, if a compressor blew or a truck backed over
        somebody,
they'd be the first ones to risk their lives dragging you out
but later you'd see them and they'd be drunk, looking for trouble, almost
        murderous,
and it would be frightening trying to figure out which person they really
        were.
Once I went home to dinner with a carpenter who'd taken me under his
        wing
and was keeping everyone off my back while he helped me. He was
        beautiful but at his house, he sulked.
After dinner, he and the kids and I were watching television while his
        wife washed the dishes
and his mother, who lived with them, sat at the table holding a big can-
        taloupe in her lap,
fondling it and staring at it with the kind of intensity people usually only
        look into fires with.

The wife kept trying to take it away from her but the old lady squawked

and my friend said, "Leave her alone, will you?" "But she's doing it on
purpose," the wife said.

I was watching. The mother put both her hands on it then, with her
thumbs spread,

as though the melon were a head and her thumbs were covering the eyes
and she was aiming it like a gun or a camera.

Suddenly the wife muttered, "You bitch!" ran over to the bookshelf, took
a book down—

A *History of Revolutions*—rattled through the pages and triumphantly
handed it to her husband.

A photograph: someone who's been garroted and the executioner, stand-
ing behind him in a business hat,

has his thumbs just like that over the person's eyes, straightening the
head,

so that you thought the thumbs were going to move away because they
were only pointing

the person at something they wanted him to see and the one with the
hands was going to say, "Look! Right there!"

"I told you," the wife said. "I swear to god she's trying to drive me crazy."

I didn't know what it all meant but my friend went wild, started breaking
things, I went home

and when I saw him the next morning at breakfast he acted as though
nothing had happened.

We used to eat at the Westfield truck stop, but I remember Fritz's, The
Victory, The Eagle,

and I think I've never had as much contentment as I did then, before
work, the light just up,

everyone sipping their coffee out of the heavy white cups and teasing the
middle-aged waitresses

who always acted vaguely in love with whoever was on jobs around there
right then

besides the regular farmers on their way back from the markets and the
long-haul truckers.

Listen: sometimes when you go to speak about life it's as though your
mouth's full of nails

but other times it's so easy that it's ridiculous to even bother.

The eggs and the toast could fly out of the plates and it wouldn't matter

and the bubbles in the level could blow sky-high and it still wouldn't.
Listen to the back-hoes gearing up and the shouts and somebody crack-
      ing his sledge into the mortar pan.
Listen again. He'll do it all day if you want him to. Listen again.

Spit

. . . then the son of the "superior race" began to spit into the Rabbi's mouth so that the Rabbi could continue to spit on the Torah . . .
    —The Black Book

After this much time, it's still impossible. The SS man with his stiff hair
    and his uniform;
the Rabbi, probably in a torn overcoat, probably with a stained beard the
    other would be clutching;
the Torah, God's word, on the altar, the letters blurring under the
    blended phlegm;
the Rabbi's parched mouth, the SS man perfectly absorbed, obsessed
    with perfect humiliation.
So many years and what is there to say still about the soldiers waiting im-
    patiently in the snow,
about the one stamping his feet, thinking, Kill him! Get it over with!
while back there the lips of the Rabbi and the other would have brushed
and if time had stopped you would have thought they were lovers,
so lightly kissing, the sharp, luger hand under the dear chin,
the eyes furled slightly and then when it started again the eyelashes of
    both of them
shyly fluttering as wonderfully as the pulse of a baby.
Maybe we don't have to speak of it at all, it's still the same.
War, that happens and stops happening but is always somehow right
    there, twisting and hardening us;
then what we make of God—words, spit, degradation, murder, shame;
    every conceivable torment.
All these ways to live that have something to do with how we live
and that we're almost ashamed to use as metaphors for what goes on in us
but that we do anyway, so that love is battle and we watch ourselves in
    love
become maddened with pride and incompletion, and God is what it is
    when we're alone
wrestling with solitude and everything speaking in our souls turns against
    us like His fury
and just facing another person, there is so much terror and hatred that
    yes,

spitting in someone's mouth, trying to make him defile his own
        meaning,
would signify the struggle to survive each other and what we'll enact to
        accomplish it.

There's another legend.
It's about Moses, that when they first brought him as a child before
        Pharaoh,
the king tested him by putting a diamond and a live coal in front of him
and Moses picked up the red ember and popped it into his mouth
so for the rest of his life he was tongue-tied and Aaron had to speak for
        him.
What must his scarred tongue have felt like in his mouth?
It must have been like always carrying something there that weighed too
        much,
something leathery and dead whose greatest gravity was to loll out like an
        ox's,
and when it moved, it must have been like a thick embryo slowly coming
        alive,
butting itself against the inner sides of his teeth and cheeks.
And when God burned in the bush, how could he not cleave to him?
How could he not know that all of us were on fire and that every word we
        said would burn forever,
in pain, unquenchably, and that God knew it, too, and would say noth-
        ing Himself ever again beyond this,
ever, but would only live in the flesh that we use like firewood,
in all the caves of the body, the gut cave, the speech cave:
He would slobber and howl like something just barely a man that beats
        itself again and again onto the dark,
moist walls away from the light, away from whatever would be light for
        this last eternity.
"Now therefore go," He said, "and I will be with thy mouth."

Toil

After the argument—argument? battle, war, harrowing; you need shrieks,
      moans from the pit—
after that woman and I anyway stop raking each other with the meat-
      hooks we've become with each other,
I fit my forehead into the smudge I've already sweated onto the window
      with a thousand other exhaustions
and watch an old man having breakfast out of a pile of bags on my front
      step.
Peas from a can, bread with the day-old price scrawled over the label in
      big letters
and then a bottle that looks so delectable, the way he carefully un-
      sheathes it
so the neck just lips out of the wrinkled foreskin of the paper and closes
      his eyes and tilts,
long and hard, that if there were one lie left in me to forgive a last rap-
      ture of cowardice
I'd go down there too and sprawl and let the whole miserable rest go to
      pieces.
Does anyone still want to hear how love can turn rotten?
How you can be so desperate that even going adrift wouldn't be
      enough—
you want to scour yourself out, get rid of all the needs you've still got in
      yourself
that keep you endlessly tearing against yourself in rages of guilt and
      frustration?
I don't. I'd rather think about other things. Beauty. How do you learn to
      believe there's beauty?
The kids going by on their way to school with their fat little lunch bags:
      beauty!
My old drunk with his bags—bottle bags, rag bags, shoe bags: beauty!
      beauty!
He lies there like the goddess of wombs and first-fruit, asleep in the
      riches,
one hand still hooked in mid-flight over the intricacies of the iron railing.

Old father, wouldn't it be a good ending if you and I could just walk
     away together?
Or that you were the king who reveals himself, who folds back the
     barbed, secret wings
and we're all so in love now, one spirit, one flesh, one generation, that
     the truces don't matter?
Or maybe a better ending would be that there is no ending.
Maybe the Master of Endings is wandering down through his herds to
     find it
and the cave cow who tells truth and the death cow who holds sea in her
     eyes are still there
but all he hears are the same old irresistible slaughter-pen bawlings.
So maybe there is no end to the story and maybe there's no story.
Maybe the last calf just ambles up to the trough through the clearing
and nudges aside the things that swarm on the water and her mouth dips
     in among them and drinks.
Then she lifts, and it pours, everything, gushes, and we're lost in both
     waters.

The Last Deaths

A few nights ago I was half-watching the news on television and half-
    reading to my daughter.
The book was about a boy who makes a zoo out of junk he finds in a
    lot—
I forget exactly; a horse-bottle, a bedspring that's a snake, things like
    that—
and on the news they were showing a film about the most recent bomb-
    ings.
There was a woman crying, tearing at her hair and breasts, shrieking
    incomprehensibly
because her husband and all her children had been killed the night
    before
and just when she'd flung herself against the legs of one of the soldiers
    watching her,
Jessie looked up and said, "What's the matter with her? Why's she crying?"

2.

I haven't lived with my daughter for a year now and sometimes it still
    hurts not to be with her more,
not to have her laughter when I want it or to be able to comfort her when
    she cries out in her sleep.
I don't see her often enough to be able to know what I can say to her,
what I can solve for her without introducing more confusions than there
    were in the first place.
That's what happened with death. She was going to step on a bug and
    when I told her she'd kill it,
it turned out that no one had ever told her about death and now she had
    to know.
"It's when you don't do anything anymore," I told her. "It's like being
    asleep."

I didn't say for how long but she's still been obsessed with it since then,
wanting to know if she's going to die and when and if I am and her
    mother and grandma and do robbers do it?
Maybe I should have just given her the truth, but I didn't: now what was
    I going to say about that woman?
"Her house fell down," I said. "Who knocked down her house?" "It just
    fell."
Then I found something for us to do, but last night, again, first thing,
"Tell me about that girl." "What girl?" "You know." Of course I know.
What could have gone on in my child's dreams last night so that woman
    was a girl now?
How many times must they have traded places back and forth in that
    innocent crib?
"You mean the lady whose house fell down?" "Yeah, who knocked her
    house down?"

3.

These times. The endless wars. The hatreds. The vengefulness.
Everyone I know getting out of their marriage. Old friends distrustful.
The politicians using us until you can't think about it anymore because
    you can't tell anymore
which reality affects which and how do you escape from it without every-
    thing battering you back again?
How many times will I lie to Jessie about things that have no meaning
    for either of us?
How many forgivenesses will I need from her when all I wanted was to
    keep her from suffering the same ridiculous illusions I have?
There'll be peace soon.
They'll fling it down like sick meat we're supposed to lick up and be
    thankful for and what then?

4.

Jessie, it's as though the whole race is sunk in an atmosphere of blood
and it's been clotting for so many centuries we can hardly move now.

Someday, you and I will face each other and turn away and the absence,
the dread, will flame between us like an enormous, palpable word that
       wasn't spoken.
Do we only love because we're weak and murderous?
Are we commended to each other to alleviate our terror of solitude and
       annihilation and that's all?

5.

I wish I could change dreams with you, baby. I've had the bad ones, what
       comes now is calm and abstract.
Last night, while you and that poor woman were trading deaths like
       horrible toys,
I was dreaming about the universe. The whole universe was happening
       in one day, like a blossom,
and during that day people's voices kept going out to it, crying, "Stop!
       Stop!"
The universe didn't mind, though. It knew we were only cursing love
       again
because we didn't know how to love, not even for a day,
but our little love days were just seeds it blew out on parachutes into the
       summer wind.
Then you and I were there. We shouted "Stop!" too. We kept wanting
       the universe to explode,
we kept wishing it would go back into its root, but the universe under-
       stood.
We were its children. It let us cry into its petals, it let its stems bend
       against us,
then it fed and covered us and we looked up sleepily—it was time to
       sleep—
and whatever our lives were, our love, this once, was enough.

The Race of the Flood

The way someone stays home, that's all, stays in the house, in the room,
          just stays,
the way she, let it be she this time, the way she stays, through the class,
          the backseat and the job;
the way she stays there for so many chapters, so many reels, not moving,
          the way the earth doesn't move;
the way one morning, one day, any day, she wakes and knows now that
          it's gone now,
that never is now, and she thinks she can feel it, the never, even her cells
          have spread over the sheets;
the way she thinks that oh, even these open-pored pores, even these
          glances butting the wall like thrown-away combs;
the way she, or these, these pores, glances, presences, so me, so within me,
as though I were she, exactly, as though I were the absence, too, the loss,
          too,
as though just beneath me was the worn, soft tallow, the unmoved and
          unmoving;
so there is this within me which has never touched life, never, never
          gone to the ball or the war,
never and never, so within and next and around me, fear and fear and
          the self-deceived,
the turned-to-the-wall, the stricken, untouched, begun ill or never be-
          gun,
the way it happens without happening, begins or doesn't, moves, gives
          way, or never does.

Or this. Messages, codes; the way he, the next one, the way he pins them
          all over himself,
on his clothes, on his skin, and then walks through the street like a sign-
          post, a billboard;
the way there are words to his wife and words to his kids, words even to
          god so our lord
is over his eyes and our father over his belly and the history of madness
          and history of cliffs;

the way there's no room now, the way every word in the world has stuck
to the skin
and is used up now, and his eyes move, roll, spin up to the top of his head
the way the eyes of those fish who try to see god or the lid of the water
roll, like dice,
so me, within me again: I cover myself with my own scrawl and wait in
the shallow,
I face the shallow and wait like a fin and I ripple the membrane of scrawl
like water;
so me, we, dear life I love you where are you, so we, dear our lord of
anguish where are you,
so zero, so void; we don't even know how to end it, how to get out of the
way of the serif or slash.

And the next, and the next, the way the next, the way all, any, any he,
any she,
any human or less or more, if not bone that leaps with its own word then
still more,
if not skin that washes its own wound then more and more, the way more
than a wound,
more than a thing which has to be spoken or born, born now, later,
again,
the way desire is born and born, the desire within me and not, within
and without and neither;
the way the next holds on to itself and the one after holds on to me, on to
my person, my human,
and I give back, the way ten times a day I offer it back with love or resent-
ment or horror,
so I bear my likeness and greet my like, and the way will, my will or not,
the way all it can say is I am or am not, or I don't, won't, cannot or will not,
and the way that it burns anyway, and the way it smiles, smiles anyway,
fills, ripens,
so that the hour or the scrawl burns and ripens; so within me, as though
I had risen,
as though I had gone to the gate and opened the lock and stepped
through;
so within me, it lifts and goes through, lifts itself through, and burns, any-
way, smiles, anyway.

Bob

If you put in enough hours in bars, sooner or later you get to hear every
    imaginable kind of bullshit.
Every long-time loser has a history to convince you he isn't living at the
    end of his own leash
and every kid has some pimple on his psyche he's trying to compensate
    for with an epic,
but the person with the most unlikely line I'd ever heard—he told me
    he'd killed, more than a few times,
during the war and then afterwards working for the mob in Philadel-
    phia—I could never make up my mind about.
He was big, bigger than big. He'd also been drinking hard and wanted to
    be everyone's friend
and until the bartender called the cops because he wouldn't stop stuffing
    money in girls' blouses,
he gave me his life: the farm childhood, the army, re-upping, the war—
    that killing—
coming back and the new job—that killing—then almost being killed
    himself by another hood and a kind of pension,
a distributorship, incredibly enough, for hairdresser supplies in the ward
    around Passyunk and Mifflin.
He left before the cops came, and before he left he shook my hand and
    looked into my eyes.
It's impossible to tell how much that glance weighed: it was like having
    to lift something,
something so ponderous and unwieldy that you wanted to call for some-
    one to help you
and when he finally turned away, it wouldn't have bothered me at all if
    I'd never seen him again.

This is going to get a little nutty now, maybe because everything was a
    little nutty for me back then.
Not a little. I'd been doing some nice refining. No work, no woman,
    hardly any friends left.
The details don't matter. I was helpless, self-pitying, angry, inert, and
    right now

I was flying to Detroit to interview for a job I knew I wouldn't get. Out-
side,
the clouds were packed against our windows and just as I let my book
drop to look out,
we broke through into a sky so brilliant that I had to close my eyes
against the glare.
I stayed like that, waiting for the stinging after-light to fade, but it seemed
to pulse instead,
then suddenly it washed strangely through me, swelling, powdering,
and when my sight came back, I was facing inwards, into the very center
of myself,
a dark, craggy place, and there was a sound that when I blocked the jets,
the hiss of the pressurization valves and the rattling silverware and
glasses, I realized was laughter.
The way I was then, I think nothing could have shocked me. I was a
well, I'd fallen in,
someone was there with me, but all I did was drift until I came to him: a
figure, arms lifted,
he was moving in a great, cumbersome dance, full of patience, full of
time, and that laughter,
a deep, flowing tumult of what seemed to be songs from someone else's
life.
Now the strange part. My ears were ringing, my body felt like water, but
I moved again,
farther in, until I saw the face of who it was with me and it was Bob, the
drunk,
or if it wasn't him, his image filled the space, the blank, the template,
better than anyone else,
and so, however doubtful it seems now, I let it be him: he was there, I let
him stay.
Understand, this happened quickly. By that night, home again, I was
broken again,
torn, crushed on the empty halves of my bed, but for that time, from
Pittsburgh, say,
until we braked down to the terminal in Detroit, I smiled at that self in
myself,
his heavy dance, his laughter winding through the wrack and detritus of
what I thought I was.

Bob, I don't know what happened to. He probably still makes the circuits
        of the clubs and corner bars,
and there must be times when strangers listen and he can tell it, the truth
        or his nightmare of it.
"I killed people," the secret heart opening again, "and Jesus God, I didn't
        even know them."

Bread

A whole section of the city I live in has been urban renewed, some of it
       torn down,
some restored to what it was supposed to have been a few hundred years
       ago.
Once you could've walked blocks without hearing English, now the
       ghettos have been cleared,
there are parks and walkways and the houses are all owned by people
       who've moved back from the suburbs.
When I lived there, at the very edge of it where the expressway is going
       in now
and the buildings are still boarded with plywood or flattened altogether,
the old market was already shuttered, the shipping depots had been relo-
       cated upriver
and the only person I ever saw was a grocer who lived across from me
       over his empty store.
I couldn't understand what he was doing there—it must have been years
since a customer had come in past the dead register and the icebox
       propped open with a carton,
but it was comforting to have him: he'd make his bed, sweep, cook for
       himself like a little wife
and when the constables came every week or so to tell us we were con-
       demned,
he never paid attention so I didn't either. I didn't want to leave. I'd been
       in love,
I thought I was healing, for all I know I might have stayed forever in the
       grim room I was camped in
but one day some boys who must have climbed up through one of the
       abandoned tenements
suddenly appeared skidding and wrestling over the steep pitch of the old
       man's roof
and when I shouted at them to get the hell off, he must have thought I'd
       meant him:
he lurched in his bed and stopped rubbing himself with the white cream
       he used to use on his breasts.

He looked up, our eyes met, and I think for the first time he really be-
  lieved I was there.
I don't know how long we stared at each other—I could hear the kids
  shrieking at me
and the road-building equipment that had just started tearing the skin
  from the avenue—
then his zincy fingers slowly subsided against his heart and he smiled,
a brilliant, total, incongruous smile, and even though I had no desire to,
the way afterwards I had no desire to cry when my children were born,
  but did,
sobbed, broke down with joy or some inadmissible apprehension, I
  smiled back.
It was as though we were lovers, as though, like lovers, we'd made speech
  again
and were listening as it gutted and fixed the space between us and then a
  violent,
almost physical loathing took me, for all I'd done to have ended in this
  place,
to myself, to everyone, to the whole business we're given the name life
  for.

I could go on with this. I could call it a victory, an exemplary triumph,
  but I'd lie.
Sometimes the universe inside us can assume the aspect of places we've
  been
so that instead of emotions we see trees we knew or touched or a path,
and instead of the face of a thought, there'll be an unmade bed, a car
  nosing from an alley.
All I know about that time is that it stayed, that something, pain or the
  fear of it,
makes me stop the wheel and reach to the silence beyond my eyes and
  it's still there:
the empty wind, the white crosses of the renewers slashed on the door-
  posts,
the last, dim layers of paint loosening from the rotted sills, drifting down.

Near the Haunted Castle

Teen Gangs Fight: Girl Paralyzed By Police Bullet
    —Headline

This is a story. You don't have to think about it, it's make-believe.
It's like a lie, maybe not quite a lie but I don't want you to worry about it.
The reason it's got to be a lie is because you already know the truth and
       I already know it
and what difference does it make? We still can't do anything: why kill
       yourself?
So here's the story. It's like the princess and the pea, remember?
Where they test her with mattresses and a pea and she's supposed not to
       sleep
and get upset and then they'll know she's the princess and marry her?
Except in this version, she comes in and nobody believes it's her and
       they lay her down
but instead of forty mattresses do you know what they lay her on? Money!
Of course, money! A million dollars! It's like a hundred mattresses, it's so
       soft, a thousand!
It's how much you cut from the budget for teachers to give the policemen.
It's how much you take from relief to trade for bullets. Soft!
And instead of the pea, what? A bullet! Brilliant! A tiny bullet stuck in at
       the bottom!
So then comes the prince. My prince, my beauty. Except he has holsters.
He has leather and badges. And what he does, he starts tearing the mat-
       tresses out.
Out? Don't forget, it's a story. Don't forget to not worry, it's pretend.
He's tearing the mattresses out and then he's stuffing them in his mouth!
This wonderful prince-mouth, this story-mouth, it holds millions, bil-
       lions,
and she's falling, slowly, or no, the pea, the bullet, is rising,
surging like some ridiculous funny snout out of the dark down there.
Does it touch you? Oh, yes, but don't worry, this is just a fib, right?
It slides next to your skin and it's cold and it goes in, in! as though you
       were a door,
as though you were the whole bedroom; in, through the backbone,
       through the cartilage,

the cords, then it freezes. It freezes and the prince is all gone,
this is the sleeping, the wrong-sleeping, you shouldn't be sleeping,
the so-heaviness in the arms, the so-heaviness in the legs, don't sleep,
        they'll leave you,
they'll throw you away . . . the dollars spinning, the prince leaving,
and you, at the bottom, on the no-turning, on the pea, like a story,
on the bullet, the single bullet that costs next to nothing, like one dollar.
People torture each other so they'll tell the whole truth, right?
And study the nervous systems of the lower orders to find the truth, right?
And tell the most obviously absurd tales for the one grain of truth?
The mother puts down her book and falls asleep watching television.
On the television they go on talking.
The father's in bed, the little gears still rip through his muscles.
The two brothers have the same dream, like Blinken and Nod, like the
        mayor and the president.
The sister . . . The sister . . . The heart furnace, the brain furnace, hot
        . . . hot . . .
Let's go back to find where the truth is. Let's find the beginning.
In the beginning was love, right? No, in the beginning . . . the bullet . . .

The Cave

I think most people are relieved the first time they actually know some-
      one who goes crazy.

It doesn't happen the way you hear about it where the person gibbers
      and sticks to you like an insect:

mostly there's crying, a lot of silence, sometimes someone will whisper
      back to their voices.

All my friend did was sit, at home until they found him, then for hours at
      a time on his bed in the ward,

pointing at his eyes, chanting the same phrase over and over. "Too much
      fire!" he'd say. "Too much fire!"

I remember I was amazed at how raggedy he looked, then annoyed be-
      cause he wouldn't answer me

and then, when he was getting better, I used to pester him to tell me
      about that fire-thing.

He'd seemed to be saying he'd seen too much and I wanted to know too
      much what

because my obsession then was that I was somehow missing everything
      beyond the ordinary.

What was only real was wrong. There were secrets that could turn you
      into stone,

they were out of range or being kept from me, but my friend, if he knew
      what I meant, wouldn't say,

so we'd talk politics or books or moon over a beautiful girl who was usu-
      ally in the visiting room when we were

who mutilated herself. Every time I was there, new slashes would've
      opened out over her forearms and wrists

and once there were two brilliant medallions on her cheeks that I
      thought were rouge spots

but that my friend told me were scratches she'd put there with a broken
      light bulb when she'd run away the day before.

The way you say running away in hospitals is "eloping." Someone who
      hurts themselves is a "cutter."

How could she do it to herself? My friend didn't think that was the ques-
      tion.

She'd eloped, cut, they'd brought her back and now she was waiting
there again,
those clowny stigmata of lord knows what on her, as tranquil and seduc-
tive as ever.
I used to storm when I'd leave her there with him. She looked so vulner-
able.
All the hours they'd have. I tormented myself imagining how they'd
come together,
how they'd tell each other the truths I thought I had to understand to
live,
then how they'd kiss, their lips, chaste and reverent, rushing over the for-
given surfaces.
Tonight, how long afterwards, watching my wife undress, letting my gaze
go so everything blurs
but the smudges of her nipples and hair and the wonderful lumpy graces
of her pregnancy,
I still can bring it back: those dismal corridors, the furtive nods, the
moans I thought were sexual
and the awful lapses that seemed vestiges of exaltations I would never
have,
but now I know whatever in the mystery I was looking for, whatever brute
or cloud I thought eluded me,
isn't lost in the frenzy of one soul or another, but next to us, in the touch,
between.
Lying down, fumbling for the light, moving into the shadow with my son
or daughter, I find it again:
the prism of hidden sorrow, the namelessness of nothing and nothing
shuddering across me,
and then the warmth, clinging and brightening, the hide, the caul, the
first mind.

Hog Heaven

for James Havard

It stinks. It stinks and it stinks and it stinks and it stinks.
It stinks in the mansions and it stinks in the shacks and the carpeted
        offices,
in the beds and the classrooms and out in the fields where there's no one.
It just stinks. Sniff and feel it come up: it's like death coming up.
Take one foot, ignore it long enough, leave it on the ground long enough
because you're afraid to stop, even to love, even to be loved,
it'll stink worse than you can imagine, as though the whole air was meat
        pressing your eyelids,
as though you'd been caught, hung up from the earth
and all the stinks of the fear drain down and your toes are the valves drip-
        ping
the giant stinks of the pain and the death and the radiance.
Old people stink, with their teeth and their hot rooms, and the kiss,
the age-kiss, the death-kiss, it comes like a wave and you want to fall
        down and be over.
And money stinks: the little threads that go through it like veins through
        an eye,
each stinks—if you hold it onto your lip it goes bad, it stinks like a vein
        going bad.
And Christ stank: he knew how the slaves would be stacked into the
        holds and he took it—
the stink of the vomit and shit and of somebody just rolling over and
        plunging in with his miserable seed.
And the seed stinks. And the fish carrying it upstream and the bird eating
        the fish
and you the bird's egg, the dribbles of yolk, the cycle: the whole thing
        stinks.
The intellect stinks and the moral faculty, like things burning, like the
        cave under justice,
and the good quiet men, like oceans of tears squeezed into one handful,
        they stink,
and the whole consciousness, like something plugged up, stinks, like
        something cut off.

Life stinks and death stinks and god and your hand touching your face

and every breath, daring to turn, daring to come back from the stop: the
turn stinks

and the last breath, the real one, the one where everyone troops into
your bed

and piles on—oh, that one stinks best! It stays on your mouth

and who you kiss now knows life and knows death, knows how it would
be to fume in a nostril

and the thousand desires that stink like the stars and the voice heard
through the stars

and each time—milk sour, egg sour, sperm sour—each time—dirt,
friend, father—

each time—mother, tree, breath—each time—breath and breath and
breath—

each time the same stink, the amazement, the wonder to do this and it
flares,

this, and it stinks, this: it stinks and it stinks and it stinks and it stinks.

Blades

When I was about eight, I once stabbed somebody, another kid, a little
      girl.
I'd been hanging around in front of the supermarket near our house
and when she walked by, I let her have it, right in the gap between her
      shirt and her shorts
with a piece of broken-off car antenna I used to carry around in my
      pocket.
It happened so fast I still don't know how I did it: I was as shocked as she
      was
except she squealed and started yelling as though I'd plunged a knife in
      her
and everybody in the neighborhood gathered around us, then they called
      the cops,
then the girl's mother came running out of the store saying, "What hap-
      pened? What happened?"
and the girl screamed, "He stabbed me!" and I screamed back, "I did
      not!" and she you did too
and me I didn't and we were both crying hysterically by that time.
Somebody pulled her shirt up and it was just a scratch but we went on
      and on
and the mother, standing between us, seemed to be absolutely terrified.
I still remember how she watched first one of us and then the other with
      a look of complete horror—
You did too! I did not!—as though we were both strangers, as though it
      was some natural disaster
she was beholding that was beyond any mode of comprehension so all
      she could do
was stare speechlessly at us, and then another expression came over her
      face,
one that I'd never seen before, that made me think she was going to cry
      herself
and sweep both of us, the girl and me, into her arms to hold us against her.
The police came just then, though, quieted everyone down, put the girl
      and the mother

into a squad-car to take to the hospital and me in another to take to jail
except they really only took me around the corner and let me go because
the mother and daughter were black
and in those days you had to do something pretty terrible to get into trou-
ble that way.

I don't understand how we twist these things or how we get them straight
again
but I relived that day I don't know how many times before I realized I
had it all wrong.
The boy wasn't me at all, he was another kid: I was just there.
And it wasn't the girl who was black, but him. The mother was real,
though.
I really had thought she was going to embrace them both
and I had dreams about her for years afterwards: that I'd be being born
again
and she'd be lifting me with that same wounded sorrow or she would
suddenly appear out of nowhere,
blotting out everything but a single, blazing wing of holiness.
Who knows the rest? I can still remember how it felt the old way.
How I make my little thrust, how she crushes us against her, how I turn
and snarl
at the cold circle of faces around us because something's torn in me,
some ancient cloak of terror we keep on ourselves because we'll do any-
thing,
anything, not to know how silently we knell in the mouth of death
and not to obliterate the forgiveness and the lies we offer one another
and call innocence.
This is innocence. I touch her, we kiss.
And this. I'm here or not here. I can't tell. I stab her. I stab her again. I
still can't.

Friends

My friend Dave knew a famous writer who used to have screwdrivers for
breakfast.
He'd start with half gin and half juice and the rest of the day he'd sit with
the same glass
in the same chair and add gin. The drink would get paler and paler,
finally he'd pass out.
Every day was the same. Sometimes, when I'm making milk for the baby,
cutting the thick,
sweet formula from the can with sterilized water, the baby, hungry again,
still hungry,
rattling his rickety, long-legged chair with impatience, I think of that
story.
Dave says the writer could talk like a god. He'd go on for hours in the
same thought.
In his books, though, you never find out why he drove so hard toward his
death.
I have a death in my memory that lately the word itself always brings
back. I'm not quite sure why.
A butterfly, during a downpour one afternoon, hooked onto my screen. I
thought it was waiting.
The light was just so. Its eyes caught the flare so it seemed to be watch-
ing me in my bed.
When I got up to come closer and it should have been frightened, it
hung on.
After the rain, it was still there. Its eyes were still shining. I touched the
screen
and it fell to the ledge. There were blue streaks on its wings. A while
later, the wind took it.
The writer drowned in his puke or his liver exploded—it depends on the
story.
He was a strong man, for all that. He must have thought it was taking for-
ever.
Dave says when he'd wake with amnesia, he wouldn't want you to fill in
the gaps.

He just wanted his gin and his juice. From all that you hear, he was
      probably right.
When we were young and we'd drink our minds to extinction, that was
      the best part: you did this, you said that.
It was like hearing yourself in a story. Sometimes real life is almost the
      same,
as though you were being recited; you can almost tell what a thought is
      before it arrives.
When I follow my mind now, another butterfly happens. It's not hard to
      see why.
It's the country this time. The butterfly walked over the white table and
      onto my hand.
I lifted it and it held. My friends were amazed. Catherine tried, too, but
      the butterfly fluttered away.
I put my hand back in the air and it found me again. It came down on a
      finger and clung.
Its sails listed. I could see it untwirling the barb of its tongue on my nail.
      I shook it away.
Those were the days and the nights when Catherine and I were first
      falling in love.
Sometimes, in the dark, I'd still be afraid but she'd touch my arm and I'd
      sleep.
The visions I had then were all death: they were hideous and absurd and
      had nothing to do with my life.
All I feel now about death is a sadness, not to be here with everyone I
      love,
but in those days, I'd dream, I'd be wracked, Catherine would have to
      reach over to hold me.
In the morning, it would be better. Even at dawn, when I'd wake first,
      trembling, gasping for air,
I'd burrow back down, Catherine would open her eyes, smiling, with me
      at her breast, and it would be better.

The Shade

A summer cold. No rash. No fever. Nothing. But a dozen times during
     the night I wake
to listen to my son whimpering in his sleep, trying to snort the sticky
     phlegm out of his nostrils.
The passage clears, silence, nothing. I cross the room, groping for the
     warm,
elusive creature of his breath and my heart lunges, stutters, tries to race
     away;
I don't know from what, from my imagination, from life itself, maybe
     from understanding too well
and being unable to do anything about how much of my anxiety is al-
     ways for myself.
Whatever it was, I left it when the dawn came. There's a park near here
where everyone who's out of work in our neighborhood comes to line up
     in the morning.
The converted school buses shuttling hands to the cannery fields in Jer-
     sey were just rattling away when I got there
and the small-time contractors, hiring out cheap walls, cheap ditches,
     cheap everything,
were loading laborers onto the sacks of plaster and concrete in the backs
     of their pickups.
A few housewives drove by looking for someone to babysit or clean cel-
     lars for them,
then the gates of the local bar unlaced and whoever was left drifted in
     out of the wall of heat
already rolling in with the first fists of smoke from the city incinerators.

It's so quiet now, I can hear the sparrows foraging scraps of garbage on
     the paths.
The stove husk chained as a sign to the store across the street creaks in
     the last breeze of darkness.
By noon, you'd have to be out of your mind to want to be here: the park
     will reek of urine,
bodies will be sprawled on the benches, men will wrestle through the
     surf of broken bottles,

but even now, watching the leaves of the elms softly lifting toward the
 day, softly falling back,
all I see is fear forgiving fear on every page I turn; all I know is every time
 I try to change it,
I say it again: my wife, my child . . . my home, my work, my sorrow.
If this were the last morning of the world, if time had finally moved in-
 side us and erupted
and we were Agamemnon again, Helen again, back on that faint, begin-
 ning planet
where even the daily survivals were giants, filled with light, I think I'd
 still be here,
afraid or not enough afraid, silently howling the names of death over the
 grass and asphalt.
The morning goes on, the sun burning, the earth burning, and between
 them, part of me lifts and starts back,
past the wash of dead music from the bar, the drinker reeling on the
 curb, the cars coughing alive,
and part, buried in itself, stays, forever, blinking into the glare, freezing.

With Ignorance

With ignorance begins a knowledge the first characteristic of which is ignorance.
    —Kierkegaard

1.

Again and again. Again lips, again breast, again hand, thigh, loin and
    bed and bed
after bed, the hunger, hunger again, need again, the rising, the spasm
    and needing again.
Flesh, lie, confusion and loathing, the scabs of clear gore, the spent seed
    and the spurt
of desire that seemed to generate from itself, from its own rising and
    spasm.
Everything waste, everything would be or was, the touching, the touch
    and the touch back.
Everything rind, scar, without sap, without meaning or seed, and every-
    one, everyone else,
every slip or leap into rage, every war, flame, sob, it was there, too, the
    stifling, the hushed,
malevolent frenzy and croak of desire, again and again, the same hunger,
    same need.
Touch me, hold me, sorrow and sorrow, the emptied, emptied again,
    touched again.
The hunger, the rising, again and again until again itself seemed to be
    need and hunger
and so much terror could rise out of that, the hunger repeating itself out
    of the fear now,
that how could you know if you lived within it at all, if there wasn't
    another,
a malediction or old prayer, a dream or a city of dream or a single, flesh-
    less, dreamless error,
whose tongue you were, who spoke with you, butted or rasped with you,
    but still, tongue or another,
word or not word, what could it promise that wouldn't drive us back to
    the same hunger and sorrow?

What could it say that wouldn't spasm us back to ourselves to be bait or a
    dead prayer?
Or was that it? Only that? The prayer hunting its prey, hunting the bait
    of itself?
Was the hunger the faith in itself, the belief in itself, even the prayer?
Was it the dead prayer?

2.

The faces waver; each gathers the others within it, the others shuddering
    through it
as though there were tides or depths, as though the depths, the tides of
    the eyes themselves
could throw out refractions, waves, shifts and wavers and each faceless
    refraction
could rise to waver beneath me, to shift, to be faceless again, beneath or
    within me,
the lying, confusion, recurrence, reluctance, the surge through into
    again.
Each room, each breast finding its ripeness of shadow, each lip and its
    shadow,
the dimming, flowing, the waver through time, through loss, gone, irre-
    deemable,
all of it, each face into regret, each room into forgetting and absence.
But still, if there were a moment, still, one moment, to begin in or go
    back to,
to return to move through, waver through, only a single moment carved
    back from the lie
the way the breast is carved from its shadow, sealed from the dross of
    darkness
until it takes the darkness itself and fills with it, taking the breath;
if, in the return, I could be taken the way I could have been taken, with
    voice or breast,
emptied against the space of the breast as though breast was breath and
    my breath,
taken, would have been emptied into the moment, it could rise here,
    now, in that moment, the same moment.

But it won't, doesn't. The moments lift and fall, break, and it shifts, wavers,
subsides into the need again, the faceless again, the faceless and the lie.

3.

Remorse? Blame? There is a pit-creature. The father follows it down with the ax.
Exile and sorrow. Once there were things we lived in, don't you remember?
We scraped, starved, then we came up, abashed, to the sun, and what was the first word?
Blame, blame and remorse, then sorrow, then the blame was the father then was ourselves.
Such a trite story, do we have to retell it? The mother took back the sun and we . . .
Remorse, self-regard, call it shame or being abashed or trying again, for the last time, to return.
Remorse, then power, the power and the blame and what did we ever suffer but power?
The head lifting itself, then the wars, remorse and revenge, the wars of humility,
the blades and the still valley, the double intention, the simple tree in the blood.
Then exile again, even the sword, even the spear, the formula scratched on the sand,
even the christening, the christened, blame again, power again, but even then,
taken out of the fire at the core and never returned, what could we not sanction?
One leg after the other, the look back, the power, the fire again and the sword again.
Blame and remorse. That gives in to desire again, in to hunger again. That gives in to . . . this . . .

4.

Someone . . . Your arm touches hers or hers finds yours, unmoving,
       unasking.
A silence, as though for the first time, and as though for the first time,
       you can listen,
as though there were chords: your life, then the other's, someone else, as
       though for the first time.
The life of the leaves over the streetlamp and the glow, swelling, chord-
       ing, under the shadows,
and the quaver of things built, one quavering cell at a time, and the song
of the cell gently bedding itself in its mortar, in this silence, this first
       attempting.
Even the shush of cars, the complex stress of a step, the word called into
       the darkness,
and, wait, the things even beyond, beyond membrane or awareness,
       mode, sense, dream,
don't they sing, too? Chord, too? Isn't the song and the silence there,
       too?
I heard it once. It changed nothing, but once, before I went on, I did
       hear:
the equation of star and plant, the wheel, the ecstasy and division, the
       equation again.
The absolute walking its planks, its long wall, its long chord of laughter
       or grief.
I heard silence, then the children, the spawn, how we have to teach
       every cell how to speak,
and from that, after that, the kiss back from the speech, the touch back
       from the song.
And then more, I heard how it alters, how we, the speakers, the can't-
       live, the refuse-to,
how we, only in darkness, groaning and thrashing into the undergrowth
       of our eternal,
would speak then, would howl, howl again, and at last, at the end, we'd
       hear it:
the prayer and the flesh crying, *Why aren't you here?* And the cry back in
       it, *I am! I am!*

5.

Imagine dread. Imagine, without symbol, without figure, history or histo-
ries; a place, not a place.
Imagine it must be risen through, beginning with the silent moment, the
secrets quieted,
one hour, one age at a time, sadness, nostalgia, the absurd pain of
betrayal.
Through genuine grief, then, through the genuine suffering for the
boundaries of self
and the touch on the edge, the compassion, that never, never quite,
breaks through.
Imagine the touch again and beyond it, beyond either end, joy or terror,
either ending,
the context that gives way, not to death, but past, past anything still with
a name,
even death, because even death is a promise offering comfort, solace,
that any direction we turn,
there'll still be the word, the name, and this the promise now, even with
terror,
the promise again that the wordlessness and the self won't be for one
instant the same enacting,
and we stay within it, a refusal now, a turning away, a never giving way,
we stay until even extinction itself, the absence, death itself, even death,
isn't longed for,
never that, but turned toward in the deepest turn of the self, the deepest
gesture toward self.
And then back, from the dread, from locution and turn, from whatever
history reflects us,
the self grounds itself again in itself and reflects itself, even its loss, as its
own,
and back again, still holding itself back, the certainty and belief tearing
again,
back from the edge of that one flood of surrender which, given space,
would, like space itself,
rage beyond any limit, the flesh itself giving way in its terror, and back
from that,
into love, what we have to call love, the one moment before we move
onwards again,

towards the end, the life again of the self-willed, self-created, embodied,
reflected again.
Imagine a space prepared for with hunger, with dread, with power and
the power
over dread which is dread, and the love, with no space for itself, no
power for itself,
a moment, a silence, a rising, the terror for that, the space for that. Imag-
ine love.

6.

Morning. The first morning of now. You, your touch, your song and
morning, but still,
something, a last fear or last lie or last clench of confusion clings,
holds back, refuses, resists, the way fear itself clings in its web of need or
dread.
What would release be? Being forgiven? No, never forgiven, never only
forgiven.
To be touched, somehow, with presence, so that the only sign is a step,
towards or away?
Or not even a step, because the walls, of self, of dread, can never release,
can never forgive stepping away, out of the willed or refused, out of the
lie or the fear
of the self that still holds back and refuses, resists, and turns back again
and again into the willed.
What if it could be, though? The first, hectic rush past guilt or remorse?
What if we could find a way through the fires that aren't with us and the
terrors that are?
What would be there? Would we be thrown back into perhaps or not yet
or not needed or done?
Could we even slip back, again, past the first step into the first refusal,
the first need, first blot of desire that still somehow exists and wants to
resist, wants to give back the hard,
immaculate shell of the terror it still keeps against respite and unclenching?
Or perhaps no release, no step or sign, perhaps only to wait and accept.
Perhaps only to bless. To bless and to bless and to bless and to bless.
Willed or unwilled, word or sign, the word suddenly filled with its own
breath.

Self and other the self within other and the self still moved through its
    word,
consuming itself, still, and consuming, still being rage, war, the fear, the
    aghast,
but bless, bless still, even the fear, the loss, the gutting of word, the gut-
    ting even of hunger,
but still to bless and bless, even the turn back, the refusal, to bless and to
    bless and to bless.

7.

The first language was loss, the second sorrow, this is the last, then:
    yours . . .
An island, summer, late dusk; hills, laurel and thorn. I walked from the
    harbor, over the cliff road,
down the long trail through the rocks. When I came to our house the
    ship's wake was just edging onto the shore
and on the stone beach, under the cypress, the low waves reassuming
    themselves in the darkness, I waited.
There was a light in a room. You came to it, leaned to it, reaching,
    touching,
and watching you, I saw you give back to the light a light more than light
and to the silence you gave more than silence, and, in the silence, I
    heard it.
You, your self, your life, your beginning, pleasure, song clear as the light
    that touched you.
Your will, your given and taken; grief, recklessness, need or desire.
Your passion or tear, step forward or step back into the inevitable veil.
Yours and yours and yours, the dream, the wall of the self that won't be
    or needn't be breached,
and the breach, the touch, yours and the otherness, yours, the separate-
    ness,
never giving way, never breached really, but as simple, always, as light, as
    silence.
This is the language of that, that light and that silence, the silence rising
    through or from you.
Nothing to bless or not bless now, nothing to thank or forgive, not to
    triumph,

surrender, mean, reveal, assume or exhaust. Our faces bent to the light, and still,

there is terror, still history, power, grief and remorse, always, always the self and the other

and the endless tide, the waver, the terror again, between and beneath, but you, now,

your touch, your light, the otherness yours, the reach, the wheel, the waves touching.

And to, not wait, not overcome, not even forget or forgive the dream of the moment, the unattainable moment again.

Your light . . . Your silence . . .

In the silence, without listening, I heard it, and without words, without language or breath, I answered.

TAR

[1983]

From My Window

Spring: the first morning when that one true block of sweet, laminar,
    complex scent arrives
from somewhere west and I keep coming to lean on the sill, glorying in
    the end of the wretched winter.
The scabby-barked sycamores ringing the empty lot across the way are
    budded—I hadn't noticed—
and the thick spikes of the unlikely urban crocuses have already broken
    the gritty soil.
Up the street, some surveyors with tripods are waving each other left and
    right the way they do.
A girl in a gym suit jogged by a while ago, some kids passed, playing
    hooky, I imagine,
and now the paraplegic Vietnam vet who lives in a half-converted ware-
    house down the block
and the friend who stays with him and seems to help him out come
    weaving towards me,
their battered wheelchair lurching uncertainly from one edge of the
    sidewalk to the other.
I know where they're going—to the "Legion": once, when I was putting
    something out, they stopped,
both drunk that time, too, both reeking—it wasn't ten o'clock—and we
    chatted for a bit.
I don't know how they stay alive—on benefits most likely. I wonder if
    they're lovers?
They don't look it. Right now, in fact, they look a wreck, careening hap-
    hazardly along,
contriving, as they reach beneath me, to dip a wheel from the curb so
    that the chair skewers, teeters,
tips, and they both tumble, the one slowly, almost gracefully sliding in
    stages from his seat,
his expression hardly marking it, the other staggering over him, spinning
    heavily down,
to lie on the asphalt, his mouth working, his feet shoving weakly and
    fruitlessly against the curb.

In the storefront office on the corner, Reed and Son, Real Estate, have
     come to see the show.
Gazing through the golden letters of their name, they're not, at least,
     thank god, laughing.
Now the buddy, grabbing at a hydrant, gets himself erect and stands
     there for a moment, panting.
Now he has to lift the other, who lies utterly still, a forearm shielding his
     eyes from the sun.
He hauls him partly upright, then hefts him almost all the way into the
     chair, but a dangling foot
catches a support-plate, jerking everything around so that he has to put
     him down,
set the chair to rights, and hoist him again and as he does he jerks the
     grimy jeans right off him.
No drawers, shrunken, blotchy thighs: under the thick, white coils of
     belly blubber,
the poor, blunt pud, tiny, terrified, retracted, is almost invisible in the
     sparse genital hair,
then his friend pulls his pants up, he slumps wholly back as though he
     were, at last, to be let be,
and the friend leans against the cyclone fence, suddenly staring up at me
     as though he'd known,
all along, that I was watching and I can't help wondering if he knows that
     in the winter, too,
I watched, the night he went out to the lot and walked, paced rather,
     almost ran, for how many hours.
It was snowing, the city in that holy silence, the last we have, when the
     storm takes hold,
and he was making patterns that I thought at first were circles, then real-
     ized made a figure eight,
what must have been to him a perfect symmetry but which, from where
     I was, shivered, bent,
and lay on its side: a warped, unclear infinity, slowly, as the snow came
     faster, going out.
Over and over again, his head lowered to the task, he slogged the path
     he'd blazed,
but the race was lost, his prints were filling faster than he made them
     now and I looked away,

up across the skeletal trees to the tall center city buildings, some, though
      it was midnight,
with all their offices still gleaming, their scarlet warning beacons signal-
      ing erratically
against the thickening flakes, their smoldering auras softening portions of
      the dim, milky sky.
In the morning, nothing: every trace of him effaced, all the field pure
      white,
its surface glittering, the dawn, glancing from its glaze, oblique, relent-
      less, unadorned.

My Mother's Lips

Until I asked her to please stop doing it and was astonished to find that
    she not only could
but from the moment I asked her in fact would stop doing it, my mother,
    all through my childhood,
when I was saying something to her, something important, would move
    her lips as I was speaking
so that she seemed to be saying under her breath the very words I was
    saying as I was saying them.

Or, even more disconcertingly—wildly so now that my puberty had
    erupted—*before* I said them.
When I was smaller, I must just have assumed that she was omniscient.
    Why not?
She knew everything else—when I was tired, or lying; she'd know I was
    ill before I did.
I may even have thought—how could it not have come into my mind?—
    that she *caused* what I said.

All she was really doing of course was mouthing my words a split second
    after I said them myself,
but it wasn't until my own children were learning to talk that I really
    understood how,
and understood, too, the edge of anxiety in it, the wanting to bring you
    along out of the silence,
the compulsion to lift you again from those blank caverns of nameless-
    ness we encase.

That was long afterward, though: where I was now was just wanting to
    get her to stop,
and considering how I brooded and raged in those days, how quickly my
    teeth went on edge,
the restraint I approached her with seems remarkable, although her so
    unprotestingly,
readily taming a habit by then three children and a dozen years old was
    as much so.

It's endearing to watch us again in that long-ago dusk, facing each other,
	my mother and me.
I've just grown to her height, or just past it: there are our lips moving
	together,
now the unison suddenly breaks, I have to go on by myself, no maestro,
	no score to follow.
I wonder what finally made me take umbrage enough, or heart enough,
	to confront her?

It's not important. My cocoon at that age was already unwinding: the
	threads ravel and snarl.
When I find one again, it's that two o'clock in the morning, a grim hotel
	on a square,
the impenetrable maze of an endless city, when, really alone for the first
	time in my life,
I found myself leaning from the window, incanting in a tearing whisper
	what I thought were poems.

I'd love to know what I raved that night to the night, what those innocent
	dithyrambs were,
or to feel what so ecstatically drew me out of myself and beyond . . .
	Nothing is there, though,
only the solemn piazza beneath me, the riot of dim, tiled roofs and im-
	passable alleys,
my desolate bed behind me, and my voice, hoarse, and the sweet, alien
	air against me like a kiss.

The Dog

Except for the dog, that she wouldn't have him put away, wouldn't let
    him die, I'd have liked her.
She was handsome, busty, chunky, early middle-aged, very black, with a
    stiff, exotic dignity
that flurried up in me a mix of warmth and sexual apprehension neither
    of which, to tell the truth,
I tried very hard to nail down: she was that much older and in those days
    there was still the race thing.
This was just at the time of civil rights: the neighborhood I was living in
    was mixed.
In the narrow streets, the tiny three-floored houses they called father-son-
    holy-ghosts
which had been servants' quarters first, workers' tenements, then slums,
    still were, but enclaves of us,
beatniks and young artists, squatted there and commerce between every-
    one was fairly easy.
Her dog, a grinning mongrel, rib and knob, gristle and grizzle, wasn't
    terribly offensive.
The trouble was that he was ill, or the trouble more exactly was that I
    had to know about it.
She used to walk him on a lot I overlooked, he must have had a tumor or
    a blockage of some sort
because every time he moved his bowels, he shrieked, a chilling, almost
    human scream of anguish.
It nearly always caught me unawares, but even when I'd see them first, it
    wasn't better.
The limp leash coiled in her hand, the woman would be profiled to the
    dog, staring into the distance,
apparently oblivious, those breasts of hers like stone, while he, not a step
    away, laboring,
trying to eject the feeble, mucus-coated, blood-flecked chains that finally
    spurted from him,
would set himself on tiptoe and hump into a question mark, one quiver-
    ing back leg grotesquely lifted.

Every other moment he'd turn his head, as though he wanted her, to no
	avail, to look at him,
then his eyes would dim and he'd drive his wounded anus in the dirt,
	keening uncontrollably,
lurching forward in a hideous, electric dance as though someone were at
	him with a club.
When at last he'd finish, she'd wipe him with a tissue like a child; he'd
	lick her hand.
It was horrifying; I was always going to call the police; once I actually
	went out to chastise her—
didn't she know how selfish she was, how the animal was suffering?—she
	scared me off, though.
She was older than I'd thought, for one thing, her flesh was loosening,
	pouches of fat beneath the eyes,
and poorer, too, shabby, tarnished: I imagined smelling something
	faintly acrid as I passed.
Had I ever really mooned for such a creature? I slunk around the block,
	chagrined, abashed.
I don't recall them too long after that. Maybe the dog died, maybe I was
	just less sensitive.
Maybe one year when the cold came and I closed my windows, I forgot
	them . . . then I moved.
Everything was complicated now, so many tensions, so much bother-
	some self-consciousness.
Anyway, those back streets, especially in bad weather when the ginkgos
	lost their leaves, were bleak.
It's restored there now, ivy, pointed brick, garden walls with broken
	bottles mortared on them,
but you'd get sick and tired then: the rubbish in the gutter, the general
	sense of dereliction.
Also, I'd found a girl to be in love with: all we wanted was to live
	together, so we did.

The Color of Time

Although the lamp is out, and although it's dusk, late, dull, stifling sum-
　　mer dusk,
a wash of the column of grimy light reflects from the airshaft the boy's
　　bedroom faces:
he can still make out his model bomber twisting and untwisting on its
　　thread from the ceiling.
Everything else is utterly still. The air, breathed, breathed again, is thick,
　　decomposed,
a dense, almost organic, almost visible volume of soiled grains suspended
　　in the liquid heat.
The boy, in briefs and T-shirt, his limp sheet disarrayed, sweats lightly,
　　not disagreeably—
his frictionless skin and the complex savor at the corners of his mouth
　　intrigue him.
Suddenly, outside, a few feet away, a voice, a woman's, harsh but affect-
　　less, droning.
"I can't go on," it says. Pause. Then, more fervor, more conviction: *I can't
go on.*
The boy looks across: the window on the other side of the shaft, a blur of
　　uncertain amber,
its panes streaked as though someone had swiped a greasy rag across
　　them, is shut,
the yellowed paint on the rotting sill beneath it has bubbled and scabbed
　　in erratic strips.
More plaintively now, almost whining, "You're drunk," the voice says,
　　"you're drunk, aren't you?"
Everything twice, the boy notes. His mother and father are out. What
　　time must it be?
"I'm beating my head." The boy lifts in a more focused, more definite
　　interest this time.
Pause. *I'm beating my head,* the voice at last reaffirms. A door crashes
　　somewhere.
The boy has only infrequently seen the woman: out back, by the trash,
　　sometimes they pass,

but her image is vivid—slippers, a housedress with a lifeless nightgown
     hanging under the hem.
Something about her repels the boy, maybe the nightgown, maybe that
     their eyes never meet.
Nothing now. The boy's testicles somehow have slipped out of the leg of
     his shorts.
Awkwardly, he tucks them back in: how wrinkled they are, the skin
     tougher than the soles of his feet.
Later, the boy sits up. Has he been sleeping? The night seems stricter,
     the other window is dark.
The boy knows that sometimes he wakes: the next morning his mother
     will say with exasperation,
"You woke up screaming again," and sometimes he'll remember her
     arms or his father's around him.
He never remembers the scream, just the embrace, usually not even
     that, but once, he knows,
he called out, his father came to him: *Listen,* the boy said, *outside, there
     are babies crying.*
Cats, his father, angry beyond what the occasion seemed to imply, had
     whispered, *Go to sleep,*
jerking roughly, irrationally, the boy had thought, the sheet up nearly
     over the boy's head.
Although it's quiet now, not a sound, it's hard—the boy doesn't know
     why—not to cry out.
He tries to imagine the bar of warm glow from his parents' room bisect-
     ing the hall
but the darkness stays stubbornly intact and whatever it is shuddering in
     his chest keeps on.
I hope I don't cry, he thinks; his thighs lock over his fists: he can hold it,
     he thinks.

Flight

The last party before I left was in an old, run-down apartment house,
        The Greystone Arms,
the owners of which were involved in a drawn-out legal wrangle with
        some of the tenants.
The building was to be razed and redeveloped, the tenants, mostly older
        women who'd lived there forever,
were contesting being evicted—I forget on what grounds—and in the
        meantime everyone else had vacated
and the apartments had been rented to anyone who'd take them month-
        to-month, without leases.
The party when I heard about it had apparently been going on all night
        every night for weeks
in the penthouse a few hippie types I knew vaguely and didn't particu-
        larly care for had taken over.
I was tempted anyway: this was still the Sixties when if anything was
        happening, you went,
besides, I was at loose ends, and, although I didn't like admitting it,
        chronically adrift and lonely.
I'd been curious about the Greystone, I could tell myself that all I
        wanted was to get inside.
The exterior had mostly kept its splendors, brass fittings, carved stone
        urns and lintels:
even the grisly old awning still somehow hung together, though all it
        seemed ever to shelter now
was the congregation of tranquillized ex–mental patients whose agencies
        had parked them in the building
and whom you'd see huddled there, day and the down and out dead of
        night, nowhere to go, nothing to do,
shuffling dreamily aside when the speed-freaks and junkies would flit out
        to make their hits
or when the ladies who still were living in all this would huff past into
        the dilapidated lobby.
The ladies: that they'd have wanted to stay on at all by now was a
        triumph of pure indignation,
the place was crawling down so fast, but they hung on, barricaded in
        their genteel cubicles.

How dire it must have been for them—the hallways with bare, under-
watted fixtures,
the rotten plumbing booming through the night, the hiss of the addicts
outside their doors.
Whatever elegance there might have been was eaten by neglect: the
wallpaper hung in ratty strips,
its ribbons and roses had bled through onto the ocher plaster under-
neath, and everything,
even the palsied elevator, emitted the spermy, scummy odor of half a
century of secret damp.
The penthouse, up an extra flight of filthy stairs, was as bad, and the
party, if possible, was worse.
Every misfit in the city, every freeloader, every blown-out druggie and
glazed teenybopper
plus the crazies from the building and no telling who or what else had
filtered up there.
Stunned on rotgut wine or grass or acid, they danced mechanically in
the daze of the deafening music,
or sprawled on the floor, offhandedly fumbling at one another as though
no one else was in the room.
There was something almost maniacally mindless about it, but at the
same time it was like a battle,
that intense, that lunatic, and, as I hesitated in the doorway, something
made me realize just how much
without noticing I'd come to be of that, to want or need it, and I swear I
must have swayed,
the way, over their imaginary chaos, Manfred must have swayed, and
Faust, before it swallowed them.

There's a park there now. The morning I came back, I wandered by and
stopped to sit awhile.
Why, after all the fuss, a park, I don't know, but at any rate, it's not a
pleasant place,
reinforced, bleak concrete mostly; a fountain, ringed with granite, out of
order, dry.
Two busloads of retarded kids were playing with their teachers on the
asphalt ball field,
twittering with glee and shrieking as they lumbered from home plate to
center field and back.

A whole platoon of them, the smallest ones—adorable—had imitation
football helmets.
Some food chain's plastic giveaways, the things had eagles stenciled on
them, and the letters GIANTS.
The other benches were populated with old women, the Greystone
ladies, back to claim their turf, I thought.
It was mild and sunny. I let my eyes close, and dozed and dreamed,
listening to the children.

The Gift

I have found what pleases my friend's chubby, rosy, gloriously shining-
   eyed year-old daughter.
She chirps, flirts with me, pulls herself up by my pants leg, and her pleas-
   ure is that I lift her,
high, by her thighs, over my head, and then that I let her suddenly fall,
   plunge, plummet,
down through my hands, to be, at the last instant, under the arms, in
   mid-gasp, caught.
She laughs when I do it, she giggles, roars; she is flushed with it, glowing,
   elated, ecstatic.
When I put her down, she whines, whimpers, claws at my lap: *Again,* she
   is saying . . . *Again: More.*
I pick up my glass, though, my friend and I chat, the child keeps at me
   but I pay no mind.

Once I would never have done that, released her like that, not until,
   satisfied, sated,
no need left, no "more," nothing would have been left for her but to fold
   sighing in my arms.
Once it was crucial that I be able to think of myself as unusually gifted
   with children,
and, even discounting the effort I put in it all, the premeditation, the
   scheming, I was.
I'd studied what they would want—at this age to rise, to fall, be tickled,
   caressed.
Older, to be heeded, attended: I had stories, dreams, ways to confide,
   take confidence back.
But beyond that, children did love me, I think, and beyond that, there
   seemed more.

I could calm crying babies, even when they were furious, shrieking, the
   mothers at wits' end.
I had rituals I'd devised, whisperings, clicks; soft, blowy whistles, a song-
   voice.
A certain firmness of hand, I remember I thought: concentration, a
   deepening of the gaze.

Maybe they'd be surprised to find me with them at all instead of the
      mother or father,
but, always, they'd stop, sometimes so abruptly, with such drama, that
      even I would be taken aback.
Tears, sometimes, would come to my eyes: I would be flooded with
      thanks that I'd been endowed with this,
or had resurrected it from some primitive source of grace I imagined
      we'd bartered away.

What else did I have? Not very much: being alone most of the time,
      retrospectively noble,
but bitter back then, brutal, abrasive, corrosive—I was wearing away with
      it like a tooth.
And my sexual hunger, how a breast could destroy me, or a haunch: not
      having the beautiful haunch.
. . . And love, too, I suppose, yes, now and then, for a girl, never for other
      men's wives yet . . .
Where did the children fit in, though, that odd want to entrance and
      enchant, to give bliss?
Did no one think I was mad? Didn't I ever wonder myself if I was using
      the children,
whether needs or compulsions, at least sublimations, were unaccounted
      for in my passion?

No, never, more sense to ask if those vulnerable creatures of the heart
      used me.
The children were light—I thought they pertained to my wish to be
      pure, a saint.
I never conjoined them with anything else, not with the loneliness or the
      vile desire,
not with my rages or the weary, nearly irrepressible urges I'd feel to let
      go, to die.
The children were light, or let intimations of light through—they were
      the way to the soul:
I wanted to think myself, too, a matrix of innocent warmth instead of the
      sorrowing brute I was,
stumbling out by myself into the moaning darkness again, thrust again
      into that murderous prowl.

On Learning of a Friend's Illness

for James Wright

The morning is so gray that the grass is gray and the side of the white
 horse grazing
is as gray and hard as the harsh, insistent wind gnawing the iron surface
 of the river,
while far off on the other shore, the eruptions from the city seem for
 once more docile and benign
than the cover of nearly indistinguishable clouds they unfurl to insinuate
 themselves among.

It's a long while since the issues of mortality have taken me this way.
 Shivering,
I tramp the thin, bitten track to the first rise, the first descent, and, toiling
 up again,
I startle out of their brushy hollow the whole herd of wild-eyed, shaggy,
 unkempt mares,
their necks, rumps, withers, even faces begrimed with patches of the
 gluey, alluvial mud.

All of them at once, their nostrils flared, their tails flung up over their
 backs like flags,
are suddenly in flight, plunging and shoving along the narrow furrow of
 the flood ditch,
bursting from its mouth, charging headlong towards the wires at the
 pasture's end,
banking finally like one great, graceful wing to scatter down the hillside
 out of sight.

Only the oldest of them all stays with me, and she, sway-backed, over at
 the knees,
blind, most likely deaf, still, when I approach her, swings her meager
 backside to me,
her ears flattening, the imperturbable opals of her eyes gazing resolutely
 over the bare,
scruffy fields, the scattered pines and stands of third-growth oak I called a
 forest once.

I slip up on her, hook her narrow neck, haul her to me, hold her for a
      moment, let her go.
I hardly can remember anymore what there ever was out here that keeps
      me coming back
to watch the land be amputated by freeways and developments, and the
      mares, in their sanctuary,
thinning out, reverting, becoming less and less approachable, more and
      more the symbols of themselves.

How cold it is. The hoofprints in the hardened muck are frozen lakes,
      their rims atilt,
their glazed opacities skewered with straw, muddled with the ancient,
      ubiquitous manure.
I pick a morsel of it up: scentless, harmless, cool, as desiccated as an
      empty hive,
it crumbles in my hand, its weightless, wingless filaments taken from me
      by the wind and strewn

in a long, surprising arc that wavers once then seems to burst into a rain
      of dust.
No comfort here, nothing to say, to try to say, nothing for anyone. I start
      the long trek back,
the horses nowhere to be seen, the old one plodding wearily away to join
      them,
the river, bitter to look at, and the passionless earth, and the grasses rush-
      ing ceaselessly in place.

Combat

Ich hatte einst ein schönes Vaterland . . . Es war ein Traum.
    —Heinrich Heine

I've been trying for hours to figure out who I was reminded of by the wel-
        terweight fighter
I saw on television this afternoon all but ruin his opponent with counter-
        punches and now I have it.
It was a girl I knew once, a woman: when he was being interviewed after
        the knockout, he was her exactly,
the same rigorous carriage, same facial structure—sharp cheekbones,
        very vivid eyebrows—
even the sheen of perspiration—that's how I'd remember her, of course
        . . . Moira was her name—
and the same quality in the expression of unabashed self-involvement,
        softened at once with a grave,
almost oversensitive attentiveness to saying with absolute precision what
        was to be said.
Lovely Moira! Could I ever have forgotten you? No, not forgotten, only
        not had with me for a time
that dark, slow voice, those vulnerable eyes, those ankles finely tendoned
        as a thoroughbred's.
We met I don't remember where—everything that mattered happened in
        her apartment, in the living room,
with her mother, whom she lived with, watching us, and in Moira's bed-
        room down the book-lined corridor.
The mother, I remember, was so white, not all that old but white: every-
        thing, hair, skin, lips, was ash,
except her feet, which Moira would often hold on her lap to massage
        and which were a deep,
frightening yellow, the skin thickened and dense, horned with calluses
        and chains of coarse, dry bunions,
the nails deformed and brown, so deeply buried that they looked like
        chips of tortoiseshell.
Moira would rub the poor, sad things, twisting and kneading at them
        with her strong hands;

the mother's eyes would be closed, occasionally she'd mutter something
under her breath in German.
That was their language—they were, Moira said, refugees, but the word
didn't do them justice.
They were well-off, very much so, their apartment was, in fact, the most
splendid thing I'd ever seen.
There were lithographs and etchings—some Klees, I think; a Munch—a
lot of very flat oriental rugs,
voluptuous leather furniture and china so frail the molds were surely cast
from butterflies.
I never found out how they'd brought it all with them: what Moira told
me was of displaced-person camps,
a pilgrimage on foot from Prussia and the Russians, then Frankfurt,
Rotterdam, and here, "freedom."
The trip across the war was a complicated memory for her; she'd been
very young, just in school,
what was most important to her at that age was her father, who she'd
hardly known and who'd just died.
He was a general, she told me, the chief of staff or something of "the war
against the Russians."
He'd been one of the conspirators against Hitler and when the plot failed
he'd committed suicide,
all of which meant not very much to me, however good the story was
(and I heard it often),
because people then were still trying to forget the war, it had been almost
ignored, even in school,
and I had no context much beyond what my childhood comic books had
given me to hang any of it on.
Moira was fascinated by it, though, and by their journey, and whenever
she wanted to offer me something—
when I'd despair, for instance, of ever having from her what I had to
have—it would be, again, that tale.
In some ways it was, I think, her most precious possession, and every
time she'd unfold it
she'd seem to have forgotten having told me before: each time the
images would be the same—
a body by the roadside, a child's—awful—her mother'd tried to hide her
eyes but she'd jerked free;

a white ceramic cup of sweet, cold milk in the dingy railroad station of
        some forgotten city,
then the boat, the water, black, the webs of rushing foam she'd made up
        creatures for, who ran beneath the waves
and whose occupation was to snare the boat, to snarl it, then . . . she didn't
        know what then,
and I'd be hardly listening anyway by then, one hand on a thigh, the
        other stroking,
with such compassion, such generous concern, such cunning twenty-
        one-year-old commiseration,
her hair, her perfect hair, then the corner of her mouth, then, so far
        away, the rich rim of a breast.
We'd touch that way—petting was the word then—like lovers, with the
        mother right there with us,
probably, I remember thinking, because we weren't lovers, not really, not
        that way (not yet, I'd think),
but beyond that there seemed something else, some complicity between
        them, some very adult undertaking
that I sensed but couldn't understand and that astonished me as did
        almost everything about them.
I never really liked the mother—I was never given anything to like—but
        I was awed by her.
If I was left alone with her—Moira on the phone, say—I stuttered, or was
        stricken mute.
It felt like I was sitting there with time itself: everything seemed some-
        how finished for her,
but there seemed, still, to be such depths, or such ascensions, to her
        unblinking brooding.
She was like a footnote to a text, she seemed to know it, suffer it, and, if
        I was wildly uneasy with her,
my eyes battering shyly in their chutes, it was my own lack, my own
        unworthiness that made it so.
Moira would come back, we'd talk again, I can't imagine what about
        except, again, obsessively, the father,
his dying, his estates, the stables, servants, all they'd given up for the
        madness of that creature Hitler.
I'd listen to it all again, and drift, looking in her eyes, and pine, ponder-
        ing her lips.

I knew that I was dying of desire—down of cheek; subtle, alien scent—
      that I'd never felt desire like this.
I was so distracted that I couldn't even get their name right: they'd kept
      the real pronunciation,
I'd try to ape what I remembered of my grandmother's Polish Yiddish but
      it still eluded me
and Moira's little joke before she'd let me take her clothes off was that
      we'd have lessons, "Von C——" "No, Von C——"
Later, when I was studying the Holocaust, I found it again, the name,
      Von C——, in Shirer's *Reich*:
it had, indeed, existed, and it had, yes, somewhere on the Eastern front,
      blown its noble head off.
I wasn't very moved. I wasn't in that city anymore, I'd ceased long before
      ever to see them,
and besides, I'd changed by then—I was more aware of history and was
      beginning to realize,
however tardily, that one's moral structures tended to be air unless you
      grounded them in real events.
Everything I did learn seemed to negate something else, everything was
      more or less up for grabs,
but the war, the Germans, all I knew about that now—no, never: what a
      complex triumph to have a nation,
all of it, beneath you, what a splendid culmination for the adolescence of
      one's ethics!
As for Moira, as for her mother, what recompense for those awful hours,
      those ecstatic unaccomplishments.
I reformulated her—them—forgave them, held them fondly, with a
      heavy lick of condescension, in my system.
But for now, there we are, Moira and I, down that hall again, in her
      room again, both with nothing on.
I can't say what she looked like. I remember that I thought her somewhat
      too robust, her chest too thick,
but I was young, and terrified, and quibbled everything: now, no doubt,
      I'd find her perfect.
In my mind now, naked, she's almost too much so, too blond, too gold,
      her pubic hair, her arm and leg fur,
all of it is brushed with light, so much glare she seems to singe the very
      tissue of remembrance,

but there are—I can see them now and didn't then—promises of dim-
ness, vaults and hidden banks of coolness.
If I couldn't, though, appreciate the subtleties, it wasn't going to hold me
back, no, it was *she* who held me back,
always, as we struggled on that narrow bed, twisted on each other, maul-
ing one another like demented athletes.
So fierce it was, so strenuous, aggressive: my thigh *here*, my hand *here*,
lips *here*, *here*,
hers *here* and *here* but never *there* or *there* . . . before it ended, she'd have
even gone into the sounds of love,
groans and whispered shrieks, glottal stops, gutturals I couldn't catch or
understand,
and all this while *nothing would be happening*, nothing, that is, in the
way I'd mean it now.
We'd lie back (this is where I see her sweating, gleaming with it,
drenched) and she'd smile.
She is satisfied somehow. This is what she wanted somehow. Only this?
Yes, only this,
and we'd be back, that quickly, in my recollection anyway, with the
mother in the other room,
the three of us in place, the conversation that seemed sometimes like a
ritual, eternally recurring.
How long we were to wait like this was never clear to me; my despera-
tion, though, was slow in gathering.
I must have liked the role, or the pretense of the role, of beast, primed,
about to pounce,
and besides, her hesitations, her fendings-off, were so warm and so bewil-
dering,
I was so engrossed in them, that when at last, once and for all, she let me
go,
the dismissal was so adroitly managed that I never realized until perhaps
right now
that what had happened wasn't my own coming to the conclusion that
this wasn't worth the bother.
It's strange now, doing it again, the business of the camps and slaughters,
the quick flicker of outrage
that hardly does its work anymore, all the carnage, all our own omissions
interposed,

then those two, in their chambers, correct, aristocratic, even with the old
     one's calcifying feet
and the younger one's intensities—those eyes that pierce me still from
     that far back with jolts of longing.
I frame the image: the two women, the young man, they, poised,
     gracious, he smoldering with impatience,
and I realize I've never really asked myself what could she, or they, possi-
     bly have wanted of me?
What am I doing in that room, a teacup trembling on my knee, that odd,
     barbed name mangled in my mouth?
If she felt a real affinity or anything resembling it for me, it must have
     been as something quaint—
young poet, brutish, or trying to be brutish—but no, I wasn't even that, I
     was just a boy, harmless, awkward,
mildly appealing in some ways, I suppose, but certainly with not a thing
     about me one could call compelling,
not compared to what, given her beauty and her means, she could have
     had and very well may have, for all I knew.
What I come to now, running over it again, I think I want to keep as
     undramatic as I can.
These revisions of the past are probably even less trustworthy than our
     random, everyday assemblages
and have most likely even more to do with present unknowables, so I
     offer this almost in passing,
with nothing, no moral distillation, no headily pressing imperatives
     meant to be lurking beneath it.
I wonder, putting it most simply, leaving out humiliation, anything like
     that, if I might have been their Jew?
I wonder, I mean, if I might have been an implement for them, not of
     atonement—I'd have nosed that out—
but of absolution, what they'd have used to get them shed of something
     rankling—history, it would be:
they'd have wanted to be categorically and finally shriven of it, or of that
     part of it at least
which so befouled the rest, which so acutely contradicted it with glory
     and debasement.
The mother, what I felt from her, that bulk of silence, that withholding
     that I read as sorrow:

might it have been instead the heroic containment of a probably reflex-
ive loathing of me?

How much, no matter what their good intentions (of which from her I
had no evidence at all)

and even with the liberal husband (although the generals' reasons
weren't that pure and got there very late),

how much must they have inevitably absorbed, that Nazi generation,
those Aryan epochs?

And if the mother shuddered, what would Moira have gone through with
me spinning at her nipple,

her own juices and the inept emissions I'd splatter on her gluing her to
me?

The purifying Jew. It's almost funny. She was taking just enough of me to
lave her conscience,

and I, so earnest in my wants, blindly labored for her, dismantling guilt
or racial squeamishness

or whatever it was the refined tablet of her consciousness deemed it
needed to be stricken of.

All the indignities I let be perpetrated on me while I lolled in that luxu-
rious detention:

could I really have believed they only had to do with virtue, maiden-
hood, or even with, I remember thinking—

I came this close—some intricate attempt Moira might be making to
redeem a slight on the part of the mother?

Or might inklings have arisen and might I, in my infatuation, have gone
along with them anyway?

I knew something, surely: I'd have had to. What I really knew, of course,
I'll never know again.

Beautiful memory, most precious and most treacherous sister: what tem-
ples must we build for you.

And even then, how belatedly you open to us; even then, with what exu-
berance you cross us.

Floor

A dirty picture, a photograph, possibly a tintype, from the turn of the cen-
        tury, even before:
the woman is obese, gigantic; a broad, black corset cuts from under her
        breasts to the tops of her hips,
her hair is crimped, wiry, fastened demurely back with a bow one incon-
        gruous wing of which shows.
Her eyebrows are straight and heavy, emphasizing her frank, unintro-
        spective plainness,
and she looks directly, easily into the camera, her expression somewhere
        between play and scorn,
as though the activities of the photographer were ridiculous or beneath
        her contempt, or,
rather, as though the unfamiliar camera were actually the much more
        interesting presence here
and how absurd it is that the lens be turned toward her and her partner
        and not back on itself.
One sees the same look—pride, for some reason, is in it, and a surpris-
        ingly sophisticated self-distancing—
in the snaps anthropologists took in backwaters during those first,
        politically preconscious,
golden days of culture-hopping, and, as Goffman notes, in certain adver-
        tisements, now.

The man is younger than the woman. Standing, he wears what looks like
        a bathing costume,
black and white tank top, heavy trousers bunched in an ungainly heap
        over his shoes, which are still on.
He has an immigrant's mustache he's a year or two too callow for, but,
        thick and dark, it will fit him.
He doesn't, like the woman, watch the camera, but stares ahead, not at
        the woman but slightly over and past,
and there's a kind of withdrawn, almost vulnerable thoughtfulness or pre-
        occupation about him
despite the gross thighs cast on his waist and the awkward, surely bother-
        some twist

his body has been forced to assume to more clearly exhibit the genital
     penetration.
He seems, in fact, abstracted—oblivious wouldn't be too strong a word—
     as though, possibly,
as unlikely as it would seem, he had been a virgin until now and was try-
     ing amid all this unholy confusion—
the hooded figure, the black box with its eye—trying and from the looks
     of it even succeeding
in obliterating everything from his consciousness but the thing itself, the
     act itself,
so as, one would hope, to redeem the doubtlessly endless nights of the
     long Victorian adolescence.

The background is a painted screen: ivy, columns, clouds; some muse or
     grace or other,
heavy-buttocked, whory, flaunts her gauze and clodhops with a half-
     demented leer.
The whole thing's oddly poignant somehow, almost, like an antique wed-
     ding picture, comforting—
the past is sending out a tendril to us: poses, attitudes of stillness we've
     lost or given back.
Also, there's no shame in watching them, in being in the tacit commerce
     of having, like it or not,
received the business in one's hand, no titillation either, not a tangle, not
     a throb,
probably because the woman offers none of the normal symptoms, even
     if minimal, even if contrived—
the tongue, say, wandering from the corner of the mouth, a glint of extra
     brilliance at the lash—
we associate with even the most innocuous, undramatic, parental sorts of
     passion, and the boy,
well, dragged in out of history, off Broome or South Street, all he is is
     grandpa:
he'll go back into whatever hole he's found to camp in, those higher-
     contrast tenements
with their rows of rank, forbidding beds, or not even beds, rags on a floor,
     or floor.
On the way there, there'll be policemen breaking strikers' heads, or
     micks', or sheenies',

there'll be war somewhere, in the sweatshops girls will turn to stone over
their Singers.
Here, at least peace. Here, one might imagine, after he withdraws, a kind
of manly focus taking him—
the glance he shoots to her is hard and sure—and, to her, a tenderness
might come,
she might reach a hand—Sweet Prince—to touch his cheek, or might—
who can understand these things?—
avert her face and pull him to her for a time before she squats to flush
him out.

Waking Jed

Deep asleep, perfect immobility, no apparent evidence of consciousness
    or of dream.
Elbow cocked, fist on pillow lightly curled to the tension of the partially
    relaxing sinew.
Head angled off, just so: the jaw's projection exaggerated slightly, almost
    to prognathous: why?
The features express nothing whatsoever and seem to call up no response
    in me.
Though I say nothing, don't move, gradually, far down within, he, or
    rather not *he* yet,
something, a presence, an element of being, becomes aware of me: there
    begins a subtle,
very gentle alteration in the structure of the face, or maybe less than that,
    more elusive,
as though the soft distortions of sleep-warmth radiating from his face and
    flesh,
those essentially unreal mirages in the air between us, were modifying,
    dissipating.
The face is now more his, Jed's—its participation in the almost Ro-
    manesque generality
I wouldn't a moment ago have been quite able to specify, not having its
    contrary, diminishes.
Particularly on the cheekbones and chin, the skin is thinning, growing
    denser, harder,
the molecules on the points of bone coming to attention, the eyelids
    finer, brighter, foil-like:
capillaries, veins; though nothing moves, there are goings to and fro
    behind now.
One hand opens, closes down more tightly, the arm extends suddenly
    full length,
jerks once at the end, again, holds: there's a more pronounced elonga-
    tion of the skull—
the infant pudginess, whatever atavism it represented, or reversion, has
    been called back.

Now I sense, although I can't say how, his awareness of me: I can feel
      him begin to *think*,
I even know that he's thinking—or thinking in a dream perhaps—of me
      here watching him.
Now I'm aware—again, with no notion how, nothing indicates it—that if
      there was a dream,
it's gone, and, yes, his eyes abruptly open although his gaze, straight
      before him,
seems not to register just yet, the mental operations still independent of
      his vision.
I say his name, the way we do it, softly, calling one another from a cove
      or cave,
as though something else were there with us, not to be disturbed, to be
      crept along beside.
The lids come down again, he yawns, widely, very consciously manifest-
      ing intentionality.
Great, if rudimentary, pleasure now: a sort of primitive, peculiarly mam-
      malian luxury—
to know, to know wonderfully that lying here, warm, protected, eyes
      closed, one can,
for a moment anyway, a precious instant, put off the lower specie onsets,
      duties, debts.
Sleeker, somehow, slyer, more aggressive now, he is suddenly more
      awake, all awake,
already plotting, scheming, fending off: nothing said but there's mild
      rebellion, conflict:
I insist, he resists, and then, with abrupt, wriggling grace, he otters down
      from sight,
just his brow and crown, his shining rumpled hair, left ineptly showing
      from the sheet.
Which I pull back to find him in what he must believe a parody of sleep,
      himself asleep:
fetal, rigid, his arms clamped to his sides, eyes screwed shut, mouth
      clenched, grinning.

Neglect

An old hill town in northern Pennsylvania, a missed connection for a
  bus, an hour to kill.
For all intents and purposes, the place was uninhabited; the mines had
  closed years before—
anthracite too dear to dig, the companies went west to strip, the miners to
  the cities—
and now, although the four-lane truck route still went through—eighteen-
  wheelers pounding past—
that was almost all: a shuttered Buick dealer, a grocery, not even a
  McDonald's,
just the combination ticket office, luncheonette and five-and-dime
  where the buses turned around.
A low gray frame building, it was gloomy and run-down, but charmingly
  old-fashioned:
ancient wooden floors, open shelves, the smell of unwrapped candy,
  cigarettes and band-aid glue.
The only people there, the only people I think that I remember from the
  town at all,
were the silent woman at the register and a youngish teen-aged boy
  standing reading.
The woman smoked and smoked, stared out the streaky window, handed
  me my coffee with indifference.
It was hard to tell how old she was: her hair was dyed and teased, iced
  into a beehive.
The boy was frail, sidelong somehow, afflicted with a devastating Nessus-
  shirt of acne
boiling down his face and neck—pits and pores, scarlet streaks and scars;
  saddening.
We stood together at the magazine rack for a while before I realized what
  he was looking at.
Pornography: two naked men, one grimaces, the other, with a fist inside
  the first one, grins.
I must have flinched: the boy sidled down, blanked his face more, and I
  left to take a walk.

It was cold, but not enough to catch or clear your breath: uncertain
    clouds, unemphatic light.
Everything seemed dimmed and colorless, the sense of surfaces dissolv-
    ing, like the Parthenon.
Farther down the main street were a dentist and a chiropractor, both
    with hand-carved signs,
then the Elks' decaying clapboard mansion with a parking space "Re-
    served for the Exalted Ruler,"
and a Russian church, gilt onion domes, a four-horned air-raid siren on a
    pole between them.
Two blocks in, the old slate sidewalks shatter and uplift—gnawed lawns,
    aluminum butane tanks—
then the roads begin to peter out and rise: half-fenced yards with scabs of
    weeks-old snow,
thin, inky, oily leaks of melt insinuating down the gulleys and the cin-
    dered cuts
that rose again into the footings of the filthy, disused slagheaps ringing
    the horizon.
There was nowhere else. At the depot now, the woman and the boy were
    both behind the counter.
He was on a stool, his eyes closed, she stood just in back of him, massag-
    ing him,
hauling at his shoulders, kneading at the muscles like a boxer's trainer
    between rounds.
I picked up the county paper: it was anti-crime and welfare bums, for
    Reaganomics and defense.
The wire-photo was an actress in her swimming suit, that famously
    expensive bosom, cream.
My bus arrived at last, its heavy, healthy white exhaust pouring in the
    afternoon.
Glancing back, I felt a qualm, concern, an ill heart, almost parental, but
    before I'd hit the step,
the boy'd begun to blur, to look like someone else, the woman had
    already faded absolutely.
All that held now was that violated, looted country, the fraying fringes of
    the town,
those gutted hills, hills by rote, hills by permission, great, naked wastes of
    wrack and spill,
vivid and disconsolate, like genitalia shaved and disinfected for an operation.

Still Life

All we do—how old are we? I must be twelve, she a little older; thirteen,
        fourteen—is hold hands
and wander out behind a barn, past a rusty hay rake, a half-collapsed old
        Model T,
then down across a barbed-wire gated pasture—early emerald ryegrass,
        sumac in the dip—
to where a brook, high with run-off from a morning storm, broadened
        and spilled over—
turgid, muddy, viscous, snagged here and there with shattered branches—
        in a bottom meadow.

I don't know then that the place, a mile from anywhere, and day, bril-
        liant, sultry, balmy,
are intensifying everything I feel, but I know now that what made simply
        touching her
almost a consummation was as much the light, the sullen surge of water
        through the grass,
the coils of scent, half hers—the unfamiliar perspiration, talc, something
        else I'll never place—
and half the air's: mown hay somewhere, crushed clover underfoot, the
        brook, the breeze.

I breathe it still, that breeze, and, not knowing how I know for certain
        that it's that,
although it is, I know, exactly that, I drag it in and drive it—rich, deli-
        cious,
as biting as wet tin—down, my mind casting up flickers to fit it—another
        field, a hollow—
and now her face, even it, frail and fine, comes momentarily to focus,
        and her hand,
intricate and slim, the surprising firmness of her clasp, how judiciously it
        meshes mine.

All we do—how long does it last? an hour or two, not even one whole afternoon:

I'll never see her after that, and, strangely (strange even now), not mind, as though,

in that afternoon the revelations weren't only of the promises of flesh, but of resignation—

all we do is trail along beside the stream until it narrows, find the one-log bridge

and cross into the forest on the other side: silent footfalls, hills, a crest, a lip.

I don't know then how much someday—today—I'll need it all, how much want to hold it,

and, not knowing why, not knowing still how time can tempt us so emphatically and yet elude us,

not have it, not the way I would, not the way I want to have *that* day, *that* light,

the motes that would have risen from the stack of straw we leaned on for a moment,

the tempered warmth of air which so precisely seemed the coefficient of my fearful ardor,

not, after all, even the objective place, those shifting paths I can't really follow now

but only can compile from how many other ambles into other woods, other stoppings in a glade—

(for a while we were lost, and frightened; night was just beyond the hills; we circled back)—

even, too, her gaze, so darkly penetrating, then lifting idly past, is so much imagination,

a portion of that figured veil we cast against oblivion, then try, with little hope, to tear away.

188

The Regulars

In the Colonial Luncheonette on Sixth Street they know everything
      there is to know, the shits.
Sam Terminadi will tell you how to gamble yourself at age sixty from
      accountant to bookie,
and Sam Finkel will tell you more than anyone cares to hear how to
      parlay an ulcer into a pension
so you can sit here drinking this shit coffee and eating these overfried
      shit eggs
while you explain that the reasons the people across the street are going
      to go bust
in the toy store they're redoing the old fish market into—the father and
      son plastering,
putting up shelves, scraping the floors; the mother laboring over the
      white paint,
even the daughter coming from school to mop the century of scales and
      splatter from the cellar—
are both simple and complex because Sam T can tell you the answer to
      anything in the world
in one word and Sam F prefaces all his I-told-you-so's with "You don't
      understand, it's complex."
"It's simple," Sam T says, "where around here is anyone going to get
      money for toys?" The end.
Never mind the neighborhood's changing so fast that the new houses at
      the end of the block
are selling for twice what the whole block would have five years ago,
      that's not the point.
Business shits, right? Besides, the family—what's that they're eating?—
      are wrong, right?
Not totally wrong, what are they, Arabs or something? but still, wrong
      enough, that's sure.
"And where do they live?" Sam F asks. "Sure as shit their last dime's in
      the lease and shit sure
they'll end up living in back of the store like gypsies, guaranteed: didn't
      I tell you or not

when the Minskys were still here that they'd bug out first chance they
    got, and did they or no?"
Everyone thought the Minsky brothers would finally get driven out of
    their auto repair shop
by zoning or by having their tools stolen so many times, Once, Frank
    Minsky would growl,
on Yom Kippur, for crying out loud, but no, at the end, they just sold,
    they'd worked fifty years,
And Shit, Frank said, that's fucking enough, we're going to Miami, what
    do you want from me?
But Sam F still holds it against them, to cave in like that, the buggers,
    bastards, shits . . .
What he really means, Sam, Sam, is that everyone misses the Minskys'
    back room, where they'd head,
come dusk, the old boys, and there'd be the bottle of schnapps and the
    tits from *Playboy*
in the grimy half-dark with the good stink of three lifetimes of grease and
    sweat and bitching,
and how good that would be, back then, oh, how far back was then? Last
    year, is that all?
"They got no class: shit, a toy store," Sam T says. What does that mean,
    Sam? What class?
No class, that's all, simple: six months there and boom, they'll have a fire,
    guaranteed.
Poor Sam, whether the last fire, at the only butcher store for blocks the
    A & P hadn't swallowed,
was arson for insurance as Sam proved the next day, or whether, the way
    the firemen saw it,
it was just a bum keeping warm in the alley, Sam's decided to take it out
    on the strangers,
glaring at them over there in their store of dreams, their damned pain-in-
    the-ass toy store.
What's the matter with you, are you crazy? is what the father finally
    storms in with one afternoon,
both Sams turning their backs, back to their shit burgers, but old Bernie
    himself is working today,
and *Hey,* Bernie says, *Don't mind them, they're just old shits, sit down, I'll*
    buy you a coffee.

190

Who the fuck do they think they are? Here have a donut, don't worry, they'll be all right,
and of course they will be. "In a month you won't get them out of your hair," says Bernie,
and he's right again, old Bernie, before you know it Sam T has got me cornered in the street.
"What is it, for Christ's sake, Sam? Let me go." "No, wait up, it's a computer for kids."
"Sam, please, I'm in a hurry." "No, hold on, just a second, look, it's simple."

Soon

The whole lower panel of the chain-link fence girdling my old grammar
      school playground
has been stripped from its stanchions and crumpled disdainfully onto the
      shattered pavement.
The upper portion sags forlornly, as though whatever maintenance man
      had to hang it last
was too disheartened doing it again to bother tensioning the guy wires to
      the true.

The building's pale, undistinguished stone is sooty, graffiti cover every
      surface within reach.
Behind their closely woven, galvanized protective mesh, the windows are
      essentially opaque,
but in the kindergarten and first grade I can make out skeletons and
      pumpkins scotch-taped up.
It's Halloween, the lower grades are having their procession and I stop
      awhile to watch.

Except that everyone is black—the kids, the parents looking on, almost
      all the teachers—
my class, when we were out there parading in our costumes, must have
      looked about the same.
Witches, cowboys, clowns, some Supermen and Batmen, a Bo-Peep and
      a vampire.
I don't think we had robots, or not such realistic ones, and they don't
      have an Uncle Sam.

Uncle Sam! *I* was Uncle Sam! I remember! With what ardor I conceived
      my passion to be him.
Uncle Sam. The war was on then, everyone was gaga with it; Uncle Sam
      was everywhere,
recruiting, selling bonds—that poster with its virile, foreshortened finger
      accusing you—
and there, at the local dime store, to my incredulous delight, his outfit was.

It must have cost enough to mean something in those days, still half in
    the Depression,
but I dwelled on it . . . The box alone: Uncle Sam was on it in his
    stovepipe, smiling this time,
and there was a tiny window you could see a square of bangles through,
    a ribbon of lapel.
It burned in me, I fretted, nagged: my first instance of our awful fever to
    consume.

When I'd had it half an hour, I hated it—even at that age, I knew when
    I'd been cheated.
Ill-made, shoddy, the gauzy fabric coarsely dyed, with the taste of some-
    thing evil in its odor,
it was waxy with a stiffening that gave it body long enough for you to get
    it on,
then it bagged, and clung, and made you feel the fool you'd been to want
    it in the first place.

My cotton-batting beard was pasted on, and itched, but I knew enough
    to hold my tongue.
The little patriot in his rage of indignation: so much anyway of education
    went against my will.
Fold your hands, raise your hands, the Pledge of Allegiance, prayers and
    air-raid drills.
We were taught obsessively to be "Good Citizens," a concept I never
    quite understood.

How the city's changed since then: downtown, businesses have fled,
    whole blocks are waste,
all that's left of what went on between the rioters and Guard tanks in the
    Sixties.
Here, even the fieldhouse on the ballpark where they gave us nature lec-
    tures is in shambles:
the grass is gone, a frowsy gorse has sprouted from the brick- and bottle-
    ridden rubble.

The baskets on their court are still intact at least, although the metal nets
    are torn.

Some men who must be from the neighborhood have got a game going
        out there now.
The children circle shyly, hand in hand, as solemn as a frieze of Greeks,
        while a yard beyond,
the backboards boom, the players sweat and feint and drive, as though
        everything depended on it.

The Gas Station

This is before I'd read Nietzsche. Before Kant or Kierkegaard, even
    before Whitman and Yeats.
I don't think there were three words in my head yet. I knew, perhaps,
    that I should suffer,
I can remember I almost cried for this or for that, nothing special, noth-
    ing to speak of.
Probably I was mad with grief for the loss of my childhood, but I wouldn't
    have known that.
It's dawn. A gas station. Route twenty-two. I remember exactly: route
    twenty-two curved,
there was a squat, striped concrete divider they'd put in after a plague of
    collisions.
The gas station? Texaco, Esso—I don't know. They were just words any-
    way then, just what their signs said.
I wouldn't have understood the first thing about monopoly or imperialist
    or oppression.
It's dawn. It's so late. Even then, when I was never tired, I'm just holding
    on.
Slumped on my friend's shoulder, I watch the relentless, wordless misery
    of the route twenty-two sky
that seems to be filming my face with a grainy oil I keep trying to rub off
    or in.
Why are we here? Because one of my friends, in the men's room over
    there, has blue balls.
He has to jerk off. I don't know what that means, "blue balls," or why he
    has to do that—
it must be important to have to stop here after this long night, but I don't
    ask.
I'm just trying, I think, to keep my head as empty as I can for as long as I
    can.
One of my other friends is asleep. He's so ugly, his mouth hanging, slack
    and wet.
Another—I'll never see this one again—stares from the window as
    though he were frightened.

Here's what we've done. We were in Times Square, a pimp found us,
    corralled us, led us somewhere,
down a dark street, another dark street, up dark stairs, dark hall, dark
    apartment,
where his whore, his girl or his wife or his mother for all I know, dragged
    herself from her sleep,
propped herself on an elbow, gazed into the dark hall, and agreed, for
    two dollars each, to take care of us.
Take care of us. Some of the words that come through me now seem to
    stay, to hook in.
My friend in the bathroom is taking so long. The filthy sky must be start-
    ing to lighten.
It took me a long time, too, with the woman, I mean. Did I mention that
    she, the woman, the whore or mother,
was having her time and all she would deign do was to blow us? Did I say
    that? Deign? Blow?
What a joy, though, the idea was in those days. Blown! What a thing to
    tell the next day.
She only deigned, though, no more. She was like a machine. When I lift
    her back to me now,
there's nothing there but that dark, curly head, working, a machine, up
    and down, and now,
Freud, Marx, Fathers, tell me, what am I, doing this, telling this, on her,
    on myself,
hammering it down, cementing it, sealing it in, but a machine, too? *Why
    am I doing this?*
I still haven't read Augustine. I don't understand Chomsky that well.
    Should I?
My friend at last comes back. Maybe the right words were there all
    along. *Complicity. Wonder.*
How pure we were then, before Rimbaud, before Blake. *Grace. Love.
    Take care of us. Please.*

Tar

The first morning of Three Mile Island: those first disquieting, uncer-
   tain, mystifying hours.
All morning a crew of workmen have been tearing the old decrepit roof
   off our building,
and all morning, trying to distract myself, I've been wandering out to
   watch them
as they hack away the leaden layers of asbestos paper and disassemble the
   disintegrating drains.
After half a night of listening to the news, wondering how to know a hun-
   dred miles downwind
if and when to make a run for it and where, then a coming bolt awake at
   seven
when the roofers we've been waiting for since winter sent their ladders
   shrieking up our wall,
we still know less than nothing: the utility company continues making
   little of the accident,
the slick federal spokesmen still have their evasions in some semblance
   of order.
Surely we suspect now we're being lied to, but in the meantime, there
   are the roofers,
setting winch-frames, sledging rounds of tar apart, and there I am, on the
   curb across, gawking.

I never realized what brutal work it is, how matter-of-factly and harrow-
   ingly dangerous.
The ladders flex and quiver, things skid from the edge, the materials are
   bulky and recalcitrant.
When the rusty, antique nails are levered out, their heads pull off; the
   underroofing crumbles.
Even the battered little furnace, roaring along as patient as a donkey,
   chokes and clogs,
a dense, malignant smoke shoots up, and someone has to fiddle with a
   cock, then hammer it,
before the gush and stench will deintensify, the dark, Dantean broth
   wearily subside.

In its crucible, the stuff looks bland, like licorice, spill it, though, on your
boots or coveralls,
it sears, and everything is permeated with it, the furnace gunked with
burst and half-burst bubbles,
the men themselves so completely slashed and mucked they seem al-
most from another realm, like trolls.
When they take their break, they leave their brooms standing at attention
in the asphalt pails,
work gloves clinging like Br'er Rabbit to the bitten shafts, and they
slouch along the precipitous lip,
the enormous sky behind them, the heavy noontime air alive with shim-
mers and mirages.

Sometime in the afternoon I had to go inside: the advent of our vigil was
upon us.
However much we didn't want to, however little we would do about it,
we'd understood:
we were going to perish of all this, if not now, then soon, if not soon,
then someday.
Someday, some final generation, hysterically aswarm beneath an atmo-
sphere as unrelenting as rock,
would rue us all, anathematize our earthly comforts, curse our surfeits
and submissions.
I think I know, though I might rather not, why my roofers stay so clear to
me and why the rest,
the terror of that time, the reflexive disbelief and distancing, all we
should hold on to, dims so.
I remember the president in his absurd protective booties, looking
absolutely unafraid, the fool.
I remember a woman on the front page glaring across the misty Susque-
hanna at those looming stacks.
But, more vividly, the men, silvered with glitter from the shingles, cling-
ing like starlings beneath the eaves.
Even the leftover carats of tar in the gutter, so black they seemed to suck
the light out of the air.
By nightfall kids had come across them: every sidewalk on the block was
scribbled with obscenities and hearts.

One of the Muses

Nor will his vision of the beautiful take the form of a face, or of hands, or of anything that is of the flesh. It will be neither words, nor knowledge, nor a something that exists in something else, such as a living creature, or the earth, or the heavens, or anything that is . . .

　　　　—*Plato,* Symposium

Where our language suggests a body and there is none: there we should like to say, is a spirit.

　　　　—*Wittgenstein,* Philosophical Investigations

1.

I will not grace you with a name . . . Even "you," however modest the
　　　convention: not here.
No need here for that much presence. Let "you" be "she," and let the
　　　choice, incidentally,
be dictated not by bitterness or fear—a discretion, simply, the most in-
　　　offensive decorum.

This was, after all, if it needs another reason, long ago, and not just in
　　　monthly, yearly time,
not only in that house of memory events, the shadowed, off-sized rooms
　　　of which
it amuses us to flip the doors of like a deck of cards, but also in the much
　　　more malleable,

mazy, convoluted matter of the psyche itself, especially the wounded
　　　psyche,
especially the psyche stricken once with furrows of potential which are
　　　afterwards untenanted:
voids, underminings, to be buttressed with the webbiest filaments of day-
　　　to-dayness.

2.

Long ago, in another place, it seems sometimes in another realm of
    being altogether,
one of those dimensions we're told intersects our own, rests there side by
    side with ours,
liable to be punched across into by charity or prayer, other skullings at
    the muscle.

How much of her essential being can or should be carried over into now
    isn't clear to me.
That past which holds her, yellowed with allusiveness, is also charged
    with unreality:
a tiny theater in whose dim light one senses fearfully the contaminating
    powers of illusion.

Here, in a relatively stable present, no cries across the gorge, no veils
    atremble,
it sometimes seems as though she may have been a fiction utterly, a
    symbol or a system of them.
In any case, what good conceivably could come at this late date of
    recapitulating my afflictions?

3.

Apparently, it would have to do with what that ancient desperation
    means to me today.
We recollect, call back, surely not to suffer; is there something then for
    me, today,
something lurking, potent with another loss, this might be meant to alter
    or avert?

No, emphatically: let it be that simple. And not any sort of longing back-
    wards, either:
no desire to redeem defeats, no humiliations to atone for, no expiations
    or maledictions.

Why bother then? Why inflict it on myself again, that awful time, those
vacillations and frustrations?

It's to be accounted for, that's all. Something happened, the time has
come to find its place.
Let it just be that: not come to terms with, not salvage something from,
not save.
There was this, it's to be accounted for: "she," for that, will certainly
suffice.

4.

She had come to me . . . *She* to *me* . . . I know that, I knew it then,
however much, at the end,
trying so to hang on to it, to keep something of what by then was noth-
ing, I came to doubt,
to call the memory into question, that futile irreducible of what had
happened and stopped happening.

She, to me, and with intensity, directness, aggression even, an aggression
that may have been,
I think, the greater part of my involvement to begin with: in the sweep of
her insistence,
it was as though she'd simply shouldered past some debilitating shyness
on my part,

some misgiving, some lack of faith I'd never dared acknowledge in
myself but which, now,
I suddenly understood had been a part of my most basic being: a tearing
shoal of self,
which, brought to light now, harrowingly recognized, had flowed away
beneath me.

5.

Later, when everything had turned, fallen, but when we still found ways, despite it all,
    through our impediments—my grief, her ever-stricter panels of reserve—
    that first consummation,
her power, the surprising counter-power I answered with, came to seem
    a myth, a primal ceremony.

Later, and not much later because the start and end were, although I couldn't bear to think it,
nearly one, it became almost a ritual, not even ritual, a repetition, and I had to recognize,
at last, how few times that first real, unqualified soaring had actually been enacted.

Maybe several times, maybe only once: once and once—that would have been enough,
enough to keep me there, to keep me trying to recuperate it, so long after I'd begun to feel,
and to acknowledge to myself, her searing hesitations, falterings, awkwardnesses.

6.

Her withholdings were so indefinite at first, it wasn't hard to fend them off, deny them.
The gasp that seemed—but did it really?—to extend a beat into a sigh, and then the sigh,
did it go on an extra instant to become a heave of tedium, impatience, resignation?

. . . Then the silences: I could have, if I'd wanted to, dared to, been certain of the silences.
They were in time, had duration, could be measured: how I must have wanted not to know.

I didn't even name them that at first, "silence," no: lapses, inattentions,
respites.

It feels as though I'd begun to try to cope with them before I'd actually
remarked them.
They weren't silences until they'd flared and fused, until her silences
became her silence,
until we seemed, to my chagrin, my anguish, horror, to be wholly in and
of them.

7.

Her silence: how begin to speak of it? I think sometimes I must have
simply gaped.
There were harmonies in it, progressions, colors, resolutions: it was a
symphony, a tone poem.
I seemed to live in it, it was always with me, a matrix, background sound:
surf, wind.

Sometimes, when I'd try to speak myself, I'd find it had insinuated into
my voice:
it would haul at me; I'd go hoarse, metallic, hollow, nothing that I said
entailed.
More and more her presence seemed preceded by it: a quiet on the stair,
hushed hall.

I'd know before I heard her step that she was with me, and when she'd
go, that other,
simpler silence, after all the rest, was like a coda, magnificent, absorbing,
one last note reverberating on and on, subdividing through its physics
toward eternity.

8.

At the same time, though, it was never, never quite, defined as being
final.

She always, I have no idea how, left her clef of reticence ajar: a lace, a
      latticework.
I thought—I think that I was meant to think—it was provisional, a stop-
      ping place.

And, to exacerbate things, it became her: with it, and within it, she
      seemed to promise more.
The sheer *focus* it demanded; such shadings were implied in how she
      turned in it;
the subtleties I hadn't been allowed, the complexities not fathomed:
      she was being re-enhanced by it.

What was inaccessible in her, what not, what—even as I'd hold her, even
      as we'd touch—
was being drawn away, marked off, forbidden: such resonance between
      potential and achieved.
The vibrations, though, as subtle as they were, crystalline, were tearing
      me apart.

9.

Sometimes, it would seem as though, still with me, she had already left
      me.
Sometimes, later, when she really had left, left again, I would seem to
      ache,
not with the shocks or after-shocks of passion, but with simply holding
      her, holding on.

Sometimes, so flayed, I would think that I was ready to accept defeat,
      ready to concede.
I may have even wished for hints of concrete evidence from her that she
      wanted us to stop.
She could, I thought, with the gentlest move, have disengaged: I was
      ready for it . . .

No, not so, I wasn't. Wasn't what was wrong so slight, so patently incon-
      sequential to the rest?

If I let her go like that, I thought, how would I ever know that what had
      brought us down
wasn't merely my own dereliction or impatience? No, there had to be a
      way to solve this.

10.

I kept thinking: there is something which, if said in precisely the right
      words to her . . .
I kept thinking, there's an explanation I can offer, an analysis, maybe just
      a way of saying,
a rhythm or a rhetoric, to fuse the strands of her ambivalence and draw
      her back.

I kept thinking—she may have kept me thinking—there's something I
      haven't understood about her,
something I've misconceived or misconstrued, something I've missed the
      message of and offended . . .
I'd set theories up from that, programs, and, with notes along the way
      toward future tries,

I'd elaborate the phrases, paragraphs, the volumes of my explication: I'd
      rehearse them,
offer them, and have her, out of hand, hardly noticing, reject, discard,
      disregard them,
until I learned myself—it didn't take me long—out of hand, hardly
      noticing, to discard them.

11.

Sometimes, though, I'd imagine that something—yes—I'd said would
      reach her.
Her presence, suddenly, would seem to soften, there would be a flood of
      ease, a decontraction.
She'd be with me, silent still, but *there*, and I would realize how far she'd
      drifted.

I wouldn't know then, having her, or thinking that I did, whether to be
    miserable or pleased.
I'd go on, even so, to try to seal it, build on it, extend, certify it somehow,
and then, suddenly again, I'd sense that she'd be gone again, or, possibly,
    much worse,

had never been there, or not the way I'd thought it for that thankful
    instant.
I'd misinterpreted, misread, I'd have to start my search again, my trial,
    travail.
Where did I ever find the energy for it? Just to think about it now
    exhausts me.

12.

Wherever I did find the strength, half of it I dedicated to absolving and
    forgiving her.
Somehow I came to think, and never stopped believing, I was inflicting
    all my anguish on myself.
She was blameless, wasn't she? Her passivity precluded else: the issue
    had to be with me.

I tried to reconceive myself, to situate myself in the syntax of our crip-
    pled sentence.
I parsed myself, searching out a different flow for the tangle of ampu-
    tated phrases I was by then.
Nothing, though, would sound, would scan, no matter how I carved,
    dissected, chopped.

I couldn't find the form, the meter, rhythm, or, by now, the barest con-
    text for myself.
I became a modifier: my only function was to alter the conditions of this
    fevered predication.
I became a word one thinks about too closely: clumps of curves and
    serifs, the arbitrary symbol of itself.

13.

I became, I became . . . Finally, I think I must have simply ceased even
        that, becoming.
I was an image now, petrified, unmediated, with no particular associa-
        tion, no connotation,
certainly no meaning, certainly no hope of ever being anything that bore
        a meaning.

It was as though my identity had been subsumed in some enormous gen-
        eralization,
one so far beyond my comprehension that all I could know was that I
        was incidental to it,
that with me or without me it would grind along the complex epicycles
        of its orbit.

It was as though the system I'd been living in had somehow suddenly
        evolved beyond me.
I had gills to breathe a stratosphere, and my hopeless project was to gen-
        erate new organs,
new lobes to try to comprehend this emotional ecology, and my extinc-
        tion in it.

14.

The hours, the labor: how I wracked my mind, how my mind revenged
        itself on me.
I was wild, helpless, incapable of anything at all by now but watching as
        I tore myself.
I huddled there at the center of myself and tried to know by some reflex-
        ive act of faith

that I'd survive all this, this thing, my self, that mauled and savaged me.
I'd behold it all, so much frenzy, so many groans and bellows; even now,
        watching now,
I seem to sink more deeply into some protective foliage: I tremble in
        here, quake,

and then I dart—even now, still, my eyes, despite me, dart: walls, floor,
    sky—
I dart across that field of fear, away, away from there, from here, from
    anywhere.
I was frightened sometimes that I might go mad. And then I did just
    that—go mad.

15.

It was like another mind, my madness, my blessèd, holy madness: no, it
    was another mind.
It arrives, my other mind, on another night when I'm without her, hop-
    ing, or past hope.
My new mind comes upon me with a hush, a fluttering, a silvery ado,
    and it has a volume,

granular and sensitive, which exactly fits the volume of the mind I
    already have.
Its desire seems to be to displace that other mind, and something in
    me—how say what?
how explain the alacrity of such a radical concurrence?—decides to let
    it,

and the split second of the decision and the onset of the workings of that
    mind are instantaneous.
In one single throb of intuition I understood what the function of my
    mind was,
because, in and of it now, convinced, absorbed, I was already working
    out its implications.

16.

I knew already that my other mind—I hardly could recall it—had had a
    flaw and from that flaw
had been elaborated a delusion, and that delusion in its turn was at the
    base of all my suffering,

all the agonies I'd been inflicting, so unnecessarily, I understood, upon
     myself.

I had thought, I realized, that reality of experience, data and events, were
     to be received,
that perception, sensory, experiential accumulation, was essentially
     passive,
that it accepted what was offered and moved within that given, the pal-
     pable or purely mental,

partaking of it as it could, jiggling the tenuous impressions here or there
     a bit,
a sentence added, or a chapter, but nothing more than that: we were
     almost victims,
or if not victims quite, not effective agents surely, not of anything that
     mattered.

17.

What my new mind made me understand, though the facts had been
     there all the while before my eyes,
was that reality, as I'd known it, as I knew it now, was being generated,
     every second,
out of me and by me: it was me, myself, and no one else, who spun it out
     this way.

It was my own will, unconscious until now but now with purpose and
     intent, which made the world.
Not made-up, which implies imagination or idea, but made, actually
     created, everything,
in a flow, a logic, a succession of events, I could trace now with my very
     blood.

Even time: looking back at the wash of time on earth, it, too, was a func-
     tion of this moment.
Then cosmic time was flowing, too, from the truth I was living now, not
     for myself now,

for my salvation or survival, but for the infinitely vulnerable fact of exis-
tence itself.

18.

Does it matter very much what the rest was, the odd conclusions I kept
coming to?
What really seems important was that even as it happened, even as I let
it happen,
even as I held it in a sort of mental gale—it wasn't necessary then to work
it out like this,

all of it was there at once, in a single block, entire, a kind of geometric
bliss—
I understood that it was all hallucination and delusion, that these in-
sights or illuminations
were wretched figments of emotion all, but I didn't care, I let them take
me further,

past proposition, syllogism, sense: I was just a premise mechanism now,
an epistemology machine;
I let my field of vision widen—everything was mine now, coal and
comet, root and moon,
all found their footing, fulfilled at last, in my felicity, and then, rendingly,
it ended.

19.

Why it stopped was as much a mystery to me as why it should have
happened in the first place,
but when it did, something else took its place, a sort of vision, or a partial
vision,
or at least a knowledge, as instantly accessible and urgent as the other,
and, I'd find, as fleeting.

Somehow, I knew, I'd touched into the very ground of self, its axioms
and assumptions,

and what was there wasn't what I'd thought—I hadn't *known* what I'd
    thought but knew it now—
not violence, not conflagration, sexual turbulence, a philosophic or emo-
    tive storm,

but a sort of spiritual erasure, a nothingness of motive and intention, and
    I understood, too,
in another bolt, that all that keeps us from that void, paradoxically per-
    haps, is trust . . .
Trust in what? Too late: that perception, too, was gone; I had to watch
    another revelation end.

20.

But not badly, even so . . . I came back, to myself, feeling not contrite,
    not embarrassed,
certainly not frightened . . . awkward, maybe, toward myself, shy,
    abashed: I couldn't, as it were,
meet the gaze of this stranger I was in a body with, but I couldn't, either,
    take my eyes away.

Something had altered, *I* had: there was something unfamiliar, incon-
    gruous about me.
I couldn't specify exactly, not at first, what I felt; it wasn't, though,
    unpleasant.
I probed myself as though I'd had an accident; nothing broken, I was all
    right, more:

a sense of lightness, somehow, a change in my specific gravity, a relief,
    unburdening,
and then I knew, with no fuss or flourish, what it was: she, she wasn't
    with me now,
she was gone from me, from either of my minds, all my minds, my
    selves—she simply wasn't there.

21.

I could say it feels as though I'm taking breaths: she is gone and gone,
        he, shriven of her,
leaps into his life, but as I went about the work of understanding what
        had happened to me,
who I was now, it was clear at once that my having torn myself from her
        was unimportant.

She was gone, why she'd been there to begin with, what I'd seen in her,
        thought she'd meant,
why I'd let that suffering come to me, became immediately the most
        theoretical of questions.
That I'd have to be without her now meant only that: without her, not
        forlorn, bereft.

I even tested cases: if she went on to someone else, touched someone
        else, would I envy them,
her touch, her fire? Not even that: her essence for me was her being with
        me for that time,
with someone else, she, too, was other than herself: a wraith, a formula
        or intellection.

22.

I felt no regret—indifference, rather, a flare of disbelief, then an unex-
        pected moment of concern.
Had she suffered, too? Had she even sensed, in her empyrean distance,
        that this,
any of it, was going on at all? I didn't answer then, if I had to now, I'd
        have to doubt it.

I think that, after those first moments, she was gone already from me:
        perhaps, though,
it's not my task to try to answer, perhaps all I really have the right to do is
        ask

what the person I am now might have to do with her, wraith or not,
     memory of a memory or not?

Was I enhanced by her? Diminished by her? All that's really sure is that
     if I was changed,
it wasn't the embrace, the touch, that would have done it, but what came
     after, her withdrawal,
her painful non-responses, her absence and the ever more incorporeal
     innuendos in that absence.

23.

And my "madness," that business of the other mind, that "trust": have I
     taken anything from that?
Perhaps. I think I'd always realized the possibility was there for us to do
     that to ourselves,
undo ourselves that way, not in suicide, but in something much more
     dire, complete, denying.

I think that I'd suspected, too, that with the means to do it, I would some-
     day have to do it.
And now, what I'd been afraid I'd do, I'd done: that she'd had to drive me
     to it didn't matter,
although probably without her, without what she'd inflicted on me, I'd
     have never come to it.

Perhaps, with her abrasive offerings and takings-back, I'd been ground
     down like a lens:
I'd had, to my horror, really to look within myself, into the greater sea of
     chaos there,
and I'd survived it, shaken but intact, with auras, even, of a kind of grati-
     tude.

24.

What I'm left with after all this time is still the certainty that something
      was attained,
though all that remain now are flickers, more and more occasional,
      more disjointed—
pale remnants of the harsh collaborations those intermediary silences
      symbolized so well.

And this . . . I mean *this*, these lines, constructions, études: these small
      histories,
where did this come from? As I said, there was no desire to go over all of
      it again,
but, after all, whatever ambivalence I felt about it, it demanded care,
      even labor.

The need for doing it never quite defined itself: it, like her, came un-
      called for.
A tone took me, an impulse toward a structure: I found it interesting, a
      question of aesthetics.
If that were so, might there be another way, another mode in which to
      come to it?

25.

The proposition now could be that this *is* she, this, itself, wholly "she."
Not an artifact, not a net in which some wingèd thing protests or pines,
      but her,
completely fused now, inspiration, outcome: she would be, now, what
      she herself effected,

the tones themselves, the systems she wrought from the conflicting
      musics of my conscience.
This time it would be that all she meant to me were these attempts, these
      uncertain colorations,
that took so long to get here, from so far, and from which she would be
      departing now at last,

not into another hesitation, pause, another looking back reluctantly on
    either of our parts—
no turnings, no farewells—but a final sundering, a seeing-off, a last, defi-
    nitely indicated,
precisely scored—no rests, diminuendos, decrescendos—silencing, and
    silence.

FLESH AND BLOOD

[1987]

I

Elms

All morning the tree men have been taking down the stricken elms
   skirting the broad sidewalks.
The pitiless electric chain saws whine tirelessly up and down their pierc-
   ing, operatic scales
and the diesel choppers in the street shredding the debris chug fever-
   ishly, incessantly,
packing truckload after truckload with the feathery, homogenized, inert
   remains of heartwood,
twig and leaf and soon the block is stripped, it is as though illusions of
   reality were stripped:
the rows of naked facing buildings stare and think, their divagations more
   urgent than they were.
"The winds of time," they think, the mystery charged with fearful clarity:
   "The winds of time . . ."
All afternoon, on to the unhealing evening, minds racing, "Insolent,
   unconscionable, the winds of time . . ."

Hooks

Possibly because she's already so striking—tall, well dressed, very clear,
   pure skin—
when the girl gets on the subway at Lafayette Street everyone notices her
   artificial hand
but we also manage, as we almost always do, not to be noticed noticing,
   except one sleeping woman,
who hasn't budged since Brooklyn but who lifts her head now, opens up,
   forgets herself,
and frankly stares at those intimidating twists of steel, the homely leather
   sock and laces,
so that the girl, as she comes through the door, has to do in turn now
   what is to be done,
which is to look down at it, too, a bit askance, with an air of tolerant,
   bemused annoyance,
the way someone would glance at their unruly, apparently ferocious but
   really quite friendly dog.

Nostalgia

In the dumbest movie they can play it on us with a sunrise and a passage
       of adagio Vivaldi—
all the reason more to love it and to loathe it, this always barely choked-
       back luscious flood,
this turbulence in breast and breath that indicates a purity residing some-
       where in us,
redeeming with its easy access the thousand lapses of memory shed in
       the most innocuous day
and cancelling our rue for all the greater consciousness we didn't have
       for past, lost presents.
Its illusion is that we'll retain this new, however hammy past more thor-
       oughly than all before,
its reality, that though we know by heart its shabby ruses, know we'll mis-
       place it yet again,
it's what we have, a stage light flickering to flood, chintz and gaud, and
       we don't care.

Artemis

The lesbian couple's lovely toddler daughter has one pierced ear with a
       thin gold ring in it
and the same abundant, flaming, almost movie-starlet hair as the
       chunkier of the women.
For an entire hour she's been busily harrying the hapless pigeons of the
       Parc Montholon
while the other two sit spooning on a bench, caressing, cradling one an-
       other in their arms
then striking up acquaintance with a younger girl who at last gets up to
       leave with them.
They call the child but she doesn't want to go just yet, she's still in the
       game she's made.
It's where you creep up softly on your quarry, then shriek and stamp and
       run and wave your arms
and watch as it goes waddle, waddle, waddle, and heaves itself to your
       great glee into the air.

Guatemala: 1964

for Loren Crabtree

The Maya-Quechua Indians plodding to market on feet as flat and tough
      as toads were semi-starving
but we managed to notice only their brilliant weaving and implacable,
      picturesque aloofness.
The only people who would talk to us were the village alcoholic, who'd
      sold his soul for *aguardiente*,
and the Bahia nurse, Jenny, middle-aged, English-Nicaraguan, the sole
      medicine for eighty miles,
who lord knows why befriended us, put us up, even took us in her jeep
      into the mountains,
where a child, if I remember, needed penicillin, and where the groups of
      dark, idling men
who since have risen and been crushed noted us with something discon-
      certingly beyond suspicion.
Good Jenny: it took this long to understand she wasn't just forgiving our
      ferocious innocence.

Herakles

A mysterious didactic urgency informs the compelling bedtime stories
      he is obsessively recounted.
Misty, potent creatures, half human, half insane with hatred and with
      lustings for the hearth:
the childhood of the race, with always, as the ground, the urgent impli-
      cation of a lesson.
Some of it he gets, that there are losses, personal and epic, but bearable,
      to be withstood,
and that the hero's soul is self-forged, self-conceived, hammered out in
      outrage, trial, abandon, risk.
The parables elude him, though: he can never quite grasp where the
      ever-after means to manifest.
Is he supposed to *be* this darkly tempered, dark fanatic of the flesh who'll
      surely consume himself?
Or should it be the opposite: would all these feats and deeds be not ex-
      emplary but cautionary?

First Desires

It was like listening to the record of a symphony before you knew any-
    thing at all about the music,
what the instruments might sound like, look like, what portion of the
    orchestra each represented:
there were only volumes and velocities, thickenings and thinnings, the
    winding cries of change
that seemed to touch within you, through your body, to be part of you
    and then apart from you.
And even when you'd learned the grainy timbre of the single violin, the
    ardent arpeggios of the horn,
when you tried again there were still uneases and confusions left, an
    ache, a sense of longing
that held you in chromatic dissonance, droning on beyond the domi-
    nant's resolve into the tonic,
as though there were a flaw of logic in the structure, or in (you knew it
    was more likely) you.

The Dirty Talker: D Line, Boston

Shabby, tweedy, academic, he was old enough to be her father and I
    thought he was her father,
then realized he was standing closer than a father would so I thought he
    was her older lover.
And I thought at first that she was laughing, then saw it was more serious,
    more strenuous:
her shoulders spasmed back and forth; he was leaning close, his mouth
    almost against her ear.
He's terminating the affair, I thought: wife ill, the kids . . . the girl won't
    let him go.
We were in a station now, he pulled back half a head from her the better
    to behold her,
then was out the hissing doors, she sobbing wholly now so that finally I
    had to understand—
her tears, his grinning broadly in—at *me* now though, as though I were a
    portion of the story.

Repression

More and more lately, as, not even minding the slippages yet, the aches
    and sad softenings,
I settle into my other years, I notice how many of what I once thought
    were evidences of repression,
sexual or otherwise, now seem, in other people anyway, to be varieties of
    dignity, withholding, tact,
and sometimes even in myself, certain patiences I would have once
    called lassitude, indifference,
now seem possibly to be if not the rewards then at least the unsuspected,
    undreamed-of conclusions
to many of the even-then-preposterous self-evolved disciplines, rigors,
    almost mortifications
I inflicted on myself in my starting-out days, improvement days, days
    when the idea alone of psychic peace,
of intellectual, of emotional quiet, the merest hint, would have meant
    inconceivable capitulation.

Como

In the Mercedes station wagon with diplomatic plates the mother has
    gone out somewhere again.
The husband is who knows and who cares where in his silver Porsche
    nine-twenty-eight.
As they come across the dismal hotel garden from their after-dinner
    promenade along the lake,
the three noisy, bratty kids are all over the pretty German teenager who
    minds them.
One tugs at one hand, another at the other, the snotty baby pulls at her
    wrinkled skirt and wails
but for all the *au pair* notices they might not be there, she might be on
    the dance floor at a ball.
It's not until the grizzled kitchen mouse-cat strolls out on the path that
    she comes to life,
kneeling, whispering, fervently coaxing the coy thing with tempting
    clicks and rubbings of her hands.

One Morning in Brooklyn

The snow is falling in three directions at once against the sienna brick of
       the houses across,
but the storm is mild, the light even, the erratic wind not harsh, and,
       tolling ten o'clock,
the usually undistinguished bells of the Sixth Street cathedral assume an
       authoritative dignity,
remarking with ponderous self-consciousness the holy singularities of
       this now uncommon day.
How much the pleasant sense, in our sheltering rooms, of warmth, en-
       closure: an idle, languid taking in,
with almost Georgian ease, voluptuous, reposeful, including titillations
       of the sin of well-being,
the gentle adolescent tempest, which still can't make up its mind quite,
       can't dig in and bite,
everything for show, flailing with a furious but futile animation wisps of
       white across the white.

Self-Knowledge

Because he was always the good-hearted one, the ingenuous one, the
       one who knew no cunning,
who, if "innocent" didn't quite apply, still merited some similar connota-
       tion of naïveté, simplicity,
the sense that an essential awareness of the coarseness of other people's
       motives was lacking
so that he was constantly blundering upon situations in which he would
       take on good faith
what the other rapaciously, ruthlessly, duplicitously and nearly always
       successfully offered as truth . . .
All of that he understood about himself but he was also aware that he
       couldn't alter at all
his basic affable faith in the benevolence of everyone's intentions and
       that because of this the world
would not as in romance annihilate him but would toy unmercifully
       with him until he was mad.

Alzheimer's: The Wife

for Renée Mauger

She answers the bothersome telephone, takes the message, forgets the
    message, forgets who called.
One of their daughters, her husband guesses: the one with the dogs, the
    babies, the boy Jed?
Yes, perhaps, but how tell which, how tell anything when all the name
    tags have been lost or switched,
when all the lonely flowers of sense and memory bloom and die now in
    adjacent bites of time?
Sometimes her own face will suddenly appear with terrifying inappropri-
    ateness before her in a mirror.
She knows that if she's patient, its gaze will break, demurely, decorously,
    like a well-taught child's,
it will turn from her as though it were embarrassed by the secrets of this
    awful hide-and-seek.
If she forgets, though, and glances back again, it will still be in there,
    furtively watching, crying.

Alzheimer's: The Husband

for Jean Mauger

He'd been a clod, he knew, yes, always aiming toward his vision of the
    good life, always acting on it.
He knew he'd been unconscionably self-centered, had indulged himself
    with his undreamed-of good fortune,
but he also knew that the single-mindedness with which he'd attended to
    his passions, needs and whims,
and which must have seemed to others the grossest sort of egotism, was
    also what was really at the base
of how he'd almost offhandedly worked out the intuitions and moves
    which had brought him here,
and this wasn't all that different: to spend his long anticipated retirement
    learning to cook,
clean house, dress her, even to apply her makeup, wasn't any sort of sec-
    ular saintliness —
that would be belittling — it was just the next necessity he saw himself as
    being called to.

The Critic

In the Boston Public Library on Boylston Street, where all the bums
      come in stinking from the cold,
there was one who had a battered loose-leaf book he used to scribble in
      for hours on end.
He wrote with no apparent hesitation, quickly, and with concentration;
      his inspiration was inspiring:
you had to look again to realize that he was writing over words that were
      already there—
blocks of cursive etched into the softened paper, interspersed with poems
      in print he'd pasted in.
I hated to think of the volumes he'd violated to construct his opus, but I
      liked him anyway,
especially the way he'd often reach the end, close his work with weary
      satisfaction, then open again
and start again: page one, chapter one, his blood-rimmed eyes as rapt as
      David's doing psalms.

New Car

Doesn't, when we touch it, that sheen of infinitesimally pebbled steel,
      doesn't it, perhaps,
give just a bit, yes, the subtlest yielding, yes, much less than flesh would,
      we realize,
but still, as though it were intending in some formal way that at last we
      were to be in contact
with the world of inorganics, as though, after all we've been through with
      it, cuts, falls, blows,
that world, the realm of carbon, iron, earth, the all-ungiving, was at-
      tempting, gently, patiently,
to reach across, respond, and mightn't we find now, not to our horror or
      even our discomfort,
that our tongue, as though in answer, had wandered gently from the
      mouth, as though it, too,
shriven of its limits, bud and duct, would sanctify this unity, would
      touch, stroke, cling, fuse?

Conscience

In how many of the miserable little life dramas I play out in my mind am
      I unforgivable,
despicable, with everything, love, kin, companionship, negotiable, mar-
      ketable, for sale,
and yet I do forgive myself, hardly marking it, although I still remember
      those fierce
if innocently violent fantasies of my eternal adolescence which could
      nearly knock me down
and send me howling through myself for caves of simple silence, black-
      ness, oblivion.
The bubble hardens, the opacities perfected: no one in here anymore to
      bring accusation,
no sob of shame to catch us in its throat, no omniscient angel, either,
      poor angel, child,
tremulous, aghast, covering its eyes and ears, compulsively washing out
      its mouth with soap.

Noise: Sinalunga

The cry of a woman making love in a room giving onto our hotel court-
      yard sounds just like Jed,
who has bronchitis, if he were saying "Ow!" in his sleep, loudly, from his
      room across the hall,
and so I am awake through another dawn in another small town in the
      country near Siena,
waiting for my son to wake up, too, and cough, or after weeks of this,
      please, not cough.
Now church bells from a nearby village; now sparrows, swallows, voices
      from a kitchen door,
as brilliant in the brilliant air as Cortona's Fra Angelico's *Annunciation*'s
      scroll of angel speech.
Now an underpowered motorscooter on a hill and from the jukebox in
      the broken-down café,
the first still blessedly indecipherable traces of the ubiquitous American
      I-Loved-You rock . . .

Anger

I killed the bee for no reason except that it was there and you were
     watching, disapproving,
which made what I would do much worse but I was angry with you any-
     way and so I put my foot on it,
leaned on it, tested how much I'd need to make that resilient, resisting
     cartridge give way
and *crack!* abruptly, shockingly it did give way and you turned sharply
     and sharply now
I felt myself balanced in your eyes—why should I feel myself so balanced
     always in your eyes;
isn't just this half the reason for my rage, these tendencies of yours, sus-
     ceptibilities of mine?—
and "Why?" your eyes said, "Why?" and even as mine sent back my an-
     swer, "None of your affair,"
I knew that I was being once again, twice now, weighed, and this time
     anyway found wanting.

Even So

Though she's seventy-four, has three children, five grown grandchildren
     (one already pregnant),
though she married and watched two men die, ran a good business—
     camping goods, tents,
not established and left to her by either of the husbands: it was her idea
     and her doing—
lived in three cities, and, since retiring, has spent a good part of the time
     traveling:
Europe, Mexico, even China, at the same time as Arthur Miller (though
     she didn't see him),
even so, when the nice young driver of their bus, starting out that day
     from Amsterdam,
asks her if she'd like to sit beside him in the jump seat where the ill tour
     guide should sit,
she's flattered and flustered and for a reason she's surprised about, feels
     herself being proud.

Drought

A species of thistle no one had ever seen before appeared almost
    overnight in all the meadows,
coarse, gray-greenish clumps scattered anywhere the dying grass had
    opened up bare earth.
The farmers knew better or were too weary to try to fight the things, but
    their children,
walking out beside them through the sunset down the hillsides toward
    the still cool woods
along the narrowed brooks, would kick the plants or try to pry them out
    with pointed sticks:
the tenacious roots would hardly ever want to give, though, and it was
    too hot still to do much more
than crouch together where the thick, lethargic water filtered up and ran
    a few uncertain feet,
moistening the pebbles, forming puddles where the thriving insects
    could repose and reproduce.

End of Drought

It is the opposite or so of the friendly gossip from upstairs who stops by
    every other evening.
It's the time she comes in once too often, or it's more exactly in the mid-
    dle of her tête-à-tête,
when she grows tedious beyond belief, and you realize that unless an eti-
    quette is violated
this will just go on forever, the way, forever, rain never comes, then
    comes, the luscious opposite,
the shock of early drops, the pavements and the rooftops drinking, then
    the scent, so heady with release
it's almost overwhelming, thick and vaginal, and then the earth, terrified
    she'd bungled it,
dwelt too long upon the problems of the body and the mind, the ancient
    earth herself,
like someone finally touching pen to page, breathes her languid, aching
    suspiration of relief.

Easter

As though it were the very soul of rational human intercourse which had
   been violated,
I can't believe you did that, the father chokes out to his little son, kneel-
   ing beside him,
tugging at the waistband of the tiny blue jeans, peering in along the split
   between the buttocks,
putting down his face at last to sniff, then saying it again, with quiet
   indignation, outrage,
a power more moral than parental: at issue here are covenants, agree-
   ments from the dawn of time.
The child, meanwhile, his eyes a little wider than they might be, is
   otherwise unblinking;
all the time the father raves, he stares, scholarly, detached, at a package
   in his hands:
a box of foil-wrapped chocolate eggs, because it's spring, because the god
   has died, and risen.

Girl Meets Boy

She would speak of "our relationship" as though it were a thing apart
   from either of us,
an entity with separate necessities, even its own criteria for appraisal,
   judgment, mode of act,
to which both of us were to be ready to sacrifice our own more momen-
   tary notions of identity.
It was as though there were a pre-existent formula or recipe, something
   from a textbook,
which demanded not only the right ingredients—attentiveness, affec-
   tion, generosity, et cetera—
but also a constant and rigorous examination and analysis of the shifting
   configurations
our emotions were assuming in their presumed movement toward some
   ultimate consummation
in whose intensity the rest of this, not an end, would be redeemed, to
   wither quietly away.

Bishop Tutu's Visit to the White House: 1984

I am afraid for you a little, for your sense of shame; I feel you are accustomed to ordinary evil.

Your assumption will be that disagreeing with your methods, he will nevertheless grasp the problems.

You will assume that he will be involved, as all humans must be, for what else is it to be human,

in a notion of personal identity as a progress toward a more conscious, inclusive spiritual condition,

so that redemption, in whatever terms it might occur, categorically will have been earned.

How will you bear that for him and those around him, righteousness and self are *a priori* the same,

that to have stated one's good intentions excuses in advance from any painful sense of sin?

I fear you will be wounded by his obtuseness, humiliated by his pride, mortified by his absurd power.

Experience

After a string of failed romances and intensely remarked sexual adventures she'd finally married.

The husband was a very formal man, handsome, elegant . . . perhaps to my taste too much so;

I sensed too much commitment in him to a life entailing . . . handsomeness and elegance, I suppose,

but he was generous with her and even their frequent arguments had a manageable vehemence.

She smiled often in those days, but behind her face an edge of animation seemed nailed shut.

You wouldn't really worry for her, by now you knew she'd be all right, but there were moments

when for no reason you could put your finger on you'd feel something in yourself too rigidly attentive:

it was as though some soft herd-alarm, a warning signal from the species, had been permanently tripped.

Resentment

What is there which so approaches an art form in its stubborn patience,
     its devotion to technique,
to elegant refinement: that relentless searching for receptacles to capture
     content and expression?
The fiercest lust of self toward self: is there anything which keeps the
     soul so *occupied*?
My slights, affronts: how I shuffle and reshuffle them, file them, index,
     code, and collate.
Justification, accusation: I permutate, elaborate, combine, condense,
     refocus, re-refine.
I mull, I ponder, convince, cajole; I prove, disprove, accomplish, reac-
     complish, satisfy, solve.
Begin again: courageous, unflinching, resigned, my conscience swoon-
     ing with projected ingenuities;
my mind's two mouths, their song, their kiss, this inaccomplishable,
     accomplished consummation!

Mornings: Catherine

Sometimes she'd begin to sing to herself before she was out of bed,
     before, I can remember thinking
as I listened from my table in the other room, she really could have even
     been all the way awake:
no sound of sheets pulled back, footsteps, just her voice, her song, so soft
     at first I wasn't sure,
rising from the silence but so close to being in it still that I couldn't hear
     the words,
only the threads of melody a car passing or a child crying in another
     house would brush away,
until it would insist again, or I'd think it would, with the volume of a
     breeze, the odor of a breeze . . .
Waiting to hear it again, to hear her again, I wouldn't move, I'd almost,
     yes, hold my breath:
her voice, her song, the meshings and unmeshings with the attending
     world, with my incredulity.

The Ladder

God was an accident of language, a quirk of the unconscious mind, but
   unhappily never of my mind.
God had risen from dream, was dream, was a dream I wanted, would do
   much to have, but never had had.
Therefore, or maybe therefore, God became functioned, with want, with
   lack, with need, denial.
Then therefore, maybe therefore, equations: God and death, God and
   war, God injustice, hatred, pain.
Then my only revelation, knowing that if God did speak what He'd say
   would be, *Your heart is dull.*
I let my sophistries and disputations fail: I knew that only in His own fire
   would God be consumed.
God, a sheet of paper scrawled with garbled cipher, flared, then cooled
   to cinder, then the cinder,
pounded by these hammerings, blended with the textures of my—could
   I still say "soul"?—my soul.

War

Jed is breathlessly, deliriously happy because he's just been deftly am-
   bushed and gunned down
by his friend Ha Woei as he came charging headlong around the corner
   of some bushes in the *bois.*
He slumps dramatically to the ground, disregarding the damp, black,
   gritty dirt he falls into,
and holds the posture of a dead man, forehead to the earth, arms and
   legs thrown full-length east and west,
until it's time for him to rise and Ha Woei to die, which Ha Woei does
   with vigor and abandon,
flinging himself down, the imaginary rifle catapulted from his hand like
   Capa's Spanish soldier's.
Dinnertime, bath time, bedtime, story time: *bam, bambambam, bam—*
   Akhilleus and Hektor.
Not until the cloak of night falls do they give themselves to the truces
   and forgivenesses of sleep.

Greed

A much-beaten-upon-looking, bedraggled blackbird, not a starling, with
    a mangled or tumorous claw,
an extra-evil air, comically malignant, like something from a folktale
    meant to frighten you,
gimps his way over the picnic table to a cube of moist white cheese into
    which he drives his beak.
Then a glister of licentious leering, a conspiratorial gleam, the cocked
    brow of common avarice:
he works his yellow scissors deeper in, daring doubt, a politician with his
    finger in the till,
a weapon maker's finger in the politician, the slobber and the licking and
    the champ and click.
It is a lovely day, it always is; the innocent daylight fades into its dying, it
    always does.
The bird looks up, death-face beside the curded white, its foot, its fist of
    dying, daintily raised.

The Past

The past is not dependent on us for existence, but exists in its own right.
    —Henry Steele Commager

All along certainly it's been there, waiting before us, waiting to receive
    us, not to waver,
flickering shakily across the mind-screen, always in another shadow, al-
    ways potentially illusion,
but out ahead, where it should be, redeemable, retrievable, accessible
    not by imagination's nets
but by the virtue of its being, simply being, waiting patiently for us like
    any other unattended,
any other hardly anticipated or not even anticipated—as much as any
    other fact rolling in . . .
All the project needs is patience, cunning, similar to that with which we
    outwit trembling death . . .
Not "history" but scent, sound, sight, the sensual fact, the beings and the
    doings, the heroes,
unmediated now, the holy and the horrid, to be worked across not like a
    wistful map, but land.

Ice

Whatever the argument the young sailor on the train is having and whomever with, he's not winning.
In his silly white starched French recruit's suit with its outsized bib and teeny ribboned cap,
he looks endearingly anachronistic, like a deckhand in *Potemkin* in the calm before they rise,
but he's gesticulating, striking one hand into the other, his feet tapping out separate rhythms,
and he's whispering, pleading, fervently, intensely, sometimes with a sweet, almost goofy grin,
sometimes angrily, most often angrily, or desperately, trying to convince himself of something,
or someone else of something, something or someone more important than he'd ever dreamed he'd know,
so it's frightening to wonder what it is, who it is, to elicit winces like that, like a lion's roar.

The Modern

Its skin tough and unpliable as scar, the pulp out of focus, weak, granular, powdery, blank,
this tomato I'm eating—wolfing, stuffing down: I'm so hungry—is horrible and delicious.
Don't tell me, I know all about it, this travesty-sham; I know it was plucked green and unripe,
then locked in a chamber and gassed so it wouldn't rot till I bought it but I don't care:
I was so famished before, I was sucking sweat from my arm and now my tomato is glowing inside me.
I muscle the juice through my teeth and the seeds to the roof of my mouth and the hard,
scaly scab of where fruit met innocent stem and was torn free I hold on my tongue and savor,
a coin, a dot, the end of a sentence, the end of the long improbable utterance of the holy and human.

The Mistress

After the drink, after dinner, after the half-hour idiot kids' cartoon special
      on the TV,
after undressing his daughter, mauling at the miniature buttons on the
      back of her dress,
the games on the bed—"Look at my pee-pee," she says, pulling her
      thighs wide, "isn't it pretty?"—
after the bath, pajamas, the song and the kiss and the telling his wife it's
      her turn now,
out now, at last, out of the house to make the call (out to take a stroll, this
      evening's lie),
he finds the only public phone booth in the neighborhood's been sav-
      aged, receiver torn away,
wires thrust back up the coin slot to its innards, and he stands there, what
      else? what now?
and notices he's panting, he's panting like an animal, he's breathing like
      a bloody beast.

The Lover

When she stopped by, just passing, on her way back from picking up the
      kids at school,
taking them to dance, just happened by the business her husband owned
      and her lover worked in,
their glances, hers and the lover's, that is, not the husband's, seemed so
      decorous, so distant,
barely, just barely touching their fiery wings, their clanging she thought
      so well muffled,
that later, in the filthy women's bathroom, in the stall, she was horrified
      to hear two typists
coming from the office laughing, about them, all of them, their boss, her
      husband, "the blind pig,"
one said, and laughed, "and her, the horny bitch," the other said, and
      they both laughed again,
"and *him*, did you see *him*, that sanctimonious, lying bastard—I thought
      he was going to *blush*."

Religious Thought

for (. . .)

Beyond anything else, he dwells on what might inhabit his mind at the
    moment of his death,
that which he'll take across with him, which will sum his being up as
    he's projected into spirit.
Thus he dwells upon the substance of his consciousness, what its con-
    tents are at any moment:
good thoughts, hopefully, of friends, recent lovers, various genres of at-
    tempted bliss.
Primitive notions of divinity and holy presence interest him not at all;
    blessèd, cursèd: less.
For life: a public, fame, companionship, arousal; for death, an endless
    calm floating on abyss.
His secret is the terror that mind will do to him again what it did that un-
    forgivable once.
Sometimes, lest he forget, he lets it almost take him again: the vile
    thoughts, the chill, the dread.

Carpe Diem

A young tourist with a two-thousand-dollar Leica and a nice-looking girl
    waiting outside the gate
has slipped into the park next to St.-Germain-des-Prés to take a picture
    with his super-fisheye
of a little girl in smock and sandals trying to balance herself on the low
    wrought-iron fence
in front of Picasso's statue for Apollinaire, the row of disattached Gothic
    arches as background.
He needs an awfully long time to focus; before you know it, she's circled
    all the way around
to the sunny bench where her mother sits intently probing at her big toe
    with a safety pin
and where a grungy Danish hippie is sound asleep, his head propped
    sideways on his old guitar.
Wait, now we're changing lenses; uh oh, girlfriend's impatient: Okay, she
    says, let's move it, maestro!

Twins

"There were two of them but nobody knew at first because only one hap-
    pened on the table,
the other was just suddenly there during the night: I felt a spasm I
    thought or dreamed
had something to do with whatever they'd done to me that afternoon and
    then there it was.
I woke up—I suppose I should have called the nurse but all I did was
    turn the light on.
He wasn't breathing, it didn't occur to me to wonder dead or not dead: I
    was very tired.
I covered us again and dozed on and off till morning; when the nurse did
    come, she was angry.
Funny: I used to think one of them was yours, the other . . . you know . . .
    That solved something for me.
That and dope, dear, darling dope: I stayed stoned an entire month, then
    I bought my diaphragm."

The Telephone

He must be her grandson: they're both very dark, she with high, broad
    cheekbones, white wiry hair,
he slightly fairer, finer featured, hair thick, rich, black, badly cropped,
    shining with oil.
I'm only watching from my car so I can't tell what language they're in,
    but it's not English.
They're standing by the phone booth arguing, the boy apparently doesn't
    want to make the call,
but the woman takes his arm—she's farm-wife muscular, he's very lean—
    and easily shoves him in.
Very rapidly, with an offhanded dexterity, he punches out a number, lis-
    tens for hardly a moment
and with an I-told-you-so exasperation holds out the receiver so that she
    can lean to it,
not quite touching, and listen, eyes focused to the middle distance, for at
    least a dozen rings.

Failure

Maybe it's not as bad as we like to think: no melodramatic rendings, sackcloths, nothing so acute
as the fantasies of conscience chart in their uncontrollably self-punishing rigors and admonitions.
Less love, yes, but what was love: a febrile, restless, bothersome trembling to continue to possess
what one was only partly certain was worth wanting anyway, and if the reservoir of hope is depleted,
neither do distracting expectations interfere with these absorbing meditations on the frailties of chance.
A certain *resonance* might be all that lacks; the voice spinning out in darkness in an empty room.
The recompense is knowing that at last you've disconnected from the narratives that conditioned you
to want to be what you were never going to be, while here you are still this far from "the end."

Crime

John the tailor had gone racing up the stairs in back of his store and because he was so frightened
had jumped right out the window into the street where he broke his arm, though not badly.
A mounted policeman who'd been with his married girlfriend around the corner heard the shouts
and came cantering up just as the holdup man with a pistol in his hand was coming out:
the policeman pulled his gun, shot once, hit the robber in the chest, and it was over.
By the time I got there, everybody was waiting for the ambulance, John was still sobbing,
the crook was lying next to that amazing clot of blood, congealed to the consistency of cow plop,
and kids were darting from the crowd, scrambling for the change he'd let spill when he fell.

Fat

The young girl jogging in mittens and skimpy gym shorts through a
      freezing rainstorm up our block
would have a perfect centerfold body except for the bulbs of grandmoth-
      erly fat on her thighs.
Who was it again I loved once . . . no, not loved truly, liked, somewhat,
      and slept with, a lot,
who when she'd brood on the I thought quite adorable blubber she had
      there would beat it on the wall?
Really: she'd post herself naked half a stride back, crouch like a skier,
      and swing her hips, bang!
onto the plaster, bang! ten times, a hundred: bang! the wall shook, bang!
      her poor body quivered.
I'd lie there aghast, I knew that mad pounding had to mean more than
      itself, of course I thought me.
For once I was right; soon after, she left me, and guess what, for all that,
      I missed her.

Fame

I recognize the once-notorious radical theater director, now suffering
      general public neglect
but still teaching and writing and still certain enough of his fame so that
      when I introduce myself
he regards me with a polite, if somewhat elevated composure, acknowl-
      edging some friends in common,
my having heard him lecture once, even the fact that I actually once
      dashed off a play
inspired by some of his more literary speculations, but never does he ask
      who I might be,
what do, where live, et cetera, manifesting instead that maddeningly
      bland and incurious cosmopolitan
or at least New Yorkian self-centeredness, grounded in the most unshak-
      able and provincial syllogism:
I am known to you, you not to me, therefore you clearly must remain be-
      neath serious consideration.

USOCA

At the United States Out of Central America rally at a run-down commu-
nity center in the Village
the audience is so sparse that the Andean musicians who've come to play
for us are embarrassed
and except for the bass guitarist who has to give the introductions ex-
plaining their songs
they all focus resolutely on their instruments, their gazes never rising,
even to one another.
Their music is vital, vigorous, sometimes almost abandoned, but in-
formed always with nostalgia,
with exile's dark alarms and melancholy, exacerbated surely by how few
and weak we are
but which we disregard, applauding when they're done so heartfeltly that
they relent a bit,
releasing shy, exotic smiles for us to pass along between us like the pre-
cious doves of hope.

Eight Months

Jed is having his bath; he lies in a few inches of water in his plastic bath-
tub on the kitchen sink.
Catherine holds a bar of white soap in one hand, her other hand rubs it,
then goes to Jed,
slipping over his gleaming skin, the bulges and crevasses, back to the
soap, back to Jed.
She's humming, Jed is gazing raptly at her and every time her hand
leaves for its journey,
he squirms with impatience, his own hands follow along as though to
hurry her return to him.
When he realizes I'm in the room, he smiles brilliantly up at me, wel-
coming me into the ritual.
Catherine stops crooning, looks up too, smiles too, but her hand goes on,
moving over Jed,
the soap, Jed, gently roiling the foamy surface: before I'm out the door,
she's singing again.

Junior High School Concert: Salle Rossini

Each movement of the Mozart has a soloist and as each appears the con-
    ductor tunes her instrument,
while they, pubescent girls all, look fiercely unconcerned with being pos-
    sibly made fools of.
Their teacher is oblivious to that, though with his graying dentures he
    seems kind enough,
he just loves music more—you can tell he might love music more than
    Toscanini or than Bach.
It might be the saddest thing about the arts that they so seldom recom-
    pense passion and commitment
with genius or with anything at all beyond a ground-floor competence,
    but *tant pis!* for that,
the old man seems to say, *Tant pis!* too if the cellos thump, if the *lento* is
    a trifle tired,
if the girl slogging through as soon would let the whole thing drop: *Tant
    pis!* everything: *Bravo!*

The Prodigy
for Elizabeth Bishop

Though no shyer than the others—while her pitch is being checked she
    beams out at the audience,
one ear sticking through her fine, straight, dark hair, Nabokov would
    surely say "deliciously"—
she's younger, slimmer, flatter, still almost a child: her bow looks half a
    foot too big for her.
Not when she begins to play, though: when she begins to play, when she
    goes swooping, leaping,
lifting from the lumbering *tutti* like a fighter plane, that bow is fire, that
    bow is song,
that bow lifts all of us, father and old uncle, yawning younger brother
    and bored best friend,
and brings us all to song, to more than song, to breaths breathed for us,
    sharp, indrawn,
and then, as she bows it higher and higher, to old sorrows redeemed, a
    sweet sensation of joy.

Souls

Bound with baling wire to the tubular jerry-built bumper of a beat-up
      old dump truck
are two of those gigantic teddy bears people win (usually shills) in cheap
      amusement parks.
It's pouring: dressed in real children's clothes, they are, our mothers
      would have said, drenched,
and they're also unrelentingly filthy, matted with the sticky, sickly,
      ghastly, dark gray sheen
you see on bums ambulating between drinking streets and on mongrels
      guarding junkyards.
Their stuffing hasn't been so crushed in them as to affect their jaunty,
      open-armed availability,
but, regarded more closely, they seem to manifest a fanatical expression-
      lessness, like soldiers,
who, wounded, captured, waiting to be shipped away or shot, must sub-
      mit now to their photograph.

Regret

Rather die than live through dying with it: rather perish absolutely now
      than perish partially
in its cold coils which would mean savaging the self from far within
      where only love, self-love,
should be allowed to measure what one was and is and to roll the bales
      of loss aside.
Or if it should survive to insinuate itself into that ceremony: not to have
      to own to it,
not to any other, anyway, at least to keep the noble cloak of reticence
      around one's self,
keep the self-contained and self-sustaining version of what was not en-
      dured but was accomplished.
Never rue: that old longing rather that the past would be always the
      portal of touching possibility:
to say I am the life and was the life, to dying say I am still the matrix and
      again the fire.

Cowboys

The science-fiction movie on the telly in which the world, threatened by
aliens with destruction,
is, as always, saved, is really just a Western with rays and jets instead of
pistols and horses.
The heroes crouch behind computers instead of rocks, but still mow
down the endlessly expendable villains
who fire back but somehow always miss the stars, except one, the extra-
lovable second lead,
nice guy, funny, a little too libidinal, who you know from minute one
will teach us to die,
in his buddy's arms, stoical, never losing sight of our side's virtues: com-
munity and self-denial.
On the other channel, Pompeii: Christians, pagans, same story, them
and us, another holy mission,
the actors resonating with deep conviction, voices of manly sanctity, like
Reagan on the news.

The Marriage

The way she tells it, they were in the Alps or somewhere, tall, snow-
capped mountains anyway,
in their hotel, a really nice hotel, she says, they'd decided that for once
they'd splurge.
They'd just arrived, they were looking from their terrace out across a lake
or bay or something.
She was sitting there, just sitting there and thinking to herself how pleas-
ant it all looked,
like a postcard, just the way for once it's supposed to look, clean and pure
and cool,
when his hand came to her shoulder and he asked her something,
"Don't you think it's lovely?"
then something else, his tone was horrid; there was something that he
wanted her to say—
how was *she* to know what he wanted her to say?—and he *shook* her
then, until she ached.

246

Fifteen

for Jessie

You give no hint how shy you really are, so thoroughly your warm and
        welcoming temperament masks
those confounding and to me still painful storms of adolescent ill at ease,
        confusion and disruption.
Our old father-daughter stroll down South Street these days is like a foray
        into the territories—
the weighings and the longings, young men, men of age, the brazen or
        sidelong subliminal proposings:
you're fair game now, but if you notice, you manage to keep it unim-
        peachably to yourself,
your newly braceless smile good-humoredly desexualizing the leering
        and licentious out-there.
Innocently you sheathe yourself in the most patently innocuous and un-
        premeditated innocence;
even with me, though, your kiss goodbye is layered: cheek toward, body
        swayed imperceptibly away.

Sixteen: Tuscany

Wherever Jessie and her friend Maura alight, clouds of young men sud-
        denly appear like bees.
We're to meet in Florence at the Ponte Vecchio at nine o'clock: they're
        twenty minutes early,
two vacationing Sicilian bees, hair agleam like fenders, are begging for a
        kiss good night when we arrive.
At San Gimignano, on the steps that go down from the church into the
        square—such clean breezes—
two Tuscan bees, lighter, handsome: great flurried conferences with ref-
        erences to pocket dictionary
to try to find out where we're staying, how long staying, how get there . . .
        impossible, poor bees.
A broad blond bee from Berkeley at the bank in Lucca; in Pisa, French
        bees, German bees . . .
The air is filled with promises of pollen, the dancing air is filled with
        honeyed wings and light.

Thinking Thought

"Oh, soul," I sometimes—often—still say when I'm trying to convince
my inner self of something.
"Oh, soul," I say still, "there's so much to be done, don't want to stop to
rest now, not already.
"Oh, soul," I say, "the implications of the task are clear, why procrasti-
nate, why whine?"
All the while I know my struggle has to do with mind being only
sometimes subject to the will,
that other portion of itself which manages to stay so recalcitrantly, obsti-
nately impotent.
"Oh, soul, come into my field of want, my realm of act, be attentive to
my computations and predictions."
But as usual soul resists, as usual soul retires, as usual soul's old act of dis-
sipation and removal.
Oh, the furious illusive unities of want, the frail, false fusions and discur-
sive chains of hope.

Jews

She could tell immediately, she said, that he was Jewish, although he
didn't of course *look* it,
it was his . . . seriousness—and she wanted to take the opportunity be-
cause she met so few these days
to ask him some questions about the vision a Jew would have of some of
the unfortunate attitudes
she felt were being promulgated—oh, Lord, again—in this terribly
provincial, conservative country.
She'd been a leftist in the old days, when it was still worth being one,
she'd admired Jews then
and still did: they were so much more aware of subtleties, of implications
in the apparently innocuous.
Here, for instance, the old anti-Semitism, little explicit, little said in pub-
lic, but people like us,
sensitive to that sort of thing, surely *we* knew: couldn't he sense it just in
the *tone* of things?

Snow: I

All night, snow, then, near dawn, freezing rain, so that by morning the
      whole city glistens
in a glaze of high-pitched, meticulously polished brilliance, everything
      rounded off,
the cars submerged nearly to their windows in the unbroken drifts lining
      the narrow alleys,
the buildings rising from the trunklike integuments the wind has molded
      against them.
Underlit clouds, blurred, violet bars, the rearguard of the storm, still
      hang in the east,
immobile over the flat river basin of the Delaware; beyond them, noth-
      ing, the washed sky,
one vivid wisp of pale smoke rising waveringly but emphatically into the
      brilliant ether.
No one is out yet but Catherine, who closes the door behind her and
      starts up the street.

Snow: II

It's very cold, Catherine is bundled in a coat, a poncho on top of that,
      high boots, gloves,
a long scarf around her neck, and she's sauntering up the middle of the
      snowed-in street,
eating, of all things, an apple, the blazing redness of which shocks
      against the world of white.
No traffic yet, the *crisp crisp* of her footsteps keeps reaching me until she
      turns the corner.
I write it down years later, and the picture still holds perfectly, precise,
      unwanting,
and so too does the sense of being suddenly bereft as she passes abruptly
      from my sight,
the quick wash of desolation, the release again into the memory of affec-
      tion, and then affection,
as the first trucks blundered past, chains pounding, the first delighted
      children rushed out with sleds.

Gardens

The ever-consoling fantasy of my early adolescence was that one day
       time would stop for me:
everything in the world, for however long I wanted it to, would stay
       frozen in a single instant,
the clock on the classroom wall, the boring teacher, the other kids . . . all
       but someone else and me,
Arlene and me, Marie and me, Barbara of the budding breasts, Sheila of
       the braids and warming smile . . .
In the nurse's room there was a narrow cot, there we would repair, there
       we would reveal ourselves.
One finds of course to one's amazement and real chagrin that such
       things actually happen,
the precocious male, the soon to be knocked-up girl, but by now that's
       no longer what we care about:
what matters now are qualities of longing, this figment, fragment, its pre-
       cious, adorable irresolutions.

The Star

Though he's sitting at the restaurant bar next to the most startlingly
       glamorous woman in the place,
who keeps leaning against him, alertly, conscientiously, even solemnly
       attending to his every word,
the very famous ex–basketball player, when he isn't dealing directly with
       her or one of his friends,
seems enormously distracted—whenever he can retreat into himself he
       does, his eyes drift away,
he takes great care to listen to what's said but the listening never really
       overtakes the waiting,
for whatever is happening to be finished so that something new can
       happen, something different, else:
even when strangers stop to offer homage, to pass a moment in his pres-
       ence, though he's gracious,
his attention never quite alights but stays tensed away, roving his dissatis-
       factions like a cat.

Kin

"You make me sick!" this, with rancor, vehemence, disgust—again, "You
      hear me? *Sick!*"
with rancor, vehemence, disgust again, with rage and bitterness, arro-
      gance and fury—
from a little black girl, ten or so, one evening in a convenience market,
      to her sister,
two or three years younger, who's taking much too long picking out her
      candy from the rack.
What next? Nothing next. Next the wretched history of the world. The
      history of the heart.
The theory next that all we are are stories, handed down, that all we are
      are parts of speech.
All that limits and defines us: our ancient natures, love and death and
      terror and original sin.
And the weary breath, the weary going to and fro, the weary always know-
      ing what comes next.

Fire

The boss, the crane operator, one of the workers, a friend of somebody in
      the junkyard—
whoever it is who watches me when I pull up to see the fire in the cab of
      the huge derrick,
the flames in crisp, hungry, emphatic shapes scaling the suddenly fragile-
      ribbed steel tower,
considers it a matter of deep, real suspicion that a stranger should bother
      to want to see this:
slouched against a stack of rusty, dismembered fenders, he regards me
      with a coolness bordering threat,
a wariness touching frank hostility, while, from a low warehouse building
      across the street,
another person, with a bulky fire extinguisher, comes, like someone from
      the UN, running,
red-faced, panting, with a look of anxious desperation, as though all the
      fault were his.

Dignity

It only exists in us so that we may lose it but then not lose it, never at all
      costs lose it:
no matter what the gaffe or awful error that we've made, on the spot we
      reassume ourselves
rapidly enough to reconvince ourselves it never happened, never could
      have happened, until,
perhaps, much later, in another life, another universe, one lonely
      evening, gently reminiscing,
sweetly sorrowing for this, sweetly fondling that, something brings to
      mind another night,
that night, when you lost . . . what? your composure? yes, you'd thought
      then you'd lost composure,
yes, the muscles of your stomach knotted up against your ribs, your
      hands trembled, but now you know
you lost more than that, yes, much more than that, but that was then,
      surely not again, never *now*.

Fast Food

Musingly she mouths the end of her ballpoint pen as she stares down at
      the sheet of paper.
A job application: lines, boxes, blanks to fill, a set of instructions, that
      logo at the top.
Name and address, she's got that; phone number, age, high school,
      height and weight: that.
Then number problems, addition, subtraction, a long, long division . . .
      she hasn't got that.
It's blank next to that, the page is white next to that, her eyes touch down
      on the white near that.
Never so white was white as that white: oh, white, angel of white, never
      were you so pure,
never were you so seared by anyone's eyes and never so sadly bereft when
      eyes lifted away,
when eyes left you and moved, indifferent and cool, across you to the
      waiting door, oh, white, white.

The Orchid
with thanks to Curtis Ingham

"Tell me to touch your breast," I wanted to say: "Please, please, please
    touch my breast,"
I thought she wanted to say, but was too frightened, like me, too over-
    whelmed, too stricken,
like me, with the surges and furies of need; our lips, locked, ground to-
    gether again and again,
we were bruised and swollen, like lovers in stories, sweating like lovers in
    bed, but no bed.
Then I heard, I thought, "Touch me," and ecstatic, I touched, but she
    brushed me away like a fly . . .
No, still held me, only my hand fell like a fly, her thirsty lips drank from
    me what they needed.
My testicles shrank, the orchid I'd paid five dollars for, hooked to the
    wires of her bra,
browned, faded, crumpled between us, as the orchid of memory crum-
    ples, mummified like a fly.

The City in the Hills

Late afternoon and difficult to tell if those are mountains, soft with mist,
    off across the lake,
the day's last luminosity pale over them, or if a dense, low-lying cloud-
    bank is holding there,
diffusing the dusk above the cottages scattered charmingly on the
    just-discernible far shore.
A tumultuous chimney of shrilly shrieking starlings wheeling and turn-
    ing over the wharves
abruptly unwinds a single undulating filament that shoots resolutely and
    unwaveringly across,
and now the old white steamer with its grainy voice of sentiment and res-
    ignation sets off, too,
to fetch the happy-ending humans implied so richly by the tiled roofs
    against the pines behind
and by the autumn air, its biting balm sensualized now by the inhala-
    tions of the eager evening.

From the Next Book by (. . .)

. . . The part where he's telling himself at last the no longer deniable
    truth about himself.
He's remembering his sins, the grosser ones he sublimated for characters
    and conflicts,
and the hardly noticeable omissions, especially from his early time,
    which he realizes now
he tended, cultivated: seeds of something which would someday bear
    fruit, achieve their grandeur.
And the woman he had lived with, and was trapped by and suffered from
    (not with), that omission . . .
Something was the matter with her heart, the doctors said, she'd need an
    operation . . .
She comes awake, sobbing in the night, holding him (although he really
    can't be held by now),
telling him she doesn't want to die, and him (this is the confession)
    astonished she'd care.

Native Americans

I'm not sure whether it was Hiawatha or a real Indian who so impressed
    me during my latency.
My father would read me Longfellow; one of our teachers taught us
    actual reservation life,
to try to make us understand that our vision of exotics and minorities was
    so contaminated
that we not only had corrupted ideas of history but didn't know what
    went on under our noses.
Whatever the person I derived from all that, I was very moved by how
    seriously he comported himself:
whether I really wanted to be him, or like him, with that intimidating
    valor and self-possession,
aren't really questions at this late date, but maybe that elaborate identity,
    warrior, victim,
hunter, obstinate survivor, muddled, split, meant more to me than just
    another semblance to be shed.

Work

Although constructed of the most up-to-date, technically advanced ele-
ments of woven glass,
carrying messages by laser pulse, the cable the telephone men are
threading down the manhole
has exactly the same thickness and tense flexibility and has to be handled
with the same delicacy
as the penis of the huge palamino stallion I saw breeding at the riding
school when I was twelve
who couldn't get it in so that Charlie Young the little stablehand had to
help him with it.
How more than horrified I was that Charlie would touch the raw, un-
peeled, violet-purple thing,
thinking nothing of it, slipping between the flaring, snorting stud and the
gleaming mare,
comely and lascivious, who, sidling under now, next year would throw a
mediocre foal, soon sold.

Gratitude

for Steve Berg

I'm scribbling suggestions on a copy of the next-to-final draft of my
friend's book of poems.
When I stop to rest, rub my eyes, and look up out the window, the phone
company, at it again,
has a sort of miniature collapsible crane outside, one member, dangling
cables from its jaws,
looming weirdly in a long, smooth, effortless arc across my line of sight,
white, clean, sleek,
enameled steel, impeccable, like something from those science-fiction
flicks my kids are so insane for.
For a moment I let myself envy the people who make those films: all that
money, all that audience . . .
The poem I'm reading now is "Gratitude": "Sunday. Nothing to do. I
park. Stumps. Weeds . . ."
And there's nothing much to do here either: all the whole poem needed
was to cut a "the."

Will

The boy had badly malformed legs, and there was a long, fresh surgical
　　　scar behind one knee.
The father, frankly wealthy, quite young, tanned, very boardroom, very
　　　well-made, self-made,
had just taken the boy's thin arm the way you would take the arm of an
　　　attractive woman,
with firmness, a flourish of affection; he was smiling directly down into
　　　the boy's face
but it was evident that this much companionability between them wasn't
　　　usual, that the father,
whatever else his relation to the boy consisted of, didn't know that if you
　　　held him that way
you would overbalance him, which, when the boy's crutches splayed and
　　　he went down, crying *"Papa!"*
must have been what informed his voice with such shrill petulance, such
　　　anguished accusation.

Pregnant

Tugging with cocked thumbs at the straps of her old overalls the way
　　　hick movie-farmers used to,
"This is the only thing I can wear," she declares, the halter hard against
　　　her heavy breasts,
then her hands encircle the impressive eight months' globe slung in its
　　　sack of comfortable denim.
Not eighteen yet, she isn't so much radiant, as brides are (she's not mar-
　　　ried), as radiantly complacent:
her two friends seem moved by the charming self-attention she gra-
　　　ciously allows them to share.
They watch closely as with affectionate familiarity she pushes on the
　　　forepart of the bulge,
as though she already felt the brow and headshape there and was com-
　　　municating arcane greetings,
which she then subtleizes into that consoling feathery, obsessive gesture,
　　　effleurage.

Peace

We fight for hours, through dinner, through the endless evening, who
    even knows now what about,
what could be so dire to have to suffer so for, stuck in one another's craws
    like fishbones,
the cadavers of our argument dissected, flayed, but we go on with it, to
    bed, and through the night,
feigning sleep, dreaming sleep, hardly sleeping, so precisely never touch-
    ing, back to back,
the blanket bridged across us for the wintry air to tunnel down, to keep
    us lifting, turning,
through the angry dark that holds us in its cup of pain, the aching dark,
    the weary dark,
then, toward dawn, I can't help it, though justice won't I know be served,
    I pull her to me,
and with such accurate, graceful deftness she rolls to me that we arrive
    embracing our entire lengths.

Some of Us

How nearly unfeasible they make it for the rest of us, those who, with
    exactly our credentials,
attain, if that's how it happens, the world of the publicly glamorous, the
    very chic, the "in."
It isn't so much being omitted, left home from the party, as knowing that
    we'll never get there,
never participate in those heady proximities our insatiable narrations
    ever tremble toward.
What would be there, we ask ourselves. Better bosoms? Better living
    rooms? Contemptibles.
Still, without it, the uneasy sense of incompletion, not really to have
    lived all that was to live,
especially knowing at this age how easy it would be now to evade en-
    croachments of the essentials,
those once impressionable, now solitude-inured, scar-tissue-tough tabu-
    las of receptive ego.

Two: Resurrections

Jed kills Catherine with a pistol he's put together himself out of some
     plastic play blocks.
Bang! you're dead. Catherine falls down on the floor: Look, you've killed
     me now, she says.
Jed is neither amused nor upset, but there is something in all this he
     takes very seriously.
I want to kill you again, he says. Before you can, Catherine says, you'll
     have to fix me.
I'll fix you, Jed says, and runs into the bathroom, coming back with
     Catherine's comb and brush.
He kneels beside her and with great solemnity places the brush in the
     center of her chest.
Then, still silent, still very serious, he slowly runs the comb over her left
     breast, right breast,
then down her belly, once across the breadth of her hips, then deep into
     the valley of her crotch.

Men

As the garbage truck is backing up, one of the garbagemen is absorbed
     watching a pretty girl pass
and a sleeve of protruding steel catches him hard enough on the bicep to
     almost knock him down.
He clutches at his arm, limping heavily across the sidewalk, obviously in
     quite serious discomfort,
but the guy who works with him and who's seen the whole thing ab-
     solutely refuses to acknowledge
that his partner might be hurt, instead he bursts out laughing and starts
     making fun of the guy,
imitating the way he's holding himself, saying, "Booby-baby want a kiss?
     What's mattah, baby?"
Now the one who's hurt, grimacing, says, "Christ," shaking his head, vig-
     orously rotating his arm.
Then, "You prick," he growls, and with a clunky leap and a great boom
     kicks the side of the truck.

Shame

A girl who, in 1971, when I was living by myself, painfully lonely, bereft, depressed,
offhandedly mentioned to me in a conversation with some friends that although at first she'd found me —
I can't remember the term, some dated colloquialism signifying odd, unacceptable, out-of-things —
she'd decided that I was after all all right . . . twelve years later she comes back to me from nowhere
and I realize that it wasn't my then irrepressible, unselective, incessant sexual want she meant,
which, when we'd been introduced, I'd naturally aimed at her and which she'd easily deflected,
but that she'd thought I really was, in myself, the way I looked and spoke and acted,
what she was saying, creepy, weird, whatever, and I am taken with a terrible humiliation.

On the Other Hand

On the other hand, in Philadelphia, long ago, at a party on Camac Street on a Sunday afternoon,
a springtime or an early autumn Sunday afternoon, I know, though the occasion's lost
and whose house it was is even lost, near the party's end, a girl, a woman, someone else's wife,
a beauty, too, a little older than I was, an "older woman," elegant and admirable and sober, too,
or nearly so, as I was coming down the stairs, put her hand on my hand on the landing,
caught me there and held me for a moment, with her hand, just her gentle hand, and with her look,
with how she looked at me, with some experience I didn't have, some delight I didn't understand,
and pulled me to her, hard, and kissed me, hard, to let me taste what subtle lusts awaited me.

The Fountain

Two maintenance men need half the morning probing just to find the
     ancient cut-off valve
which is locked tight with rust so that they have to wrestle it with pene-
     trating oil and wrenches
until the flow begins to falter, then arrests, the level in the basin hesi-
     tantly lowering.
Now they shovel at the copper drains, mossed and caked with leaves and
     scraps of sandwich paper;
now a fishy fragrance fills the atmosphere although there weren't and
     never have been any fish,
and all the gods and goddesses, the Neptunes and the dolphins and
     Dianas, shed their sheen,
their streaked bronze re-emerging, dimmer now, paler, to its other ele-
     ment, while underneath,
a million filters from a million cigarettes tremble in the final suction,
     worming at the slits.

The Latin Quarter

All the Greek restaurants in the old student neighborhood have pigs
     roasting in their windows.
From morning until dinnertime the plump sucklings deliciously darken,
     rotating dutifully
on the blackened spits which enter by the anus and exit from angry
     wounds between the eyes.
One's front legs have been neatly trussed beneath it, like a running horse
     from *Horn and Hound.*
Another's have been wittily arranged to cover its squinting eyes, like
     someone being "it."
In one place, no pig, just a singer, on a platform on a stool: a young man
     with a *balalaika.*
On the floor in front of him, a television screen in grainy blues shows
     him again, but from behind,
so that, standing listening to his voice come through the squeaky speaker,
     we can be there, too.

Rungs

When we finally tracked him down, the old man (not really all that very
   old, we thought)
who'd made the comfortable, graceful, elegantly mortised chairs for all
   the farmers' kitchens
told us, never even opening the heavy iron gate into his yard, that he was
   through, retired,
done with it, and no, he didn't know anybody else who made them now,
   no one, he was the last.
He seemed to say it all with satisfaction, or at least was anyway unmoved
   by what it may have meant,
leaving us to back away, apologize, get into our car to make an awkward
   U-turn in his unpaved lane,
suffering meanwhile pangs of conscience and regret for honest good
   things gone for good,
all the innocence the world was losing, all the chances we'd once had,
   and lost, for beauty.

Normality

"Sometimes I feel as though all I really want is to take his little whizzer
   in my mouth . . .
Didn't you ever feel anything like that? I mean, I'll be changing him,
   and he's smiling,
kicking his legs like crazy, and I can tell he's really excited and I know
   I'm excited
and I think how clean and pure and soft he is down there, and that won-
   derful *smell*, you know,
at first you think it's the powder you put on them but then you realize it's
   them, *him*,
it's his goddamned intrinsic odor, I could eat it up, and what would be so
   wrong with it?
I'm not trying to shock you; I mean, maybe if you let yourself, you'd feel
   things like that . . .
Maybe it's you who's fucked up and repressed; I'll bet what I feel for my
   baby's *normal*."

The Storm

A dense, low, irregular overcast is flowing rapidly in over the city from
the middle South.
Above it, the sky holds blue, with scattered, intricate conglomerations of
higher clouds
sidling in a much more even, stately procession across the dazzling,
unsullied azure.
Now the lower level momentarily thins, fragments, and the early sun,
still sharply angled,
breaks through into a finer veil and simmers, edges sharp, its ardent disk
gently mottled.
Down across the roof lines, the decorative dome of Les Invalides looms,
intruding on all this,
and suddenly a swallow banks around its gilded slopes, heading out but
veering quickly back
as though the firmament, figured by so many volumes now, were too
intimidating to row out in alone.

Blame

Where no question possibly remains—someone crying, someone dead—
blame asks: whose fault?
It is the counterpart, the day-to-day, the real life, of those higher faculties
we posit,
logic, reason, the inductions and deductions we yearningly trace the
lines of with our finger.
It also has to do with nothing but itself, a tendency, a habit, like smoking
or depression:
the unaccountable life quirks forecast in neither the soured milk nor the
parents' roaring bed.
Relationship's theodicy: as the ever-generous deity leaves the difficult
door of faith ajar
in a gesture of just-fathomable irony, so our beloved other, in the pain of
partial mutuality,
moves us with its querulous "Look what you made me do!" toward the
first clear glimpses of terrible self.

Medusa

Once, in Rotterdam, a whore once, in a bar, a sailors' bar, a hooker bar,
   opened up her legs—
her legs, my god, were logs—lifted up her skirt, and rubbed herself, with
   both hands rubbed herself,
there, right there, as though what was there was something else, as
   though the something else
was something she just happened to have under there, something that
   she wanted me to see.
All I was was twenty, I was looking for a girl, the girl, the way we always,
   all of us,
looked for the girl, and the woman leaned back there and with both
   hands mauled it,
talked to it, asked it if it wanted me, laughed and asked me if I wanted it,
   while my virginity,
that dread I'd fought so hard to lose, stone by stone was rising back inside
   me like a wall.

Rush Hour

Someone has folded a coat under the boy's head, someone else, an Arab
   businessman in not very good French,
is explaining to the girl, who seems to have discovered, like this, in the
   crowded Métro,
her lover is epileptic, that something must be done to keep the boy from
   swallowing his tongue:
he works a billfold between the rigidly clenched teeth as the kneeling
   girl silently looks on,
her expression of just-contained terror transfiguring her, generalizing her
   almost to the mythic,
the very image of our wonder at what can befall the most ordinary after-
   noon of early love.
The spasms quiet, the boy, his left ear scarlet from rubbing the wool,
   comes to, looks up at the girl,
and she, as the rest of us begin to move away, hesitates, then lays her
   cheek lightly on his brow.

Philadelphia: 1978

I'm on my way to the doctor to get the result of chest X-rays because I
   coughed blood
a few weeks ago while we were still in California; I am more or less a
   wreck of anxiety
and just as I turn the corner from Spruce Street onto Sixteenth where
   my doctor's is,
a raggedy-looking guy coming toward me on the sidewalk yells to me
   from fifty feet away:
"I know that walk! I sure know *that* walk!" smiling broadly, with genuine
   good feeling.
Although I don't recognize him—he looks druggy, wasted—I smile back,
   then, as we come closer,
he suddenly seems dubious, asking, "Don't I know you?" "Maybe not."
   "Weren't you in 'Nam?"
and before I can answer, "Shit!" he spits out, "shit!" furious with me:
   "You fucking *shit!*"

Midas

It wasn't any mewling squeamishness about how "hard" he'd become:
   if his responsibilities as chief
sometimes spilled over in impatience, with subordinates, even at home,
   well, that came with the territory.
And it wasn't either any unaccounted-for sentimentality, no degrading
   longings for the lost good days
when never enough had somehow been just enough, before more than
   he'd ever need became insufficient.
No, his preoccupation had to do with his desire: not with anything he
   wanted and didn't have—
what after all was left to have?—but with something askew in the very
   quality of desire itself.
It was as though he had to will himself to want, had to drag himself
   awake even to pay attention,
and then, when he'd ungaraged his lust, he'd half forget it, the ache
   would fade before it flowered.

The Park

In that oblivious, concentrated, fiercely fetal decontraction peculiar to
        the lost,
a grimy derelict is flat out on a green bench by the sandbox, gazing
        blankly at the children.
"Do you want to play with me?" a small boy asks another, his fine head
        tilted deferentially,
but the other has a lovely fire truck so he doesn't have to answer and
        emphatically he doesn't,
he just grinds his toy, its wheels immobilized with grit, along the low
        stone wall.
The first child sinks forlornly down and lays his palms against the earth
        like Buddha.
The ankles of the derelict are scabbed and swollen, torn with aching
        varicose and cankers.
Who will come to us now? Who will solace us? Who will take us in their
        healing hands?

Travelers

He drives, she mostly sleeps; when she's awake, they quarrel, and now, in
        a violet dusk,
a rangy, raw-boned, efficient-looking mongrel loping toward them down
        the other shoulder
for no apparent reason swerves out on the roadbed just as a battered taxi
        is going by.
Horrible how it goes under, how it's jammed into the asphalt, com-
        pressed, abraded, crumpled,
then is ejected out behind, still, a miracle, alive, but spinning wildly on
        itself, tearing,
frenzied, at its broken spine, the mindless taxi never slowing, never
        noticing or caring,
they slowing, only for a moment, though, as, "Go on," she says, "go on,
        go on," face averted,
she can't look, while he, guilty as usual, fearful, fascinated and uncouth,
        can't not.

Second Persons: Café de L'Abbaye

Without quite knowing it, you sit looking for your past or future in the
    couples strolling by,
the solitaries stalking by, saddened that you never seem to find what
    you've been looking for
although you've no idea or at least you tell yourself you don't what you
    might be looking for,
you only have the vaguest, vagrant sense that it would be someone you
    knew once, lover, friend,
and lost, let drift away, not out of your life, for they were meant to drift
    away that way,
but from some portion of your meaning to yourself, or from the place
    such meaning should reside:
the other would recuperate essences, would be the link from where you
    were to where you would be,
if consciousness were able, finally, to hold all of this together, even not
    quite ever knowing why.

The Lens

Snapshots of her grandchildren and great-grandchildren are scattered on
    the old woman's lap.
How are you, Ma? her son asks, then, before she answers, to the nurse:
    How's she doing?
The old woman, smiling, tilts her head back, centering her son in the
    thick, unfamiliar lenses.
Her head moves left, then right, farther back now, forward, then finally
    she has and holds him.
She is beaming now, an impression of almost too-rapt attentiveness, ad-
    miration, even adoration.
Do you want to eat, Ma? the son asks; the woman starts to nod and in
    doing so loses him again
and has to track him again, that same, slow, methodically circular, back-
    and-forth targeting in.
You want to go downstairs for lunch? the son asks, a bit impatient: Ma,
    you want to get a bite?

The Body

Jed says: How come I'm afraid to climb on the jungle game when even
    the littler kids aren't?
I say: But you did go up on it, I saw you before, you were going across the
    vine bridge.
Jed says: Yeah, I went up there, but I was afraid of the hard part, where
    you swing down.
I say: Well, people do things at different rates, there are things you can
    do that they can't.
Jed says: Am I a coward? Why couldn't I just swing right down there; I'm
    like the cowardly lion.
I say: When I was a kid I was just like you, I was always timid, I thought
    I was weak.
I say: I started doing sports late, like you, but look, now you're swimming
    and everything.
Jed says: I'm tired of swimming. What time is it? Can I get a crêpe? I
    don't think I'm weak.

Racists

Vas en Afrique! Back to Africa! the butcher we used to patronize in the
    Rue Cadet market,
beside himself, shrieked at a black man in an argument the rest of the
    import of which I missed
but that made me anyway for three years walk an extra street to a shop of
    definitely lower quality
until I convinced myself that probably I'd misunderstood that other thing
    and could come back.
Today another black man stopped, asking something that again I didn't
    catch, and the butcher,
who at the moment was unloading his rotisserie, slipping the chickens
    off their heavy spit,
as he answered—how get this right?—casually but accurately *brandished*
    the still-hot metal,
so the other, whatever he was there for, had subtly to lean away a little, so
    as not to flinch.

The Dream

How well I have repressed the dream of death I had after the war when I
was nine in Newark.
It would be nineteen-forty-six; my older best friend tells me what the
atom bomb will do,
consume me from within, with fire, and that night, as I sat, bolt awake,
in agony, it did:
I felt my stomach flare and flame, the edges of my heart curl up and char
like burning paper.
All there was was waiting for the end, all there was was sadness, for in
that awful dark,
that roar that never ebbed, that frenzied inward fire, I knew that every-
one I loved was dead,
I knew that consciousness itself was dead, the universe shucked clean of
mind as I was of my innards.
All the earth around me heaved and pulsed and sobbed; the orient and
immortal air was ash.

Dawn

The first morning of mist after days of draining, unwavering heat along
the shore: a *breath*:
a plume of sea fog actually visible, coherent, intact, with all of the
quieter mysteries
of the sea implicit in its inconspicuous, unremarkable gathering in the
weary branches
of the drought-battered spruce on its lonely knoll; it thins now, sidles
through the browning needles,
is penetrated sharply by a sparrow swaying precipitously on a drop-
glittering twiglet,
then another bird, unseen, is there, a singer, chattering, and another,
long purls of warble,
which also from out of sight insinuate themselves into that dim, fragile,
miniature cloud,
already now, almost with reluctance, beginning its dissipation in the
overpowering sunlight.

II

Reading: Winter

He's not sure how to get the jack on—he must have recently bought the
    car, although it's an ancient,
impossibly decrepit, barely holding-together Chevy: he has to figure out
    how each part works,
the base plate, the pillar, the thing that hooks to the bumper, even the
    four-armed wrench,
before he can get it all together, knock the hubcap off and wrestle free
    the partly rusted nuts.
This all happens on a bed of sheet ice: it's five below, the coldest January
    in a century.
Cars slip and skid a yard away from him, the flimsy jack is desperately,
    precariously balanced,
and meanwhile, when he goes into the trunk to get the spare, a page of
    old newspaper catches his attention
and he pauses, rubbing his hands together, shoulders hunched, for a full
    half minute, reading.

Reading: The Subway

First he finishes *The Chief*, "New York's Civil Employee's Weekly," then
    folds it carefully
and slips it into his much-wrinkled *Duane Reade* shopping bag ("The
    Chain of Experience"),
from which he retrieves a thick, green, double-cellophane-bound vol-
    ume, *Successful Investing*,
balancing it on the waistband of his slick designer jeans: *Lewis*, they say,
    instead of *Levi's*.
The train is going very fast, the car sways frighteningly, almost lifting us
    from our seats,
but he stands firmly planted, with an imperturbably athletic dexterity,
    not even holding on,
only glancing up from time to time to gaze with an apparently real inter-
    est at an advertisement—
Un buen baño con jabón Ivory—as though to decathect a moment, let-
    ting go, the better to absorb.

Reading: The Bus

As she reads, she rolls something around in her mouth, hard candy it
       must be, from how long it lasts.
She's short, roundish, gray-haired, pleasantly pugnacious-looking, like
       Grace Paley, and her book,
Paint Good and Fast, must be fascinating: she hasn't lifted her eyes since
       Thirty-fourth Street,
even when the corner of a page sticks so that she has to pause a bit to lick
       her index finger . . .
No, now she does, she must have felt me thinking about her: she blinks,
       squints out the window,
violently arches her eyebrows as though what she'd just read had really to
       be nailed down,
and, stretching, she unzips a pocket of her blue backpack, rummages
       through it, and comes out with,
yes, hard candy, red and white, a little sackful, one of which she offers
       with a smile to me.

Reading: The Gym

The bench he's lying on isn't nearly wide enough for the hefty bulk of
       his torso and shoulders.
Shielding his eyes with his sheaf of scrawled-on yellow paper from the
       bare bulb over his head,
legs lifted in a dainty V, he looks about to tip, but catches himself with
       unconscious shrugs.
Suddenly he rises—he's still streaming from his session on the Nautilus
       and heavy bag—
goes into the shower, comes back, dries off with a gray, too-small towel
       and sits to read again,
applying as he does an oily, evil-looking lotion from a dark brown bottle
       onto his legs and belly.
Next to his open locker, a ragged equipment bag, on top a paperback:
       The Ethical System of Hume.
The smell of wintergreen and steam-room steam; from the swimming
       pool echoes of children screaming.

Reading: The Cop

Usually a large-caliber, dull-black, stockless machine gun hangs from a
     sling at his hip
where a heavily laden cartridge belt in the same blue as his special-forces
     uniform cinches his waist,
and usually he stands directly in the doorway, so that people have to edge
     their way around him—
there was some sort of bombing in the building, and presumably this is
     part of his function.
He often seems ill at ease and seems to want to have but doesn't quite
     because he's so young
that menacingly vacant expression policemen assume when they're un-
     sure of themselves or lonely,
but still, today, when I noticed him back in the hallway reading what
     looked like a political pamphlet,
I was curious and thought I'd just stop, go back, peek in, but then I
     thought, no, not.

Reading: Early Sorrow

The father has given his year-old son *Le Monde* to play with in his
     stroller and the baby does
just what you'd expect: grabs it, holds it out in front of him, stares impor-
     tantly at it,
makes emphatic and dramatic sounds of declamation, great pronounce-
     ments of analytic probity,
then tears it, pulls a page in half, pulls the half in quarters, shoves a
     hearty shred in his mouth—
a delicious editorial on unemployment and recession, a tasty *jeu de mots*
     on government ineptitude.
He startles in amazement when the father takes the paper back from
     him: *What in heaven's name?*
Indignation, impotence, frustration, outrage, petulance, rebellion, real-
     ism, resignation.
Slumping back, disgusted . . . *Hypocrite lecteur, semblable* . . . Just wait,
     he's muttering, just wait . . .

Suicide: Elena

She was fourteen and a half; she'd hanged herself: how had she ever
    found the resource for it,
the sheer *strength*, as frail as she was, skinny even for her age, breastless
    and hipless,
with a voice so subdued and without resonance she seemed to play it to
    herself, like a clavichord?
My co-therapist had made a "megaphone" for her by tearing out the bot-
    tom of a paper coffee cup.
She agreed to try it, then seemed relieved to have it, becoming more vol-
    uble and animated.
She only visited our group once, though, with a boy I didn't see again
    until the day it happened.
"Do you know about Elena?" I asked him; I said the name the Spanish
    way, "El-*lay*-nah"—
I knew a Mexican Elena then, from Monterey—"El-*leh*-nah," the boy
    said, "not El-*lay*-nah. Yeah."

Suicide: Ludie

The whole time I've been walking down the block the public phone at
    the corner's been ringing
so when I get there just to try to help somebody out I stop and pick it up
    and say "Hello."
A woman's voice: "Is Ludie there?" "You have a wrong number," I an-
    swer, "I'm in a phone booth."
"I know you are," the voice says, "but isn't Ludie anywhere around
    there?" "No, no one is."
"You *sure*? Look again. She just called me, Ludie, and she says she's go-
    ing to commit *su*-icide."
"She really isn't here, I'd have seen her down the street: there isn't any-
    body around here."
"Well, what am I supposed to do? What are you supposed to do when
    somebody's gonna kill herself?"
"The police. Where does Ludie live?" "That's the whole thing, she don't
    live where she lives."

Suicide: Anne

for Anne Sexton

Perhaps it isn't as we like to think, the last resort, the end of something,
 thwarted choice or attempt,
but rather the ever-recurring beginning, the faithful first to mind, the
 very image of endeavor,
so that even the most patently meaningless difficulties, a badly started
 nail, a lost check,
not to speak of the great and irresolvable emotional issues, would bring
 instantly to mind
that unfailingly reliable image of a gesture to be carried out for once
 with confidence and grace.
It would feel less like desperation, being driven down, ground down, and
 much more a reflex, almost whim,
as though the pestering forces of inertia that for so long had held you
 back had ebbed at last,
and you could slip through now, not to peace particularly, not even to
 escape, but to completion.

Love: Youth

Except for the undeniable flash of envy I feel, the reflexive competitive-
 ness, he's inconsequential:
all I even see of him is the nape of his neck with his girlfriend's fingers
 locked in his hair.
She, though, looks disturbingly like a girl I wanted and pestered and who
 I thought broke my heart
when I was at that age of being all absorbed in just the unattainabilities
 she represented.
With what unashamed ardor this one is kissing, head working, that hand
 tugging him ever tighter,
and when at last they come apart, with what *gratitude* she peers at him,
 staring into his eyes
with what looks like nothing but relief, as though she'd waited her whole
 life for this, died for this,
time has taken so long for this, I thought you'd never get here, I thought
 I'd wither first and fade.

Love: Beginnings

They're at that stage where so much desire streams between them, so
    much frank need and want,
so much absorption in the other and the self and the self-admiring entity
    and unity they make—
her mouth so full, breast so lifted, head thrown back *so* far in her laugh-
    ter at his laughter,
he so solid, planted, oaky, firm, so resonantly factual in the headiness of
    being craved so,
she almost wreathed upon him as they intertwine again, touch again,
    cheek, lip, shoulder, brow,
every glance moving toward the sexual, every glance away soaring back
    in flame into the sexual—
that just to watch them is to feel again that hitching in the groin, that fill-
    ing of the heart,
the old, sore heart, the battered, foundered, faithful heart, snorting again,
    stamping in its stall.

Love: Habit

He has his lips pressed solidly against her cheek, his eyes are wide open,
    though, and she, too,
gazes into the distance, or at least is nowhere in the fragile composition
    they otherwise create.
He breaks off now, sulkily slouches back; his hand, still lifted to her face,
    idly cups her chin,
his fingers casually drumming rhythms on her lips, a gesture she finds
    not at all remarkable—
she still gazes away, looking for whatever she's been looking for, her inat-
    tention like a wall.
Now he kisses her *again*, and they both, like athletes, hold that way
    again, perversely persevering . . .
O, Paolo, O, Francesca: is this all it comes to, the perturbations and the
    clamor, the broken breath,
the careenings on the wheel: just this: the sorrowing flame of conscious-
    ness so miserably dimmed?

Love: Loss

He's the half-respectable wino who keeps to himself, camping with his
    bags on the steps of the *Bourse*.
She's the neighborhood schizo, our nomad, our pretty post-teen princess
    gone to the grim gutter:
her appalling matted hair, vile hanging rags, the engrossing shadow plays
    she acts out to herself.
Tonight, though, something takes her, she stops, waits, and smiling cun-
    ningly asks him for a smoke.
They both seem astonished, both their solitudes emerge, stiff-legged,
    blinking, from their lairs.
The air is charged with timid probings, promises, wants and lost wants,
    but suddenly she turns,
she can't do it, she goes, and he, with a stagy, blasé world-weariness leans
    back and watches,
like Orpheus watches as she raptly picks her way back to the silver path,
    back to the boiling whispers.

Love: Sight

When she's not looking in his eyes, she looks down at his lips, his chin,
    collar, tie, back again.
When he's not looking in her eyes—her cheek, parted mouth, neck,
    breasts, thighs, back again.
Sometimes their four hands will lock and in a smooth contortion end up
    at her waist, then his waist,
then up between them, weaving, writhing, with so much animation that
    their glances catch there.
The first time he looks away, she still smiles at him, smugly, with a lus-
    ciousness almost obscene,
then her gaze goes trailing after, as if afraid to be abandoned, as if desir-
    ing even what he sees.
The second time, it might be with some small suspicion that her eyes go
    quickly chasing his;
the third, they're hardening, triangulating, calculating, like a combat
    sergeant's on the line.

Love: Petulance

She keeps taking poses as they eat so that her cool glance goes off at
    perpendiculars to him.
She seems to think she's hiding what she feels, that she looks merely
    interested, sophisticated.
Sometimes she leans her head on her hand, sometimes with a single
    finger covers her lower lip.
He, too, will prop his temple on his fist, as though to make her believe
    he's lost in thought.
Otherwise he simply chews, although the muscles of his jaws rise vio-
    lently in iron ridges.
Their gazes, when they have to go that way, pass blankly over one an-
    other like offshore lights.
So young they are for this, to have arrived at this, both are suffering so
    and neither understands,
although to understand wouldn't mean to find relief or overcome, that
    this, too, is part of it.

Love: Intimacy

They were so exceptionally well got-up for an ordinary Sunday afternoon
    stop-in at Deux Magots,
she in very chic deep black, he in a business suit, and they were so evi-
    dently just out of bed
but with very little to say to one another, much gazing off, elaborate
    lightings of her cigarettes,
she more proper than was to be believed, sipping with a flourished pinky
    at her Pimm's Cup,
that it occurred to me I was finally seeing one of those intriguing *Herald
    Tribune* classifieds —
a woman's name, a number — for "escorts" or "companions," but then I
    had to change my mind:
she'd leaned toward him, deftly lifted a line of his thinning hair, and idly,
    with a mild pat,
had laid it back — not commiserating, really, just keeping record of the
    progress of the loss.

Love: Shyness

By tucking her chin in toward her chest, she can look up darkly through
       her lashes at him,
that look of almost anguished vulnerability and sensitivity, a soft, near-cry
       of help,
the implication of a deeply privileged and sole accessibility . . . yours
       alone, yours, yours alone,
but he's so flagrantly uncertain of himself, so clearly frightened, that he
       edges into comedy:
though everybody at the party is aware she's seducing him, he doesn't
       seem to understand;
he diddles with his silly mustache, grins and gawks, gabbles away around
       her about this and that.
Now she's losing interest, you can see it; she starts to glance away, can't
       he see it? Fool!
Touch her! Reach across, just caress her with a finger on her cheek: fool,
       fool—only touch her!

Love: Wrath

He was very much the less attractive of the two: heavyset, part punk, part
       L. L. Bean,
both done ineptly; his look as brutal as the bully's who tormented you in
       second grade.
She was delicate and pretty; what she was suffering may have drawn her
       features finer.
As I went by, he'd just crossed his arms and said, "*You're* the one who's
       fucking us all up!"
He snarled it with a cruelty which made him look all the more a thug,
       and which astonished me,
that he would dare to speak to her like that, be so unafraid of losing her
       unlikely beauty . . .
But still, I knew, love, what he was feeling: the hungering for reason, for
       fair play,
the lust for justice; all the higher systems "Go": the need, the fear, the
       awe, burned away.

Love: The Dance

They're not quite overdressed, just a bit attentively, flashily for seventy-
    five or eighty.
Both wear frosted, frozen, expensive but still delicately balanced and
    just-adhering wigs,
and both have heavy makeup: his could pass for a Miami winter tan, but
    hers goes off the edge—
ice-pink lipstick, badly drawn, thick mascara arching like a ballerina's
    toward the brow.
All things considered, she's not built that badly; he has his gut sucked
    nearly neatly in;
their dancing is flamboyant, well rehearsed, old-time ballroom swirls,
    deft romantic dips and bows.
If only they wouldn't contrive to catch our eyes so often, to acknowledge
    with ingratiating grins:
the waltz of life, the waltz of death, and still the heart-work left undone,
    the heavy heart, left undone.

Good Mother: The Métro

Why is he wearing a white confirmation suit—he's only about three—on
    a Thursday morning,
in the Métro station Richelieu-Drouot, and what possibly has he done
    wrong, so wrong,
that his mother should be shrieking at him in a language I don't under-
    stand or even recognize
but whose syllables of raging accusation still pierce and fluster me with
    an intimate anguish?
He *has* done something, too, the way he sits curled up, you know it, the
    way he cries heartfeltly:
it's clearly not the mother's ordinary worries or preoccupations that could
    bring such awful anger . . .
What then? Is it something of the body? Has he disgraced himself? Or is
    it something of the soul?
Has he hurt her very soul? That's how she acts. Did I do that? Ever?
    Please, forgive me if I did.

Good Mother: The Plane

Bulging overnight bags on both shoulders, in one hand a sack with extra
        diapers, cookies, toys,
in the other a translucent plastic bag, a giant Snoopy grinning with
        malevolent cuteness through,
"Move, move, move," she keeps saying, nudging the child with her knee,
        "Can't you just move?"
but he, as he's been doing all flight long, obstinately fusses, whines,
        whimpers, dawdles,
and when she pushes him again lets out a real, really loud, though not a
        really heartfelt howl.
It's midnight, the plane is hours late, for hours she's been reading,
        singing, telling stories,
and now, the gluey California summer air filling up the plane like sweat,
        she finally loses patience,
puts the Snoopy down, an overnight bag, grabs the kid and swats him, to
        the great relief of all.

Good Mother: The Car

At last he's being allowed to play in his mother's car the way he always
        wants to, by himself.
She's brushed some choky pale stuff on her cheeks, smeared the shiny
        red grease on her lips,
made the funny eye-face she makes playing with her lashes, perfume
        now behind her ears,
her wrists, down along her chest, and now she's left him here, smiling at
        him: "Back soon."
He turns the wheel, fast, left and right, clicks the lights, on, off,
        scrunches down to the pedals,
then in not at all a long time here she is again, opening the door, kissing
        him, but, strange,
she puts the makeup on again, exactly as before, no perfume, but the
        powder and the lips:
even the fleck of scarlet on a tooth, which with a pinky must be precisely
        fingernailed away.

Good Mother: Out

"I want," he says again, through his tears, in this unfamiliar voice, again,
  "I want, I want,"
not even knowing why he says it now, says it yet again, only knowing that
  he has to say it,
even when she's told him calmly why he can't, then hissed the reasons
  why of course he can't,
then hit him, on the bottom, hard, again, again, and meaning it, so that
  he's crying, sobbing,
but though he sees her growing desperate, though he knows she'll hit
  him again, he says again,
"I want, I want, I want," though he really doesn't care now, doesn't even
  want what might be wanted:
why keep saying it? Tears aflow, sobs like painful stones, why must he
  keep on with it?
Does he love her less? Is their relationship ever henceforth to be this?
  Desire, denial, despair?

Good Mother: The Street

He lets the lunch bag fall, he doesn't mean to, really, but there it is, on
  the pavement,
and naturally the little jar of applesauce inside is shattered, naturally the
  paper melts,
and to his horror naturally the gook comes oozing through now, sickly
  now, filthy now; vile.
His fault, his fault, except today it doesn't seem to matter, his mother says
  it doesn't matter,
she's been humming to herself this morning, maybe that's the reason;
  anyway, she bends to it,
uses pieces of the glass to scoop it, carries it to someone's trash: all
  done—she smiles.
Her fingers are still sticky, though; she holds them hanging limply for a
  moment, then,
one by one, she brings them to her pursed lips and with a tiny smack
  licks them clean.

Good Mother: The Bus

Mommy and Daddy are having one of their fights, he can tell by the way
    when Daddy asks something,
Mommy smiles brightly, looking not at Daddy but at him, as though he'd
    asked the question.
He doesn't mind that much at first; it's pleasant being in her arms, being
    smiled at so nicely.
Daddy looks away, out the window, Mommy looks too, out there, with
    the same wide-eyed smile,
but when Daddy looks at her again her smile suddenly is back in *his*
    face, Daddy's somewhere else,
the smile is on *his* forehead—now Mommy kisses it, and finds a smudge
    there to be rubbed away.
What Daddy whispers now *makes* Mommy look, but there's an advertise-
    ment to the left of Daddy's ear,
it's *that* she smiles at this time, a picture of a *dog* . . . How quickly weari-
    some this gets, how saddening.

Good Mother: Home

It was worse than being struck, that tone, that intensity, that abnegating
    fervor and furor.
It seemed to open on a kind of limitless irrationality, uncontrollability,
    chaos, an abyss,
as though no matter what the cause had been, the occasion that released
    this, there might never be
available to them the new antithesis, the new alignment of former senti-
    ments which would let it stop.
Sometimes he would feel that both of them were bound in it, as in a
    force beyond either of them;
sometimes he thought he felt beneath her rage anxiety, as though she
    were frightened by it too.
He wanted to submit, capitulate, atone, if only she would *stop*, but he
    could never say, "Please stop,"
because somehow he knew that their connection was as firm in this—
    firmer—as in their affection.

Vehicle: Conscience

That moment when the high-wire walker suddenly begins to falter, wob-
ble, sway, arms flailing,
that breathtakingly rapid back-and-forth aligning-realigning of the dis-
placed center of gravity,
weight thrown this way, no, too far; that way, no, too far again, until the
movements themselves
of compensation have their rhythms established so that there's no way
possibly to stop now . . .
that very moment, wheeling back and forth, back and forth, appeal,
repeal, negation,
just before he lets it go and falls to deftly catch himself going by the wire,
somersaulting up,
except for us it never ceases, testing moments of the mind-weight this
way, back and back and forth,
no re-establishing of balance, no place to start again, just this, this force,
this gravity and fear.

Vehicle: Forgetting

The way, playing an instrument, when you botch a passage you have to
stop before you can go on again—
there's a chunk of time you have to wait through, an interval to let the
false notes dissipate,
from consciousness of course, and from the muscles, but it seems also
from the room, the actual air,
the bad try has to leak off into eternity, the volumes of being scrubbed to
let the true resume . . .
So, having loved, and lost, lost everything, the other and the possibility of
other and parts of self,
the heart rushes toward forgetfulness, but never gets there, continuously
attains the opposite instead,
the senses tensed, attending, the conductors of the mind alert, waiting for
the waiting to subside:
when will tedious normality begin again, the old calm silences recur, the
creaking air subside?

Vehicle: Insecurity

The way the voice always, always gives it away, even when you weren't
aware yourself you felt it,
the tightness in the middle range, the hollow hoarseness lower toward
the heart that chips, abrades,
shoves against the hindpart of the throat, then takes the throat, then takes
the voice as well,
as though you'd lost possession of the throat and then the voice or what it
is that wills the voice
to carry thoughtlessly the thought through tone and word, and then the
thoughts themselves are lost
and the mind that thought the thoughts begins to lose itself, despairing
of itself and of its voice,
this infected voice that infects itself with its despair, this voice of terror
that won't stop,
that lays the trap of doubt, this pit of doubt, this voiceless throat that swal-
lows us in doubt.

Vehicle: Indolence

The way it always feels like the early onset of an illness, the viral armies
mobilizing in the breast,
a restlessness of breath as though the air weren't giving nourishment . . .
and the way, always, it's not . . .
Gazing into the indifferently insisting morning, trees, sky, great patches
won't come into focus,
or more exasperatingly come clear, hold a moment, are taken in the
moire of lapse and inattention.
The way we know that what is being called for is affirmation, the inser-
tion of the self into the moral:
this is sin, the very throat of luxury; more than sleep it holds us, more
than love betrays us . . .
The way we know that if we step across the sluggish stream to act, our
hovering holiness is saved,
if we submit and sink, we're lost . . . the way, always, we're lost, in these
irresistible inertias, lost . . .

Vehicle: Circles

It was like simply wanting to give up at last, the saying fifty times a day,
      not quite to yourself,
"I'm tired, so tired of this, of everything," until you'd forgotten somehow
      what you were tired of,
and realized, unavailingly, hopelessly, that saying it meant something
      else, to you, to life,
something closer to the "Help me! Please!" you used to want to cry out,
      aloud, again, to no one,
for no reason, for simply being there, here, baffled by these quantities of
      need and groundless sorrow . . .
How could you have gone past that, only to arrive at this, this about
      which there is nothing whatsoever
you can feel except the certainty of knowing that you're doing what
      you're doing to yourself, but why?
And if you pass this, what will that have meant, what will it have cost to
      accomplish *this* undoing?

Vehicle: Absence

The way, her father dead a day ago, the child goes in his closet, finds her-
      self inside his closet,
finds herself atop the sprawl of emptied shoes, finds herself enveloped in
      the heavy emptied odor,
and breathes it in, that single, mingled gust of hair and sweat and father-
      flesh and father,
breathes it in and tries to hold it, in her body, in her breath, keep it in
      her breath forever . . .
so we, in love, in absence, in an absence so much less than death but still
      shaped by need and loss,
so we too find only what we want in sense, the drive toward sense, the
      hunger for the actual flesh;
so we, too, breathe in, as though to breathe was now itself the end of all,
      as though to scent,
to hold the fading traces of an actual flesh, was all, the hungering senses
      driven toward all . . .

Vehicle: Violence

The way boxers postulate a feeling to label that with which they over-
    come the body's vile fears,
its wish to flinch, to flee, break and run . . . they call it anger, pride, the
    primal passion to prevail;
the way, before they start, they glare at one another, try to turn them-
    selves to snarling beasts . . .
so we first make up something in the soul we name and offer credence
    to—"meaning," "purpose," "end"—
and then we cast ourselves into the conflict, turn upon our souls, snarl
    like snarling beasts . . .
And the way the fighters fight, coolly until strength fails, then desper-
    ately, wildly, as in a dream,
and the way, done, they fall in one another's arms, almost sobbing with
    relief, sobbing with relief:
so we contend, so we wish to finish, wish to cry and end, but we never
    cry, never end, as in a dream.

III

Le Petit Salvié

for Paul Zweig
1935–1984

1.

The summer has gone by both quickly and slowly. It's been a kind of eternity, each day spinning out its endlessness, and yet with every look back, less time is left . . .

So quickly, and so slowly . . . In the tiny elevator of the flat you'd borrowed on the Rue de Pondicherry,
you suddenly put your head against my chest, I thought to show how tired you were, and lost consciousness,
sagging heavily against me, forehead oiled with sweat, eyes ghastly agape . . . so quickly, so slowly.
Quickly the ambulance arrives, mewling at the curb, the disinterested orderlies strap you to their stretcher.
Slowly at the clinic, waiting for the doctors, waiting for the ineffectual treatments to begin.
Slowly through that night, then quickly all the next day, your last day, though no one yet suspects it.
Quickly those remaining hours, quickly the inconsequential tasks and doings of any ordinary afternoon.
Quickly, slowly, those final silences and sittings I so regret now not having taken all of with you.

2.

"I don't think we'll make the dance tonight," I mumble mawkishly. "It's
      definitely worse," you whisper.
Ice pack hugged to you, you're breathing fast; when you stop answering
      questions, your eyes close.
You're there, and then you slip away into your meditations, the way, it
      didn't matter where,
in an airport, a café, you could go away into yourself to work, and so
      we're strangely comforted.
It was dusk, late, the softening, sweetening, lingering light of the endless
      Paris evening.
Your room gave on a garden, a perfect breeze washed across your bed, it
      wasn't hard to leave you,
we knew we'd see you again: we kissed you, Vikki kissed you, "Goodbye,
      my friends," you said,
lifting your hand, smiling your old warming smile, then you went into
      your solitude again.

3.

We didn't know how ill you were . . . we knew how ill but hid it . . . we
      didn't know how ill you were . . .
Those first days when your fever rose . . . if we'd only made you go into
      the hospital in Brive . . .
Perhaps you could have had another year . . . but the way you'd let death
      touch your life so little,
the way you'd learned to hold your own mortality before you like an un-
      familiar, complex flower . . .
Your stoicism had become so much a part of your identity, your virtue,
      the system of your self-regard;
if we'd insisted now, you might have given in to us, when we didn't,
      weren't we cooperating
with what wasn't just your wish but your true passion never to be dying,
      sooner dead than dying?
You did it, too: composed a way from life directly into death, the ignoble
      scribblings between elided.

4.

It must be some body-thing, some species-thing, the way it comes to take
      me from so far,
this grief that tears me so at moments when I least suspect it's there,
      wringing tears from me
I'm not prepared for, had no idea were even there in me, this most
      unmanly gush I almost welcome,
these cries so general yet with such power of their own I'm stunned to
      hear them come from me.
Walking through the street, I cry, talking later to a friend, I try not to but
      I cry again,
working at my desk I'm taken yet again, although, again, I don't want to
      be, not now, not again,
though that doesn't mean I'm ready yet to let you go . . . what it does
      mean I don't think I know,
nor why I'm so ill prepared for this insistence, this diligence with which
      consciousness afflicts us.

5.

I imagine you rising to something like heaven: my friend who died last
      year is there to welcome you.
He would know the place by now, he would guide you past the ledges
      and the thorns and terror.
Like a child I am, thinking of you rising in the rosy clouds and being up
      there with him,
being with your guru Baba, too, the three of you, all strong men, all
      partly wild children,
wandering through my comforting child's heaven, doing what you're
      supposed to do up there forever.
I tell myself it's silly, all of this, absurd, what we sacrifice in attaining
      rational mind,
but there you are again, glowing, grinning down at me from somewhere
      in the heart of being,
ablaze with wonder and a child's relief that this after all is how astonish-
      ingly it finishes.

6.

In my adult mind, I'm reeling, lost—I can't grasp anymore what I even
        think of death.
I don't know even what we hope for: ecstasy? bliss? or just release from
        being, not to suffer anymore.
At the grave, the boring rabbi said that you were going to eternal rest:
        rest? why rest?
Better say we'll be absorbed into the "Thou," better be consumed in
        light, in Pascal's "Fire"!
Or be taken to the Godhead, to be given meaning now, at last, the mean-
        ing we knew eluded us.
God, though, Godhead, Thou, even fire: all that is gone now, gone the
        dark night arguments,
gone the partial answers, the very formulations fail; I grapple for the
        questions as *they* fail.
Are we to be redeemed? When? How? After so much disbelief, will
        something be beyond us to receive us?

7.

Redemption is in life, "beyond" unnecessary: it is radically demeaning to
        any possible divinity
to demand that life be solved by yet another life: we're compressed into
        this single span of opportunity
for which our gratitude should categorically be presumed; this is what
        eternity for us consists of,
praise projected from the soul, as love first floods outwards to the other
        then back into the self . . .
Yes, yes, I try to bring you to this, too; yes, what is over now is over; yes,
        we offer thanks,
for what you had, for what we all have: this portion of eternity is no
        different from eternity,
they both contract, expand, cast up illusion and delusion and all the
        comfort that we have is love,
praise, the grace not to ask for other than we have . . . yes and yes, but
        this without conviction, too.

8.

What if after, though, there is something else, will there be judgment
     then, will it be retributive,
and if it is, if there is sin, will you have to suffer some hellish match with
     what your wrongs were?
So much good you did, your work, your many kindnesses, the befriend-
     ings and easy generosities.
What sort of evil do we dare imagine we'd have to take into those awful
     rectifications?
We hurt one another, all of us are helpless in that, with so much vulner-
     able and mortal to defend.
But that vulnerability, those defenses, our belittling jealousies, resent-
     ments, thrusts and spites
are the very image of our frailty: shouldn't our forgiveness for them and
     our absolution be assumed?
Why would our ultimate identities be burdened with absolutes, impera-
     tives, lost discordant hymns?

9.

How ambiguous the triumphs of our time, the releasing of the intellect
     from myth and magic.
We've gained much, we think, from having torn away corrupted modes
     of aggrandizement and giantism,
those infected and infecting errors that so long held sway and so bloated
     our complacencies
that we would willingly inflict even on our own flesh the crippling im-
     plications of our metaphysic.
How much we've had to pay, though, and how dearly had to suffer for
     our liberating dialectics.
The only field still left to us to situate our anguish and uncertainty is in
     the single heart,
and how it swells, the heart, to bear the cries with which we troubled the
     startled heavens.
Now we have the air, transparent, and the lucid psyche, and gazing in-
     ward, always inward, to the wound.

10.

The best evidence I have of you isn't my memory of you, or your work,
     although I treasure both,
and not my love for you which has too much of me in it as subject, but
     the love others bore you,
bear you, especially Vikki, who lived out those last hard years with you,
     the despairs and fears,
the ambivalences and withdrawals, until that final week of fever that
     soaked both your pillows.
Such a moving irony that your last days finally should have seared the
     doubt from both of you.
Sometimes it's hard to tell exactly whom I cry for—you, that last night as
     we left you there,
the way you touched her with such solicitude, or her, the desolation she
     keeps coming to:
*"I've been facing death, touched death, and now I have a ghost I love and
     who loves me."*

11.

Genevieve, your precious Gen, doesn't quite know when to cry, or how
     much she's supposed to cry,
or how to understand those moments when it passes, when she's dis-
     tracted into play and laughter
by the other kids or by the adults who themselves don't seem to grasp this
     terrible non-game.
At the cemetery, I'm asked to speak to her, comfort her: never more im-
     possible to move beyond cliché.
We both know we're helplessly embedded in ritual: you wanted her, I tell
     her, to be happy,
that's all, all her life, which she knows, of course, but nods to, as she
     knows what I don't say,
the simplest self-revealing truths, your most awful fear, the brutal fact of
     your mortality:
how horribly it hurt to go from her, how rending not being here to help
     bear this very pain.

12.

Nothing better in the world than those days each year with you, your
    wife, my wife, the children,
at your old stone house in the Dordogne, looking over valleys one way,
    chestnut woods the other,
walks, long talks, visits to Lascaux or Les Eyzies, reading, listening to
    each other read.
Our last night, though, I strolled into the moonless fields, it might have
    been a thousand centuries ago,
and something suddenly was with me: just beyond the boundaries of my
    senses presences were threatening,
something out of childhood, mine or humankind's; I felt my fear, famil-
    iar, unfamiliar, fierce,
might freeze me to the dark, but I looked back—I wasn't here alone,
    your house was there,
the zone of warmth it made was there, you yourself were there, circled in
    the waiting light.

13.

I seem to have to make you dead, dead again, to hold you in my mind so
    I can clearly have you,
because unless I do, you aren't dead, you're only living somewhere out of
    sight, I'll find you,
soon enough, no need to hurry, and my mind slips into this other tense,
    other grammar of condition,
in which you're welded to banalities of fact and time, the reality of what
    is done eluding me.
If you're accessible to me, how can you be dead? You are accessible to
    me, therefore . . . something else.
So what I end with is the death of death, but not as it would have been
    elaborated once,
in urgencies of indignation, resignation, faith: I have you neither here,
    nor there, but not not-anywhere:
the soul keeps saying that you might be here, or there—the incessant
    passions of the possible.

14.

Here's where we are: out behind the house in canvas chairs, you're read-
        ing new poems to me,
as you have so often, in your apartment, a park in Paris—anywhere: side-
        walk, restaurant, museum.
You read musically, intensely, with flourishes, conviction: I might be the
        audience in a hall,
and you are unimaginably insecure, you so want me to admire every
        poem, every stanza, every line,
just as I want, need, you, too, to certify, approve, legitimize, all without a
        doubt or reservation,
and which neither of us does, improving everything instead, suggesting
        and correcting and revising,
as we knew, however difficult it was, we had to, in our barely overcome
        but overcome competitiveness.
How I'll miss it, that so tellingly accurate envy sublimated into warmth
        and brothership.

15.

Here's where we are: clearing clumps of shrub and homely brush from
        the corner of your yard,
sawing down a storm-split plum tree, then hacking at the dozens of
        malevolently armored maguey:
their roots are frail as flesh and cut as easily, but in the August heat the
        work is draining.
Now you're resting, you're already weak although neither of us will admit
        it to the other.
Two weeks later, you'll be dead, three weeks later, three months, a year,
        I'll be doing this,
writing this, bound into this other labor that you loved so much and that
        we also shared,
still share, somehow always will share now as we shared that sunny late-
        summer afternoon,
children's voices, light; you, pale, leaning on the wall, me tearing at the
        vines and nettles.

16.

"A man's life cannot be silent; living is speaking, dying, too, is speaking,"
    so you wrote,
so we would believe, but still, how understand what the finished life
    could have meant to say
about the dying and the death that never end, about potential gone,
    inspiration unaccomplished,
love left to narrow in the fallacies of recall, eroding down to partial ges-
    ture, partial act?
And we are lessened with it, amazed at how much our self-worth and joy
    were bound into the other.
There are no consolations, no illuminations, nothing of that long-
    awaited flowing toward transcendence.
There is, though, compensation, the simple certainty of having touched
    and having been touched.
The silence and the speaking come together, grief and gladness come
    together, the disparates fuse.

17.

Where are we now? Nowhere, anywhere, the two of us, the four of us,
    fifty of us at a *fête*.
Islands of relationship, friends and friends, the sweet, normal, stolid ma-
    trix of the merely human,
the circles of community that intersect within us, hold us, touch us al-
    ways with their presence,
even as, today, mourning, grief, themselves becoming memory, there still
    is that within us which endures,
not in possession of the single soul in solitude, but in the covenants of
    affection we embody,
the way an empty house embodies elemental presences, and the way,
    attentive, we can sense them.
Breath held, heart held, body stilled, we attend, and they are there,
    covenant, elemental presence,
and the voice, in the lightest footfall, the eternal wind, leaf and earth, the
    constant voice.

18.

"The immortalities of the moment spin and expand; they seem to have
      no limits, yet time passes.
These last days here are bizarrely compressed, busy, and yet full of sup-
      pressed farewells . . ."
The hilly land you loved, lucerne and willow, the fields of butterfly and
      wasp and flower.
Farewell the crumbling house, barely held together by your ministra-
      tions, the shed, the pond.
Farewell your dumb French farmer's hat, your pads of yellow paper, your
      joyful, headlong scrawl.
The coolness of the woods, the swallow's swoop and whistle, the confi-
      dent call of the owl at night.
Scents of dawn, the softening all-night fire, char, ash, warm embers in
      the early morning chill.
The moment holds, you move across the path and go, the light lifts,
      breaks: goodbye, my friend, farewell.

A DREAM OF MIND

[1992]

I

When

As soon as the old man knew he was actually dying, even before anyone
   else would admit it,
he wanted out of the business, out of the miserable game, and he told
   whoever would listen,
whenever they'd listen, wife, family, friends, that he'd do it himself but
   how could he,
without someone to help, unable to walk as he was, get out of bed or up
   from the toilet himself?

At first he'd almost been funny: "Somebody comes, somebody goes,"
   he'd said on the birth of a niece,
and one day at lunch, "Please pass the cream cheese," then, deadpan,
   "That's all I'll miss."
But now he's obsessed: "Why won't you help me?" he says to his chil-
   dren, ten times a day,
a hundred and ten, but what if such meddling's wrong, and aren't these
   last days anyway precious?

Still, he was wearing them down: "This is no fun," he said to a son help-
   ing him hobble downstairs,
and the son, knowing full well what he meant, dreading to hear what he
   meant, had to ask "What?"
so the old man, the biopsy incision still lumping the stubble of hair on
   the side of his skull,
could look in his eyes and say, if not as an accusation then nearly,
   "Death, dying: you know."

By then they knew, too, that sooner or later they'd have to give in, then
   sooner was over,
only later was looming, aphasiac, raving too late, so they held council
   and argued it out,
and though his daughter, holding on to lost hopes, was afraid, they de-
   cided to help him,
and told the old man, who said, "Finally, at last," and then to his daugh-
   ter, "Don't be afraid."

On the day it would happen, the old man would be funny again: wolfing
      down handfuls of pills,
"I know this'll upset my stomach," he'd say, but for now he only asks how
      it will happen.
"You'll just sleep," he's told, and "That's great" is his answer: "I haven't
      slept for weeks."
Then "Great" again, then, serious, dry-eyed, to his weeping family: "Just
      don't tell me when."

The Vessel

I'm trying to pray; one of the voices of my mind says, "God, please help
    me do this,"
but another voice intervenes: "How conceive God's interest would be to
    help you believe?"

Is this prayer? Might this exercise be a sign, however impure, that such
    an act's under way,
that I'd allowed myself, or that God had allowed me, to surrender to this
    need in myself?

What makes me think, though, that the region of my soul in which all
    this activity's occurring
is a site which God might consider an engaging or even an acceptable
    spiritual location?

I thought I'd kept the lack of a sacred place in myself from myself, there-
    fore from God.
Is *this* prayer, recognizing that my isolation from myself is a secret I no
    longer can keep?

Might prayer be an awareness that even our most belittling secrets are
    absurd before God?
Might God's mercy be letting us think we haven't betrayed those secrets
    to Him until now?

If I believe that there exists a thing I can call God's mercy, might I be
    praying at last?
If I were, what would it mean: that my sad loneliness for God might be
    nearing its end?

I imagine that were I in a real relation with God instead of just being
    lonely for Him,
the way I'd apprehend Him would have nothing to do with secrets I'd
    kept, from Him or myself.

I'd empty like a cup: that would be prayer, to empty, then fill with a sub-
stance other than myself.
Empty myself of what, though? And what would God deign fill me with
except my own prayer?

Is this prayer now, believing that my offering to God would be what He'd
offered me?
I'm trying to pray, but I know that whatever I'm doing I'm not: why aren't
I, when will I?

Allies: According to Herodotus

"Just how much are you worth?" Xerxes asks Pythius, reputedly the richest man in Lydia,
at the entertainment Pythius was holding in his palace for Xerxes and his chiefs of staff.
"Exactly three million nine hundred and ninety-three thousand golden darics," Pythius answers,
"and all of it is yours, my humble contribution towards your glorious war against the Greeks."

Xerxes is pleased: since he's left Persia with his troops, only Pythius along their route
has offered hospitality without being compelled to; all this might indicate a welcome drift.
"Consider yourself my personal friend," he says to Pythius: "Keep your fortune, you've earned it,
and furthermore I'm awarding you another seven thousand darics of my own to round it off."

Later, as Xerxes is preparing to go on, an eclipse is sighted, which irrationally alarms Pythius,
but also encourages him to ask Xerxes for a favor. "Anything you want, just ask," says Xerxes.
"I have five sons," Pythius replies, "and all of them are leaving to take part in your campaign.
I'm getting on: let me keep my eldest here, to help take care of me and see to my estates."

Xerxes is incensed. "You ungrateful scum," he snarls, "you have the gall to talk about your son,
when I myself, Xerxes himself, is going off to fight with all my sons and friends and relatives?
It would have pleased my ears if you'd offered me your *wife*, and thrown in your old carcass.
You saved yourself by your generosity the other night, but now you'll know a real king's rage."

Some ancients doubt Herodotus, but not in this; Xerxes, after all, angry
at the Hellespont,
had it lashed and branded; we can trust therefore that near the moment
when history begins,
Xerxes commanded that the beloved eldest son of Pythius be brought to
him and cut in half,
and that the halves be placed along the roadside for his army to march
out towards Greece between.

Harm

With his shopping cart, his bags of booty and his wine, I'd always found
      him inoffensive.
Every neighborhood has one or two these days; ours never rants at you at
      least or begs.

He just forages the trash all day, drinks and sings and shadowboxes, then
      at nightfall
finds a doorway to make camp, set out his battered little radio and slab of
      rotting foam.

The other day, though, as I was going by, he stepped abruptly out be-
      tween parked cars,
undid his pants, and, not even bothering to squat, sputtered out a nox-
      ious, almost liquid stream.

There was that, and that his bony shanks and buttocks were already
      stained beyond redemption,
that his scarlet testicles were blown up bigger than a bull's with some sor-
      rowful disease,

and that a slender adolescent girl from down the block happened by
      right then, and looked,
and looked away, and looked at me, and looked away again, and made
      me want to say to her,

because I imagined what she must have felt, It's not like this, really, it's
      not this,
but she was gone, so I could think, But isn't it like this, isn't this just what
      it is?

The Insult

Even here, in a forest in the foothills of a range of mountains, lucent air,
  the purest dawn,
a continent and years away from where it happened, it comes back to
  me, simmering and stinging,
driving me farther down along the pathway to a hidden brook I hadn't
  realized was there.

The thrust came first, accurate, deft, to the quick, its impetus and reason-
  ings never grasped.
Then my pain, my sullen, shocked retort, harsh, but with nothing like an
  equivalent rancor.
Then the subsiding: nothing resolved, only let slide; nothing forgiven,
  only put by.

The stream bends here under a bridge, its voice lifts more loudly from
  the rocks of its bed.
The quickly hardening light slants in over the tough, sparse wild grasses
  on the far hill.
Wind rattling the aspens; a hawk so tiny it seems almost a toy hovering in
  a socket of updraft.

Even now, I have no real wish to tell it, I know it so well why have to
  recite it again?
What keeps bringing us back to those fissures so tenaciously holding our
  furious suffering?
Are there deeper wounds in us than we know; might grief itself be com-
  munion and solace?

So many footprints crossing and recrossing the trail through the boulders
  edging the bank;
the swarms of apparently purposeless insects ticking their angular circuits
  over the water.
The song of the water, the mindless air, the hawk beyond sight, the in-
  audible cry of its prey.

Child Psychology

for Loren Crabtree and Barbara Cram

In that stage of psychosexual development called latency, when not that
    much, at least supposedly,
is going on—libido sleeps, the engrossing Oedipal adventure is forgotten
    for a time—
we were going somewhere and without telling him I took my father's
    keys and went outside to wait.
House, car, office keys: how proud I was to be the keeper of that weighty,
    consequential mass.
I stood there, tossing it from hand to hand, then, like my father, high into
    the air.
And then I missed, and saw it fall, onto the narrow grating of a storm
    sewer, and then in.

I gazed, aghast, down into those viscous, unforgiving depths, intestinal,
    malignant, menacing.
What happened? Had I dropped the keys on purpose? God no: I well
    knew my father's hand.
They'd just fallen, by themselves, that's what I'd say; no, say nothing, that
    was even better,
keep still, lips sealed, stoicism, silence—what other mechanism did I
    have beside denial?
Which is what I implemented when my father came to question me, and
    question me again.
Wholly taken in the burning ardor of my virtue, I was as innocent as
    Isaac, and as dumb.

Months pass, the doorbell rings, as always I'm the one to run to answer;
    a man is there,
he holds the long-forgotten ring of keys, my father's name, address, and
    number legible, intact.
I don't remember what men wore back then to muck about in filth for
    us, but it didn't matter;
the second I saw him I knew him—*the return of the repressed* . . . so soon,
    though, so very soon.

The shudderings I drove within were deafening; I couldn't bring myself
      to speak, but knew he would,
as I knew what he would say: "Is your father home?" He was, he was:
      how could he not be?

Chapter Eleven

As in a thousand novels but I'll never as long as I live get used to this
      kind of thing,
the guy who works as director of something or other in the business my
      friend owns and who,
I'm not sure why, we're out, my friend and I, for an after-work drink
      with, keeps kidding around,
making nice, stroking us, both of us, but of course mostly my friend, say-
      ing "Yes, boss, yes, boss,"
which is supposed to be funny but isn't because joke or no joke he's
      really all over my friend,
nodding, fawning, harking hard, and so intense it all is, with such edges
      of rage or despair—
is my friend letting him go? is his job as they say in that world, that hard
      world, on the line?—
that finally even my friend, who must have suspected something like this
      was going to happen
(why bring me then?), gets edgy, there are lapses, we all shift, then my
      friend says something,
"I don't feel great," something, "I have a headache," and, without think-
      ing, I'm sure without thinking,
it happens so quickly, the guy reaches, and, with the back of his hand,
      like a nurse or a mother,
feels my friend's forehead, as though to see if he has a fever, and my
      friend, what else? jerks back,
leaving the hand hung there in mid-air for a moment, almost saluting,
      almost farewelling,
until finally the poor man hauls the hand in, reels it back in, and does
      what with it?
Puts it for a moment lightly on the back of his head, lightly on his collar,
      the table, his drink?
All right, yes, the back of his head, lightly; lightly, his collar, the table,
      his drink.
But what does it matter anyway what the poor man does with his poor
      marooned hand?

Besides, he's fine now, we're all fine, it was all just a blink, the man's folded his hands,

you'd think he was just saying grace or something, and probably nothing happened at all,

you probably just blinked and drifted and imagined it all; if you asked the man how he was,

what would he say, except "What do you mean?" and what would you do but shut up and smile,

this isn't *Death of a Salesman*, nobody here is going to turn into a Gregor Samsa;

if you were him, wouldn't the last thing you'd want be for someone like me to me-too you?

My friend beckons, the check comes on its little salver and my friend stares down at it hard.

"I'm dead," he says finally. "I'm on such a short leash with the bank, I can't make a dime."

The Loneliness

Not even when my gaze had gone unmet so long, starved so long, it went
    out of my control;
the most casual passing scrutiny would make my eyes, though I'd im-
    plore them not to,
scurry, slither, dart away to execute again their cowardly, abject cere-
    mony of submission.

It was as though my pupils had extruded agonizing wires anyone who
    wanted to could tug.
What I looked at, what let approach me, had virtue only in so much as it
    would let me be,
let me hide further back within myself, let that horrid, helpless, sideways
    cringing stop.

Not even when my voice became so riddled with disuse my only re-
    course seemed to be to cry.
Some pointless pride, though, wouldn't let me: I'd ransack the layers of
    numb, resisting tissue,
but when I'd touch my cheeks they'd still be dry, even that benign re-
    lease had been proscribed.

I'd think there might be something I could tell myself that would be
    equivalent to crying,
an idea or locution that would excavate a route through those impacted
    wells of desolation.
Thought hurt now, though; I couldn't concentrate: the most elementary
    logic lay beyond me.

Not even when, near sleep, it seemed somewhere in my mental boil my
    name was being called.
I'd reach out to hold the voice, then I'd realize that "name" and "call"
    were only symbols,
that some more painful aural stuff was solidifying in the echoing am-
    phitheater of my skull.

No wonder my fascination turned to those as lost as me, the drugged, the drunk, the mad.
Like ancient wounds they were, punctured with their solitude and sorrow, suppurating, stinking;
I'd recoil from what the soul could come to, but I knew within my soul that they were me.

My life, too, eluded me; I, too, learned to shun what of myself I saw in those around me.
No face now without its screen of categorical resistance, no glance untainted by denial.
I was being spoored by my imaginations; I felt guilt, and then remorse, as though I'd sinned.

I thought I'd come to know it then, when it began to turn on me, become its own exacerbation,
when the most unpremeditated look or smile or gesture, coming from it didn't matter who,
roused only rage in me, rejection, fire . . . I was close then, closer, but no, not even then.

By then, though, I was near the end; I'd never thought I would, but I was looking back,
almost apprehensive for the innocent I'd been, wondering if it all had been a romance,
if I might have really sanctioned all that hard annealing, and even then I hadn't understood.

When I knew, it was long after I imagined that I'd let it go; when I saw it come upon my children;
when I knew that they believed as I'd believed they'd never be sufficient to themselves again;
when I realized there was nothing I could do or say to help them: then, and only then.

Scar

As though the skin had been stripped and pulled back onto the skull like
      a stocking and soldered
too tightly so that it mottled to yellow and ocher, the pores and follicles
      thumbed out of the clay
by the furious slash of flame that must have leapt on her and by the heal-
      ing that hurt her—

if it is healing that leaves her, age three, in a lassitude lax on her mother's
      broad lap,
bleak, weary, becalmed, what's left of her chin leaned heavily onto what's
      left of her fingers,
those knobs without nails, diminished, blunted, as though someone had
      hammered them thicker;

nares gone, ears gone, most of the dear lips gone so that your gaze is
      taken too deeply, terribly,
into the pool of the mouth as into a genital; the eyelids upper and lower
      wrinkled like linen,
the blood rims of the eyes too graphically vivid; harsh, tearless, porno-
      graphically red—

and you are supposed not to look or look and glance quickly away and
      not look at the mother,
who signs with a stone shoulder and eyes fixed to the child's white-gauze
      surgical cap
that if you do look you are cursed, if you do look you will and you well
      know it be damned.

Lascivious pity, luxurious pity, that glances and looks and looks twice
      and delivers the tear
and hauls out of the blind, locked caves of the breast these silent stran-
      gles of sobs
that ache but give something like tremulous whispers of sanctity back,
      psalms of gratification.

Lascivious pity, idle, despicable pity, pity of the reflexive half-thought
      holy thought
thinking the mindless threnody of itself once again: I watched, I couldn't
      not watch her,
as she so conscientiously, carefully wouldn't watch me; rapacious, pillag-
      ing pity: forgive me.

II

SOME OF THE FORMS OF JEALOUSY

Signs

My friend's wife has a lover; I come to this conclusion—not suspicion,
       mind, conclusion,
not a doubt about it, not a hesitation, although how I get there might be
       hard to track;
a blink a little out of phase, say, with its sentence, perhaps a word or two
       too few;
a certain tenderness of atmosphere, of aura, almost like a pregnancy,
       with less glow, perhaps,
but similar complex inward blushes of accomplishment, achievement,
       pride—during dinner,
as she passes me a dish of something, as I fork a morsel of it off, as our
       glances touch.

My friend's manner, or his guise, is openness, heartiness and healthy
       haleness in all things;
the virtue of conviction, present moment, that sort of thing: it is his pas-
       sion and his ethic,
so I don't know now if he knows or doesn't know, or knows and might be
       hiding it, or doesn't care.
He is hearty, open, present; he is eating dinner in the moment with his
       wife and old dear friend.
The wife, wifely, as she pours my wine and hands it to me looks across
       the glass's rim at me.
Something in the wifely glance tells me now she knows I know, and
       when I shyly look away,
reach across for bread and butter, she looks down at my hand, and up
       again: she is telling me
she doesn't care the least bit if I know or don't know, she might in fact
       wish me to know.

My friend is in the present still, taking sustenance; it's sustaining, good;
       he smiles, good.
Down below, I can just make out the engines of his ship, the stresses,
       creaks and groans;

everything's in hand; I hear the happy workers at their chugging furnaces
and boilers.
I let my friend's guise now be not my guise but truth; in truth, I'm like
him, dense, convinced,
involved all in the moment, hearty, filled, fulfilled, not just with manner,
but with fact.
I ply my boilers, too; my workers hum: light the deck lamps, let the string
quartet play.

My friend's wife smiles and offers me her profile now; she is telling me
again: but why?
She smiles again, she glows, she plays me like a wind chime; I sit here
clanging to myself.
My friend doesn't seem to see me resonating; he grins, I grin, too, I flee
to him again.
I'm with him in his moment now, I'm in my mouth just as he's in his,
munching, hungrily, heartily.
My safe and sane and hungry mouth hefts the morsels of my sustenance
across its firmament.
The wife smiles yet again, I smile, too, but what I'm saying is if what she
means is so,
I have no wish to know; more, I never did know; more, if by any chance
I might have known,
I've forgotten, absolutely, yes: if it ever did come into my mind it's
slipped my mind.
In truth, I don't remember anything; I eat, I drink, I smile; I hardly even
know I'm there.

The Cautionary

A man who's married an attractive, somewhat younger woman conceives
    a painful jealousy of her.
At first he's puzzled as to why he should brood so fretfully on her faithful-
    ness or lack of it.
Their lovemaking is fulfilling: he enjoys it, his wife seems to, too, as
    much as he does,
or, to his surprise (he's never had this experience before), maybe more
    than he does.
When they married, it had seemed a miracle, he'd hardly been able to
    believe his great luck:
the ease and grace with which she'd come to him, the frank, good-
    humored way she'd touch him.
But now . . . it isn't that she gives too much meaning to sex, or exhibits
    insufficient affection,
it's how *involved* in it she gets, so nearly oblivious, in a way he can never
    imagine being.
He finds that he's begun to observe their life in bed with what he thinks
    is a degree of detachment.
He sees himself, his blemishes, the paunch he can't always hide, then
    her, her sheen, her glow.
Why, he asks, would such a desirable woman have committed herself so
    entirely to such as him?
And, more to the point: why this much passion, these urgencies and
    wants, this blind delight?
By a train of logic he can't trace to its source but which he finds chill-
    ingly irrefutable,
he decides that it's not he himself, as himself, his wife desires, but that
    she simply *desires.*
He comes to think he's incidental to this desire, which is general, unspe-
    cific, without object,
almost, in its intensity and heat, without a subject: she herself seems sec-
    ondary to it,
as though the real project of her throaty, heaving passion was to melt her
    mindlessly away.

Why would such need be limited to him: wouldn't it sweep like a search-
light across all maleness?
He can't help himself, he begins to put to the proof his disturbing but
compelling observations.
When they're out together, it's self-evident to him that every man who
sees her wants her:
all the furtive glances, behind, aside, even into surfaces that hold her
image as she passes.
It dawns on him in a shocking and oddly exciting insight that for so
many to desire her
some *signal* would have to be sent, not an actual gesture perhaps, noth-
ing so coarse as a beckoning,
but something like an aura, of eagerness, availability, which she'd be sub-
consciously emitting.
Hardly noticing, he falls a step behind her, the better to watch her, to
keep track of her.
Then he realizes to his chagrin that his scrutiny might very well be work-
ing on his wife.
In a sadly self-fulfilling prophecy, she might begin to feel vulnerable,
irritated, disconnected;
yes, alone, she must often feel alone, as though he, wretch that he is,
wasn't even there.
This is the last way he'd have thought that his obsession would undo
him, but why not?
A woman among admiring men is already in the broadest sense a poten-
tial object of desire,
but a woman with a sharply heightened awareness of her most elemen-
tary sexual identity,
as his wife by now would have, with this jackal, as he now sees himself,
sniffing behind her:
wouldn't she, even against her best intentions, manifest this in a primi-
tive, perceptible way,
and wouldn't men have to be aware, however vaguely, that some sexual
event was taking place?
Mightn't the glances she'd inspire reflect this, bringing an intriguing
new sense of herself,
and mightn't this make even more likely that she'd betray him in just the
way that he suspects?

Yes. No. Yes. He knows that he should stop all this: but how can he, without going to the end?

The end might be just the thing he's driving them both towards, he can't help himself, though,

he'll dissemble his fixations, but if there's to be relief, it will have to wait till then.

Baby Talk

Willa Selenfriend likes Paul Peterzell better than she likes me and I am
    dying of it.
"Like" is what we say in eighth grade to mean a person has a secret crush
    on someone else.
I am dying of Willa liking Paul without knowing why she likes him
    more, or what it means.
It doesn't matter, Willa has insinuated cells of doubt in me, I already feel
    them multiplying,
I know already that a single lifetime won't be long enough to extirpate
    their progeny.
Willa likes Paul better than me but one summer day she'll come out to
    the park with me.
Why? Did she pity me? I don't care. We're there, we've walked, now
    we're resting on the grass.
Is this rest, though, to lie here, Willa so close, as lovely as ever, and as
    self-possessed?
I try, too, to calm myself, but the silence is painful; is this because Paul's
    in it, too?
Do I suspect it's that of which Willa's silence is composed? If so, of what
    is mine composed?
We lie there just a minute, or a year, the surgings and the pulsings in my
    heart and groin
are so intense that finally Paul's forgotten, only Willa's there with me, my
    docile longings.
Willa's turned towards me, her eyes are closed, I bring my face down
    closer, next to hers.
Astonishing that Willa should be in the visible with me, glowing in the
    world of pertinent form.
I move my lips towards hers, I can't resist, only this much, this gently, but
    then, no,
with one subtle shift, the mildest movement of the angle of her brow,
    Willa repositions us
so that my awkwardness makes absurd my plot of our participation in a
    mutual sensual accord.

With what humiliating force I have to understand I'd been suffering an
      unforgivable illusion;
I'd believed that for a little moment Paul had left us, but he'd been there
      all along,
with the unwavering omniscience of a parent, the power of what some-
      day I'll call a conscience.
What had ever made me think I'd so easily obliterate him from the fray-
      ing dusk of childhood?
Weren't we contained in him, held in him; wouldn't fearful heart forever
      now falter in its flight?

The Question

The middle of the night, she's wide awake, carefully lying as far away as
she can from him.
He turns in his sleep and she can sense him realizing she's not in the
place she usually is,
then his sleep begins to change, he pulls himself closer, his arm comes
comfortably around her.
"Are you awake?" she says, then, afraid that he might think she's asking
him for sex,
she hurries on, "I want to know something; last summer, in Cleveland,
did you have someone else?"
She'd almost said—she was going to say—"Did you have a *lover*?" but
she'd caught herself;
she'd been frightened by the word, she realized; it was much too definite,
at least for now.
Even so, it's only after pausing that he answers, "No," with what feeling
she can't tell.
He moves his hand on her, then with a smile in his voice asks, "Did you
have somebody in Cleveland?"
"That's not what I was asking you," she says crossly. "But that's what I
asked *you*," he answers.
She's supposed to be content now, the old story, she knows that she's sup-
posed to be relieved,
but she's not relieved, her tension hasn't eased the slightest bit, which
doesn't surprise her.
She's so confused that she can't really even say now if she wants to be-
lieve him or not.
Anyway, what about that pause? Was it because in the middle of the
night and six months later
he wouldn't have even known what she was talking about, or was it be-
cause he needed that moment
to frame an answer which would neutralize what might after all have
been a shocking thrust
with a reasonable deflection, in this case, his humor: a laugh that's like a
lie and is.

"When would I have found the time?" he might have said, or, "Who in Cleveland could I love?"

Or, in that so brief instant, might he have been finding a way to stay in the realm of truth,

as she knew he'd surely want to, given how self-righteously he esteemed his ethical integrities?

It comes to her with a start that what she most deeply and painfully suspects him of is a *renunciation*.

She knows that he has no one now; she thinks she knows there's been no contact from Cleveland,

but she still believes that there'd been something then, and if it was as important as she thinks,

it wouldn't be so easily forgotten, it would still be with him somewhere as a sad regret,

perhaps a precious memory, but with that word, renunciation, hooked to it like a price tag.

Maybe that was what so rankled her, that she might have been the object of his charity, his *goodness*.

That would be too much; that he would have wronged her, then sacrificed himself for her.

Yes, "Lover," she should have said it, "Lover, lover," should have made him try to disavow it.

She listens to his breathing; he's asleep again, or has he taught himself to feign that, too?

"No, last summer in Cleveland I didn't have a lover, I have never been to Cleveland, I love you.

There is no Cleveland, I adore you, and, as you'll remember, there was no last summer:

the world last summer didn't yet exist, last summer still was universal darkness, chaos, pain."

Meditation

You must never repeat this to him, *but when I started seeing my guru was when I got pregnant.*
I'm not bothered to think there's a connection—we'd been trying so long— but he would be.
He doesn't like my Baba, he says that he's repelled by him; I think he's really envious.
But why? Just because I believe in one person doesn't hurt my feelings for someone else.
You're supposed to give yourself to the guru, that's the whole idea, not that way, though.
He makes so much fuss: Baba is a fake, Baba is a pig; he says that I should leave him,
but he knows I won't: if he made me choose, I don't know what I'd do; and there's the baby.
When we made the baby, after my first visit to the ashram, I was so quiet inside, so serene,
as though I'd never been alive before; I felt Baba with me, just like when I met him.
I knew right away the pregnancy had taken, I knew I'd finally get my child; I was so happy.
I'm not lying to him, just not telling him; I can't, I won't. Don't you, either—promise!

Politics

They're discussing the political situation they've been watching evolve in
     a faraway country.
He's debating intensely, almost lecturing, about fanaticism and religion,
     the betrayal of ideals.
He believes he's right, but even as he speaks he knows within himself
     that it's all incidental;
he doesn't really care that much, he just can't help himself, what he's
     really talking about
is the attraction that he feels she feels towards those dark and passionate
     young men
just now glowing on the screen with all the unimpeachable righteous-
     ness of the once-oppressed.
He says that just because they've been afflicted isn't proof against their
     lying and conniving.
What he means is that they're not, because she might find them virile,
     therefore virtuous.
He says that there are always forces we don't see that use these things for
     evil ends.
What he means is that he's afraid that she might turn from him towards
     someone suffering,
or, as possible, towards someone who'd share with similar conviction her
     abhorrence of suffering.
He means he's troubled by how *sure* she is, how her compassions are so
     woven into her identity.
Isn't the degree to which she's certain of her politics, hence of her right-
     ness in the world,
the same degree to which she'd be potentially willing to risk herself, and
     him, and everything?
Also, should she wish to justify an action in her so firmly grounded socio-
     ethical system,
any action, concupiscence, promiscuity, orgy, wouldn't it not only let her
     but abet her?
Sometimes he feels her dialectics and her assurance are assertions of
     some ultimate availability.

Does he really want someone so self-sufficient, who knows herself so
    well, knows so much?
In some ways, he thinks—has he really come to this?—he might want
    her knowing *nothing*.
No, not nothing, just . . . a little less . . . and with less fervor, greater prag-
    matism, realism.
More and more in love with her, touched by her, he still goes on, to his
    amazement, arguing.

Pillow Talk

*Please try to understand, it was only one small moment, it didn't mean a
     thing, not really.*
*He was nice enough, but I didn't like him that much, I just felt, you've felt
     it, too, I'm sure,*
*a burden in my chest, as though I couldn't catch my breath, or get my
     heartbeat straight.*
*You know, I know you know: there's an ache in you, you want to make it
     stop, that awful flurrying;*
*you can't get back to where you used to like to be, everything is out of bal-
     ance in you,*
*and you realize, even if you'd rather not, that the only way is with this
     other person,*
*you can't tell how you come to that conclusion, you feel silly, you hardly
     even know him,*
*he's almost not important anyway, he just represents release from all of it,
     a correction,*
*but you know that nothing else will get this settled in you, that you'll al-
     ways be like this,*
*with this sense of incompletion, unless you act, even though you might not
     really want to,*
*so you go ahead and while it's happening you don't think of things like evil
     or betrayal,*
*you just want your inner world back in order so you can start to live your
     life again,*
*and then it's over, ended, you won't ever need him anymore, you realize it's
     finished, done.*
*I thought that you should know, that if you knew you'd understand: tell
     me, do you? Understand?*

Ethics

The only time, I swear, I ever fell more than abstractly in love with some-
one else's wife,
I managed to maintain the clearest sense of innocence, even after the
woman returned my love,
even after she'd left her husband and come down on the plane from
Montreal to be with me,
I still felt I'd done nothing immoral, that whole disturbing category had
somehow been effaced;
even after she'd arrived and we'd gone home and gone to bed, and even
after, the next morning,
when she crossed my room undressed—I almost looked away; we were
both as shy as adolescents—
and all that next day when we walked, made love again, then slept, cling-
ing to each other,
even then, her sleeping hand softly on my chest, her gentle breath gently
moving on my cheek,
even then, or not until then, not until the new day touched upon us, and
I knew, knew absolutely,
that though we might love each other, something in her had to have the
husband, too,
and though she'd tried, and would keep trying to overcome herself, I
couldn't wait for her,
did that perfect guiltlessness, that sure conviction of my inviolable virtue,
flee me,
to leave me with a blade of loathing for myself, a disgust with who I
guessed by now I was,
but even then, when I took her to the airport and she started up that cor-
ridor the other way,
and we waved, just waved—anybody watching would have thought that
we were separating friends—
even then, one part of my identity kept claiming its integrity, its non-
involvement, even chastity,
which is what I castigate myself again for now, not the husband or his
pain, which he survived,
nor the wife's temptation, but the thrill of evil that I'd felt, then kept
myself from feeling.

The Mirror

The way these days she dresses with more attention to go out to pass the
    afternoon alone,
shopping or just taking walks, she says, than when they go together to a
    restaurant or party:
it's such a subtle thing, how even speak of it, how imagine he'd be able to
    explain it to her?
The way she looks for such long moments in the mirror as she gets ready,
    putting on her makeup;
the way she looks so deeply at herself, gazes at her eyes, her mouth,
    down along her breasts:
what is he to say, that she's looking at herself in ways he's never seen
    before, more *carnally*?
She would tell him he was mad, or say something else he doesn't want
    no matter what to hear.
The way she puts her jacket on with a flourish, the way she gaily smiles
    going out the door,
the door, the way the door slams shut, the way its latch clicks shut be-
    hind her so emphatically.
What is he to think? What is he to say, to whom? The mirror, jacket,
    latch, the awful door?
He can't touch the door, he's afraid he'll break the frightening covenant
    he's made with it.
He can't look into the mirror, either, that dark, malicious void: who
    knows what he might see?

The Call

When one of my oldest and dearest friends died and another friend
      called to console me,
I found myself crying—I hadn't thought I would—and said, "I didn't
      know I'd feel this bad."
Now, a year later, the second friend calls again, this time because his
      mistress has left him.
He's anguished, his voice torn; "I didn't know," he tells me, "that I'd feel
      this bad."
I'm shocked to hear him use precisely the words I had in my grief, but of
      course I understand.
There are more calls, and more, but in the end they all add up to much
      the same thing.
The mistress had warned him time and again, if not in so many words,
      that this might happen;
she'd asked him to leave his wife, he hadn't yet, but thought his honest
      oath to was in effect.
How was he to know that what he'd taken as playful after-intercourse
      endearments were threats?
Now that this terrible thing has happened, he's promised he'll really do
      it, but too late:
his beloved has found someone else, she's in love, no question now of
      beginning over.
At first my friend's desperation is sad to behold, his self-esteem is in har-
      rowing decline;
decisiveness, or a lack of it, his lack of it, has become the key factor in his
      value system.
Gradually, though, he begins to focus on the new lover, on his insipid-
      ness, his pitiful accomplishments.
There are flaws to this attack, though, because with each new proof of
      the other's shortcomings,
with each attempt to neutralize his effectiveness, my friend's self-blame
      becomes more acute.
Still, he can't say to himself, "Behold this giant competitor, this
      (Freudian) father of a man,"

so he keeps diminishing the other, which only augments his sense of the capriciousness of fate.

Then, to his relief (though he won't quite admit it), he finds sometimes he's furious at the woman.

How could she have done this? She'd known the risks he'd taken in doubling his affections,

shouldn't she simply have accepted his ambivalence and hesitation as a part of their relation?

And what about his wife; yes, some innocence, some purity has been transgressed there, too.

Her suspicions had been hot; she'd accepted his denials; wasn't that an offering to the mistress?

Aren't there violations, then, not just of his own good intentions but of his wife's generosity?

He's often torn with rage now, he doesn't even know at whom, but then he has to stop himself.

He doesn't want to blame the mistress *too* much, in case she should, despite all, come back,

and he doesn't want to hate his wife, who still doesn't know, or is even kinder than he thought.

So he keeps dutifully forgiving everyone, which throws the whole fault back on him again

and makes him wonder what kind of realignment could possibly redeem so much despair.

No, it's all ruined in advance, everything is stuck, the only thing he can do now is forget.

They're so degrading, these issues which can be resolved by neither consolation nor forgiveness.

No wonder my friend would cast his misery as mourning; no wonder, biting my tongue, I'd let him.

The Image

She began to think that jealousy was only an excuse, a front, for some-
thing even more rapacious,
more maniacally pathological in its readiness to sacrifice its own well-
being for its satisfaction.
Jealousy was supposed to be a fact of love, she thought, but this was a
compulsion, madness,
it didn't have a thing to do with love, it was perfectly autonomous, love
was just its vehicle.
She thought: wasn't there a crazy hunger, even a delight, in how he'd
pounced on her betrayal?
There hadn't even *been* betrayal until he'd made it so; for her, before
that, it had been a whim,
a frivolity she'd gone to for diversion, it hadn't had anything to do with
him, or them.
Her apologies meant nothing, though, nor her fervent promise of repen-
tance, he *held* his hurt,
he cultivated, stroked it, as though that was all that kept him in relation-
ship with her.
He wanted her to think she'd maimed him: what was driving him to such
barbarous vindictiveness?
She brought to mind a parasite, waiting half a lifetime for its victim to
pass beneath its branch,
then coming to fully sentient, throbbing, famished life and without hesi-
tation letting go.
It must have almost starved in him, she thinks, all those years spent
scenting out false stimuli,
all that passive vigilance, secreting bitter enzymes of suspicion, ingesting
its own flesh;
he must have eaten at himself, devouring his own soul until his chance
had finally come.
But now it had and he had driven fangs in her and nothing could con-
tain his terrible tenacity.
She let the vision take her further; they had perished, both of them,
there they lay, decomposing,

one of them drained white, the other bloated, gorged, stale blood oozing
through its carapace.
Only as a stupid little joke, she thought, would anybody watching dare
wonder which was which.

The Idyll

*I just don't want to feel put down; if she decides she wants to sleep with
        someone, listen,*
*great, go ahead, but I want to know about it and I want the other guy to
        know I know;*
*I don't want some mother sliming in her sack, using her and thinking he's
        one up on me.*

*She's always touching men, she sort of leans at them, she has to have them
        notice her,*
*want to grab her; it's like she's always telling me she's on the lookout for
        some stud,*
*some gigantic sex-machine who's going to get it on with her a hundred
        times an hour.*

*Once it really happened: she looked me in the eye and said, "I balled
        someone else last night."*
*Christ, I felt these ridges going up and down my jaw, I thought my teeth
        were going to break.*
*What'd I do? I took her home, we made out like maniacs. What else was I
        supposed to do?*

*Sometimes I wonder if I need it. I mean, she'll be coming on to somebody,
        as usual,*
*I'll want to crack her head for her, but if I think about it, I might get a
        buzz from it,*
*it must be what going into battle's like: sometimes I think going nuts from
        her is my religion.*

*I don't know if she fools around much now; I guess I'm not a whole lot into
        other women either.*
*The last time I was with another chick—she was a little knockout, too—I
        wasn't hardly there.*
*I realized who I wanted to be with was her. I turned off. Hell, is that how
        you get faithful?*

The Silence

He hasn't taken his eyes off you since we walked in, although you seem
    not to notice particularly.
Only sometimes, when your gaze crosses his, mightn't it leave a very tiny
    tuft behind?
It's my imagination surely, but mightn't you be all but imperceptibly
    acknowledging his admiration?
We've all known these things; the other, whom we've never seen before,
    but whose ways we recognize,
and with whom we enter into brilliant complicities; soul's receptors
    tuned and armed;
the concealed messages, the plots, the tactics so elegant they might have
    been rehearsed:
the way we wholly disregard each other, never, except at the most casu-
    ally random intervals,
let our scrutinies engage, but then that deep, delicious draft, that eager
    passionate appreciation . . .
I tell myself that I don't care, as I might not sometimes, when no rival's
    happened by,
but I do care now, I care acutely, I just wonder what the good would be
    if I told you I can see
your mild glances palpably, if still so subtly, furtively, intertwining now
    with his.
I'd only be insulting you, violating my supposed trust in you, belittling
    both of us.
We've spent so much effort all these years learning to care for one an-
    other's sensitivities.
In an instant that's all threatened; your affections seem as tenuous as
    when we met,
and I have to ask myself, are you more valuable to me the more that
    you're at risk?
Am I to you? It's degrading, thinking we're more firmly held together by
    our mutual anxiety.
If my desire is susceptible to someone else's valuations of its object, then
    what am I?

Can I say that my emotions are my own if in my most intimate affection
such contaminations lurk?
Still, though, what if this time I'd guessed right, and what if I should try
to tell you,
to try to laugh about it with you, to use our union, and our hard-earned
etiquettes to mock him,
this intruder—look—who with his dream of even daring to attempt you
would be ludicrous?
There would still be risks I almost can't let myself consider: that you'd
be humoring me,
that the fierce intensity of your attraction to him would already consti-
tute a union with him,
I'd be asking you to lie, and doing so you'd be thrown more emphatically
into his conspiracy;
your conniving with him would relegate me to the status of an obliga-
tion, a teary inconvenience.
This is so exhausting: when will it relent? It seems never, not as long as
consciousness exists.
Therefore, as all along I knew I would, as I knew I'd have to, I keep still,
conceal my sorrow.
Therefore, when you ask, "Is something wrong?" what is there to answer
but, "Of course not, why?"

Soliloquies

1.

Strange that sexual jealousy should be so much like sex itself: the same engrossing reveries,
the intricate, voluptuous pre-imaginings, the impatient plottings towards a climax, then climax . . .
Or, not quite climax, since jealousy is different in how uninvolved it is in consummation.
What is its consummation but negation? Not climax but relief, a sigh of resignation, disappointment.
Still, how both depend upon a judicious intermingling of the imaginary and the merely real,
and how important image is for both, the vivid, breath-held unscrolling of fugitive inner effigies.
Next to all our other minds, how pure both are, what avid concentration takes us in them.
Maybe this is where jealousy's terrific agitation comes from, because, in its scalding focus,
a desperate single-mindedness is imposed upon the soul and the sad, conditioned soul responds,
so fervently, in such good faith, it hardly needs the other person for its delicious fever.
Is there anything in life in which what is fancied is so much more intense than what's accomplished?
We know it's shadow, but licentious consciousness goes on forever manufacturing . . . fever.

2.

The stupidity of it, the repetitiveness, the sense of all one's mental mechanisms run amok.
Knowing that pragmatically, statistically, one's fantasies are foolish, but still being trapped.

The almost unmanageable foreboding that one's character won't be up
to its own exigencies.
Knowing one is one's own victim; how self-diminishing to have to ask,
"Who really *am* I, then?"
I am someone to be rescued from my mind, but the agent of my suffer-
ing is its sole redemption;
only someone else, a specific someone else, can stop me from inflicting
this upon myself.
And so within myself, in this unsavory, unsilent solitude of self, I fall into
an odious dependency.
I'm like an invalid relying absolutely on another's rectitude; but the
desperate invalid, abandoned,
would have at least the moral compensation of knowing that he wasn't
doing this to himself;
philosophically, his reliance would be limited by the other's sense of
obligation, or its absence.
This excruciating, groundless need becomes more urgent, more to be
desired the more it's threatened,
while its denouement promises what one still believes will be an un-
imaginably luxurious release.

3.

I try to imagine the kind of feeling which would come upon me if I
really were betrayed now.
How long would I remain in that abject state of mind? When would it
end? Am I sure it would?
What constitutes a state of mind at all? Certain chunks of feeling, of
pleasure or pain?
I postulate the pain, but can I really? My mood prevents it. Is that all I
am, then, mood?
Sometimes I feel firmly socketed within myself; other moments, I seem
barely present.
Which should I desire? Mightn't it be better not to feel anything if I'm
helpless anyway?
I try to reconceive the problem: I am he who will forgive his being
wronged, but can I know I will?

All my mind will tell me absolutely and obsessively is that its future isn't
    in my governance.
Might that be why the other's possible offense seems much more *rank*
    than mine would ever be?
My betrayal would be whimsical, benign, the hymen of my innocence
    would be quickly reaffirmed.
Hers infects, contaminates, is ever the first premeditated step of some
    squalid longer term.
I would forgive, but suspect that she might already be beyond forgive-
    ness: whose fault then?

4.

What would be the difference? The way jealousy seeps into my notions
    of intention and volition,
the annihilating force it has: mightn't it be grounded in the furies of
    more radical uncertainty?
That nothing lasts, that there's no real reason why it doesn't last, and that
    there's death,
and more maddening still that existence has conjectured possibilities of
    an after-death,
but not their certainty, rather more the evidence that any endlessness is
    mental fiction.
And that there might be a God, a potentially beloved other who *would*
    know, this, and everything,
who already has sufficient knowledge of our fate to heal us but may well
    decide not to do so.
How not rage, how, in love, with its promises of permanence, the only
    answer to these doubts,
not find absurd that this, too, should suffer from foreboding, and one so
    mechanically averted?
Might jealousy finally suggest that what we're living isn't ever what we
    think we are?
What, though, would more require our love, our being loved, our vow of
    faithfulness and faith?
And what would more compel that apprehensive affirmation: *I'll love you
    forever, will you me?*

III

She, Though

Her friend's lover was dying, or not "friend," they weren't that yet, if they
      ever really were;
it was another girl she'd found to share the studio she'd rented in an old
      commercial building.
Both of them were painters, the other serious, hardworking, she floun-
      dering and unconfident.
She gave you the feeling people fresh from art school often do that the
      painter's life
would be just fine except for all those hours you had to put in with the
      bothersome canvas.
"Lover" isn't quite the right word, either: the couple were too young,
      "boyfriend" would be better,
although, given the strenuousness of their trial, the more grown-up term
      could well apply.
He was twenty-three or -four, a physicist who'd already done his doctor-
      ate and published papers;
he had cancer of the brain; it had only recently been diagnosed but the
      news had all been bad.
I forget exactly how I met them: there weren't that many writers or artists
      in our city then,
we mostly knew each other, even if our fellowship seemed more
      grounded in proximity than sympathy.
She and I, I suppose I should say, once almost had a thing; she asked me
      to sit for her,
and when she'd posed me and was fussing with her charcoal, I under-
      stood why I was really there.
I was surprised; though we'd known each other for a while we were
      casual friends at best,
we'd never expressed attraction for each other, and I remember feeling
      sometimes that she resented me.
I had a reputation as a worker, even if I hadn't published anything except
      some book reviews
and a criticism of an art show, but she may have felt I had more prestige
      than I should have.

I had nothing particularly against her; maybe the tenuousness of her
     involvement in her work
and what it represented to me of myself made her less attractive than she
     might have been.
I distrusted her, wasn't sure why she wanted me, but wasn't anyway about
     to get in bed.
Her signaling was pretty raw: she'd take my head in her hands to move
     me to a new position,
then hold me longer than she had to, and she'd look intently *in* my eyes
     instead of at them.
Finally she just said, "Let's do it," but I turned her down, in a way which
     at the time
I thought was very bright but which may certainly have had to do with
     how badly things turned out.
I told her that I liked her but that I could only sleep with girls I loved,
     really loved.
She accepted my refusal in the spirit I'd hoped she would, as an example
     of my inner seriousness,
and as also having to do—through I don't recall what track—with my
     dedication as an artist.
That dedication, or obsession, or semblance of obsession, counted for
     much in those days.
For most of us it was all we had, struggling through our perplexed, in-
     terminable apprenticeships.
We were trying to create identities as makers and as thinkers, and that
     entailed so much.
I never realized until lately just how traumatic the project of my own
     self-remaking was.
I wreaked such violence on myself; the frivolous, not unsuccessful ado-
     lescent I had been
had to be remolded from such contradictory clues as I could find into a
     wholly other person.
I'd been an *athlete*, for heaven's sake, I'd been a party boy, I hung out, I
     drank, I danced:
one New Year's Eve I'd set out to kiss a hundred girls, and nearly had;
     that kind of thing.
Now who was I? Someone sitting hours on end going crazy looking at
     an empty piece of paper.

Everything I'd learned in college seemed garbled and absurd: I knew
   nothing about anything.
All I understood was that I wasn't ready for this yet, that I'd have to reach
   some higher stage
before I'd have the right to even think that I was someone who could call
   himself a poet.
We must have all felt more or less like that, though it seemed important
   never to admit it.
"Morally perfect yourself, then you'll write a poem," I read somewhere
   not long ago: is it true?
I don't think I know yet, I surely didn't then, but that was what we'd
   somehow come to,
a mix of saint and genius, neither of which we ever in our wildest ravings
   dreamed we'd be.
Maybe that was why we liked extremities so much, and mental dramas;
   we spoke forever about *limits*,
things like microcosm-macrocosm, or the way the solar system and
   atomic model seemed to match:
probably we thought that, on that wide a scale, we'd at least be sure of
   being *somewhere*.
We loved it when things went so far they turned into their opposites; the
   courteous criminal,
the rake who in his single-minded lust achieves a sanctity, the cabalist
   obscene with bliss.
There were always remnants of religion in our schemes; somehow from
   the mishmash of our education
we'd decided that you didn't practice art for its own sake or even to be
   competent or famous;
it was all supposed to be a part of a something that would lift you to an-
   other realm,
another mode of being, where you'd attain the "absolute"—a word we
   loved—along with "mystic."
But there was even more than that; art was going to be the final word on
   all else, too:
morality, philosophy, religion; if there was a God, wasn't He the God of
   Dante or Bach,
rather than a theologian's or a prophet's, unless they dreamed their vi-
   sions, too, in poetry?

When we thought of social issues or of politics, it was always with as
    audacious an immoderation.
"Justice" meant the universe of justice; the ideal, platonic shape, some-
    thing in your soul
that mirrored an imaginary, perfect state, at which the particulars of real
    life could only hint.
History for us was the history of arts and letters, anything of moment was
    attached to that.
So young we were; we had theories about everything, life, the soul: Did
    art spring from neurosis?
Was its insanity redemptive? Were you damned by art, exalted? It all
    depended on the day.
But being young wasn't the whole problem; there was moral character
    to be considered, too.
That girl, for instance, in that enormous studio: it irritated me the way
    she'd waste her time,
puttering, reading magazines; she spent more effort sending slides to
    galleries than painting.
She'd been in some group exhibitions—she wasn't without talent—now
    she'd convinced herself
that being "professional" meant not picking up a brush unless a dealer
    promised you a show.
I knew all that was posturing, self-deception, sham; I knew from what I
    went through myself
how repugnant working was when you didn't know if there was ever go-
    ing to be a recompense.
I don't mean to make light of it, what we were trying to do was hard, and
    not just the work,
in some ways that was easy: what was really difficult was waiting for the
    labor to begin;
you had to tell yourself every minute that you did it why you did and
    what it was for.
So little really happened, and no one but a friend or two even noticed
    what you were doing.
The dropout rate among us was impressive: over time so many drifted
    off, some to law school,
some into endless therapies; a black sculptor began to drink and disap-
    peared into the ghetto;

someone else became an "art consultant," choosing prints and paintings
for corporate boardrooms.

It did seem easier for some, though; some were seen as having been suc-
cessful from the start.

I suppose it had to do with confidence; they weren't necessarily the ones
who'd won the prizes,

but they seemed certified, legitimized, they had clues about their ulti-
mate trajectories;

you felt they'd freed themselves from thinking they were being *watched*,
those chosen few,

they were on their own and, though they hadn't done much yet, were
envied and looked up to.

What happens to those younger masters isn't always happy; maybe that
much unquestioning admiration,

that much carrying of so many other people's hopes, even at that level,
isn't good for you.

Also, when everyone's that young, there's much misreading of charisma
and eccentricity as talent.

Some, anyway, would turn out to have the gift, but not enough of what
you could call the *cunning*,

the kind of objectivity artists seem to need to keep their work evolving in
meaningful ways.

They'd find a mode of doing what their gift had offered them, then stay
with it too long,

and find later that they'd used it up and gotten stuck in some too flashy
segment of themselves.

Others would have the cunning, and the drive it seemed to go with, but
too much of it;

they'd become impatient, and move off to something close to art—
usually involving money—

to which they'd bring their ingenuity and energy, becoming rich or cel-
ebrated, but so what?

She, I don't have to say, wasn't one of the elect, no more than I'd dare
claim I was.

The other girl may have been; if so, she controlled the arrogance it
sometimes went with.

The boyfriend for all we knew was a genius; we had to take his mysteri-
ous accomplishments on faith.

He was brilliant enough in conversation, at any rate, and had an attractive calm about him.

In the face of his illness, and though no one dared speak of it, his at least possible death,

the two of them had evolved one of those surprising complicities of resignation and acceptance

which can take the most unexceptional people at such times, and they were hardly unexceptional.

They had an admirably mature relationship; they respected and encouraged one another's work,

and were solicitous towards each other in gentle, complicated ways the rest of us found heartening.

But with all that, the dignity they seemed committed to achieving now was of another order.

For one thing, there was no denial in it, no trying to behave more fittingly before the facts.

They stayed mostly to themselves, and worked; if they did go anywhere, to an opening, say,

they left early, refusing to let anything intrude on their resolute and by now ennobling composure.

The rest of us must have been a little awed; being with them was like being with a movie star.

We may have been excited, too, and secretly inspired, but all they seemed to want from us

was that we act as though nothing unusual was happening, and we were all too happy to comply.

She, though, once she'd found out about it—the girl apparently at first had kept it from her—

wasn't taking anything so calmly, wasn't having any of this stoicism, this holding back.

I don't know how, but she was all at once their chum, their confidante, their social secretary.

She was blazing with consideration for them, some unsuspected energy had been released in her.

She dropped her painting altogether now, and did good deeds for them instead: she was everywhere,

organizing quiet dinners, getting people to throw parties; she even once promoted a recital,

which was supposed to give some of our musicians an opportunity to play
        but which she turned—
and not in an unpleasantly pretentious way—into an elegant soiree and
        cocktail honoring them.
They became, in fact, as she took over, the unofficial guests of honor
        everywhere they went.
They hardly seemed to notice, though, and to hardly notice her; she was
        like a stage director,
rushing back and forth behind the scenes, keeping all the action moving
        unobtrusively along,
except it wasn't the audience which was supposed to be oblivious to all
        the cable-hauling,
the changing sets and lighting, but the innocent creatures out on the
        apron of the stage.
I often wondered, considering what they seemed to have wanted before
        she started in on that,
whether they were ever bothered by her benevolent chicanery; they
        didn't appear to be.
They could have stopped her, but their sorrow may have been more
        oppressive than we knew;
maybe there was something that they needed after all, maybe it was just
        that much attention.
Or it could all have been just another factor to be balanced in their bril-
        liant equation,
the way one of their mothers' clutching a tissue to an irrepressible tear
        would have been.
If they didn't have a problem with her machinations, though, I did; I
        found it all depressing.
I thought I knew what she was up to—a naked compensation for her fail-
        ures at the easel—
and I began to stay away from functions she was overseeing, which
        meant most of them by now.
I just kept to myself more, even if it meant afflicting myself with still
        more loneliness,
a loneliness the opposite of what I found in books, where you went off on
        your holy pilgrimage,
enriched yourself with arcane meditations on the universe, and then pro-
        duced your masterpiece.

My masterpiece, if I still could have a fantasy of such a thing, seemed
more buried every day
beneath the layers of confusion, uncertainty, and mental maladroitness
to which I was so susceptible.
I don't remember what finally brought me to the party where I saw the
three of them again.
It was just a night at someone's house; everyone was there, I was glad to
be there, too,
hearing other people's voices, breathing other people's breath, feeling
ordinary human warmth.
The young man still looked well enough, the two of them were sitting at
the piano, whispering.
She was near them; when she saw me, she came over, she was glad to see
me, where had I been?
There was something she'd been wanting to ask me; no, not right now,
wait, later on.
I couldn't conceive what question she might have for me, but I'd been by
myself so much
that any contact was intriguing, and besides, she looked, with her new air
of purpose, quite aglow.
As the party swirled on, I watched her; it was remarkable how she'd
involved herself with them.
I'd never thought of her as subtle but I had to recognize how much intel-
ligence she had for this.
She was always near them, but never overbearingly so; she was just
available to them,
they were always in a triangle with her, as though she possessed some
benign, proprietary power.
She'd bring them drinks and sandwiches, lead people over to them, lean
down to listen, laugh.
It seemed natural when she'd lightly touch the lover's shoulder, or stroke
the girl's hair.
Later on, I caught her hand and led her to the bedroom; what had she
been going to ask?
What she asked was if I knew anything to read on death; could I recom-
mend a book on death.
At first I didn't understand what she was saying, I couldn't register it, get
it down.

What? "You've read a lot of books," she said. "I need one to give to some-
    body who's dying."
She said it quietly, she was serious, almost solemn, but she was looking
    at my eyes this time.
"Something to comfort them," she added with conspiratorial intensity,
    "in their ordeal."
I don't remember what I answered, if I did—I may have said they're all
    on death, all books,
I still believed it sometimes in those days, it sometimes seemed the core
    of my aesthetic code.
What I'm hearing now is "Timor mortis conturbat me"—"The fear of
    death is killing me"—
but what I remember thinking then, with a desperate conviction, was
    that she'd beaten me:
she'd held her grudge this long, and then attacked, prevailed and won
    our little agon.
By assuming, or making believe that she assumed, I'd be so unaware of
    something of such moment,
she'd let me know I was an outcast among outcasts, subtracted from what
    society I had, a pretender,
and by turning my own medium against me, showing how absurd it
    would have been for me to think
that writing could heal or solace real grief, she'd proved that my preten-
    sions were a farce.
I think I was amazed that she'd have used her own good deeds to get at
    me, but more importantly,
I knew she'd touched some truth, and that something in me had been
    undermined so profoundly
that as I turned from her, although of course I wouldn't let her know, I
    must have almost staggered.
I think I doubted even then, though, how much my psychic storm really
    had to do with her.
I knew she didn't hate me *that* much, and that what had happened to us
    wasn't very deep.
No, it wasn't me she'd hated and wanted vengeance from, it was *art*; I
    was just the medium,
a handy means to rebel against art, to degrade it, express how much she
    despised it.

She'd chosen me to use—and this *had* hurt—because she knew I knew I
    wasn't really pure.
All my narcissism, all the juvenile self-indulgence that had let me think
    that as I was
I could still be an initiate in art's exalted realm, no matter how I lied and
    twisted my identity,
she'd long ago intuited, and finally struck with, and she may have even
    guessed—I hope not—
that in this moment I was living out what in turning to a life by art I'd
    been trying to evade.
I don't think I cared if she was taking satisfaction from my turmoil, she
    didn't matter anymore.
I beheld myself, and I was mortified, not because of anybody else's ideas
    or norms or values,
but for my own, all I'd studied and prepared for, which had suddenly
    become shameful to me.
"You must change your life": I knew Rilke's line already, now I had a
    hint of how it happened.
It's not easy to remember how much of what I later came to understand
    revealed itself that evening:
a mass of sad intention was set under way in me I've spent all these years
    trying to enact.
Right then I was most likely struck by just the wrongness of how I'd so far
    conceived my task.
I'd believed that art was everything, the final resolution of all my insecu-
    rity and strivings.
Now I realized that in attempting to create a character in art, someone
    who would live for art,
I'd turned away from something in myself, some lapse I hadn't glimpsed,
    and, more shocking still,
I knew that architecture, poetry, and painting weren't the self-containing
    glories I'd imagined,
but that they, too, could have evasions lurking in them, grievous cosmic
    flinchings from reality.
Art wasn't everything, nothing could be everything, but more crucially,
    art *needed* you:
I knew now that if you hated art, as she did, that was what you hated in it,
    that responsibility,

not to making up a self which might someday be worthy of ecstasy or
　　fame, but to art itself,
to the negating force it could become unless you understood what its
　　decisive limits were.
The power, the willed resolve I'd believed you needed for your work, I
　　knew now were elementary,
that arduous and obscure responsibility was what mattered most, and I
　　intuited, and *knew*,
that what it consisted of was a concern, for all of us, for every human
　　being: one by one.
The forms and substances were incidental, *we* were form and substance;
　　subject, object, reason.
"You must change your life." I knew then, or began to know, that what
　　art needed at the end
was an acceptance of what's muddled and confused in us, what's broken
　　by our lives and living.
To love art meant to love our errors; what we owed art was ourselves and
　　our imperfect world.
"Timor mortis conturbat me." "You must change your life." I was left
　　with my forbidding mottoes,
my attempts to overcome my unconfidence and indolence, and every
　　day my sorry stabs at poems.
Whether I used well what I learned that night, or if it changed me, how
　　am I to know?
Can we ever say in all good conscience we've really changed? We only
　　have our single story.
In mine, the physicist, the young man, the boy—what else would I think
　　he was by now?—
the poor boy dies sooner even than predicted; this all takes place in just
　　some months.
The boy dies, the girlfriend moves away; I see her work reviewed, years
　　later, in the *Times*;
they loved her: she was praised especially for her "mastery of expression":
　　good for her.
She—how specify her now? my antagonist? my demon other? the an-
　　tithesis in my groping dialectic?—
she drops from sight: I forgave her, but never heard another breath about
　　her, and never wanted to.

IV

A DREAM OF MIND

for Adam Zagajewski

The Method

A dream of method first, in which mind is malleable, its products as
        revisable as sentences,
in which I'll be able to extract and then illuminate the themes of being
        as I never have.
I'm intrigued—how not be?—but I soon realize that though so much
        flexibility is tempting—
whole zones of consciousness wouldn't only be reflected or referred to,
        but embodied, as themselves,
before the sense-stuff of the world is attached to them, adulterating and
        misrepresenting them—
I have only the sketchiest notion of how to incorporate this exotic and
        complicated methodology,
and when I try, something in my character resists manipulating elements
        of mind so radically.
Imagine being offered an instrument to play that violated all your previ-
        ous aesthetic norms,
with a fleshy, tender, sensitive component, crudely sewn or soldered to
        an innocently inorganic,
and a shape that hinted at the most contradictory techniques—brute
        force, a delicate dexterity.
You know you're supposed to draw this hybrid to your breast, to try to
        coax from it its music,
but under the tension of so many formal contradictions, what actually
        would you bring forth?
Isn't this like that? I'd be dreaming dreams of dreams, hammering out
        ideas of dreams:
wouldn't anything I'd come up with have to be a monstrous mix of sub-
        stance and intention?
Making something out of nothing; surely more than matters of order or
        proportion are at stake.
I feel myself go cold now, taken by a clarity that makes me ask if I'm not
        already in the dream,
if I'm not merely being tempted by it, in the sense that one is tempted by
        an ill desire.

What if all this theory's the equivalent of nightmare, its menace mas-
       querading as philosophy?
Can mind contort itself so recklessly and not endanger its most basic
       links to common sense?
I dream a dream of method, comprehending little of the real forces or
       necessities of dream,
and find myself entangled in the dream, entrapped, already caught in
       what the dream contrived,
in what it made, of my ambitions, or of what it itself aspired to for its
       darker dreaming.

Shadows

They drift unobtrusively into the dream, they linger, then they depart,
    but they emanate, always,
an essence of themselves, an aura, of just the frequency my mind needs
    to grasp and contain them.
Sometimes, though, the identity that I sense there, the person I feel inti-
    mated or implied,
is so fluid and changes so rapidly and dramatically that often I hardly
    know who I'm with.
Someone is there, then they're someone from another moment of my
    life, or even a stranger.
At first I find such volatile mutability surprisingly less agitating than I'd
    have thought,
probably because these others brought and taken away by the dream
    manifest such careless unconcern.
Before long, though, I feel apprehensive: I find that whenever someone
    in the dream changes,
I subtly alter who I am as well, so as to stay in a proper relation with this
    new arrival
who may already be somebody else, someone for whom the self I've
    come up with is obsolete.
Suddenly I'm never quite who I should be; beset by all this tenuous veer-
    ing and blurring,
my character has become the function of its own revisions; I'm a by-
    stander in my own dream.
Even my response to such flux is growing unstable; until now I've con-
    sidered it speculatively,
but what says I'm not going to stay in this epistemologically tremulous
    state forever?
I find I'm trying to think how to stop this, but trying to think in dream
    means, as always,   ·
trying to *do*, and what do now with this presence moving towards me,
    wavering, shifting,
now being itself, now another, webbed now in the shadows of memory,
    now brilliant, burning?

Am I to try to engage it, or turn back to myself to steel myself in a more
   pure concentration?
Even as I watch, it transfigures again; I see it, if it is it, as through ice, or
   a lens.
I feel a breath touch me now, but is it this breath I feel or someone's I
   haven't met yet,
is it a whisper I hear or the murmur of multitudes sensing each other
   closer within me?
How even tell who I am now, how know if I'll ever be more than the
   field of these interchangings?

Vocations

Blocks of time fall upon me, adhere for a moment, then move astonish-
ingly away, fleeting, dissolving,
but still I believe that these parcels of experience have a significance
beyond their accumulation,
that though they bear no evident relation besides being occasionally ad-
jacent to each other,
they can be considered in a way that implies consequence, what I come
to call the dream's "meaning."
Although I can't quite specify how this ostensible meaning differs from
the sum of its states,
it holds an allure, *solutions* are implied, so I keep winding the dream's
filaments onto its core.
The problem is that trying to make the recalcitrant segments of the
dream cohere is distracting;
my mind is always half following what happens while it's half involved in
this other procedure.
Also, my ideas about meaning keep sending directives into the dream's
already crowded circuits,
and soon I'm hard put keeping the whole intractable mechanism mov-
ing along smoothly enough
to allow me to believe that at least I'm making a not overly wasteful use
of my raw materials.
Although, doesn't the notion of "use" seem questionable, too? Use how,
and to what end?
To proliferate more complexities when I haven't come to terms with
those I've already proposed?
Mightn't all of this be only a part of the mind's longing to be other or
more than it is?
Sometimes I think I'd be better off letting the dream make its own way
without butting in so,
but no, I understand the chaos I might wreak if I left off these indispens-
able cohesions.
How depressing dream can feel now, nothing in it can move, everything
is suspended, waiting,

or, worse, not waiting, going on as it's always gone on but with such fear-
    ful, timid resolve
that I begin to wonder if all that keeps me going is my fear of random-
    ness, regression, chance.
It doesn't matter anymore: whatever dream meant once, whatever it
    might come to mean,
I know the only way I'll ever finish with this anguish is to understand
    it, and to understand
was what the dream promised, and what, with all its blundering hopes, it
    promises still.

The Solid

Although I'm apparently alone, with a pleasant but unextraordinary feel-
 ing of self-sufficiency,
I know I'm actually a part of a group of people who for reasons the dream
 never makes clear
are unavailable to any of my senses, though I'm always aware of the pres-
 sure of their presence.
No matter what else I'm doing, no matter how scant the attention I pay,
 I know they're there,
only my response to being in relation with beings I can only imagine
 alters now and again.
Usually I'm comforted: this intuition seems to impart to the dream such
 stability as it has.
Immersed with my mysterious companions in an enormous, benign,
 somehow consoling solid,
all that's required is that I not carelessly set jolts out into that sensitive
 bulk of otherness.
At other, nearly simultaneous moments, I feel signals sent, intentionally
 or not, I can't tell,
which arrive to my consciousness as an irritation, almost an abrasion of
 the material of thought.
In some far corner of dream, someone wants, needs, with such vehe-
 ment, unreasonable fervor,
that even from here I'm afflicted with what I can only believe is an
 equivalent chagrin.
I try to think of ways to send back if not reassurance then an acknowledg-
 ment of my concern,
but I realize this would require not only energy and determination but a
 discernment, a delicacy,
the mere thought of which intimidates me, reinforcing the sense I have
 of my ineffectiveness.
I begin to be afraid then, the dream is deteriorating; how vulnerable I am
 in my very connections.
Don't my worst anxieties rise out of just such ambiguous feelings of com-
 munion and debt?

I'm suddenly swamped, overwhelmed in these tangles of unasked-for
      sympathies and alliances.
Always then, though, through an operation whose workings I'm never
      forced to explain to myself,
I'm released, the limits of my selfhood are reestablished, the nascent
      nightmare subsides,
and I'm able to reassume the not-incongruous sense of being alone and
      with so many others,
with nothing asked of me more than what any reasonable dream needs
      for its reasonable dreaming,
and the most minor qualms as to what I may have traded for my peace of
      mind, and what lost.

The Charge

An insistence in dream on a succession of seemingly urgent but possibly
      purposeless tasks
to be executed for no evident reason beyond the tautological one that
      dream says they must.
The nature of these undertakings is unclear, imprecise, they can even
      change definition,
I can never find more than the most ambiguous grounds to justify my
      obsession with them.
It seems sometimes that far away in the past of the dream a shameful
      error was committed,
and that these obligations are only my share of a more general rectifica-
      tion or atonement.
Often I can't tell if what I'm doing is by any sane measure what I'm
      supposed to be doing,
or whether all my efforts are the groundwork for yet another, still more
      illogical dream.
I'm never unaware either that I'm squandering time; this undermines my
      self-assurance still more,
so, the dream still driving me through it, me still helplessly driving my-
      self through the dream,
I begin to think that persisting in this will put me into a state of such un-
      manageable consternation
that everything in me will simply go awry, leaving me tearing at myself in
      rages of frustration.
How long this has been under way, I can't tell; forever, it seems, all the
      time of the dream,
but maybe because I've looked back now, it comes to me that even
      should these needs be satisfied,
their compulsions slaked, it won't have been my doing: dream will just
      have pitied me,
given me surcease, not the satisfaction I'd anticipated despite all, but
      deflection and distraction.
All I'm left to hope for is that something other than nostalgia or regret
      awaits me,

that I won't end up longing for my labors, yearning for the solaces of
        goals I'd never grasped,
trying to remember when the dream of finishing what can't be finished
        ended, or if it did.

The Crime

Violence in the dream, violation of body and spirit; torment, mutilation,
   butchery, debasement.
At first it hardly feels real, there's something ceremonial in it, something
   of the dance.
The barbarisms seem formulaic, restrained, they cast a stillness about
   them, even a calm.
Then it comes once again, the torment, the debasement, and I have to
   accept that it's real.
Human beings are tearing each other to pieces, their rancor is real, and
   so is their pain.
Violence in the dream, but I still think—something wants me to think—
   there are *reasons*:
ideas are referred to, ideals, propositions of order, hierarchies, mores,
   structures of value.
Even in dream, though, I know it's not true, I know that if reasons there
   are, they're ill reasons.
Even in dream, I'm ashamed, and then, though I'm frightened, I steel
   myself and protest.
I protest, but the violence goes on, I cry out, but the pain, the rage, the
   rancor continue.
Then I suddenly realize I've said nothing at all, what I dreamed was spo-
   ken wasn't at all.
I dreamed I protested, I dreamed I cried out: I was mute, there was only
   an inarticulate moan.
What deceived me to think I'd objected when really I'd only cowered,
   embraced myself, moaned?
My incompetent courage deceived me, my too-timid hopes for the hu-
   man, my qualms, my doubts.
Besides the suspicion perhaps that the dream doesn't reveal the horror
   but draws it from itself,
that dream's truth is its violence, that its pity masks something I don't
   want to find there.
What I hear now in the dream is the dream lamenting, its sorrow, its fear,
   its cry.
Caught in the reasons of dream, I call out; caught in its sorrow, I know
   who I hear cry.

Shells

Shells of fearful insensitivity that I keep having to disadhere from my
   heart, how dream you?
How dream away these tireless reflexes of self-protection that almost
   define heart
and these sick startles of shame at confronting again the forms of fear the
   heart weaves,
the certitudes and the hatreds, the thoughtless fortifications of scarred,
   fearful self?
How dream you, heart hiding, how dream the products of heart foul with
   egotism and fear?
Heart's dream, the spaces holding you are so indistinct and the hurt
   place you lurk so tender,
that even in dream membranes veil and distort you, only fancy and
   falsehood hint where you are.
How can I dream the stripping away of the petrified membranes muf-
   fling the tremulous heart?
I reach towards the heart and attain only heart's stores of timidity, self-
   hatred, and blame;
the heart I don't dare bring to my zone of knowledge for fear it will
   shame me again,
afflict me again with its pettiness, coyness, its sham zeal, false pity, and
   false pride.
Dream of my heart, am I only able to dream illusions of you that touch
   me with pity or pride?
How dream the heart's sorrow to redeem what it contains beyond its self-
   defense and disdain?
How forgive heart when the part of me that beholds heart swells so in its
   pride and contempt?
Trying to dream the dream of the heart, I hide myself from it, I veil my
   failures and shame.
Heart, ever unworthy of you, lost in you, will I ever truly dream you, or
   dream beyond you?

Room

I wanted to take up room. What a strange dream! I wanted to take up as
    much room as I could,
to swell up, enlarge, crowd into a corner all the others in the dream with
    me, but why?
Something to do with love, it felt like, but what love needs more volume
    than it has?
Lust, then: its limitlessness, the lure of its ineluctable renewal — but this
    came before lust.
Fear? Yes, the others were always more real than I was, more concrete,
    emphatic: why not fear?
Though I knew that this was my dream, they were the given and I the
    eccentric, wobbling variable.
A dubious plasma, drifting among them, self-consciously sidling, flowing,
    ebbing among them,
no wonder my atoms would boil, trying to gel, and no wonder I'd some-
    times resent them,
brood on them, trying to understand what they were, what my connec-
    tion to them really was.
Sometimes I'd think the point of the dream was to find what of me was
    embodied in them.
What I was with them, though, what they finally were in themselves, I
    hardly could tell.
Sometimes they seemed beasts; I could see them only as beasts, captives
    of hunger and fear.
Sometimes they were angels, nearly on fire, embracing, gleaming with
    grace, gratitude, praise.
But when their lips touched, were they kissing, or gnawing the warmth
    from a maw?
So much threatening pain to each other, so much pain accomplished:
    no surprise I'd think beasts.
But still, I loved them; I wasn't just jealous of them, I loved them, was of
    them, and, more,
I'd grown somehow to know in the dream that part of my love meant ac-
    counting for them.

Account for them: how, though, why? Did they account for each other,
    would they for me?
That wasn't what the dream meant to be now; I loved them, I wasn't to
    ask if they loved me.
The fear, the loving and being loved, the accounting for and the wish to
    had all become one.
Dream, where have you brought me? What a strange dream! Who would
    have thought to be here?
Beasts, angels, taking up room, the ways of duty and love: what next,
    dream, where now?

History

I have escaped in the dream; I was in danger, at peril, at immediate, furi-
ous, frightening risk,
but I deftly evaded the risk, eluded the danger, I conned peril to think I'd
gone that way,
then I went this, then this way again, over the bridges of innocence, into
the haven of sorrow.
I was so shrewd in my moment of risk, so cool: I was as guileful as
though I were guilty,
sly, devious, cunning, though I'd done nothing in truth but be who I was
where I was
when the dream conceived me as a threat I wasn't, possessed of a power
I'd never had,
though I had found enough strength to flee and the guileful wherewithal
to elude and be free.
I have escaped and survived, but as soon as I think it, it starts again, I'm
hounded again:
no innocence now, no unlikeliest way, only this frenzied combing of the
countries of mind
where I always believed I'd find safety and solace but where now are con-
fusion and fear
and a turmoil so total that all I have known or might know drags me with
it towards chaos.
That, in this space I inhabit, something fearsome is happening, head-
long, with an awful momentum,
is never in doubt, but that's all I can say—no way even to be sure if I'm
victim or oppressor;
absurd after all this not to know if I'm subject or object, scapegoat, per-
petrator, or prey.
The dream is of beings like me, assembled, surrounded, herded like
creatures, driven, undone.
And beings like me, not more like me but like me, assemble and herd
them, us; undo us.
No escape now, no survival: captured, subjugated, undone, we all move
through dreams of negation.

Subject, object, dream doesn't care; accumulate or subtract, self as so-
lace, self-blame.

Thou shalt, thou shalt not; thus do I, thus I do not: dream is indifferent,
bemused, abstracted.

Formulation, abstraction; assembly, removal: the dream detached; exal-
tation, execration, denial.

The Gap

So often and with such cruel fascination I have dreamed the implacable
      void that contains dream.
The space there, the silence, the scrawl of trajectories tracked, traced,
      and let go;
the speck of matter in non-matter; sphere, swing, the puff of agglutinate
      loose-woven tissue;
the endless pull of absence on self, the sad molecule of the self in its
      chunk of duration;
the desolate grain, flake, fragment of mind that thinks when the mind
      thinks it's thinking.
So often, too, with equal absorption, I have dreamed the end of it all:
      mind, matter, void.
I'm appalled, but I do it again, I dream it again, it comes uncalled for but
      it comes, always,
rising perhaps out of the fearful demands consciousness makes for link-
      age, coherence, congruence,
connection to something beyond, even if dread: mystery exponentially
      functioned to dread.
Again, premonitions of silence, the swoop through a gulf that might be
      inherent in mind
as though mind bore in its matter its own end and the annulment of
      everything else.
Somehow I always return in the dream from the end, from the meaning-
      less, the mesh of despair,
but what if I don't once, what if the corrections fail once and I can't re-
      cover the thread
that leads back from that night beyond night that absorbs night as night
      absorbs innocent day?
The whole of being untempered by self, the great selves beyond self all
      wholly wound out;
sense neutered, knowledge betrayed: what if this is the real end of dream,
      facing the darkness
and subjecting the self yet again to imperious laws of doubt and denial
      which are never repealed?

How much can I do this, how often rejuvenate and redeem with such
      partial, imperfect belief?
So often, by something like faith, I'm brought back in the dream; but
      this, too; so often this, too.

The Knot

Deciphering and encoding, to translate, fabricate, revise; the abstract
    star, the real star;
crossing over boundaries we'd never known were there until we found
    ourselves beyond them.
A fascination first: this was why the dream existed, so our definitions
    would be realized.
Then more than fascination as we grasped how dream could infiltrate
    the mundane with its radiance.
There'd be no mundane anymore: wholly given to the dream, our debil-
    itating skepticisms overcome,
we'd act, or would be acted on—the difference, if there'd been one,
    would have been annulled—
with such purity of motive and such temperate desire that outcome
    would result from inspiration
with the same illumination that the notion of creation brings when it
    first comes upon us.
No question now of fabricating less ambiguous futures, no trying to re-
    cast recalcitrant beginnings.
It would be another empire of determination, in which all movement
    would be movement towards—
mergings, joinings—and in which existence would be generated from
    the qualities of our volition:
intention flowing outwards into form and back into itself in intricate
    threadings and weavings,
intuitions shaped as logically as crystal forms in rock, a linkage at the
    incandescent core,
knots of purpose we would touch into as surely as we touch the rippling
    lattice of a song.
No working out of what we used to call identity; our consummations
    would consist of acts,
of participating in a consciousness that wouldn't need, because it grew
    from such pure need,
acknowledgment or subject: we'd be held in it, always knowing there
    were truths beyond it.

Cleansed even of our appetite for bliss, we'd only want to know the ground of our new wonder,

and we wouldn't be surprised to find that it survived where we'd known it had to all along,

in all for which we'd blamed ourselves, repented and corrected, and never for a moment understood.

The Fear

In my dream of unspecific anxiety, nothing is what it should be, nothing
    acts as it should;
everything shifts, shudders, won't hold still long enough for me to name
    or constrain it.
The fear comes with no premonition, no flicker in the daily surges and
    currents of dream.
Momentums, inertias, then logic distends, distorts, bends in convulsive
    postures of scorn.
All I hold dear rushes away in magnetic repulsion to me, ravaged as
    though by a storm,
but I know that I myself am the storm, I am the force that daunts, threat-
    ens, rages, repels.
I am like time, I gather the things of creation and drive them out from
    me towards an abyss.
All I call beauty is ravaged, transcendence hauled back in a gust to cor-
    poreal swarm.
I never believe that the part of me which is fear can raze all the rest with
    such fury,
even the flesh is depleted, forsaken; I'm no longer spirit or flesh but lost
    within both,
negated, forlorn, a thing the dream can capture and propel through itself
    any way it desires.
Nothing to hope for now but more concrete fears that at least might re-
    veal their reason.
Nothing to dream but silence and forgetting; everything failing, even the
    wanting to be.

You

Such longing, such urging, such warmth towards, such force towards, so
       much ardor and desire;
to touch, touch into, hold, hold against, to feel, feel against and long to-
       wards again,
as though the longing, urge and warmth were ends in themselves, the
       increase of themselves,
the force towards, the ardor and desire, focused, increased, the incarna-
       tion of themselves.
All this in the body of dream, all in the substance of dream; allure, at-
       traction and need,
the force so consumed and rapt in its need that dream might have
       evolved it from itself,
except the ardor urges always towards the other, towards you, and with-
       out you it decays,
becomes vestige, reflex, the defensive attempt to surmount instinctual
       qualms and misgivings.
No qualms now, no misgivings; no hesitancy or qualifications in longing
       towards you;
no frightened wish to evolve ideals to usurp qualm, fear or misgiving, not
       any longer.
The longing towards you sure now, ungeneralized, certain, the urge now
       towards you in yourself,
your own form of nearness, the surface of desire multiplied in the need
       that urges from you,
your longing, your urging, the force and the warmth from you, the sure
       ardor blazing in you.

To Listen

In the dream of death where I listen, the voices of the dream keep dimin-
 ishing, fading away.
The dead are speaking, my dead are speaking, what they say seems ur-
 gent, to me, to themselves,
but as I try to capture more clearly what I heard just moments ago, the
 voices ebb and it's lost;
what's more, my impatience to know what was said seems to drive it fur-
 ther out of my ken.
In the dream of death where I listen, I keep thinking my dead have a
 message for me:
maybe they'll tell me at last why they must always die in the dream, live,
 die, die again.
I still can't hear what they say, though; I force my senses into the silence
 but nothing is there.
Sometimes I listen so hard I think what I'm waiting to hear must already
 have been spoken,
it's here, its echo surrounds me, I just have to learn to bring it more
 clearly within me
and I'll know at last what I never thought I would know about death and
 the dead and the speech
of affection the dead speak that stays on in the sentient space between
 living and after.
For the dead speak from affection, dream says, there's kindness in the
 voices of the dead.
I listen again, but I still hear only fragments of the elaborate discourse
 the dead speak;
when I try to capture its gist more is effaced, there are only faded words
 strewn on the page
of my soul that won't rest from its need to have what it thinks it can have
 from the dead.
Something is in me like greed now, I can't stop trying to tear the silence
 away from the voices,
I tear at the actual voices, though I know what the dead bring us is not to
 be held,

that the wanting to hold it is just what condemns dream to this pained,
    futile listening,
is what brings dream finally to its end, in silence, in want, in believing
    it's lost,
only for now, my dream thinks, at least let it be only for now, my forsaken
    dream thinks,
what the dead brought, what the dead found in their kind, blurred, weary
    voices to bring.

The Covenant

In my unlikeliest dream, my dead are with me again, companions again,
      in an ordinary way;
nothing of major moment to accomplish, no stains to cleanse, no oaths
      or debts to redeem:
my dead are serene, composed, as though they'd known all along how
      this would be.
Only I look aslant, only I brood and fret, marvel; only I have to know
      what this miracle is:
I'm awed, I want to embrace my newly found dead, to ask why they had
      to leave me so abruptly.
In truth, I think, I want pity from them, for my being bereft, for my grief
      and my pain.
But my dead will have none of my sorrow, of my asking how they came
      to be here again.
They anoint me with their mild regard and evidence only the need to
      continue, go on
in a dream that's almost like life in how only the plainest pastimes of love
      accumulate worth.
Cured of all but their presence, they seem only to want me to grasp their
      new way of being.
At first I feel nothing, then to my wonder and perhaps, too, the wonder
      of the dead,
I sense an absence in them, of will, of anything like will, as though will
      in the soul
had for the dead been all given over, transfigured, to humility, resigna-
      tion, submission.
I know without knowing how that the dead can remember the move-
      ments of will, thought willing,
the gaze fixed at a distance that doesn't exist, the mind in its endless war
      with itself—
those old cravings—but the striving to will themselves from themselves is
      only a dream,
the dead know what death has brought is all they need now because all
      else was already possessed,

all else was a part of the heart as it lived, in what it had seen and what it
    had suffered,
in the love it had hardly remarked coming upon it, so taken it was with
    its work of volition.
I can hardly believe that so little has to be lost to find such good fortune
    in death,
and then, as I dream again the suspensions of will I'm still only just able
    to dream,
I suddenly know I've beheld death myself, and instead of the terror, the
    flexions of fear,
the repulsion, recoil, impatience to finish, be done with the waiting once
    and for all,
I feel the same surge of acceptance, patience, and joy I felt in my dead
    rising in me:
I know that my dead have brought what I've restlessly waited all the life
    of the dream for.
I wait in joy as they give themselves to the dream once again; waiting,
    I'm with them again.

Light

Always in the dream I seemed conscious of myself having the dream
    even as I dreamed it.
Even now, the dream moving towards light, the field of light flowing
    gently towards me,
I watch myself dreaming, I watch myself dreaming and watching, I
    watch both watchers together.
It almost seems that this is what dream is about, to think what happens as
    it's happening.
Still, aren't there disturbing repercussions in being in such an active re-
    lation with dream?
What about nightmare, for instance; nightmare is always lurking there
    out at the edges,
it's part of dream's definition: how be so involved in the intimate work-
    ings of dream
without being an accomplice of nightmare, a portion of its cause or even
    its actual cause?
Doesn't what comes to me have to be my fault, and wouldn't the alterna-
    tive be more troubling still —
that I might *not* be the one engendering this havoc, that I'm only al-
    lowed to think so,
that the nightmare itself, hauling me through its vales of anguish, is the
    operative force?
What do I mean by nightmare itself, though? Wouldn't that imply a
    mind here besides mine?
But how else explain all the *care*, first to involve me, then to frighten me
    out of my wits?
Mustn't something with other agendas be shaping the dream; don't all
    the enticements and traps
suggest an intention more baleful than any I'd have for visiting such
    mayhem on myself?
And if this isn't the case, wouldn't the alternative be as bad; that each
    element of the dream
would contain its own entailment so that what came next would just do
    so for no special reason?

How frivolous dream would be, then: either way, though, so much subjugation, so little choice.

Either way, isn't the real nightmare my having so little power, *even over my own consciousness?*

Sometimes, when I arrive in dream here, when I arrive nearly overwhelmed with uncertainty here,

I feel a compulsion to renounce what so confounds me, to abdicate, surrender, but to what?

I don't even know if my despair might not be another deception the devious dream is proposing.

At last, sometimes, perhaps driven to this, perhaps falling upon it in exhaustion or resignation,

I try to recapture how I once dreamed, innocently, with no thought of being beside or beyond:

I imagine myself in that healing accord I still somehow believe must precede or succeed dream.

My vigilance never flags, though; I behold the infernal beholder, I behold the uncanny beheld,

this mind streaming through me, its turbulent stillness, its murmur, inexorable, beguiling.

V

Helen

1.

More voice was in her cough tonight: its first harsh, stripping sound
    would weaken abruptly,
and he'd hear the voice again, not hers, unrecognizable, its notes from
    somewhere else,
someone saying something they didn't seem to want to say, in a tongue
    they hadn't mastered,
or a singer, diffident and hesitating, searching for a place to start an un-
    familiar melody.

Its pitch was gentle, almost an interrogation, intimate, a plea, a moan,
    almost sexual,
but he could hear assertion, too, a straining from beneath, a forcing at
    the withheld consonant,
and he realized that she was holding back, trying with great effort not to
    cough again,
to change the spasm to a tone instead and so avert the pain that lurked
    out at the stress.

Then he heard her lose her almost-word, almost-song: it became a groan,
    the groan a gasp,
the gasp a sigh of desperation, then the cough rasped everything away,
    everything was cough now,
he could hear her shuddering, the voice that for a moment seemed the
    gentlest part of her,
choked down, effaced, abraded, taken back, as all of her was being taken
    from him now.

2.

In the morning she was standing at the window; he lay where he was and
    quietly watched her.

A sound echoed in from somewhere, she turned to listen, and he was
        shocked at how she moved:
not *enough* moved, just her head, pivoting methodically, the mecha-
        nisms slowed nearly to a halt,
as though she was afraid to jar herself with the contracting tendons and
        skeletal leverings.

A flat, cool, dawn light washed in on her: how pale her skin was, how
        dull her tangled hair.
So much of her had burned away, and what was left seemed draped list-
        lessly upon her frame.
It was her eye that shocked him most, though; he could only see her pro-
        file, and the eye in it,
without fire or luster, was strangely isolated from her face, and even from
        her character.

For the time he looked at her, the eye existed not as her eye, his wife's,
        his beloved's eye,
but as *an* eye, an object, so emphatic, so pronounced, it was separate
        both from what it saw
and from who saw with it: it could have been a creature's eye, a member
        of that larger class
which simply indicated sight and not that essence which her glance had
        always brought him.

It came to him that though she hadn't given any sign, she knew that he
        was watching her.
He was saddened that she'd tolerate his seeing her as she was now, weak,
        disheveled, haggard.
He felt that they were both involved, him watching, her letting him, in a
        depressing indiscretion:
she'd always, after all their time together, only offered him the images
        she thought he wanted.

She'd known how much he needed beauty, how much presumed it as
        the elemental of desire.
The loveliness that illuminated her had been an engrossing narrative his
        spirit fed on;

he entered it and flowed out again renewed for having touched within
and been a part of it.
In his meditations on her, he'd become more complicated, fuller, more
essential to himself.

It was to her beauty he'd made love at first, she was there within its cap-
tivating light,
but was almost secondary, as though she was just the instance of some
overwhelming generality.
She herself was shy before it; she, too, as unassumingly as possible was
testing this abstraction
which had taken both of them into its sphere, rendering both subservient
to its serene enormity.

As their experience grew franker, and as she learned to move more con-
fidently towards her core,
became more overtly active in elaborating needs and urges, her beauty
still came first.
In his memory, it seemed to him that they'd unsheathed her from the
hazes of their awe,
as though her unfamiliar, fiery, famished nakedness had been disclosed
as much to her as to him.

She'd been grateful to him, and that gratitude became in turn another
fact of his desire.
Her beauty had acknowledged him, allowed him in its secret precincts,
let him be its celebrant,
an implement of its luxurious materiality, and though he remained as-
tonished by it always,
he fulfilled the tasks it demanded of him, his devotions reinvigorated and
renewed.

3.

In the deepest sense, though, he'd never understood what her beauty was
or really meant.
If you only casually beheld her, there were no fanfares, you were taken
by no immolating ecstasies.

It amused him sometimes seeing other men at first not really understand-
　　ing what they saw;
no one dared to say it, but he could feel them holding back their disap-
　　pointment or disbelief.

Was this Helen, mythic Helen, this female, fleshed like any other, im-
　　perfect and approachable?
He could understand: he himself, when he'd first seen her, hadn't really;
　　he'd even thought,
before he'd registered her spirit and intelligence, before her laughter's
　　melodies had startled him—
if only one could alter such and such, improve on this or that: he hardly
　　could believe it now.

But so often he'd watched others hear her speak, or laugh, look at her
　　again, and fall in love,
as puzzled as he'd been at the time they'd wasted while their raptures of
　　enchantment took.
Those who hadn't ever known her sometimes spoke of her as though she
　　were his thing, his toy,
but that implied something static in her beauty, and she was surely just
　　the opposite of that.

If there was little he'd been able to explain of what so wonderfully ab-
　　sorbed him in her,
he knew it was a movement and a process, that he was taken towards and
　　through her beauty,
touched by it but even more participating in its multiplicities, the revela-
　　tions of its grace.
He felt himself becoming real in her, tangible, as though before he'd
　　only half existed.

Sometimes he would even feel it wasn't really him being brought to such
　　unlikely fruition.
Absurd that anyone so coarse and ordinary should be in touch with such
　　essential mystery:
something else, beyond him, something he would never understand,
　　used him for its affirmations.

What his reflections came to was something like humility, then a grati-
tude of his own.

4.

The next night her cough was worse, with a harsher texture, the spasms
came more rapidly,
and they'd end with a deep, complicated emptying, like the whining flat-
tening of a bagpipe.
The whole event seemed to need more labor: each cough sounded more
futile than the last,
as though the effort she'd made and the time lost making it had added to
the burden of illness.

Should he go to her? He felt she'd moved away from him, turning more
intently towards herself.
Her sickness absorbed her like a childbirth; she seemed almost like some-
one he didn't know.
There'd been so many Helens, the first timid girl, then the sensual Helen
of their years together,
then the last, whose grace had been more intricate and difficult to know
and to exult in.

How childishly frightened he'd always been by beauty's absence, by its
destruction or perversity.
For so long he let himself be tormented by what he knew would have to
happen to her.
He'd seen the old women as their thighs and buttocks bloated, then with-
ered and went slack,
as their dugs dried, skin dried, legs were sausaged with the veins that rose
like kelp.

He'd tried to overcome himself, to feel compassion towards them, but,
perhaps because of her,
he'd felt only a shameful irritation, as though they were colluding in
their loss.
Whether they accepted what befell them, even, he would think, gladly
acquiescing to it,

or fought it, with all their sad and valiant unguents, dyes, and ointments,
    was equally degrading.

His own body had long ago become a ruin, but beauty had never been a
    part of what he was.
What would happen to his lust, and to his love, when time came to sav-
    age and despoil her?
He already felt his will deserting him; for a long time, though, nothing
    touched or dulled her:
perhaps she really was immortal, maybe his devotion kept her from the
    steely rakings of duration.

Then, one day, something at her jowls; one day her hips; one day the
    flesh at her elbows . . .
One day, one day, one day he looked at her and knew that what he'd
    feared so was upon them.
He couldn't understand how all his worst imaginings had come to pass
    without his noticing.
Had he all this while been blind, or had he not wanted to acknowledge
    what he'd dreaded?

He'd been gazing at her then; in her wise way, she'd looked back at him,
    and touched him,
and he knew she'd long known what was going on in him: another admi-
    ration took him,
then another fire, and that simply, he felt himself closer to her: there'd
    been no trial,
nothing had been lost, of lust, of love, and something he'd never
    dreamed would be was gained.

5.

With her in the darkness now, not even touching her, he sensed her
    fever's suffocating dryness.
He couldn't, however much he wanted to, not let himself believe she
    was to be no more.
And there was nothing he could do for her even if she'd let him; he tried
    to calm himself.

400

Her cough was hollow, soft, almost forgiving, ebbing slowly through the
volumes of her thorax.

He could almost hear that world as though from in her flesh: the current
of her breath,
then her breastbone, ribs, and spine, taking on the cough's vibrations,
giving back their own.
Then he knew precisely how she was within herself as well, he was with
her as he'd never been:
he'd unmoored in her, cast himself into the night of her, and perceived
her life with her.

All she'd lived through, all she'd been and done, he could feel accumu-
lated in this instant.
The impressions and sensations, feelings, dreams, and memories were
tearing loose in her,
had disconnected from each other and randomly begun to float, collide,
collapse, entangle;
they were boiling in a matrix of sheer chance, suspended in a purely
mental universe of possibility.

He knew that what she was now to herself, what she remembered, might
not in truth have ever been.
Who, then, was she now, who was the person she had been, if all she
was, all he still so adored,
was muddled, addled, mangled: what of her could be repository now, the
place where she existed?
When everything was shorn from her, what within this flux of fragments
still stayed her?

He knew then what he had to do: he was so much of her now and she of
him that she was his,
her consciousness and memory both his, he would will her into him,
keep her from her dissolution.
All the wreckage of her fading life, its shattered hours taken in this fear-
ful flood,
its moments unrecoverable leaves twirling in a gust across a waste of loss,
he drew into himself,

and held her, kept her, all the person she had been was there within his
    sorrow and his longing:
it didn't matter what delirium had captured her, what of her was being
    lacerated, rent,
his pain had taken on a power, his need for her became a force that he
    could focus on her;
there was something in him like triumph as he shielded her within the
    absolute of his affection.

Then he couldn't hold it, couldn't keep it, it was all illusion, a confec-
    tion of his sorrow:
there wasn't room within the lenses of his mortal being to contain what
    she had been,
to do justice to a single actual instant of her life and soul, a single mo-
    ment of her mind,
and he released her then, let go of this diminished apparition he'd cre-
    ated from his fear.

But still, he gave himself to her, without moving moved to her: she was
    still his place of peace.
He listened for her breath: was she still here with him, did he have her
    that way, too?
He heard only the flow of the silent darkness, but he knew now that in it
    they'd become it,
their shells of flesh and form, the old delusion of their separateness and
    incompletion, gone.

When one last time he tried to bring her image back, she was as vivid as
    he'd ever seen her.
What they were together, everything they'd lived, all that seemed so frag-
    ile, bound in time,
had come together in him, in both of them: she had entered death, he
    was with her in it.
Death was theirs, she'd become herself again; her final, searing loveli-
    ness had been revealed.

THE VIGIL

[1997]

I

The Neighbor

Her five horrid, deformed little dogs, who incessantly yap on the roof
      under my window;
her cats, god knows how many, who must piss on her rugs—her landing's
      a sickening reek;
her shadow, once, fumbling the chain on her door, then the door slam-
      ming fearfully shut:
only the barking, and the music, jazz, filtering as it does day and night
      into the hall.

The time it was Chris Conner singing "Lush Life," how it brought back
      my college sweetheart,
my first real love, who, till I left her, played the same record, and, head
      on my shoulder,
hand on my thigh, sang sweetly along, of regrets and depletions she was
      too young for,
as I was too young, later, to believe in her pain: it startled, then bored,
      then repelled me.

My starting to fancy she'd ended up in this firetrap in the Village, that
      my neighbor was her;
my thinking we'd meet, recognize one another, become friends, that I'd
      accomplish a penance;
my seeing her—it wasn't her—at the mailbox, grey-yellow hair, army
      pants under a nightgown:
her turning away, hiding her ravaged face in her hands, muttering an
      inappropriate "Hi."

Sometimes, there are frightening goings-on in the stairwell, a man shout-
      ing *Shut up!*
the dogs frantically snarling, claws scrabbling, then her, her voice,
      hoarse, harsh, hollow,
almost only a tone, incoherent, a note, a squawk, bone on metal, metal
      gone molten,

calling them back, Come back, darlings; come back, dear ones, my
sweet angels, come back.

Medea she was, next time I saw her, sorceress, tranced, ecstatic, stock-
still on the sidewalk,
ragged coat hanging agape, passersby flowing around her, her mouth
torn suddenly open,
as though in a scream, silently though, as though only in her brain or
breast had it erupted:
a cry so pure, practiced, detached, it had no need of a voice or could no
longer bear one.

These invisible links that allure, these transfigurations even of anguish
that hold us:
the girl, my old love, the last, lost time I saw her, when she came to find
me at a party:
her drunkenly stumbling, falling, sprawling, skirt hiked, eyes veined red,
swollen with tears;
her shame, her dishonor; my ignorant, arrogant coarseness; my secret
pride, my turning away.

Still life on a roof top: dead trees in barrels, a bench, broken; dogs, excre-
ment, sky.
What pathways through pain, what junctures of vulnerability, what cross-
ings and counterings?
Too many lives in our lives already, too many chances for sorrow, too
many unaccounted-for pasts.
Behold me, the god of frenzied, inexhaustible love says, rising in bloody
splendor: *Behold me!*

Her making her way down the littered vestibule stairs, one agonized step
at a time;
my holding the door, her crossing the fragmented tiles, faltering at the
step to the street,
droning, not looking at me, "Can you help me?" taking my arm, leaning
lightly against me;
her wavering step into the world, her whispering, "Thanks, love," lightly,
lightly against me.

Dominion: Depression

I don't know what day or year of their secret cycle this blazing golden
     afternoon might be,
but out in the field in a shrub hundreds of pairs of locusts are locked in
     a slow sexual seizure.

Hardly more animate than the few leaves they haven't devoured, they
     seethe like a single being,
limbs, antennas, and wings all tangled together as intricately as a layer of
     neurons.

Always the neat, tight, gazeless helmet, the exoskeleton burnished like
     half-hardened glue;
always the abdomen twitched deftly under or aside, the skilled rider, the
     skillfully ridden.

One male, though, has somehow severed a leg, it sways on the spike of a
     twig like a harp:
he lunges after his female, tilts, falls; the mass horribly shudders, shifts,
     realigns.

So dense, so hard, so immersed in their terrible need to endure, so un-
     like me but like me,
why do they seem such a denial, why do I feel if I plunged my hand in
     among them I'd die?

This must be what god thinks, beholding his ignorant, obstinate, libidi-
     nally maniacal offspring:
wanting to stop them, to keep them from being so much an image of his
     impotence or his will.

How divided he is from his creation: even here near the end he sees
     moving towards him
a smaller, sharper, still more gleaming something, extracting moist mat-
     ter from a skull.

No more now: he waits, fists full of that mute, oily, crackling, crystalline
    broil,
then he feels at last the cool wingbeat of the innocent void moving in
    again over the world.

Fragment

This time the holdup man didn't know a video-sound camera hidden up
     in a corner
was recording what was before it or more likely he didn't care, opening
     up with his pistol,
not saying a word, on the clerk you see blurredly falling and you hear—I
     keep hearing—
crying, "God! God!" in that voice I was always afraid existed within us,
     the voice that knows
beyond illusion the irrevocability of death, beyond any dream of being
     not mortally injured—
*"You're just going to sleep, someone will save you, you'll wake again, loved
     ones beside you . . ."*
Nothing of that: even torn by the flaws in the tape it was a voice that
     knew it was dying,
knew it was being—horrible—slaughtered, all that it knew and aspired to
     instantly voided;
such hopeless, astonished pleading, such overwhelmed, untempered pity
     for the self dying;
no indignation, no passion for justice, only woe, woe, woe, as he felt
     himself falling,
even falling knowing already he was dead, and how much I pray to my-
     self I want not, ever,
to know this, how much I want to ask why I must, with such perfect, de-
     tailed precision,
know this, this anguish, this agony for a self departing wishing only to
     stay, to endure,
knowing all the while that, having known, I always will know this torn,
     singular voice
of a soul calling "God!" as it sinks back through the darkness it came
     from, cancelled, annulled.

The Hovel

Slate scraps, split stone, third hand splintering timber; rusted nails and
      sheet-tin;
dirt floor, chinks the wind seeps through, the stink of an open sewer
      streaming behind;
rags, flies, stench, and never, it seems, clear air, light, a breeze of benev-
      olent clemency.

My hut, my home, the destiny only deferred of which all I live now is
      deflection, illusion:
war, plunder, pogrom; crops charred, wife ravished, children starved,
      stolen, enslaved;
muck, toil, hunger, never a moment for awareness, of birdsong, of dawn's
      immaculate stillness.

Back bent, knees shattered, teeth rotting; fever and lesion, the physical
      knowledge of evil;
illiterate, numb, insensible, superstitious, lurching from lust to hunger to
      unnameable dread:
the true history I inhabit, its sea of suffering, its wave to which I am froth,
      scum.

My Fly

for Erving Goffman, 1922–1982

One of those great, garishly emerald flies that always look freshly gener-
      ated from fresh excrement
and who maneuver through our airspace with a deft intentionality that
      makes them seem to think,
materializes just above my desk, then vanishes, his dense, abrasive buzz
      sucked in after him.

I wait, imagine him, hidden somewhere, waiting, too, then think, who
      knows why, of you—
don't laugh—that he's a messenger from you, or that you yourself (you'd
      howl at this),
ten years afterwards have let yourself be incarnated as this pestering anti-
      angel.

Now he, or you, abruptly reappears, with a weightless pounce alighting
      near my hand.
I lean down close, and though he has to sense my looming presence, he
      patiently attends,
as though my study of him had become an element of his own observa-
      tions—maybe it is you!

Joy! To be together, even for a time! Yes, tilt your fuselage, turn it towards
      the light,
aim the thousand lenses of your eyes back up at me: how I've missed the
      layers of your attention,
how often been bereft without your gift for sniffing out pretentiousness
      and moral sham.

Why would you come back, though? Was that other radiance not intri-
      cate enough to parse?
Did you find yourself in some monotonous century hovering down the
      tidy queue of creatures
waiting to experience again the eternally unlikely bliss of being matter
      and extension?

You lift, you land—you're rushed, I know; the interval in all our termi-
    nals is much too short.
Now you hurl against the window, skid and jitter on the pane: I open it
    and step aside
and follow for one final moment of felicity your brilliant ardent atom
    swerving through.

Hercules, Deianira, Nessus

from Ovid, Metamorphoses, *Book IX*

There was absolutely no reason after the centaur had pawed her and
      tried to mount her,
after Hercules waiting across the raging river for the creature to carry her
      to him
heard her cry out and launched an arrow soaked in the hydra's incurable
      venom into the monster,
that Deianira should have believed him, Nessus, horrible thing, as he
      died but she did.

We see the end of the story: Deianira anguished, aghast, suicide-sword in
      her hand;
Hercules' blood hissing and seething like water in which molten rods are
      plunged to anneal,
but how could a just-married girl hardly out of her father's house have
      envisioned all that,
and even conjecturing that Nessus was lying, plotting revenge, how
      could she have been sure?

We see the centaur as cunning, malignant, a hybrid from the savage time
      before ours
when emotion always was passion and passion was always unchecked by
      commandment or conscience;
she sees only a man-horse, mortally hurt, suddenly harmless, eyes sud-
      denly soft as a foal's,
telling her, "Don't be afraid, come closer, listen": offering homage,
      friendship, a favor.

In our age of scrutiny and dissection we know Deianira's mind better
      than she does herself:
we know the fortune of women as chattel and quarry, objects to be won
      then shunted aside;
we understand the cost of repression, the repercussions of unsatisfied
      rage and resentment,
but consciousness then was still new, Deianira inhabited hers like the
      light from a fire.

Or might she have glimpsed with that mantic prescience the gods hadn't
  yet taken away
her hero a lifetime later on the way home with another king's daughter,
  callow, but lovely,
lovely enough to erase from Hercules' scruples not only his vows but the
  simple convention
that tells you you don't bring a rival into your aging wife's weary, sorrow-
  ful bed?

. . . No, more likely the centaur's promise intrigued in itself: an infalli-
  ble potion of love.
"Just gather the clots of blood from my wound: here, use my shirt, then
  hide it away.
Though so exalted, so regal a woman as you never would need it, it
  might still be of use:
whoever's shoulders it touches, no matter when, will helplessly, hope-
  lessly love you forever."

See Hercules now in the shirt Deianira has sent him approaching the
  fire of an altar,
the garment suddenly clinging, the hydra, his long-vanquished foe, alive
  in its threads,
each thread a tentacle clutching at him, each chemical tentacle acid,
  adhering, consuming,
charring before his horrified eyes skin from muscle, muscle from tendon,
  tendon from bone.

Now Deianira, back then, the viscous gouts of Nessus' blood dyeing her
  diffident hands:
if she could imagine us watching her there in her myth, how would she
  want us to see her?
Surely as symbol, a petal of sympathy caught in the perilous rift between
  culture and chaos,
not as the nightmare she'd be, a corpse with a slash of tardy self-
  knowledge deep in its side.

What Hercules sees as he pounds up the bank isn't himself cremated
  alive on his pyre,

shrieking as Jove his Olympian father extracts his immortal essence from
      its agonized sheathing—
he sees what's before him: the woman, his bride, kneeling to the dark,
      rushing river,
obsessively scrubbing away, he must think, the nocuous, mingled reek of
      horse, hydra, human.

Instinct

Although he's apparently the youngest (his little Rasta-beard is barely
        down and feathers),
most casually connected (he hardly glances at the girl he's with, though
        she might be his wife),
half-sloshed (or more than half) on picnic-whiskey teenaged father,
        when his little son,
two or so, tumbles from the slide, hard enough to scare himself, hard
        enough to make him cry,
really cry, not partly cry, not pretend the fright for what must be some
        scarce attention,
but really let it out, let loudly be revealed the fear of having been so close
        to real fear,
he, the father, knows just how quickly he should pick the child up, then
        how firmly hold it,
fit its head into the muscled socket of his shoulder, rub its back, croon
        and whisper to it,
and finally pull away a little, about a head's length, looking, still con-
        cerned, into its eyes,
then smiling, broadly, brightly, as though something had been shared,
        something of importance,
not dreadful, or not very, not at least now that it's past, but rather some-
        thing . . . funny,
funny, yes, it was funny, wasn't it, to fall and cry like that, though one
        certainly can understand,
we've all had glimpses of a premonition of the anguish out there, you're
        better now, though,
aren't you, why don't you go back and try again, I'll watch you, maybe
        have another drink,
yes, my son, my love, I'll go back and be myself now: you go be the per-
        son you are, too.

Time: 1976

1.

Time for my break; I'm walking from my study down the long hallway
      towards the living room.
Catherine is there, on the couch, reading to Jed, the phonograph is play-
      ing Bach's *Offering*.
I can just hear Catherine's voice as she shows Jed the pictures: *Voilà le*
      château, voilà Babar,
and with no warning I'm taken with a feeling that against all logic I rec-
      ognize to be regret,
as violent and rending a regret as anything I've ever felt, and I under-
      stand immediately
that all of this familiar beating and blurring, the quickening breath, the
      gathering despair,
almost painful all, has to do with the moment I'm in, and my mind, rac-
      ing to keep order,
thrusts this way and that and finally casts itself, my breath along with it,
      into the future.

2.

Ten years from now, or twenty; I'm walking down the same hallway, I
      hear the same music,
the same sounds—Catherine's story, Jed's chirps of response—but I
      know with anxiety
that most of this is only in my mind: the reality is that Catherine and Jed
      are no longer there,
that I'm merely constructing this—what actually accompanies me down
      that corridor is memory:
here, in this tentative but terribly convincing future I think to myself that
      it must be the music—
the Bach surely is real, I can *hear* it—that drives me so poignantly, ex-
      pectantly back

to remember again that morning of innocent peace a lifetime ago when
      I came towards them;
the sunny room, the music, the voices, each more distinct now: *Voilà le
      château, voilà Babar* . . .

3.

But if I'm torn so with remembrance in *this* present, then something
      here must be lost.
Has Jed grown, already left home? Has Catherine gone on somewhere,
      too, to some other life?
But no, who'd have played the record: perhaps they, or one of them,
      either one would be enough,
will still be out there before me, not speaking, perhaps reading, looking
      out the window, waiting.
Maybe all this grief, then, was illusion; a sadness, not for loss, but for the
      nature of time:
in my already fading future, I try to find a reconciliation for one more
      imaginary absence . . .
All this, sensation, anxiety, and speculation, goes through me in an in-
      stant, then in another,
a helplessness at what mind will do, then back into the world: *Voilà
      Babar, voilà la vieille dame* . . .

The Coma

for the memory of S. J. Marks

"My character wound," he'd written so shortly before, "my flaw," and
     now he was dying,
his heart, his anguished heart stopping, maiming his brain, then being
     started again;
"my loneliness," in his childish square cursive, "I've been discarded but
     I've earned it,
I'd like to grow fainter and fainter then disappear; my arrogant, inauthen-
     tic false self."

"My weak, hopeless, incompetent reparations," he'd written in his loneli-
     ness and despair,
"there's so much I'm afraid of facing, my jealousy, my inertia; roots are
     tearing from my brain."
And now, as he lay in his coma, I thought I could hear him again, "I'm
     insensitive, ineffectual,
I seethe with impatience," hear him driving himself with the shattered
     bolt of his mind deeper,

"It's my fault, my arrogant doubt, my rage," but I hoped, imagining him
     now waking downwards,
hoped he'd believe for once in the virtues his ruined past had never let
     him believe in,
his gifts for sympathy, kindness, compassion; in the ever-ascending down-
     wards of dying,
I hoped he'd know that his passion to be goodness had made him good-
     ness, like a child;

not "my malaise, my destructive neurosis": let him have known for him-
     self his purity and his warmth;
not "my crippled, hateful disdain": let have come to him, in his last lift
     away from himself,
his having wanted to heal the world he'd found so wounded in himself;
     let him have known,
though his crushed heart wouldn't have wanted him to, that, in his love
     and affliction, he had.

Proof

Not to show off, but elaborating some philosophical assertion, "Watch
      her open her mouth,"
says the guardian of an elderly, well-dressed retarded woman to the little
      circle of ladies
companionably gathered under a just-flowering chestnut this lusciously
      balmy Sunday.

She moves her hand in to everyone else an imperceptible gesture, her
      charge opens wide,
a peanut, to murmurs of approbation, is inserted, though all absorbed
      again as they are,
nobody sees when a moment later it slips from the still-visible tongue to
      the lip, then falls,

the mouth staying tensely agape, as though news of a great calamity had
      just reached it,
as though in eternity's intricate silent music someone had frighteningly
      mis-struck a chord,
so everything else has to hold, too, lovers strolling, children setting boats
      out on the pond,

until the guardian takes notice and says not unkindly, "Close, dear,"
      which is dutifully done,
and it all can start over: voices, leaves, water, air; always the yearning,
      sensitive air,
urging against us, aspiring to be us, the light striking across us: signs,
      covenants, codes.

Secrets

I didn't know that the burly old man who lived in a small house like ours
    down the block in Newark
was a high-up in the mob on the docks until I was grown and my father
    finally told me.

Neither did it enter my mind until much too much later that my superior
    that year at Nisner's,
a dazzlingly bright black man, would never in those days climb out of his
    mindless stockroom.

The councilman on the take, the girl upstairs giving free oral sex, the
    loansharks and addicts —
it was all news to me: do people hide things from me to protect me? Do
    they mistrust me?

Even when Sid Mizraki was found beaten to death in an alley, I didn't
    hear until years later.
Sid murdered! God, my God, was all I could say. Poor, sad Sidney; poor
    hard-luck Sid!

I hadn't known Sidney that long, but I liked him: plump, awkward, he
    was gentle, eager to please,
the way unprepossessing people will be; we played ball, went to China-
    town with the guys.

He'd had a bleak life: childhood in the streets, bad education, no
    women, irrelevant jobs;
in those days he worked for the city, then stopped; I had no idea of his
    true tribulations.

As the tale finally found me, Sid had a boss who hated him, rode him,
    drove him insane,
and Sid one drunk night in a bar bribed some burglars he knew to kill
    the creep for him.

I can't conceive how you'd dream up something like that, or how you'd
     know people like that,
but apparently Sid had access to tax rolls, and rich people's addresses he
     was willing to trade.

Then suddenly he was transferred, got a friendlier boss, forgot the whole
     witless affair,
but a year or so later the thieves were caught and as part of their plea bar-
     gain sold Sid.

He got off with probation, but was fired, of course, and who'd hire him
     with that record?
He worked as a bartender, went on relief, drifted, got into drugs, some
     small-time dealing.

Then he married—"the plainest woman on earth," someone told me—
     but soon was divorced:
more drugs, more dealing, run-ins with cops, then his unthinkable cal-
     vary in that alley.

It was never established who did it, or why; no one but me was surprised
     it had happened.
A bum found him, bleeding, broken, inert; a friend from before said,
     "His torments are over."

Well, Sid, what now? Shall I sing for you, celebrate you with some truth?
     Here's truth:
add up what you didn't know, friend, and I don't, and you might have
     one conscious person.

No, this has nothing to do with your omissions or sins or failed rectifica-
     tions, but mine:
to come so close to a life and not comprehend it, acknowledge it, truly
     know it is life.

How can I feel so clearly the shudder of blows, even the blessèd oblivion
     breaking on you,
and not really grasp what you were in yourself to yourself, what secrets
     sustained you?

So, for once I know something, that if anyone's soul should be singing,
Sidney, it's yours.
Poor poet, you'd tell me, *poor sheltered creature: if you can't open your
eyes, at least stay still.*

The Widower

He'd tried for years to leave her, then only months ago he finally had;
    now she's dead,
and though he claims he hates her still, I can tell he really loves and is
    obsessed by her.
I commiserate with him about her faults, her anarchic temperament, her
    depressing indolence,
the way she'd carried on when he'd moved out, spying on him, telephon-
    ing at all hours,
until his anger moves towards malice, bitterness, and he attacks her even
    for her virtues,
her mildness, her impulsive generosity, then I don't quite disagree, it's
    too soon for that,
but I at least demur, firmly enough to alleviate my already overcompro-
    mised conscience
but discreetly enough to allow him to reexpound his thesis that her fren-
    zied desperation
at their parting was one more proof of her neurosis, and had nothing to
    do with her dying,
which was just a cardiac, a circulation thing—how primitively Freudian
    to think otherwise—
though he and I both know, as surely as we're going on with this, on and
    on with this,
she brought about her death herself, as much as if she'd shot herself, and
    he,
because he still loved her so but found her still so impossible to love, as
    much as let her.

Money

How did money get into the soul; how did base dollars and cents ascend
        from the slime
to burrow their way into the crannies of consciousness, even it feels like
        into the flesh?

Wants with no object, needs with no end, like bacteria bringing their
        fever and freezing,
viruses gnawing at neurons, infecting even the sanctuaries of altruism
        and self-worth.

We asked soul to be huge, encompassing, sensitive, knowing, all-
        knowing, but not this,
not money roaring in with battalions of pluses and minus, setting up
        camps of profit and loss,

not joy become calculation, life counting itself, compounding itself like
        a pocket of pebbles:
fester, it feels like; a weeping, unhealable wound, an affront at all costs to
        be avenged.

Greed, taint and corruption, this sickness, this buy and this miserable
        sell;
soul against soul, talons of caustic tungsten: *what has been done to us,
        what have we done?*

My Book, My Book

The book goes fluttering crazily through the space of my room towards
    the wall like a bird
stunned in mid-flight and impacts and falls not like a bird but more bru-
    tally, like a man,
mortally sprawling, spine torn from its sutures, skeletal glue fragmented
    to crystal and dust.

Submissive, inert, it doesn't as would any other thing wounded shudder,
    quake, shiver,
act out at least desperate, reflexive attempts towards persistence, en-
    durance, but how could it,
wasn't it shriven already of all but ambition and greed; rote, lame emula-
    tions of conviction?

. . . Arrives now to my mind the creature who'll sniff out someday what in
    this block of pretension,
what protein, what atom, might still remain to digest and abstract, trans-
    figure to gist,
what trace of life substance wasn't burned away by the weight of its love-
    lessness and its sham.

Come, little borer, sting your way in, tunnel more deeply, blast, mine,
    excavate, drill:
take my book to you, etherealize me in the crunch of your gut; refine
    me, release me:
let me cling to your brainstem, dissolve in your dreaming: verse, page,
    quire; devour me, devourer.

Time: 1975

My father-in-law is away, Catherine and I and Renée, her mother, are
      eating in the kitchen;
Jed, three weeks old, sleeps in his floppy straw cradle on the counter next
      to the bread box;
we've just arrived, and I'm so weary with jet lag, with the labor of tending
      to a newborn
that my mind drifts and, instead of their words, I listen to the music of
      the women's voices.

Some family business must be being resolved: Renée is agitated, her tone
      suddenly urgent,
there's something she's been waiting to tell; her eyes hold on Catherine's
      and it's that,
the intensity of her gaze, that brings back to me how Catherine looked
      during her labor—
all those hours—then, the image startlingly vivid, I see Renée giving
      birth to Catherine.

I see the darkened room, then the bed, then, sinews drawn tight in her
      neck, Renée herself,
with the same abstracted look in her eyes that Catherine had, layer on
      layer of self disadhering,
all the dross gone, all but the fire of concentration, the heart-stopping
      beauty, and now,
at last, my Catherine, our Catherine, here for us all, blazing, bawling,
      lacquered with gore.

Cave

Not yet a poet, not yet a person perhaps, or a human, or not so far as I'd
      know now,
I lurk in the lobe of a cave, before me sky, a tangle of branch, a tree I
      can't name.

Not yet in a myth, tale, history, chronicle of a race, or a race, I don't
      know if I speak,
and if I do speak, I don't know if I pray—to what pray?—or if I sing; do I
      dare sing?

Who would be with me? Would there be indication of household past
      the scatter of seed,
the cracked-open, gnawed-open bones there would have to have been to
      sustain me?

Cold, cold ending; rain rising and ending, ever-menacing night circling
      towards me;
might I dream, at least, singing; toneless nearly, two notes or three,
      modeless, but singing?

Not yet in a garden, of morality or of mind, not yet in the shimmering
      prisms of reflection,
there must still be past the prattle and haggle of breath some aspiration to
      propel me.

A gust of upgroaning ardor, flurries of sad meditation, nostalgia for so
      much already lost:
in a stumble of uncountable syllables spun from pulse and passion some-
      thing sings, and I sing.

Grief

Dossie Williams, 1914–1995

1.

Gone now, after the days of desperate, unconscious gasping, the reflexive
      staying alive,
tumorous lungs, tumorous blood, ruined, tumorous liver demanding to
      live, to go on,
even the innocent bladder, its tenuous, dull golden coin in the slack
      translucent bag;
gone now, after the months of scanning, medication, nausea, hair loss
      and weight loss;
remission, partial remission, gratitude, hope, lost hope, anxiety, anger,
      confusion,
the hours and days of everyday life, something like life but only as dying
      is like life;
gone the quiet at the end of dying, the mouth caught agape on its last
      bite at a breath,
bare skull with its babylike growth of new hair thrown back to open the
      terrified larynx;
the flesh given way but still of the world, lost but still in the world with
      the living;
my hand on her face, on her brow, the sphere of her skull, her arm, so
      thin, so wasted;
gone, yet of us and with us, a person, not yet mere dream or imagination,
      then, gone, wholly,
under the earth, cold earth, cold grasses, cold winter wind, freezing eter-
      nity, cold, forever.

2.

Is this grief? Tears took me, then ceased; the wish to die, too, may have
      fled through me,
but not more than with any moment's despair, the old, surging wish to
      be freed, finished.

I feel pain, pain for her fear, pain for her having to know she was going,
  though we must;
pain for the pain of my daughter and son, for my wife whose despair for
  her mother returned;
pain for all human beings who know they will go and still go as though
  they knew nothing,
even pain for myself, my incomprehension, my fear of stories never be-
  gun now never ending.
But still, is this grief: waking too early, tiring too quickly, distracted, im-
  patient, abrupt,
but still waking, still thinking and working; is this what grief is, is this
  pain enough?
I go to the mirror: someone who might once have felt something merely
  regards me,
eyes telling nothing, mouth saying nothing, nothing reflected but the
  things of the world,
nothing told not of any week's, no, already ten days now, any ten days'
  normal doings.
Shouldn't the face evidence anguish, shouldn't its loving sadness and
  loss be revealed?
Ineffable, vague, elusive, uncertain, distracted: shouldn't grief have a
  form of its own,
and shouldn't mind know past its moment of vague, uncertain distrac-
  tion the sureness of sorrow;
shouldn't soul flinch as we're taught proper souls are supposed to, in rev-
  erence and fear?
Shouldn't grief be pure and complete, reshaping the world in itself, in
  grief for itself?

3.

Eighty, dying, in bed, tubes in her chest, my mother puts on her morn-
  ing makeup;
the broad, deft strokes of foundation, the blended-in rouge, powder, eye
  shadow, lipstick;
that concentration with which you must gaze at yourself, that ravenous,
  unfaltering focus.

Grief for my mother, for whatever she thought her face had to be, to be
    made every morning;
grief for my mother-in-law in her last declining, destroying dementia,
    getting it wrong,
the thick ropes of rouge, garish green paint on her lips; mad, misplaced
    slash of mascara;
grief for all women's faces, applied, created, trying to manifest what the
    soul seeks to be;
grief for the faces of all human beings, our own faces telling us so much
    and no more,
offering pain to all who behold them, but which when they turn to
    themselves, petrify, pose.
Grief for the faces of adults who must gaze in their eyes deeply so as not
    to glimpse death,
and grief for the young who see only their own relentless and grievous
    longing for love.
Grief for my own eyes that try to seek truth, even of pain, of grief, but
    find only approximation.

4.

My face beneath your face, face of grief, countenance of loss, of fear, of
    irrevocable extinction;
matrix laid upon matrix, mystery on mystery, guise upon guise, sem-
    blance, effigy, likeness.
Oh, to put the face of grief on in the morning; the tinting, smoothing,
    shining and shaping;
and at the end of the day, to remove it, detach it, emerge from the sor-
    rowful mask.
Stripped now of its raiment, the mouth, caught in its last labored breath,
    finds last resolution;
all the flesh now, stripped of its guises, moves towards its place in the
    peace of the earth.
Grief for the earth, accepting the grief of the flesh and the grief of our
    grieving forever;
grief for the flesh and the body and face, for the eyes that can see only
    into the world,

and the mind that can only think and feel what the world gives it to think
and to feel;
grief for the mind gone, the flesh gone, the imperfect pain that must stay
for its moment;
and grief for the moment, its partial beauties, its imperfect affections, all
severed, all torn.

II

Symbols

1. / WIND

Night, a wildly lashing deluge driving in great gusts over the blind, de-
   feated fields,
the usually stoical larches and pines only the mewling of their suddenly
   malleable branches;
a wind like a knife that never ceased shrieking except during the stun-
   ning volleys of thunder.

By morning, half the hundred pullets in the henhouse had massed in a
   corner and smothered,
an inert, intricate structure of dulled iridescence and still-distracted, still-
   frenzied eyes,
the vivid sapphire of daybreak tainted by a vaporous, gorge-swelling fetor.

The tribe of survivors compulsively hammered their angular faces as
   usual into the trough:
nothing in the world, they were saying, not carnage or dissolution, can
   bear reflection;
the simplest acts of being, they were saying, can obliterate all, all mad-
   ness, all mourning.

2. / GUITAR

For long decades the guitar lay disregarded in its case, unplucked and
     untuned,
then one winter morning, the steam heat coming on hard, the maple
     neck swelling again,
the sixth, gravest string, weary of feeling itself submissively tugged to and
     fro

over the ivory lip of the bridge, could no longer bear the tension preced-
     ing release,
and, with a faint thud and a single, weak note like a groan stifled in a fist,
     it gave way,
its portions curling agonizingly back on themselves like sundered seg-
     ments of worm.

. . . The echoes abruptly decay; silence again, the other strings still stead-
     fast, still persevering,
still feeling the music potent within them, their conviction of timeless-
     ness only confirmed,
of being essential, elemental, like earth, fire, air, from which all beauty
     must be evolved.

3. / OWL

The just-fledged baby owl a waiter has captured under a tree near the
    island restaurant
seems strangely unfazed to be on display on a formica table, though she
    tilts ludicrously,
all her weight on one leg as though she had merely paused in her lift
    towards departure.

Immobile except for her constantly swiveling head, she unpredictably
    fixes her gaze,
clicking from one far focus to another—sea, tree, sky, sometimes it seems
    even star—
but never on hand or eye, no matter how all in the circle around her
    chirp and cajole.

Thus the gods once, thus still perhaps gods: that scrutiny densely grained
    as granite,
the rotation calibrated on chromium bearings; dilation, contraction;
    wrath, disdain and remove . . .
But oh, to be slipping ever backwards in time, the savage memories, the
    withheld cry!

4. / DOG

Howl after pitiful, aching howl: an enormous, efficiently muscular
      doberman pinscher
has trapped itself in an old-fashioned phone booth, the door closed
      firmly upon it,
but when someone approaches to try to release it, the howl quickens and
      descends,

and if someone in pity dares anyway lean on and crack open an inch the
      obstinate hinge,
the quickened howl is a snarl, the snarl a blade lathed in the scarlet gape
      of the gullet,
and the creature powers itself towards that sinister slit, ears flattened,
      fangs flashing,

the way, caught in the deepest, most unknowing cell of itself, heart's
      secret, heart's wound,
decorous usually, seemly, though starving now, desperate, will turn
      nonetheless, raging,
ready to kill, or die, to stay where it is, to maintain itself just as it is, deco-
      rous, seemly.

5. / FIRE

The plaster had been burnt from the studs, the two-by-four joists were
      eaten with char;
ceilings smoke-blackened, glass fragments and foul, soaked rags of old
      rug underfoot:
even the paint on the outside brick had bubbled in scabs and blisters and
      melted away.

Though the fire was ostensibly out, smoke still drifted up through cracks
      in the floor,
and sometimes a windowsill or a door frame would erupt in pale, insidi-
      ous flames,
subtle in the darkness, their malignancies masked in blushes of temper-
      ate violet and rose.

Like love it was, love ill and soiled; like affection, affinity, passion, mis-
      used and consumed;
warmth betrayed, patience exhausted, distorted, all evidence of kindness
      now unkindness . . .
Yet still the hulk, the gutted carcass; fuming ash and ember; misery and
      shame.

6. / DAWN

Herds of goats puttering by on the rock-strewn path in what sounded like
    felt slippers;
before that (because the sudden awareness of it in sleep always came
    only after it passed),
the church bell, its cry in the silence like a swell of loneliness, then lone-
    liness healed.

The resonant *clock* of the fisherman's skiff being tethered to the end of
    the jetty;
the sad, repetitive smack of a catch of squid being slapped onto a slab of
    concrete;
the waves, their eternal morning torpor, the cypress leaning warily back
    from the shore.

A voice from a hill or another valley, expanding, concretizing like light,
    falling, fading,
then a comic grace-note, the creak of rickety springs as someone turns in
    their bed:
so much beginning, and now, sadness nearly, to think one might not
    even have known!

7. / WIG

The bus that won't arrive this freezing, bleak, pre-Sabbath afternoon
      must be Messiah;
the bewigged woman, pacing the sidewalk, furious, seething, can be only
      the mystic Shekinah,
the presence of God torn from Godhead, chagrined, abandoned, long-
      ing to rejoin, reunite.

The husband in his beard and black hat, pushing a stroller a step behind
      her as she stalks?
The human spirit, which must slog through such degrading tracts of
      slush and street-filth,
bound forever to its other, no matter how incensed she may be, how
      obliviously self-absorbed.

And the child, asleep, serene, uncaring in the crank and roar of traffic,
      his cheeks afire,
ladders of snowy light leaping and swirling above him, is what else but
      psyche, holy psyche,
always only now just born, always now just waking, to the ancient truths
      of knowledge, suffering, loss.

8. / GARDEN

A garden I usually never would visit; oaks, roses, the scent of roses I usu-
  ally wouldn't remark
but do now, in a moment for no reason suddenly unlike any other, numi-
  nous, limpid, abundant,
whose serenity lifts and enfolds me, as a swirl of breeze lifts the leaves
  and enfolds them.

Nothing ever like this, not even love, though there's no need to measure,
  no need to compare:
for once not to be waiting, to be in the world as time moves through and
  across me,
to exult in this fragrant light given to me, in this flow of warmth given to
  me and the world.

Then, on my hand beside me on the bench, something, I thought some-
  body else's hand, alighted;
I flinched it off, and saw—sorrow!—a warbler, gray, black, yellow, in
  flight already away.
It stopped near me in a shrub, though, and waited, as though unstartled,
  as though unafraid,

as though to tell me my reflex of fear was no failure, that if I believed I
  had lost something,
I was wrong, because nothing can be lost, of the self, of a lifetime of
  bringing forth selves.
Then it was gone, its branch springing back empty: still oak, though, still
  rose, still world.

444

III

Realms

Often I have thought that after my death, not in death's void as we usu-
ally think it,
but in some simpler after-realm of the mind, it will be given to me to
transport myself
through all space and all history, to behold whatever and converse with
whomever I wish.

Sometimes I might be an actual presence, a traveler listening at the edge
of the crowd;
at other times I'd have no physical being; I'd move unseen but seeing
through palace or slum.
Sophocles, Shakespeare, Bach! Grandfathers! Homo erectus! The uni-
verse bursting into being!

Now, though, as I wake, caught by some imprecise longing, you in the
darkness beside me,
your warmth flowing gently against me, it comes to me that in all my
after-death doings,
I see myself as alone, always alone, and I'm suddenly stranded, forsaken,
desperate, lost.

To propel myself through those limitless reaches without you! Never! Be
with me, come!
Babylon, Egypt, Lascaux, the new seas boiling up life; Dante, Delphi,
Magyars and Mayans!
Wait, though, it must be actually you, not my imagination of you, how-
ever real: for myself,

mind would suffice, no matter if all were one of time's terrible toys, but I
must have you,
as you are, the unquenchable fire of your presence, otherwise death truly
would triumph.
Quickly, never mind death, never mind mute, oblivious, onrushing time:
wake, hold me!

Storm

Another burst of the interminable, intermittently torrential dark after-
   noon downpour,
and the dozens of tirelessly garrulous courtyard sparrows stop hectoring
   each other
and rush to park under a length of cornice endearingly soiled with
   decades of wing-grease.

The worst summer in memory, thermal inversion, smog, swelter, intima-
   tions of global warming;
though the plane trees still thrust forth buds as though innocent April
   were just blooming,
last week's tentative pre-green leaflings are already woefully charred with
   heat and pollution.

Thunder far off, benign, then closer, slashes of lightning, a massive, con-
   cussive unscrolling,
an answering tremor in the breast, the exaltation at sharing a planet with
   this, then sorrow;
that we really might strip it of all but the bare wounded rock lumbering
   down its rote rail.

A denser veil of clouds now, another darkening downlash, the wind rises,
   the sparrows scatter,
the leaves quake, and Oh, I throw myself this way, the trees say, then that
   way, I tremble,
I moan, and still you don't understand the absence I'll be in the void of
   unredeemable time.

. . . Twelve suns, the prophecies promise, twelve vast suns of purification
   will mount the horizon,
to scorch, sear, burn away, then twelve cosmic cycles of rain: no tree left,
   no birdsong,
only the vigilant, acid waves, vindictively scouring themselves again and
   again on no shore.

Imagine then the emergence: Oh, this way, the sky streaked, Oh, that
      way, with miraculous brightness;
imagine us, beginning again, timid and tender, with a million years
      more this time to evolve,
an epoch more on all fours, stricken with shame and repentance, before
      we fire our forges.

Interrogation II

after the painting by Leon Golub

(Four interrogators; a victim, bound and hooded; red walls, a ladderlike device with chain; a chair)

1.

There will always be an issue: doctrine, dogma, differences of con-
    science, politics, or creed.
There will always be a reason: heresy, rebellion, dissidence, inadequate
    conviction or compliance.

There will always be the person to command it: president or king, dicta-
    tor or chief of staff,
and the priest or parson to anoint it, consecrate it, bless it, ground its
    logic in the sacred.

There will always be the victim; trembling, fainting, fearful, abducted,
    bound, and brought here;
there will always be the order, and the brutes, thugs, reptiles, scum, to
    carry out the order.

There will always be the room, the chair, the room whose walls are
    blood, the chair of shame.
There will always be the body, hooded, helpless; and the soul within,
    trembling, fearful, shamed.

2.

If I am here, hooded, helpless,
within these walls of blood,

upon this chair of shame,
something had to think me here.

I lived within my life,
I only thought my life,

I was stolen from it:
something *thought* me from it.

If something thought me,
there had to be a mind,

and if there was a mind,
it had to be contained, revealed,

as I thought mine was,
within a strip of temporal being.

If it was another mind,
like mine, that thought

and bound and brought me here,
some other consciousness

within its strip of being,
didn't it, that bit of being,

have to feel as I must feel
the nothingness against it,

the nothingness encroaching
on the rind of temporality,

the strand of actuality,
in which it is revealed?

Wasn't it afraid
to jeopardize the sensitivity

with which it knows itself,
with which it senses being

trembling upon nothingness,
struggling against nothingness,

with which it holds away
the nothingness within itself

which seems to strive to join
into that greater void?

When it stole me from my life,
abducted me and bound me,

wouldn't it have felt itself
being lost within the void

of nothingness within it?
Wasn't it afraid?

3.

Why are you crying?
Nothing is happening.

No one is being tortured,
no one beaten.

Why are you crying?
Nothing is happening.

No one's genitals nails spine
crushed torn out shattered.

No one's eardrums burst with fists,
no one's brain burst with bludgeons.

Why are you crying?
Nothing is happening.

No one's bones unsocketed
fractured leaching marrow.

No one flayed, flogged, maimed,
seared with torches,

set afire racked
shot electrocuted hung.

Why are you crying?
Nothing is happening.

There is only a chair,
a room, a ladder,

flesh indelibly marked
with pain and shame.

Why are you crying?
Nothing is happening.

4.

The human soul, the soul
we share, the single soul,

that by definition
which is our essential being,

is composed of other souls,
inhabited by other beings:

thus its undeniable power,
its purity, its vision,

thus its multiplicity
in singularity.

I understand the composition
of the soul, its communality,

but must I share my soul
with brutes and reptiles,

must I share my being,
vision, purity, with scum?

Impossible that in the soul
the human species

should be represented
as these brutes and thugs;

mortal substance
bodied as these reptiles.

Soul would loathe itself,
detest its very substance,

huddle in its lurk of essence
howling out its grief

of temporality, snarling out
its rage of mutability,

rather than be represented
by these beasts of prey.

The human soul is being
devoured by beasts of prey.

The human soul is prey.

5.

I didn't know the ladder to divinity on which were dreamed ascending
      and descending angels,
on which sodden spirit was supposed to rarify and rise, had become an
      instrument of torment,
wrist-holes punctured in its rungs, chains to hold the helpless body ham-
      mered in its uprights.

I didn't know how incidental life can seem beside such implements of
      pain and degradation;
neither did I know, though, how much presence can be manifested in
      the hooded, helpless body:
brutalized and bound, sinews, muscles, skin, still are lit with grace and
      pride and hope.

We cry from shame, because the body and the soul within are mocked,
      displayed, and shamed.
There will always be a reason, there will always be a victim, rooms of
      blood, chairs of pain.
But will there be the presence, grace and hope and pride enduring past
      the pain and shame?

Song

A city square, paths empty, sky clear; after days of rain, a purified sunlight
   blazed through;
all bright, all cool, rinsed shadows all vivid; the still-dripping leaves sated,
   prolific.

Suddenly others: voices, anger; sentences started, aborted; harsh, honed
   hisses of fury:
two adults, a child, the grown-ups raging, the child, a girl, seven or eight,
   wide-eyed, distracted.

"You, you," the parents boiled on in their clearly eternal battle: "you
   creature, you cruel,"
and the child stood waiting, instead of going to play on the slide or the
   swing, stood listening.

I wished she would weep; I could imagine the rich, abashing gush
   springing from her:
otherwise mightn't she harden her heart; mightn't she otherwise without
   knowing it become scar?

But the day was still perfect, the child, despite her evident apprehension,
   slender, exquisite:
when she noticed me watching, she precociously, flirtily, fetchingly
   swept back her hair.

Yes, we know one another, yes, there in the sad broken music of mind
   where nothing is lost.
Dear one, love, they were so sweetly singing: *where shall I refuge seek if
   you refuse me?*

Insight

1.

All under the supposition that he's helping her because she's so often
    melancholy lately,
he's pointing out certain problems with her character, but he's so serious,
    so vehement,
she realizes he's *attacking* her, to hurt, not help; she doesn't know what
    might be driving him,
but she finds she's thinking through his life for him, the losses, the long-
    forgotten sadnesses,
and though she can't come up with anything to correlate with how hate-
    fully he's acting,
she thinks *something* has to be there, so she listens, nods, sometimes she
    actually agrees.

2.

They're only arguing, but all at once she feels anxiety, and realizes she's
    afraid of him,
then, wondering whether she should risk expressing it to him, she under-
    stands she can't,
that the way he is these days he'll turn it back on her, and so she keeps it
    to herself,
then, despite herself, she wonders what their life's become to have to
    hide so much,
then comes a wave of disappointment, with herself, not him, and not for
    that initial fear,
but for some cowardice, some deeper dread that makes her ask, why not
    him?

3.

He's very distant, but when she asks him what it is, he insists it's nothing,
     though it's not,
she knows it's not, because he never seems to face her and his eyes won't
     hold on hers;
it makes her feel uncertain, clumsy, then as though she's somehow sup-
     plicating him:
though she wants nothing more from him than she already has—what
     would he think she'd want?—
when she tries to trust him, to believe his offhanded reassurance, she
     feels that she's pretending,
it's like a game, though very serious, like trying to talk yourself out of an
     imminent illness.

4.

If there are sides to take, he'll take the other side, against anything she
     says, to anyone:
at first she thinks it's just coincidence; after all, she knows she's some-
     times wrong,
everyone is sometimes wrong, but with him now all there seem to be are
     sides, she's always wrong;
even when she doesn't know she's arguing, when she doesn't care, he
     finds her wrong,
in herself it seems she's wrong, she feels she should apologize, to some-
     one, anyone, to him;
him, him, him; what is it that he wants from her: remorse, contrition,
     should she just *die?*

5.

He's telling her in much too intricate detail about a film he's seen: she
     tries to change the subject,
he won't let her, and she finds she's questioning herself—must she be so
     critical, judgmental?—
then she's struck, from something in his tone, or absent from his tone,
     some lack of resonance,
that why he's going on about the movie is because there's nothing else to
     say to her,
or, worse, that there are things to say but not to her, they're too intimate
     to waste on her:
it's *she*, she thinks, who's being measured and found wanting, and what
     should she think now?

6.

This time her, her story, about something nearly noble she once did, a
     friend in trouble,
and she helped, but before she's hardly started he's made clear he thinks
     it's all a fantasy,
and she as quickly understands that what he really means is that her love,
     her love for him,
should reflexively surpass the way she loved, or claims she loved, the
     long-forgotten friend,
and with a cold shock, she knows she can't tell him that, that the be-
     trayal,
and certainly there is one, isn't his desire to wound, but her thinking that
     he shouldn't.

7.

She sits in his lap, she's feeling lonely, nothing serious, she just wants
       sympathy, company,
then she realizes that though she hasn't said a word, he's sensed her sad-
       ness and is irked,
feels that she's inflicting, as she always does, he seems to think, her mis-
       ery on him,
so she tells herself not to be so needy anymore, for now, though, she just
       wants to leave,
except she can't, she knows that if he suspects he's let her down he'll be
       more irritated still,
and so she stays, feeling dumb and out of place, and heavy, heavier, like
       a load of stone.

8.

She experiences a pleasurable wave of nostalgia, not for her own past,
       but for his:
she can sense and taste the volume and the textures of the room he slept
       in as a child,
until she reminds herself she's never been there, never even seen the
       place, so, reluctantly,
she thinks reluctantly, she wonders if she might not be too close, too
       devoted to him,
whether she might actually be trying to become him, then she feels her-
       self resolve, to her surprise,
to disengage from him, and such a sense of tiredness takes her that she
       almost cries.

9.

As usual these days he's angry with her, and because she wants him not
      to be she kisses him,
but perhaps because he's so surprised, she feels him feel her kiss came
      from some counter-anger,
then she starts to doubt herself, wondering if she might have meant it as
      he thinks she did,
as a traitor kiss, a Judas kiss, and if that's true, his anger, both his angers,
      would be justified:
look, though, how he looks at her, with bemusement, hardly hidden, he
      knows her so well,
he senses her perplexity, her swell of guilt and doubt: how he cherishes
      his wrath!

10.

Such matters end, there are healings, breakings-free; she tells herself
      they end, but still,
years later, when the call she'd dreaded comes, when he calls, asking
      why she hasn't called,
as though all those years it wasn't her who'd called, then stopped calling
      and began to wait,
then stopped waiting, healed, broke free, so when he innocently suggests
      they get together,
she says absolutely not, but feels uncertain—is she being spiteful?
      small?—and then she knows:
after this he'll cause her no more pain, though no matter how she wished
      it weren't, this is pain.

In Darkness

That old documentary about the miners' strike in Harlan County, the
        company hireling, the goon,
who's brought in as a guard for the scabs and ends up blowing a miner's
        brains out:
how he, the thug, the enforcer, confronting the strikers, facing them
        down, pistol in hand,
ready to kill, maim, slaughter, destroy, evidences no compunction, no
        trepidation, no fear,
and you know it's because he has no reverence for creaturely existence,
        even his own,
to deflect him from what for him are the only true issues, obedience,
        wealth, property, power;
how he posed, strutted, snarled in contempt at those he conceived were
        beneath him,
the way, now, so many in power, assuming that same stance of righteous
        rectitude and rage,
snarl their contempt at those who'd dare hold differing notions of gover-
        nance and justice.

And when, after, the strikers met in the bare, scrufty yard of their dead
        friend's house,
and found there in the dust a shining shard, an arch of perfectly white
        human skull-bone;
though it was midnight, with just enough faint moonlight to make out
        the circle of faces,
you could see that despite their resolve they were frightened, despite
        their desperate need
they were awed at having to know once again how brief our mortal mo-
        ment of time is,
while behind them, the thug, the enforcer, prowled and raved, teeth
        clenched, jaw grinding,
his ravenous craving for order unslaked, his fear and his longing for love
        extracted forever,

as now, they, the political thugs, crazed with power, prowl, waiting to
   wreak social mayhem,
not for charity's sake but submission's, not for compassion but for ap-
   peasement of limitless greed.

The Demagogue

As on the rim of a cup crusted with rancid honey a host of hornets sud-
　　denly settles,
congealing in a mindless, ravenous mass, bristling with stingers of men-
　　ace and rage, thus they,

so muddled with the rich intoxicant bliss of his resentment they forget
　　who they are,
congregate, mass, swarm on his lips, to suck at his sanctimonious syrups
　　of indignation,

that which once was love in them so corrupted that when he urges
　　them—warriors, hornets—
to lift the cup of spiritual violence to their lips and drink, they do lift,
　　they do drink.

The Bed

Beds squalling, squealing, muffled in hush; beds pitching, leaping, im-
      mobile as mountains;
beds wide as a prairie, strait as a gate, as narrow as the plank of a ship to
      be walked.

*I squalled, I squealed, I swooped and pitched; I covered my eyes and fell
      from the plank.*

Beds proud, beds preening, beds timid and tense; vanquished beds wish-
      ing only to vanquish;
neat little beds barely scented and dented, beds so disused you cranked
      them to start them.

*I admired, sang praises, flattered, adored: I sighed and submitted, solaced,
      comforted, cranked.*

Procrustean beds with consciences sharpened like razors slicing the dark-
      ness above you;
beds like the labors of Hercules, stables and serpents; Samson blinded,
      Noah in horror.

*Blind with desire, I wakened in horror, in toil, in bondage, my conscience
      in tatters.*

Beds sobbing, beds sorry, beds pleading, beds mournful with histories
      that amplified yours,
so you knelled through their dolorous echoes as through the depths of
      your own dementias.

*I echoed, I knelled, I sobbed and repented, I bandaged the wrists, sighed
      for embryos lost.*

A nation of beds, a cosmos, then, how could it still happen, the bed at
      the end of the world,

as welcoming as the world, ark, fortress, light and delight, the other beds
all forgiven, forgiving.

A bed that sang through the darkness and woke in song as though world it-
self had just wakened;
two beds fitted together as one; bed of peace, patience, arrival, bed of un-
waning ardor.

The Heart

When I saw my son's heart blown up in bland black and white on the
      sonogram screen,
an amoebic, jellylike mass barely contained by invisible layers of mem-
      brane, I felt faint.

Eight years old, Jed lay, apparently unafraid, wires strung from him into
      the clicking machine,
as the doctor showed us a pliable, silvery lid he explained was the valve,
      benignly prolapsed,

which to me looked like some lost lunar creature biting too avidly, ur-
      gently at an alien air,
the tiniest part of that essence I'd always allowed myself to believe could
      stand for the soul.

Revealed now in a nakedness nearly not to be looked upon as the muscu-
      lar ghost of itself,
it majestically swelled and contracted, while I stood trembling before it,
      in love, in dread.

Exterior: Day

Two actors are awkwardly muscling a coffin out of a doorway draped in
        black funeral hangings;
a third sobs, unconvincingly though: the director cries "Cut!" and they
        set up again.

Just then an old woman, blind, turns the corner; guiding herself down
        the side of the building,
she touches the velvet awning and visibly startles: has someone died and
        she not been told?

You can almost see her in her mind move through the entrance, and feel
        her way up the stairs,
knocking, trying doors—who might be missing?—but out here every-
        thing holds.

For a long moment no one knows what to do: the actors fidget, the cam-
        eraman looks away;
the woman must be aware that the street is unnaturally quiet, but she still
        doesn't move.

It begins to seem like a contest, an agon; illusion and truth: crew, on-
        lookers, and woman;
her hand still raised, caught in the cloth, her vast, uninhabited gaze
        sweeping across us.

Time: 1978

1.

What could be more endearing, on a long, too quiet, lonely evening in
    an unfamiliar house,
than, on the table before us, Jed's sneakers, which, finally, at eleven
    o'clock, I notice,
tipped on their sides, still tied, the soles barely scuffed since we just
    bought them today,
or rather submitted to Jed's picking them out, to his absolutely having to
    have them,
the least practical pair, but the first thing besides toys he's ever cared so
    much about,
and which, despite their impossible laces and horrible color, he passion-
    ately wanted, *desired*,
and coerced us into buying, by, when we made him try on the sensible
    pair we'd chosen,
limping in them, face twisted in torment: his first anguished ordeal of a
    violated aesthetic.

2.

What more endearing except Jed himself, who, now, perhaps because of
    the new night noises,
wakes, and, not saying a word, pads in to sit on Catherine's lap, head on
    her breast, silent,
only his breathing, sleep-quickened, as I write this, trying to get it all in,
    hold the moments
between the sad desolation I thought if not to avert then to diminish in
    writing it down,
and this, now, my pen scratching, eyes rushing to follow the line and not
    lose Jed's gaze,
which dims with sleep now, wanders to the window—hills, brush, field
    cleft with trenches—

and begins to flutter so that I can't keep up with it: quick, quick, before
       you're asleep,
listen, how and whenever if not now, now, will I speak to you, both of
       you, of all this?

Hawk

Whatever poison it had ingested or injury incurred had flung it in agony
      onto its back,
and it drove itself with shuddering, impotent flails of its wings into the
      dirt.

When it stopped, I came closer, thinking its sufferings over, but it sav-
      agely started again,
talons retracted, spine cramped grotesquely, pinions beginning to shatter
      and fray.

I knew what to do, but, child of the city, I couldn't: there was no one to
      help me;
I could only—forgive me—retreat from that frantic, irrational thrashing,
      thinking as I went,

Die, please, the way, it came to me with a startling remorse, I did when
      my father was dying,
when he woke from the probe in his brain to the worse than death wait-
      ing for him.

There'd be long moments he'd seem not to breathe: absolute stillness,
      four long beats, more,
between huge inhalations, and, Go, I'd think, *die, be released from the
      toil of your dying.*

I'd think it again and again, with the fierce anguished impatience of the
      child I was now again,
then I'd wonder: might this be only my unpardonably wanting my own
      anxiety to be over?

When at last he'd open his eyes, I'd think, No, *stay, be with us as long as
      you can,*
relieved I at least could think that; but that other shock of misgiving still
      holds me.

I was frightened, then, too; then, too, something was asked and I wasn't
     who I wanted to be.
How seldom I am, how much more often this self-sundering doubt, this
     bewildering contending.

The Lover

for Michel Rétiveau

Maybe she missed the wife, or the wife's better dinner parties, but she
     never forgave him,
the lover, not for having caused the husband to switch gender prefer-
     ence, but for being,
she must have said, or sighed, a thousand times, so difficult to be with, so
     crude, so *tiresome*.

But it was she who began to bore, the way she kept obsessively question-
     ing his legitimacy—
so *arch* he was, she'd say, so *bitchy*—and all after the rest of us had come
     to appreciate
his mildly sardonic, often brilliant bantering, his casual erudition in so
     many arcane areas.

It's true that at first he may have seemed at least a little of what she said
     he was—
obstreperously, argumentatively, if wittily, abrasive—but we assigned that
     to what,
considering the pack of friends' old friends with which he was faced, was
     a reasonable apprehension

about being received into a society so elaborate in the intricacies of its
     never articulated
but still forbiddingly solidified rituals of acceptance: he really handled it
     quite graciously.
What after all did she expect of him? Shyness? Diffidence? The diffi-
     dence of what? A bride?

The Game

"Water" was her answer and I fell instantly and I knew self-destructively
     in love with her,
had to have her, would, I knew, someday, I didn't care how, and soon,
     too, have her,
though I guessed already it would have to end badly though not so disas-
     trously as it did.

My answer, "lion" or "eagle," wasn't important: the truth would have
     been anything but myself.
The game of that first fateful evening was what you'd want to come back
     as after you died;
it wasn't the last life-or-death contest we'd have, only the least erotically
     driven and dangerous.

What difference if she was married, and perhaps mad (both only a little,
     I thought wrongly)?
There was only my jealous glimpse of her genius, then my vision of
     vengeance: midnight, morning—
beneath me a planet possessed: cycles of transfiguration and soaring,
     storms crossing.

Spider Psyche

The mummified spider hung in its own web in the rafters striped legs
    coiled tightly
into its body head hunched a bit into what would be shoulders if it had
    been human
indicating a knowledge perhaps of the death coming to take it indicating
    not fear of death
I surmise but an emotion like wanting to be ready or ready on time trying
    to prepare psyche
for death so psyche won't fall back into the now useless brain the core
    imprinted with all
it knew in the world until now but only a nub now no longer receptor
    receptacle rather
and perhaps psyche did it didn't flinch rather just gazed out of the web of
    perception
watching the wave of not-here take the shore-edge of here acknowledg-
    ing rather its portion
of being the blare of light in the corner the grain in the wood the old
    odors and the space
a great cup underneath a great gaping under the breadth of your being so
    that you want
no matter what this last moment of holding even if shoulders and brain
    can hardly abide it
even if brain swoons nearly trying to hold its last thought last fusion of
    will and cognition
and there is no end in this ending no contingent condition of being this
    glare of perception
hurl of sensation all one sense and intention act and love my psyche my
    spider love and hope
take us dear spider of self into your otherness into having once been and
    the knowledge of having
in all this been once in wonder so every instant was thanks and all else
    was beneath and adrift
my spider psyche all awe now all we ever wanted to be now in this great
    gratitude gone

Grace

Almost as good as her passion, I'll think, almost as good as her presence,
      her physical grace,
almost as good as making love with her, I'll think in my last aching
      breath before last,
my glimpse before last of the light, were her good will and good wit, the
      steadiness of her affections.

Almost, I'll think, sliding away on my sleigh of departure, the rind of my
      consciousness thinning,
the fear of losing myself, of—worse—losing her, subsiding as I think,
      hope it must,
almost as good as her beauty, her glow, was the music of her thought, her
      voice and laughter.

Almost as good as kissing her, being kissed back, I hope I'll have strength
      still to think,
was watching her as she worked or read, was beholding her selfless sym-
      pathy for son, friend, sister,
even was feeling her anger, sometimes, rarely, lift against me, then be
      forgotten, put aside.

Almost, I'll think, as good as our unlikely coming together, was our con-
      stant, mostly unspoken debate
as to whether good in the world was good in itself, or (my side) only the
      absence of evil:
no need to say how much how we lived was shaped by her bright spirit,
      her humor and hope.

Almost as good as living at all—improbable gift—was watching her once
      cross our room,
the reflections of night rain she'd risen to close the window against flar-
      ing across her,
doubling her light, then feeling her come back to bed, reaching to find
      and embrace me,

as I'll hope she'll be there to embrace me as I sail away on that last voyage out of myself,

that last passage out of her presence, though her presence, I'll think, will endure,

as firmly as ever, as good even now, I'll think in that lull before last, almost as ever.

Time: 1972

As a child, in the half-dark, as you wait on the edge of her bed for her to
        sleep,
will lift her hand to your face and move it over your brow, cheeks, the
        orbits of your eyes,
as though she'd never quite seen you before, or really remarked you, or
        never like this,
and you're taken for a time out of your own world into hers, her world of
        new wonder,
and are touched by her wonder, her frank, forthright apprehending,
        gentle and knowing,
somehow already knowing, creating itself—you can feel it—in this out-
        flow of bestowal,

so, sometimes, in the sometimes somber halls of memory, your life as
        you've known it,
in the only way you can know it, in these disparate, unpredictable up-
        surges of mind,
gathers itself, gathers what seem like the minds behind mind that shim-
        mer within mind,
and turns back on itself, suspending itself, caught in the marvel of
        memory and time,
and, as the child's mind, so long ago now, engendered itself in attach-
        ment's touch and bestowal,
life itself now seems engendered from so much enduring attachment, so
        much bestowal.

Villanelle of the Suicide's Mother

Sometimes I almost go hours without crying,
Then I feel if I don't, I'll go insane.
It can seem her whole life was her dying.

She tried so hard, then she was tired of trying;
Now I'm tired, too, of trying to explain.
Sometimes I almost go hours without crying.

The anxiety, the rage, the denying;
Though I never blamed her for my pain,
It can seem her whole life was her dying,

And mine was struggling to save her: prying,
Conniving: it was the chemistry in her brain.
Sometimes I almost go hours without crying.

If I said she was easy, I'd be lying;
The lens between her and the world was stained:
It can seem her whole life was her dying

But the fact, the *fact*, is stupefying:
Her absence tears at me like a chain.
Sometimes I almost go hours without crying.
It can seem her whole life was her dying.

Thirst

Here was my relation with the woman who lived all last autumn and
      winter day and night
on a bench in the Hundred and Third Street subway station until finally
      one day she vanished:

we regarded each other, scrutinized one another: me shyly, obliquely,
      trying not to be furtive;
she boldly, unblinkingly, even pugnaciously; wrathfully even, when her
      bottle was empty.

I was frightened of her, I felt like a child, I was afraid some repressed part
      of myself
would go out of control and I'd be forever entrapped in the shocking
      seethe of her stench.

Not excrement, merely, not merely surface and orifice going unwashed,
      rediffusion of rum:
there was will in it, and intention, power and purpose; a social, ethical
      rage and rebellion.

. . . Despair, too, though, grief, loss: sometimes I'd think I should take
      her home with me,
bathe her, comfort her, dress her: she wouldn't have wanted me to, I
      would think.

Instead I'd step into my train: how rich, I would think, is the lexicon of
      our self-absolving;
how enduring our bland, fatal assurance that reflection is righteousness
      being accomplished.

The dance of our glances, the clash; pulling each other through our per-
      ceptual punctures;
then holocaust, holocaust: host on host of ill, injured presences squan-
      dered, consumed.

Her vigil, somewhere, I know, continues: her occupancy, her absolute,
    faithful attendance;
the dance of our glances: challenge, abdication, effacement; the per-
    fume of our consternation.

Old Man

Special: Big Tits, says the advertisement for a soft-core magazine on our
      neighborhood newsstand,
but forget her breasts—a lush, fresh-lipped blonde, skin glowing gold,
      sprawls there, resplendent.
Sixty nearly, yet these hardly tangible, hardly better than harlots can still
      stir me.

Maybe coming of age in the American sensual darkness, never seeing an
      unsmudged nipple,
an uncensored vagina, has left me forever infected with an unquench-
      able lust of the eye:
always that erotic murmur—I'm hardly myself if I'm not in a state of in-
      cipient desire.

God knows, though, there are worse twists your obsessions can take: last
      year, in Israel,
a young ultra-Orthodox rabbi, guiding some teenaged girls through the
      shrine of the *Shoah*,
forbade them to look in one room because there were images in it he
      said were licentious.

The display was a photo: men and women, stripped naked, some trying
      to cover their genitals,
others too frightened to bother, lined up in snow waiting to be shot and
      thrown in a ditch.
The girls to my horror averted their gaze: what carnal mistrust had their
      teacher taught them?

Even that, though . . . Another confession: once, in a book on pre-war
      Poland, a studio-portrait,
an absolute angel, with tormented, tormenting eyes; I kept finding my-
      self at her page;
that she died in the camps made her, I didn't dare wonder why, more
      present, more precious.

"Died in the camps": that, too, people, or Jews anyway, kept from their
        children back then,
but it was like sex, you didn't have to be told. Sex and death: how close
        they can seem.
So constantly conscious now of death moving towards me, sometimes I
        think I confound them.

My wife's loveliness almost consumes me, my passion for her goes be-
        yond reasonable bounds;
when we make love, her holding me, everywhere all around me, I'm
        there and not there,
my mind teems, jumbles of faces, voices, impressions: I live my life over
        as though I were drowning.

. . . Then I am drowning, in despair, at having to leave her, this, every-
        thing, all: unbearable, awful . . .
Still, to be able to die with no special contrition, not having been slaugh-
        tered or enslaved,
and not having to know history's next mad rage or regression—it might
        be a relief.

No, again no, I don't mean that for a moment, what I mean is the world
        holds me so tightly,
the good and the bad, my own follies and weakness, that even this coun-
        terfeit Venus,
with her sham heat and her bosom probably plumped with gel, so moves
        me my breath catches.

Vamp, siren, seductress, how much more she reveals in her glare of ink
        than she knows;
how she incarnates our desperate human need for regard, our passion to
        live in beauty,
to be beauty, to be cherished, by glances if by no more, of something like
        love, or love.

REPAIR

[1999]

Ice

That astonishing thing that happens when you crack a needle-awl into a
    block of ice:
the way a perfect section through it crazes into gleaming fault-lines, frac-
    tures, facets;
dazzling silvery deltas that in one too-quick-to-capture instant madly
    complicate the cosmos of its innards.
Radiant now with spines and spikes, aggressive barbs of glittering light, a
    treasure hoard of light,
when you stab it again it comes apart in nearly equal segments, both
    faces grainy, gnawed at, dull.

An icehouse was a dark, low place of raw, unpainted wood,
always dank and black with melting ice.
There was sawdust and sawdust's tantalizing, half-sweet odor, which, so
    cold, seemed to pierce directly to the brain.
You'd step onto a low-roofed porch, someone would materialize,
take up great tongs and with precise, placating movements like a lion-
    tamer's slide an ice-block from its row.

Take the awl yourself now, thrust, and when the block splits do it again,
    yet again;
watch it disassemble into smaller fragments, crystal after fissured crystal.
Or if not the puncturing pick, try to make a metaphor, like Kafka's
    frozen sea within:
take into your arms the cake of actual ice, make a figure of its ponderous
    inertness,
of how its quickly wetting chill against your breast would frighten you
    and make you let it drop.

Imagine how even if it shattered and began to liquefy
the hope would still remain that if you quickly gathered up the slithery,
    perversely skittish chips,
they might be refrozen and the mass reconstituted, with precious little of
    its brilliance lost,

just this lucent shimmer on the rough, raised grain of water-rotten floor, just this single drop, as sweet and warm as blood, evaporating on your tongue.

The Train

Stalled an hour beside a row of abandoned, graffiti-stricken factories,
the person behind me talking the whole while on his portable phone,
every word irritatingly distinct, impossible to think of anything else,
I feel trapped, look out and see a young hare moving through the sooty
      scrub;
just as I catch sight of him, he turns with a start to face us, and freezes.

Gleaming, clean, his flesh firm in his fine-grained fur, he's very endear-
      ing;
he reminds me of the smallest children on their way to school in our
      street,
their slouchy, unself-conscious grace, the urge you feel to share their
      beauty,
then my mind plays that trick of trying to go back into its wilder part,
to let the creature know my admiration, and have him acknowledge me.

All the while we're there, I long almost painfully out to him,
as though some mystery inhabited him, some semblance of the sacred,
but if he senses me he disregards me, and when we begin to move
he still waits on the black ballast gravel, ears and whiskers working,
to be sure we're good and gone before he continues his errand.

The train hurtles along, towns blur by, the voice behind me hammers
      on;
it's stifling here but in the fields the grasses are stiff and white with rime.
Imagine being out there alone, shivers of dread thrilling through you,
those burnished rails before you, around you a silence, immense, stupen-
      dous,
only now beginning to wane, in a lift of wind, the deafening creaking of
      a bough.

Archetypes

Often before have our fingers touched in sleep or half-sleep and enlaced,
often I've been comforted through a dream by that gently sensitive pres-
    sure,
but this morning, when I woke your hand lay across mine in an awkward,
unfamiliar position so that it seemed strangely external to me, removed;
an object whose precise weight, volume and form I'd never remarked:
its taut, resistant skin, dense muscle-pads, the subtle, complex structure,
with delicately elegant chords of bone aligned like columns in a temple.

Your fingers began to move then, in brief, irregular tensions and releas-
    ings;
it felt like your hand was trying to hold some feathery, fleeting creature,
then you suddenly, fiercely, jerked it away, rose to your hands and knees,
and stayed there, palms flat on the bed, hair tangled down over your
    face,
until with a coarse sigh almost like a snarl you abruptly let yourself fall
and lay still, your hands drawn tightly to your chest, your head turned
    away,
forbidden to me, I thought, by whatever had raised you to that defiant
    crouch.

I waited, hoping you'd wake, turn, embrace me, but you stayed in your-
    self,
and I felt again how separate we all are from one another, how even our
    passions,
which seem to embody unities outside of time, heal only the most be-
    nign divisions,
that for our more abiding, ancient terrors we each have to find our own
    valor.
You breathed more softly now, though; I took heart, touched against you,
and, as though nothing had happened, you opened your eyes, smiled at
    me,
and murmured—how almost startling to hear you in your real voice—
    "Sleep, love."

After Auschwitz

We'd wanted to make France
but by dusk we knew we wouldn't,
so in a Bavarian town
just off the autobahn,
we found a room, checked in,
and went out to look around.

The place was charming: hushed,
narrow, lamp-lit streets,
half-timbered houses,
a dark-stoned church
and medieval bridges
over a murmuring river.

I didn't sleep well, though,
and in the morning, early,
I took another stroll
and was surprised to realize
that all of it, houses,
bridges, all except

as far as I could tell
the sleeping church, were deft
replicas of what
they must have been before
the war, before the Allied
bombers flattened them.

At Auschwitz, there was nothing
I hadn't imagined beforehand.
I'd been through it in my mind
so much, so often, I felt
only unutterably weary.
All that shocked me was

to find the barracks and bleak
paths unoccupied,
and the gas and torture chambers,
and the crematoria;
so many silent spaces,
bereft, like schools in summer.

Now, in a pleasant square,
I came on a morning market;
farmers, tents and trucks,
much produce, flowers,
the people prosperous,
genial, ruddy, chatty,

and it was then there arose
before me again the barbed
wire and the bales of hair,
the laboratories and
the frozen ash. I thought
of Primo Levi, reciting

Dante to the all but dead,
then, I don't know why,
of the Jewish woman, Masha,
of whom Levi tells
how, when she'd escaped,
been informed on, caught,

and now was to be hanged
before the other prisoners,
someone called out to her,
"Masha, are you all right?"
and she'd answered, answered, answered,
"I'm always all right."

A village like a stage set,
a day's drive back
that other place which always

now everywhere on earth
will be the other place
from where one finds oneself.

Not risen from its ruins
but caught in them forever,
it demands of us how
we'll situate this so
it doesn't sunder us
between forgivenesses

we have no right to grant,
and a reticence
perhaps malignant, heard
by nothing that exists,
yet which endures, a scar,
a broken cry, within.

The Dress

In those days, those days which exist for me only as the most elusive
  memory now,
when often the first sound you'd hear in the morning would be a storm
  of birdsong,
then the soft clop of the hooves of the horse hauling a milk wagon down
  your block

and the last sound at night as likely as not would be your father pulling
  up in his car,
having worked late again, always late, and going heavily down to the
  cellar, to the furnace,
to shake out the ashes and damp the draft before he came upstairs to fall
  into bed;

in those long-ago days, women, my mother, my friends' mothers, our
  neighbors,
all the women I knew, wore, often much of the day, what were called
  "housedresses,"
cheap, printed, pulpy, seemingly purposefully shapeless light cotton
  shifts,

that you wore over your nightgown, and, when you had to go to look for
  a child,
hang wash on the line, or run down to the grocery store on the corner,
  under a coat,
the twisted hem of the nightgown, always lank and yellowed, dangling
  beneath.

More than the curlers some of the women seemed constantly to have in
  their hair,
in preparation for some great event, a ball, one would think, that never
  came to pass;
more than the way most women's faces not only were never made up
  during the day,

but seemed scraped, bleached, and, with their plucked eyebrows, scarily
    masklike;
more than all that it was those dresses that made women so unknowable
    and forbidding,
adepts of enigmas to which men could have no access, and boys no con-
    ception.

Only later would I see the dresses also as a proclamation: that in your
    dim kitchen,
your laundry, your bleak concrete yard, what you revealed of yourself was
    a fabulation;
your real sensual nature, veiled in those sexless vestments, was utterly
    your dominion.

In those days, one hid much else, as well: grown men didn't embrace
    one another,
unless someone had died, and not always then; you shook hands, or, at a
    ball game,
thumped your friend's back and exchanged blows meant to be codes for
    affection;

once out of childhood you'd never again know the shock of your father's
    whiskers
on your cheek, not until mores at last had evolved, and you could hug
    another man,
then hold on for a moment, then even kiss (your father's bristles white
    and stiff now).

What release finally, the embrace: though we were wary—it seemed so
    audacious—
how much unspoken joy there was in that affirmation of equality and
    communion,
no matter how much misunderstanding and pain had passed between
    you by then.

We knew so little in those days, as little as now, I suppose, about healing
    those hurts:

even the women, in their best dresses, with beads and sequins sewn on
the bodices,
even in lipstick and mascara, their hair aflow, could only stand wringing
their hands,

begging for peace, while father and son, like thugs, like thieves, like
Romans,
simmered and hissed and hated, inflicting sorrows that endured, the
worst anyway,
through the kiss and embrace, bleeding from brother to brother into the
generations.

In those days there was still countryside close to the city, farms, corn-
fields, cows;
even not far from our building with its blurred brick and long shadowy
hallway
you could find tracts with hills and trees you could pretend were moun-
tains and forests.

Or you could go out by yourself even to a half-block-long empty lot, into
the bushes:
like a creature of leaves you'd lurk, crouched, crawling, simplified, sav-
age, alone;
already there was wanting to be simpler, wanting when they called you,
never to go back.

The Blow

I saw a man strike a beggar,
a rank, filthy, though not,
truly, insufferable beggar.
He had touched the man, though,
from behind, to stop him,
which startled the man,

so he blindly swept out
his fist, not thinking—
but didn't that make it worse?—
and hit the beggar, harder
than he'd have meant to
if he'd meant to, on the chest.

He knew at once, I saw,
he'd made a mistake;
the beggar, as tipsy
as he was, was insulted,
indignant, but did the man
regret what he'd done

for the sake of the dignity
of the beggar, or for the years
he'd tried to attain
innocence, all for naught
now, or because, really,
he was a little afraid?

The beggar was shouting,
the man wondered whether
to offer him money,
but he guessed the beggar
would lord it over him,
so he looked angry instead.

Walking faster, the beggar
haranguing him still,
the man suddenly saw himself
and the beggar as atoms,
nullities, passing beside
one another, or through.

How we toil, he mused,
from this aimless hour
to that, from one intractable
quandary to the next, until
we're left only a horrible
fear of our own existence.

Which, he remembered,
a famous thinker thought once,
as the image rose in him
of a youth he'd seen in a madhouse,
". . . entirely idiotic, sitting
on a shelf in the wall."

"That shape am I,"
the sage despaired,
beholding his own mind
flickering desperately over
the great gush of the real,
to no end, no avail.

Bone

An erratic, complicated shape, like a tool for some obsolete task:
the hipbone and half the gnawed shank of a small, unrecognizable ani-
  mal on the pavement in front of the entrance to the museum;
grimy, black with tire-dust, soot, the blackness from our shoes, our ink,
  the grit that sifts out of our air.

Still, something devoured all but this much, and if you look more
  closely,
you can see tiny creatures still gnawing at the shreds of decomposing
  meat, sucking at the all but putrefying bone.

Decades it must be on their scale that they harvest it, dwell and generate
  and age and die on it.
Where will they transport the essence of it when they're done?
How far beneath the asphalt, sewers, subways, mains and conduits is the
  living earth to which at last they'll once again descend?
Which intellect will register in its neurons the great fortune of this ex-
  ceptional adventure? Which poet sing it?
Such sweetness, such savor: luxury, satiety, and no repentance, no regret.

But Maman won't let you keep it.
"Maman, please . . ."
"It's filthy. Drop it. *Drop it! Drop it! Drop it!*"

Shock

Furiously a crane
in the scrapyard out of whose grasp
a car it meant to pick up slipped,
lifts and lets fall, lifts and lets fall
the steel ton of its clenched pincers
onto the shuddering carcass
which spurts fragments of anguished glass
until it's sufficiently crushed
to be hauled up and flung onto
the heap from which one imagines
it'll move on to the shredding
or melting down that awaits it.

Also somewhere a crow
with less evident emotion
punches its beak through the dead
breast of a dove or albino
sparrow until it arrives at
a coil of gut it can extract,
then undo with a dexterous twist
an oily stretch just the right length
to be devoured, the only
suggestion of violation
the carrion jerked to one side
in involuntary dismay.

Splayed on the soiled pavement
the dove or sparrow; dismembered
in the tangled remnants of itself
the wreck, the crane slamming once more
for good measure into the all
but dematerialized hulk,
then luxuriously swaying
away, as, gorged, glutted, the crow

with savage care unfurls the full,
luminous glitter of its wings,
so we can preen, too, for so much
so well accomplished, so well seen.

The Poet

I always knew him as "Bobby the poet," though whether he ever was one
   or not,
someone who lives in words, making a world from their music, might be
   a question.

In those strange years of hippiedom and "people-power," saying you were
   an artist
made you one, but at least Bobby acted the way people think poets are
   supposed to.

He dressed plainly, but with flair, spoke little, yet listened with genuine
   attention,
and a kind of preoccupied, tremulous seriousness always seemed to ab-
   sorb him.

Also he was quite good-looking, and mysterious, never saying where he'd
   come from,
nor how he lived now: I thought he might be on welfare, but you didn't
   ask that.

He'd been around town for a while, had dropped from sight for a few
   months when
one evening he came up to me in the local bookstore; I could see he
   hadn't been well.

He looked thin, had a soiled sling tied on one arm, the beret he usually
   wore was gone,
and when I turned to him he edged back like a child who's afraid you
   might hit him.

He smiled at himself then, but without humor; his eyes were partly
   closed, from dope,

I guessed, then changed my mind: this seemed less arbitrary, more pur-
          poseful.

Still, he had to tilt his head back a little to keep me in focus in his field
          of vision:
it was disconcerting, I felt he was looking at me from a place far away in
          himself.

"Where've you been, Bobby?" I asked. He didn't answer at first, but
          when I asked again,
he whispered, "In the hospital, man; I had a breakdown . . . they took me
          away there."

Then he subsided into his smile, and his silence. "What happened to
          your arm?"
He dipped his shoulder, his sling opened, and cradled along his arm was
          a long knife.

"That looks dangerous," I said; "I need it," he came back with, and the
          sling came closed.
I was startled. Did he think someone was out to hurt him? Might he
          think it was me?

He never stopped looking at me; his agitation was apparent, and not
          reassuring;
we'd been friendly, but I didn't know him that well. "Where's your
          book?" I asked finally.

He'd always carried an old-fashioned bound accountant's ledger, its
          pages scrawled
with columns of poems: his "book," though as far as I knew no one but
          he ever read it.

Again no response; I remember the store was well-lit, but my image of
          him is shadow;
the light seemed extracted from his presence, obliterated by the mass of
          his anguish.

Poets try to help one another when we can: however competitive we are, and we are,
the life's so chancy, we feel so beleaguered, we need all the good will we can get.

Whether you're up from a slum or down from a carriage, how be sure you're a poet?
How know if your work has enduring worth, or any? Self-doubt is almost our definition.

Now, waiting with Bobby, I could tell he'd had enough of all that, he wanted out;
that may have explained his breakdown, but what was it he expected from me?

I was hardly the most visible poet around; I'd published little, didn't give readings,
or teach, although, come to think of it, maybe that's just what Bobby was after.

Someone once said that to make a poem, you first have to invent the poet to make it:
Bobby'd have known I'd understand how the first-person he'd devised had betrayed him.

Bobby from nowhere, Bobby know-nothing, probably talentless Bobby: wasn't that me?
I'd know as well as he did how absurd it could be to take your trivial self as the case.

But if Bobby'd renounced poetry, what was my part to be? To acknowledge it for him?
Flatter him? Tell him to keep on? I might well have, but not without knowing his work.

Then it came to me that his being here meant more than all that—it was a challenge;

Bobby wanted to defy me, and whatever he'd taken into his mind I rep-
resented.

The truth is I was flattered myself, that it was me he'd chosen, but there
was that knife;
though the blade was thin, serrated, to cut bread, not tendon or bone, it
still was a knife,

it could hurt you: despite myself, I felt my eyes fall to its sorry scabbard,
and as I did,
I could see Bobby'd caught my concern: he seemed to come to attention,
to harden.

Though he still hadn't threatened me quite—he never did—I knew now
I was afraid,
and Bobby did, too: I could sense his exaltation at having so invaded my
emotions;

an energy all at once emanated from him, a quaver, of satisfaction, or an-
ticipation:
"This is my poem," he might have been saying, "are you sure yours are
worth more?"

Then the moment had passed; it was as though Bobby had flinched,
though he hadn't,
torn his gaze from mine, though it clung, but we both knew now nothing
would happen,

we both realized Bobby's menace was a mask, that it couldn't conceal his
delicacy,
the gentle sensitivity that would have been so useful if he'd been able to
keep writing.

He must have felt me thinking that, too; something in him shut down,
and I wondered:
would he take this as a defeat? Whose, though? And what would a vic-
tory have been?

He turned then and without a word left, leaving me stranded there with
      my books
while he drifted out into the rest of his life, weighed down with his eva-
      sions, and mine.

I never found out what he came to in the end; I've always kept him as
      "Bobby the poet."
I only hope he didn't suffer more rue, that the Muse kept watch on her
      innocent stray.

Stone

These things that came into my mind,
that were unbearable, unthinkable.
Certain visions I suppose they could be called,
abominations that afflicted me with agony.

To think of them even now requires awful effort.
Like the hero going into battle
needing four strong men to lift his eyelids.
The unforgiving eyelids of my memory.

Like Perseus, the Gorgon in his mirror-shield,
how he could strike and not be turned to stone.
The stone slabs in my mind. All they hide.
All I've tried so to forget which stays in me.

Even, once, a head; it only matters whose to me.
A head hacked off, set bleeding on a table.
I had thought that only warriors, only Perseus,
could do these things. And yet it glared at me.

Though I knew it was my mind that had done
this thing, mind reeled away in agony.
The agonizing plasma consciousness can be.
Stone. Slabs of stone. Eyelids. Memory.

Droplets

Even when the rain falls relatively hard,
only one leaf at a time of the little tree
you planted on the balcony last year,
then another leaf at its time, and one more,
is set trembling by the constant droplets,

but the rain, the clouds flocked over the city,
you at the piano inside, your hesitant music
mingling with the din of the downpour,
the gush of rivulets loosed from the eaves,
the iron railings and flowing gutters,

all of it fuses in me with such intensity
that I can't help wondering why my longing
to live forever has so abated that it hardly
comes to me anymore, and never as it did,
as regret for what I might not live to live,

but rather as a layering of instants like this,
transient as the mist drawn from the rooftops,
yet emphatic as any note of the nocturne
you practice, and, the storm faltering, fading
into its own radiant passing, you practice again.

Tender

A tall-masted white sailboat works laboriously across a wave-tossed bay;
when it tilts in the swell, a porthole reflects a dot of light that darts to-
   wards me,
skitters back to refuge in the boat, gleams out again, and timidly retreats,
like a thought that comes almost to mind but slips away into the general
   glare.

An inflatable tender, tethered to the stern, just skims the commotion of
   the wake:
within it will be oars, a miniature motor, and, tucked into a pocket, life
   vests.
Such reassuring redundancy: don't we desire just such an accessory, faith
   perhaps,
or at a certain age to be comforted, not daunted, by knowing one will
   really die?

To bring all that with you, by compulsion admittedly, but on such a slen-
   der leash,
and so maneuverable it is, tractable, so nearly frictionless, no need to
   strain;
though it might have to rush a little to keep up, you hardly know it's
   there:
that insouciant headlong scurry, that always ardent leaping forwards into
   place.

Risk

Difficult to know whether humans are inordinately anxious
about crisis, calamity, disaster, or unknowingly crave them.
These horrific conditionals, these expected unexpecteds,
we dwell on them, flinch, feint, steel ourselves:
but mightn't our forebodings actually precede anxiety?
Isn't so much sheer heedfulness emblematic of *desire*?

How do we come to believe that wrenching ourselves to attention
is the most effective way for dealing with intimations of catastrophe?
Consciousness atremble: might what makes it so
not be the fear of what the future might or might not bring,
but the wish for fear, for concentration, vigilance?
As though life were more convincing resonating like a blade.

Of course, we're rarely swept into events, other than domestic tumult,
from which awful consequences will ensue. Fortunately rarely.
And yet we sweat as fervently
for the most insipid issues of honor and unrealized ambition.
Lost brothership. Lost lust. We engorge our little sorrows,
beat our drums, perform our dances of aversion.

Always, "These gigantic inconceivables."
Always, "What will have been done to me?"
And so we don our mental armor,
flex, thrill, pay the strict attention we always knew we should.
A violent alertness, the muscularity of risk,
though still the secret inward cry: What else, what more?

House

The way you'd renovate a ruined house, keeping the "shell," as we call it,
     brick, frame or stone,
and razing the rest: the inside walls—partitions, we say—then stairs,
     pipes, wiring, commodes,
saving only . . . no, save nothing this time; take the self-shell down to its
     emptiness, hollowness, void.

Down to the scabrous plaster, down to the lining bricks with mortar
     squashed through their joints,
down to the eyeless windows, the forlorn doorless doorways, the sprung
     joists powdery with rot;
down to the slab of the cellar, the erratically stuccoed foundation, the
     black earth underneath all.

Down under all to the ancient errors, indolence, envy, pretension, the
     frailties as though in the gene;
down to where consciousness cries, "Make me new," but pleads as
     pitiably, "Cherish me as I was."
Down to the swipe of the sledge, the ravaging bite of the pick; rubble,
     wreckage, vanity: the abyss.

Naked

Pissing out the door of a cottage
in an after-squall wind before dawn
in the tame hill country of Wales,
farms everywhere, fences and hedgerows,
but still enough strangeness, precipitous
pastures, patches of woods shadowing
tangles of one-car-wide lanes,
to take you out of yourself for a time,

so, naked under the low lintel,
an unaffrighting darkness before you,
so much of a washed-clean breeze
with so many temperate pulses and currents
of sleek, sensitive air languorously
touching across then seemingly through you,
how not delight to imagine dawn's
first wash moving through you as well,

barns, trees, and crouched shrubs
blockily coming to themselves within you;
then cockcrow, birds chirring
awake, and the silence, too, within
and without, as you turn away, leaving
the old patched door ajar
to breathe in the last wisps of night,
the already headily fragrant field-scents.

Glass

I'd have thought by now it would have stopped,
as anything sooner or later will stop, but still it happens

that when I unexpectedly catch sight of myself in a mirror,
there's a kind of concussion, a cringe; I look quickly away.

Lately, since my father died and I've come closer to his age,
I sometimes see him first, and have to focus to find myself.

I've thought it's that, my precious singularity being diluted,
but it's harsher than that, crueler, the way, when I was young,

I believed how you looked was supposed to *mean*,
something graver, more substantial: I'd gaze at my poor face

and think, "It's still not there." Apparently I still do.
What isn't there? Beauty? Not likely. Wisdom? Less.

Is how we live or try to live supposed to embellish us?
All I see is the residue of my other, failed faces.

But maybe what we're after is just a less abrasive regard:
not "It's still not there," but something like "Come in, be still."

Shoe

A pair of battered white shoes have been left out all night on a sill across
the way.
One, the right, has its toe propped against the pane so that it tilts oddly
upwards,
and there's an abandon in its attitude, an elevation, that reminds me of a
satyr on a vase.

A fleece of summer ivy casts the scene into deep relief, and I see the
creature perfectly:
surrounded by his tribe of admiring women, he glances coolly down at
his own lifted foot,
caught exactly at the outset of the frenzied leaping which will lift all of
them to rapture.

The erotic will diffused directly into matter: you can sense his menacing
lasciviousness,
his sensual glaze, his delight in being flagrant, so confidently more than
merely mortal,
separate from though hypercritically aware of earthly care, of our so
amusing earthly woe.

All that carnal scorn which in his dimension is a fitting emblem for his
energy and grace,
but which in our meager world would be hubris, arrogance, compensa-
tion for some lack or loss,
or for that passion to be other than we are that with a shock of longing
takes me once again.

Dream

Strange that one's deepest split from oneself
should be enacted in those banal and inevitable
productions of the double dark of sleep.
Despite all my broodings about dream,
I never fail to be amazed by the misery
I inflict on myself when I'm supposedly at rest.

Rest? In last night's dream my beloved announced to me,
and to others in the dream as well, that her desire was . . .
to not limit her range of sexual choice.
I implored her, but she wouldn't respond.
Why would characters in one's own dream
share with the waking world such awful unknowability?

Dreams are said to enact unfulfilled needs,
discords we can't admit to ourselves,
but I've never been able to believe that.
I dream pain, dream grief, dream shame,
I cry out, wake in terror:
is there something in me that *requires* such torment?

There used to be books of dream:
every dream had symbolic meaning.
And the old Chinese believed
that dreams implied their reversal:
a dream of travel meant you'd stay home,
to dream of death meant longer life.

Yes, yes! Surely my beloved in my dream
was saying she loved only me.
The coolness in your eyes, love, was really heat,
your wish to range was your renewal of allegiance;
those prying others were you and I ourselves,
beholding one another's fealty, one another's fire.

Mad dreams! Mad love!

The Cup

What was going through me at that time of childhood
when my mother drinking her morning coffee would drive me wild with
loathing and despair?
Every day, her body hunched with indignation at having had to leave its
sleep,
her face without its rouge an almost mortal pale,
she'd stand before the stove and wait until the little turret on the cof-
feepot subsided,
then she'd fill her cup and navigate her way across the kitchen.

At the table, she'd set the cup down in its saucer, pour in milk, sit,
let out a breath charged with some onerous responsibility I never under-
stood,
and lift the cup again.
There'd be a tiny pause as though she had consciously to synchronize
her mouth and hand,
then her lips would lengthen and reach out, prehensile as a primate's
tail,
and seem to *grasp* the liquid with the sputtering suctioning of gravity im-
perfectly annulled.
Then, grimacing as though it were a molten metal she was bringing into
herself—
always grimacing, I'd think: did she never know what temperature the
stuff would be?—
she'd hold about a spoonful just behind her teeth before she'd slide it
thickly down.

Thickly, much too thickly:
she must have changed its gravity in there to some still more viscous,
lavalike elixir.
Then there'd be a grateful lowering of her shoulders.
Also then her eyes would lift to focus on a point beyond my head
as though always then a thought had come to her that needed rarer
ranges of reflection.

She'd do that twice, all that always twice, and put the coffee down.
In its porcelain cauldron, the military-brownish broth would sway—
was her passion for it going to make it boil again?—and finally come to
    rest.

. . . As *I* never came to rest, as I had to watch, I knew the interval by
    heart,
her hand come down to it again, her head lower to it again,
that excruciating suction sound again, her gaze loosening again.
I'd be desperate, wild, my heart would pound.
There was an expression then, "to tell on someone": that was what I
    craved, to *tell* on her,
to have someone bear witness with me to her awful wrong.
What was I doing to myself? Or she to me?
Oh, surely she to me!

Lost Wax

My love gives me some wax,
so for once instead of words
I work at something real:
I knead until I see emerge
a person, a protagonist;
but I must overwork my wax,
it loses its resiliency,
comes apart in crumbs.

I take another block:
this work, I think, will be a self;
I can feel it forming, brow
and brain; perhaps it will be me,
perhaps, if I can create myself,
I'll be able to amend myself;
my wax, though, freezes
this time, fissures, splits.

Words or wax, no end
to our self-shaping, our forlorn
awareness at the end of which
is only more awareness.
Was ever truth so malleable?
Arid, inadhesive bits of matter.
What might heal you? Love.
What make you whole? Love. My love.

Space

The space within me, within which I partly, or possibly mostly exist:
so familiar it is yet how little I know it, I'm not even sure of its volume;
sometimes it expands behind me like a wing, sometimes it contracts,
and while the world is often in it, it's rarely wholly congruent with it.

I'm not even certain when or why the world happens to appear there,
in a way that means something, brings with it more than my perceptions
at that instant, something that arrives with an insistence, a *friction*,
so that I have to move myself aside within myself to make a place for it.

If this space, at any rate, were a room, its color would be beige, or umber,
with fleetings of gold, not the gold of icons, but paler, less emphatic:
when my eyes first close there's a momentary darkening there as well,
sometimes the dimness smolders more intensely, almost to blood red.

Reestablishing myself in myself like this always comes to pass,
it seems it can't not come to pass, but an effort is needed, too,
something like faith: my vision rolls back through the bell of the skull,
all my ordinary thoughts are deferred, time becomes purely potential,

then clumps of light, glowing, pulsing patterns stutter in, then images,
usually of where I am just then, then others, then I hear my breath,
feel my body, become aware of thoughts and language; but even then,
the unexpected can occur: right now, a sharp, rolling, planetary horizon.

Such a strange interval: I wonder if this is what the last, indivisible instant
before death might be, before the absolutely unluminous absence.
To open one's tangible eyes just then, as I do now: light, shapes, color!
Close again; darkness without end, but wait, still glow, still sentience: bliss.

Tantrum

A child's cry out in the street, not of pain or fear,
rather one of those vividly inarticulate
yet perfectly expressive trumpet thumps of indignation:
something wished for has been denied,
something wanted *now* delayed.

So useful it would be to carry that preemptive howl
always with you; all the functions it performs,
its equivalents in words are so unwieldy,
take up so much emotive time,
entail such muffling, qualifying, attenuation.

And in our cries out to the cosmos, our exasperation
with imperfection, our theodicies, betrayed ideals:
to keep that rocky core of rage within one's rage
with which to blame, confront, accuse, bewail
all that needs retaliation for our absurdly thwarted wants.

Not Soul

Not soul,
not that tired tale anyway about preliterate
people believing cameras would extract
their spiritual essence, nothing so obvious,

but what is it I feel has been stripped,
stolen, negated, when I look out across
this valley of old farms, mist, trees,
a narrow, steep-banked brook,

and have the thought take me that all this
is a kind of reservation, a museum,
of land, plants, houses, even people—
a woman now, crossing a field—

that it all endures only by the happenstance
of no one having decided to "develop" it,
bring in a highway from the turnpike,
construct subdivisions, parking lots, malls?

Not soul,
soul is what religions believed subsumes
experience and will, what philosophers
surmised compels us to beauty and virtue,

is what even the most skeptical still save
for any resolving description of inner life,
this intricately knotted compound
which resists any less ambiguous locution.

How imagine so purely human a term
applying to things, to the rushing brook
which follows the slant of soil beneath it,
the mist functioned by the warmth of air,

even the houses to be torn down or crowded
into anonymity according to patterns
which have no discernible logic, certainly
nothing one mind might consider sufficient?

Not soul,
but still, anthropomorphism or not,
the very shape and hue and texture of reality,
the sheen of surface, depth of shadow,

seem unfocused now, hollowed out,
as though the pact between ourselves and world
that lets the world stand for more than itself
were violated, so that everything I see,

the lowering clouds, the tempered light,
and even all I only bring to mind, is dulled,
despoiled, as though consciousness no longer
could distill such truths within itself,

as though a gel of sadness had been interposed
between me and so much loveliness
so much at risk, as though a tear
had ineradicably fixed upon the eye.

Depths

I'm on a parapet looking down
into a deep cleft in the earth
at minuscule people and cars
moving along its narrow bottom.
Though my father's arms are around me
I feel how far it would be to fall,
how perilous: I cringe back,
my father holds me more tightly.
Was there ever such a crevice?
No, I realized much, much later
we were on an ordinary building
looking down into a city street.

A picture book: desert sunlight,
a man and woman clad in sandals,
pastel robes, loose burnooses,
plying a material like dough,
the man kneading in a trough,
the woman throwing at a wheel.
Somehow I come to think they're angels,
in heaven, fashioning human beings.
Was there ever such a story?
No, the book, at Sunday school,
showed daily life in the Bible,
the people were just making jars.

Just jars, and yet those coils of clay,
tinted light to dark like skin,
swelled beneath the woman's hands
as I knew already flesh should swell,
and as I'd know it later, when,
alone with someone in the dark,
I'd close my eyes, move my hands
across her, and my mouth across her,

trying to experience an ideal,
to participate in radiances
I passionately believed existed,
and not only in imagination.

Or, with love itself, the love
that came to me so readily, so
intensely, so convincingly each time,
and each time ravaged me
when it spoiled and failed, and left
me only memories of its promise.
Could real love ever come to me?
Would I distort it if it did?
Even now I feel a frost of fear
to think I might not have found you,
my love, or not believed in you,
and still be reeling on another roof.

Tree

One vast segment of the tree, the very topmost, bows ceremoniously
    against a breath of breeze,
patient, sagacious, apparently possessing the wisdom such a union of
    space, light and matter should.

Just beneath, though grazed by the same barely perceptible zephyr, a
    knot of leaves quakes hectically,
as though trying to convince that more pacific presence above it of its
    anxieties, its dire forebodings.

Now some of the individual spreads that make up the higher, ponderous,
    stoic portion are caught, too,
by a more insistent pressure: their unity disrupted, they sway irrationally;
    do they, too, sense danger?

Harried, quaking, they seem to wonder whether some untoward response
    will be demanded of them,
whether they'll ever graze again upon the ichor with which such benign
    existences sustain themselves.

A calming now, a more solid, gel-like weight of heat in the air, in the tree
    a tense, tremulous subsiding;
the last swelling and flattening of the thousand glittering armadas of sun-
    light passing through the branches.

The tree's negative volume defines it now; the space it contains con-
    tained in turn by the unmoving warmth,
by duration breathlessly suspended, and, for me, by a languorous sense
    of being all at once pacified, quelled.

King

1.

A tall, handsome black man, bearded, an artist, in nineteen sixty-eight, in Philadelphia,
you're walking down Market Street two days after Martin Luther King's murder
on your way to the memorial service scheduled that morning near the Liberty Bell.
Thirty years later, and I can still picture you there: you're walking fast, preoccupied,
when suddenly a police car swerves over the curb in front of you, blocking your way.

And I can see the two policemen, both white, cold, expressionless, glaring at you:
a long moment passes, then I see you looking over your shoulder, turning away,
moving towards the street, to the back of the squad car, passing behind it off the curb,
around it to the sidewalk on the other side and continuing down Market again,
to Nineteenth, then right to Rittenhouse Square where someone's waiting for you.

When you see the person (he's white, like the policemen), you don't say anything;
though you'd made an appointment not an hour ago to go to the service together,
you don't even glance at him again until he runs after you, calling for you to wait.
You stop to talk to him then, but only long enough to tell him in a harsh, low voice
everything that had happened with the policemen, then a few hard sentences more.

2.

Maybe my trying to relive this with you should stop there; this after all is
       your story,
but something still feels unresolved between us, as so much does in our
       culture.
I've heard black friends say that in some ways race matters were easier
       then,
at least then the prejudice was out in the open, you knew where you
       were:
even the police were only the most visible edge of a hardly covert white
       racism.

But if the police were a symbol of something else, they were brutal
       enough at it.
You could, if you were black, man or woman, be beaten to death by
       policemen.
You could, at a cop's whim, be arrested for "disturbing the peace," or
       "resisting arrest,"
which meant you'd done nothing, but had been battered badly enough
       for it to show,
necessitating if not an excuse then a reason, which incidentally added to
       your sentence.

Back then, too, even if you could afford a good lawyer, who might get
       you off,
if the police were angry enough, you had reason to fear that in the bus
       from jail
to the courtroom, you'd be raped, gang-raped, and no one would dare say
       a thing.
All that had to have come to your mind as you stood, that idling squad
       car before you,
the cops inside it with their clubs and guns, impassive, their eyes chal-
       lenging, hard.

3.

They'd have known when they'd spotted you where you were going;
      everyone was.
And they'd have seen that you were confident, full of yourself: an "uppity
      nigger."
However they'd have put it to themselves, they'd have believed that by
      insulting you
they could denigrate King with you, debase what he'd stood for, demon-
      strate to you
that if you thought he had released you from the trap of history you were
      deluded.

But there would have been even more they'd have wanted to be sure you
      understood,
were ready to break their fists on you, maim or kill you so that you'd un-
      derstand:
that their world would prevail, that authority, power, and absolute physi-
      cal coercion
with no ethical dimension whatsoever must and will precede all and
      resolve all
and break everything down again and again into an unqualified domin-
      ion of force.

All that would have passed between you in an instant, what came next,
      though,
would have driven their rage to a level where you knew the situation
      might explode:
it was their suspicion, and your certainty, that even if they did apparently
      intimidate you,
they couldn't make you renounce in yourself the conviction of your
      moral worth,
the inextinguishable truth that would supersede even what might seem
      submission.

4.

Wasn't that what would have made you know you'd have to turn and go
    around them?
Surely your fury outstripped your fear, but didn't you make a truce with
    them, and a wager?
The truce was your walking away and their acceptance of that as a sign of
    compliance;
the wager, on their part, was that in your pretense of capitulation there'd
    be uncertainty,
that one day you'd have to forgive yourself for your humiliation, and
    wouldn't be able to.

And wasn't the wager on your side that though you might be hurt by your
    seeming yielding,
the lesion of your doubt, your shame and possible self-accusations would
    be outweighed
by knowing that nothing would have justified letting them exert their
    thuggery on you,
that, no matter what they believed, they wouldn't, couldn't have negated
    your anger?
But wouldn't your surrender have scorched you? Wasn't that what you
    were saying to me?

Don't tell me you know what I feel, and don't give me that crap about be-
    ing with us,
you wouldn't know how to be with us, you don't know the first thing about
    us.
For three hundred years we've coddled you, protected your illusions of inno-
    cence,
letting you go on thinking you're pure: well you're not pure, you're the
    same as those pigs.
And please, please, don't tell me again you can understand because you're
    a Jew.

5.

A black man, a white man, three decades of history, of remembering and
       forgetting.
The day was Good Friday: after a long winter, the first warm, welcoming
       odors of spring.
People flowed to Independence Hall Park from all directions, everyone
       was subdued;
if there were tensions, they were constrained by our shared grief; we held
       hands.
The night before, though, in some cities there were riots: gunfire, sol-
       diers, buildings burning.

Sometimes it's hard to know why they stopped: I often think if I were
       black in America,
I might want to run riot myself with the sheer hypocritical unendingness
       of it all:
a so-called politics of neglect, families savaged, communities fractured
       and abandoned.
Black man, white man: I can still see us, one standing stricken, the other
       stalking away;
I can still feel your anger, feel still because it's still in me my helpless
       despair.

And will you by now have been able to leave behind the indignities and
       offense
of both halves of that morning? Isn't that what we're supposed to do in
       our country;
aren't we given to believe our wounds will heal, our scars fade, our in-
       sults be redeemed?
Later, during the service, when the "overcome" anthem was sung, I
       started to cry;
many others in the crowd around were crying, black and white, but I
       couldn't see you.

Owen: Seven Days

for Owen Burns, born March 5, 1997

Well here I
go again into my
grandson's eyes

seven days
old and he knows
nothing logic tells me

yet when I
look into his eyes
darkish grayish blue

a whole tone
lighter
than his mother's

I feel myself almost
with a *whoosh*
dragged

into his consciousness
and processed
processed processed

his brows knit
I'm in there now
I don't know

in what form but
his gaze hasn't
faltered an instant

though still his
brows knit and
knit as though to

get just right
what I am no
what I'm thinking

as though to get
what I'm thinking
just exactly right

in perplexity perhaps
his brows knit
once again

perhaps because
of how little
inscrutability

with which the
problem of me
is presented

not "Who are you?"
but more something
like "Why?

Why are you? Out
there? Do you
know?"

then his eyelids
start to flutter
time to sleep

and once again with
something like
another *whoosh*

I'm ejected back
out into my
world

bereft? no
but for an instant
maybe just a little

lonely just a
little desolated
just for a while

utterly confounded
by the sheer
propulsive

force of
being taken
by such love

Gas

Wouldn't it be nice, I think, when the blue-haired lady in the doctor's
     waiting room bends over the magazine table
and farts, just a little, and violently blushes, wouldn't it be nice if intes-
     tinal gas came embodied in visible clouds
so she could see that her really quite inoffensive *pop* had only barely
     grazed my face before it drifted away?

Besides, for this to have happened now is a nice coincidence because not
     an hour ago, while we were on our walk,
my dog was startled by a backfire and jumped straight up like a horse
     bucking and that brought back to me
the stable I worked on weekends when I was twelve and a splendid
     piebald stallion who whenever he was mounted

would buck just like that, though more hugely, of course, enormous,
     gleaming, resplendent, and the woman,
her face abashedly buried in her *Elle* now, reminded me I'd forgotten
     that not the least part of my awe
consisted of the fact that with every jump he took the horse would pow-
     erfully fart, *fwap, fwap, fwap,*

something never mentioned in the dozens of books about horses and
     their riders I devoured in those days.
All that savage grandeur, the steely glinting hooves, the eruptions driven
     from the creature's mighty innards:
breath stopped, heart stopped, nostrils madly flared, I didn't know if I
     wanted to break him or be him.

Last Things

for John Stewart

In a tray of dried fixative in a photographer friend's darkroom,
I found a curled-up photo of his son the instant after his death,
his glasses still on, a drop of blood caught at his mouth.

Recently, my friend put a book together to commemorate his son;
near the end, there's a picture taken the day before the son died;
the caption says: "This is the last photo of Alex."

I'm sure my friend doesn't know I've seen the other picture.
Is telling about it a violation of confidence?
Before I show this to anyone else, I'll have to ask his permission.

If you're reading it, you'll know my friend pardoned me,
that he found whatever small truth his story might embody
was worth the anguish of remembering that reflexive moment

when after fifty years of bringing reality into himself through a lens,
his camera doubtlessly came to his eye as though by itself,
and his finger, surely also of its own accord, convulsed the shutter.

The Lie

As one would praise a child or dog, or punish it,
as one would chastise it, or hit it, *hit* it;
as one would say, *sit, sit down, be still*:
so don't we discipline ourselves, disparage,
do as thoughtlessly unto ourselves?

As one would tell a lie, a faithless lie,
not with good intention, to obviate a harm,
but just to have one's way, to win, *prevail*:
so don't we deceive ourselves,
and not even know we are?

A self which by definition cannot tell
itself untruths, yet lies, which, wanting
to tell itself untruths, isn't able to, not then,
and would like sometimes not to know
it's lied, but can't deny it has, not then.

And our righteousness before ourselves,
how we're so barbarous towards ourselves,
so mercilessly violate ourselves;
as one would never, with a loved one, harm,
never, with a dear one, strike, not *strike*.

As one would with an enemy, implacable,
as one would with an animal, intractable,
as one would with a self which savagely resists:
this amputating, this assailing, this self-slashing.
As one would lie, as one so fervently would lie.

The Nail

Some dictator or other had gone into exile, and now reports were com-
        ing about his regime,
the usual crimes, torture, false imprisonment, cruelty and corruption,
        but then a detail:
that the way his henchmen had disposed of enemies was by hammering
        nails into their skulls.
Horror, then, what mind does after horror, after that first feeling that
        you'll never catch your breath,
mind imagines—how not be annihilated by it?—the preliminary tap,
        feels it in the tendons of the hand,
feels the way you do with *your* nail when you're fixing something, mak-
        ing something, shelves, a bed;
the first light tap to set the slant, and then the slightly harder tap, to em-
        bed the tip a little more . . .

No, no more: this should be happening in myth, in stone, or paint, not
        in reality, not here;
it should be an emblem of itself, not itself, something that would *mean*,
        not really have to happen,
something to go out, expand in implication from that unmoved mass of
        matter in the breast;
as in the image of an anguished face, in grief for us, not us as us, us as in
        a myth, a moral tale,
a way to tell the truth that grief is limitless, a way to tell us we must al-
        ways understand
it's we who do such things, we who set the slant, embed the tip, lift the
        sledge and drive the nail,
drive the nail which is the axis upon which turns the brutal human
        world upon the world.

Canal

The almost deliciously ill, dank, dark algae on the stone of its sides,
the putrid richness of its flow which spontaneously brings forth refuse,
dead fish, crusts, condoms, all slowly surging in its muck of gruel,
under the tonnage of winter sky which darkens everything still more,
soils the trash, fruit, paper, dead leaves, water, impossibly still more.

Yet trudging, freezing, along beside it, I seem taken by it, to be of it,
its shape, its ooze; in the biting wind it and I make one single thing,
this murky, glass-hard lid with gulls fixed in it lifting and falling,
this dulled sheet, dense as darkness, winding by indifferent buildings,
we compose a single entity, a unity, not as fanciful speculation

but as though one actually might be the sentient mind of something,
as though only watching this indolent swell would bring into me
all that ever touched it, went across, perished and dissolved in it,
all caught lymphlike in this mortal trench, this ark, this cognizance;
a craving spirit flung across it, a tranquil stillness deep within it.

The Dance

A middle-aged woman, quite plain, to be polite about it, and somewhat
    stout, to be more courteous still,
but when she and the rather good-looking, much younger man she's with
    get up to dance,
her forearm descends with such delicate lightness, such restrained but
    confident ardor athwart his shoulder,
drawing him to her with such a firm, compelling warmth, and moving
    him with effortless grace
into the union she's instantly established with the not at all rhythmically
    solid music in this second-rate café,

that something in the rest of us, some doubt about ourselves, some sad
    conjecture, seems to be allayed,
nothing that we'd ever thought of as a real lack, nothing not to be ad-
    mired or be repentant for,
but something to which we've never adequately given credence,
which might have consoling implications about how we misbelieve our-
    selves, and so the world,
that world beyond us which so often disappoints, but which sometimes
    shows us, lovely, what we are.

Biopsy

Have I told you, love, about the experience
I used to have before I knew you?
At first it seemed a dream—I'd be in bed—
then I'd realize I was awake, which made it—
it was already frightening—appalling.

A dense, percussive, pulsing hum,
too loud to bear as soon as I'd hear it,
it would become a coil of audible matter
tightening over me, so piercing
I was sure I'd tear apart in it.

I'd try to say a word to contradict it,
but its hold on me was absolute,
I was paralyzed; then, my terror
past some limit, I'd try again: this time
I'd cry out aloud, and it would stop.

Trembling, I'd come to myself, as,
the night of your tests, I came shuddering
awake, my fear for you, for both of us,
raging more terribly through me
than that vision of annihilation ever did.

It was like the desolate time before you:
I couldn't turn to you for reassurance
lest I frighten you, couldn't embrace you
for fear I'd wake you to your own anxiety,
so, as I had then, I lay helpless, mute.

The results were "negative"; now
I'll tell you of those hours in which my life,
not touching you but holding you,
not making a sound but crying for you,
divided back into the half it is without you.

The Island

Glorious morning, the sun still mild on the eastward hills, the hills still
hushed;
only sometimes will a placeless voice find its way across the softly sleep-
ing valley,
a slightly higher wave rise and wash in sighing over the stony beach.

So pleasant in such peace the way self inhabits its perceptual containers,
luxurious to descend so insouciantly from the inwardly armored helmet
of thought;
consciousness dilates, there's a feeling of lubrication, acceleration,

my attention, as though freed of me, darts from a here which often isn't
here,
to a there which usually remains resolutely an *away*; darts now from a
white house
to an even whiter church up behind it, then down across a thistled slope

before it lifts abruptly, captured by the apparition of a single yellow
flower petal
soaring in a magnifying gush of light unwaveringly *upwards*, towards the
firmament.
A sign? To reinforce the fittingness with which vision and its contents
coincide?

Now a burly, gray-white, rather short-winged gull lifts into the square of
window
and with a visibly potent muscling of its pinions banks from sight. An-
other sign?
Of more strenuous felicities? But if one believed such things, what
wouldn't be?

What about the fisherman out on his boat? What of the slowly moving
boat itself?
How productive mind can seem, wheeling through such doing-
something doing-nothing,

how pure its feeling of achievement in these world-spun strandings of
  connection.

But now comes an intimation of distraction; might the moment be al-
  ready being lost?
No matter: let the swaying cypress, the ever-sweetening breezes be their
  own reprieve.
Another swell sweeps across the still-calm bay; everything ripples, every-
  thing holds.

Dirt

My grandmother is washing my mouth
out with soap; half a long century gone
and still she comes at me
with that thick, cruel, yellow bar.
All because of a word I said,
not even said really, only repeated,
but *Open*, she says, *open up!*
her hand clawing at my head.

I know now her life was hard;
she lost three daughters as babies,
then her husband died, too,
leaving young sons, and no money.
She'd stand me in the sink to pee
because there was never room in the toilet.
But, oh, her soap! Might its bitter burning
have been what made me a poet?

The street she lived on was unpaved,
her flat two cramped rooms and a fetid
kitchen where she stalked and caught me.
Dare I admit that after she did it
I never really loved her again?
She lived to a hundred, even then.
All along it was the sadness, the squalor,
but I never, until now, loved her again.

Swifts

Why this much fascination with you, little loves, why this what feels like,
     oh, hearts,
almost too much exultation in you who set the day's end sky ashimmer
     with your veerings?
Why this feeling one might stay forever to behold you as you bank,
     swoop, swerve, soar,
make folds and pleats in evening's velvet, and pierce and stitch, dissect,
     divide,
cast up slopes which hold a beat before they fall away into the softening
     dusk?
That such fragile beings should concoct such sky-long lifting bends
     across the roofs,
as though human work counted for as little as your quickly dimming in-
     tersecting cries.

Tiniest dear ones, but chargers, too, gleaming, potent little coursers of
     the firmament,
smaller surely, lighter, but with that much force, that much insistence
     and enchantment;
godlings, nearly, cast upon the sky as upon a field of thought until then
     never thought,
gravity exempting from its weary weight its favorite toy, oh, you, and its
     delights, you and you,
as you hurl yourself across the tint of sinking sunlight that flows behind
     you as a wake of gold.
And the final daylight sounds you wing back to your eaves with you to
     weave into the hush,
then your after-hush which pulses in the sky of memory one last beat
     more as full dark falls.

Invisible Mending

Three women old as angels,
bent as ancient apple trees,
who, in a storefront window,
with magnifying glasses,
needles fine as hair, and shining
scissors, parted woof from warp
and pruned what would in
human tissue have been sick.

Abrasions, rents and frays,
slits and chars and acid
splashes, filaments that gave
way of their own accord
from the stress of spanning
tiny, trifling gaps, but which
in a wounded psyche
make a murderous maze.

Their hands as hard as horn,
their eyes as keen as steel,
the threads they worked with
must have seemed as thick
as ropes on ships, as cables
on a crane, but still their heads
would lower, their teeth bare
to nip away the raveled ends.

Only sometimes would they
lift their eyes to yours to show
how much lovelier than these twists
of silk and serge the garments
of the mind are, yet how much
more benign their implements
than mind's procedures
of forgiveness and repair.

And in your loneliness you'd notice
how really very gently they'd take
the fabric to its last, with what
solicitude gather up worn edges
to be bound, with what severe
but kind detachment wield
their amputating shears:
forgiveness, and repair.

THE SINGING

[2003]

I

The Doe

Near dusk, near a path, near a brook,
we stopped, I in disquiet and dismay
for the suffering of someone I loved,
the doe in her always incipient alarm.

All that moved was her pivoting ear
the reddening sun shining through
transformed to a color I'd only seen
in a photo of a child in a womb.

Nothing else stirred, not a leaf,
not the air, but she startled and bolted
away from me into the crackling brush.

The part of my pain which sometimes
releases me from it fled with her, the rest,
in the rake of the late light, stayed.

The Singing

I was walking home down a hill near our house on a balmy afternoon
        under the blossoms
Of the pear trees that go flamboyantly mad here every spring with their
        burgeoning forth

When a young man turned in from a corner singing no it was more of a
        cadenced shouting
Most of which I couldn't catch I thought because the young man was
        black speaking black

It didn't matter I could tell he was making his song up which pleased me
        he was nice-looking
Husky dressed in some style of big pants obviously full of himself hence
        his lyrical flowing over

We went along in the same direction then he noticed me there almost
        beside him and "Big"
He shouted-sang "Big" and I thought how droll to have my height incor-
        porated in his song

So I smiled but the face of the young man showed nothing he looked in
        fact pointedly away
And his song changed "I'm not a nice person" he chanted "I'm not I'm
        not a nice person"

No menace was meant I gathered no particular threat but he did want to
        be certain I knew
That if my smile implied I conceived of anything like concord between
        us I should forget it

That's all nothing else happened his song became indecipherable to me
        again he arrived
Where he was going a house where a girl in braids waited for him on the
        porch that was all

No one saw no one heard all the unasked and unanswered questions
were left where they were
It occurred to me to sing back "I'm not a nice person either" but I
couldn't come up with a tune

Besides I wouldn't have meant it nor he have believed it both of us knew
just where we were
In the duet we composed the equation we made the conventions to
which we were condemned

Sometimes it feels even when no one is there that someone something is
watching and listening
Someone to rectify redo remake this time again though no one saw nor
heard no one was there

Bialystok, or Lvov

A squalid wayside inn, reeking barn-brewed vodka,
cornhusk cigarettes that cloy like acrid incense
in a village church, kegs of rotten, watered wine,
but then a prayer book's worn-thin pages,
and over them, as though afloat in all that fetidness,
my great-grandfather's disembodied head.

Cacophonous drunkenness, lakes of vomit
and oceans of obscenities; the smallpox pocked
salacious peasant faces whose carious breath
clots one's own; and violence, the scorpion-
brutal violence of nothing else, to do, to have,
then the prayers again, that tormented face,

its shattered gaze, and that's all I have,
of whence I came, of where the blood came from
that made my blood, and the tale's not even mine,
I have it from a poet, the Russian-Jewish then
Israeli Bialik, and from my father speaking of
his father's father dying in his miserable tavern,

in a fight, my father said, with berserk Cossacks,
but my father fabulated, so I omit all that,
and share the poet's forebears, because mine
only wanted to forget their past of poverty
and pogrom, so said nothing, or perhaps
where someone came from, a lost name,

otherwise nothing, leaving me less
history than a dog, just the poet's father's
and my great-grandfather's inn, that sty,
the poet called it, that abyss of silence, I'd say,
and that soul, like snow, the poet wrote,
with tears of blood, I'd add, for me and mine.

This Happened

A student, a young woman, in a fourth floor hallway of her *lycée*,
perched on the ledge of an open window chatting with friends between
      classes;
a teacher passes and chides her, *Be careful, you might fall,*
almost banteringly chides her, *You might fall,*
and the young woman, eighteen, a girl really, though she wouldn't think
      that,
as brilliant as she is, first in her class, *and beautiful, too,* she's often told,
smiles back, and leans into the open window, which wouldn't even be
      open if it were winter,
if it were winter someone would have closed it (*Close it!*)
leans into the window, farther, still smiling, farther and farther,
though it takes less time than this, really an instant, and lets herself fall.
      Herself fall.

A casual impulse, a fancy, never thought of until now, hardly thought of
      even now . . .
No, more than impulse or fancy, the girl knows what she's doing,
the girl means something, the girl means to *mean,*
because, it occurs to her in that instant, that beautiful or not, bright yes
      or no,
she's not who she is, *she's not the person she is,* and the reason, she sud-
      denly knows,
is that there's been so much premeditation where she is, so much plot-
      ting and planning,
there's hardly a person where she is, or if there is, it's not her, or not
      wholly her,
it's a self inhabited, lived in by her, and seemingly even as she thinks it
she knows what's been missing: grace, not premeditation but grace,
a kind of being in the world spontaneously, with *grace.*

Weightfully upon me was the world.
Weightfully this self which graced the world yet never wholly itself.
Weightfully this self which weighed upon me,

the release from which is what I desire and what I achieve.
And the girl remembers, in this infinite instant already so many times
    divided,
the grief she felt once, hardly knowing she felt it, to merely inhabit her-
    self.
Yes, the girl falls, absurd to fall, even the earth with its compulsion to
    take unto itself all that falls
must know that falling is absurd, yet the girl falling isn't myself,
or she is myself, but a self I took of my own volition unto myself.
Forever. With grace. *This happened.*

Self-Portrait with Rembrandt Self-Portrait

I put my face inches from his
and look into his eyes
which look back,
but whatever it is
so much beyond suffering
I long towards in his gaze
and imagine inhabiting mine
eludes me.

I put my face inches from his
face palette-knifed nearly raw,
scraped down to whatever it is
that denies flesh yet is flesh
but whatever it is
which still so exalts flesh,
even flesh scraped nearly raw,
eludes me.

My face inches from his
face neither frowning
nor smiling nor susceptible
any longer to any expression
but this watch, this regard;
whatever it is
I might keep of any of that
eludes me.

My face inches from his,
his inches from mine,
whatever it is beyond
dying and fear of dying,
whatever it is beyond solace
which remains solace
eludes me,
yet no longer eludes me.

Gravel

Children love gravel, kneeling to play in gravel,
even gravel covering dry, irrelevant dust.

It's not "Look what I found!" but the gravel itself,
which is what puzzles adults, that nothing's there,

even beneath, but it's just what Catherine most likes,
that there's no purpose to it, no meaning.

So, that day in the metro when the pickpocket
she'd warned a tourist against knelt, a hand at his ankle,

glowering at her, I wonder if one layer of her mind
had drift through it, *"Like a child, with gravel."*

That the thief may have been reaching into his boot
for a knife or a razor didn't come to her until later,

when she told me about it; only then was she frightened,
even more than when the crook, the creep, the slime,

got up instead and shoved her, and spit at her face,
and everyone else stood there as blank as their eyes,

only then did she lean against me, and shudder, as I,
now, not in a park or playground, not watching a child

sift through her shining fingers those bits of shattered
granite which might be our lives, shudder again.

Lessons

1.

When I offered to help her and took the arm
of the young blind woman standing
seemingly bewildered on my corner,
she thanked me, disengaged my hand
and tucked one of hers under my elbow
with a forthright, somehow heartening firmness;
we walked a few blocks to the subway
and rode awhile in the same direction;
she studied history, she told me, then here
was my stop, that's all there was time for.

2.

Something about feeling the world
come towards her in irrational jags,
a hundred voices a minute, honks,
squeals, the clicking blur of a bike,
and how she let herself flow across it
with the most valiant, unflinching unsurprise
made the way I dwell in my own cognition,
the junctures of perception and thought,
seem suddenly hectic, blunt;
the sense of abundances squandered, misused.

3.

My first piano teacher was partially blind;
her sister, whom she lived with,
was entirely so; she had a guidedog,
a shepherd, who'd snarl at me from their yard—

I feared him nearly as much as the teacher.
She, of the old school, cool and severe,
because of her sight would seem to scowl at my fingers,
and she kept a baton on the keyboard to rap them
for their inexhaustible store of wrong notes
and for lags of my always inadequate attention.

4.

Still, to bring her back just to berate her
is unfair, I mustn't have been easy either;
I keep being drawn to that place, though:
there was some scent there, some perfume, some powder;
my ears would ring and my eyes widen and tear.
Rank, wild, it may have been perspiration—
they were poor—or old music, or books;
two women, a dog: despite myself,
stumbling out into the dusk—dear dusk—
I'd find myself trying to breathe it again.

5.

. . . And the way one can find oneself strewn
so inattentively across life, across time.
Those who touch us, those whom we touch,
we hold them or we let them go
as though it were such a small matter.
How even know in truth how much
of mind should be memory, no less
what portion of self should be others
rather than self? Across life, across time,
as though it were such a small matter.

Oh

Oh my, Harold Brodkey, of all people, after all this time appearing to
    me,
so long after his death, so even longer since our friendship, our last
    friendship,
the third or fourth, the one anyway when the ties between us definitively
    frayed,
(Oh, Harold's a handful, another of his ex-friends sympathized, to my
    relief);

Harold Brodkey, at a Christmas Eve dinner, of all times and places,
because of my nephew's broken nose, of all reasons, which he suffered in
    an assault,
the bone shattered, reassembled, but healing a bit out of plumb,
and when I saw him something Harold wrote came to mind, about Mar-
    lon Brando,

how until Brando's nose was broken he'd been pretty, but after he was
    beautiful,
and that's the case here, a sensitive boy now a complicatedly handsome
    young man
with a sinewy edge he hadn't had, which I surely remark because of
    Harold,
and if I spoke to the dead, which I don't, or not often, I might thank him:

It's pleasant to think of you, Harold, of our good letters and talks;
I'm sorry we didn't make it up that last time, I wanted to but I was worn
    out
by your snits and rages, your mania to be unlike and greater than anyone
    else,
your preemptive attacks for inadequate acknowledgment of your ge-
    nius . . .

But no, leave it alone, Harold's gone, truly gone, and isn't it unforgiv-
    able, vile,

to stop loving someone, or to stop being loved; we don't mean to lose
      friends,
but someone drifts off, and we let them, or they renounce us, or we
      them, or we're hurt,
like flowers, for god's sake, when really we're prideful brutes, as blunt as
      icebergs.

Until something like this, some Harold Brodkey wandering into your
      mind,
as exasperating as ever, and, oh my, as brilliant, as charming, unwound
      from his web
to confront you with how ridden you are with unthought regret, how di-
      minished,
how well you know you'll clunk on to the next rationalization, the next
      loss, the next lie.

Narcissism

. . . The word alone sizzles like boiling acid, moans like molten lead, but ah my dear, it leaves the lips in such a sweetly murmuring hum.

Dissections

Not only have the skin and flesh and parts of the skeleton
of one of the anatomical effigies in the *Musée de l'Homme*
been excised, stripped away, so that you don't look just at,
but through the thing—pink lungs, red kidney and heart,
tangles of yellowish nerves he seems snarled in, like a net;

not only are his eyes without eyelids, and so shallowly
embedded beneath the blade of the brow, that they seem,
with no shadow to modulate them, flung open in pain or fear;
and not only is his gaze so frenziedly focused that he seems to be
receiving everything, even our regard scraping across him as *blare*;

not only that, but looking more closely, I saw he was real,
that he'd been constructed, reconstructed, on an actual skeleton:
the nerves and organs were wire and plaster, but the armature,
the staring skull, the spine and ribs, were varnished, oxidizing bone;
someone was there, his personhood discernible, a self, a soul.

I felt embarrassed, as though I'd intruded on someone's loneliness,
or grief, and then, I don't know why, it came to me to pray,
though I don't pray, I've unlearned how, to whom, or what,
what fiction, what illusion, or, it wouldn't matter, what true thing,
as mostly I've forgotten how to weep . . . Only mostly, though,

sometimes I can sense the tears in there, and sometimes, yes,
they flow, though rarely for a reason I'd have thought—
a cello's voice will catch in mine, a swerve in a poem, and once,
a death, someone I hardly knew, but I found myself sobbing, sobbing,
for everyone I had known who'd died, and some who almost had.

In the next display hall, evolution: half, then quarter creatures,
Australopithecus, Pithecanthropus, Cro-Magnon,
sidle diffidently along their rocky winding path towards us.
Flint and fire, science and song, and all of it coming to this,
this unhealable self in myself who knows what I should know.

Scale: I

Catherine shrieks
a little then comes
over to show me
where something bit her.

Parking herself
flank to my face
she jerks her shirt
out of her jeans—

the smallest segment
of skin, so smooth,
though, so densely
resilient, so *present*,

that the whole inside
of my body goes
achingly hollow,
and floods with lust.

•

No sign of a sting;
Catherine tucks
herself in and goes
back to her work-

bench to hammer
again at the links
she's forging
for a necklace,

leaving me to act
as though nothing
had changed,
as though this moment

I'm caught in
could go on expanding
like this forever,
with nothing changed.

Scale: II

Once, hearing you behind me, I turned,
you were naked, I hadn't known you would be,

and something in my sense of dimension went awry,
so your body, the volumes of your shoulders and hips,

the broad expanse of your chest over your breasts
and the long, sleek slide down between

seemed all at once larger, more than that—
you were lavish, daunting, a deluge of presence.

I wanted to touch you, but I looked away;
it wasn't desire I felt, or not only desire,

I just didn't want ordinary existence to resume,
as though with you there could be such a thing.

Doves

So much crap in my head,
so many rubbishy facts,
so many half-baked
theories and opinions,
so many public figures
I care nothing about
but who stick like pitch;
so much political swill.

So much crap, yet
so much I don't know
and would dearly like to:
I recognize nearly none
of the birdsongs of dawn—
all I'm sure of is
the maddeningly vapid *who*,
who-who of the doves.

And I don't have half
the names of the flowers
and trees, and still less
of humankind's myths,
the benevolent ones,
from the days before ours;
water-plashed wastes,
radiant intercessions.

So few poems entire,
such a meager handful
of precise recollections of paintings:
detritus instead, junk,
numbers I should long ago
have erased, inane
"information," I'll doubtless
take with me to the grave.

So much crap, and yet,
now, morning, that first
sapphire dome of glow,
the glow! The first sounds
of being awake, *the sounds!* —
a wind whispering, but even
trucks clanking past,
even the idiot doves.

And within me, along
with the garbage, faces, faces
and voices, so many
lives woven into mine,
such improbable quantities
of memory; so much already
forgotten, lost, pruned away —
the doves though, the doves!

Flamenco

I once met a guitarist,
in Spain, in Granada,
an American, of all things,
and on top of that Jewish,
who played flamenco like a fiend.

He called himself "Juan,"
then something with an "S,"
not the "S" it was once,
but Sastres, or something;
whatever: he played like a fiend.

He lived in a seedy hotel,
which was really a whorehouse,
he told me, though mostly
what he told me were lies;
still, he did play like a fiend.

That he was a drug addict
he didn't say, but he'd often
have to go for a shot, he said
because he was sick, but who cared,
when he played like a fiend?

Or perhaps I should say
he played like a fiend
when he played, because often,
as they say, he was "nodding,"
and no one like that plays like a fiend.

He lived in a whorehouse, did drugs,
and lied. How had it happened?
It came to him, it could have
to you or me, and I for one
never played anything like a fiend.

Inculcations

Only heartbreaking was it much later to first hear someone you loved
      speak of strangers with disdain.
They, them, those: this accent, that hue, these with their filth and squalor,
      those in their shacks, their slums.

We were intelligent, ambitious, appropriately acquisitive; they untrustwor-
      thy, ignorant, feckless;
worse, they were presumed to need less than we, and therefore merited yet
      more scorn and contempt.

Only saddening a lifetime after to recall those cosmologies of otherness
      settling comfortably within you;
you knew from the tone of their formulation they were despicable, base,
      but, already tamed, you stayed still.

Whence dullness, whence numbness, for so much had to be repudiated or
      twisted that the senses became stone;
whence distrust, and anxiety, for isn't their origin just there, in the impo-
      tence and contradiction it all implied?

Only appalling now to comprehend that reality could be constructed of
      expediency, falsehood, self-lies;
only worth lamenting now when at last you might but hopelessly won't,
      for so much else demands rectification.

Even our notions of beauty, even our modes of adornment; whence suspi-
      cion of one's own sensual yearnings,
whence dejection, whence rage, all with such labor to be surmounted,
      while love waited, life waited; whence woe.

Whence woe, and the voice far distant within crying out still of what was
      lost or despoiled.
And the cellular flares incessantly flashing, evil and good, yes, no;
      whence desolation, what never would be.

Sully: Sixteen Months

One more thing to keep:
my second grandson, just
pre-speech, tripping on a toy,
skidding, bump and yowl,

and tears, real tears,
coursing down his cheeks,
until Jessie, cooing, lifts
and holds him to her,

so it's over, but as
they're leaving for home,
he and I alone a moment
in the room where he fell,

he flops down again,
to show me, look,
how it came to pass,
this terrible thing, trilling

syllables for me, no
words yet, but notes,
with hurt in them, and cries,
and that greater cry

that lurks just behind:
right here, he's saying,
on this spot precisely,
here it happened, and yes,

I answer, yes, and so
have the chance to lift him
too, to hold him, light
and lithe, against me, too.

The World

Splendid that I'd revel even more in the butterflies harvesting pollen
from the lavender in my father-in-law's garden in Normandy
when I bring to mind Francis Ponge's poem where he transfigures them
to levitating matches, and the flowers they dip into to unwashed cups;
it doesn't work with lavender, but still, so lovely, matches, cups,
and lovely, too, to be here in the fragrant summer sunlight reading.

Just now an essay in *Le Monde*, on Fragonard, his oval oil sketch
of a mother opening the bodice of her rosily blushing daughter
to demonstrate to a young artist that the girl would be suitable as a
            "model";
the snide quotation marks insinuate she might be other than she seems,
but to me she seems entirely enchanting, even without her top
and with the painter's cane casually lifting her skirt from her ankle.

Fragonard needs so little for his plot; the girl's disarranged underslips
a few quick swirls, the mother's compliant mouth a blur, her eyes
two dots of black, yet you can see how crucial this transaction is to her,
how accommodating she'd be in working through potential complica-
            tions.
In the shadows behind, a smear of fabric spills from a drawer,
a symbol surely, though when one starts thinking symbol, what isn't?

Each sprig of lavender lifting jauntily as its sated butterfly departs,
Catherine beneath the beech tree with her father and sisters, me watch-
            ing,
everything and everyone might stand for something else, *be* something
            else.
Though in truth I can't imagine what; reality has put itself so solidly
            before me
there's little need for mystery . . . Except for us, for how we take the
            world
to us, and make it more, more than we are, more even than itself.

II

Of Childhood the Dark

Here

Uncanny to realize one was *here*, so much
came before the awareness of being here.

Then to suspect your place here was yours only
because no one else wanted or would have it.

A site, a setting, and you the matter to fill it,
though you guessed it could never be filled.

Therefore, as much as a presence, you were a problem,
a task; insoluble, so optional, so illicit.

Then the first understanding: that you
yourself were the difficult thing to be done.

Outsets

Even then, though surely I was a "child,"
which implied sense and intent, but no power,

I wasn't what I'd learned a child should be:
I was never naïve, never without guile.

Hardly begun, I was no longer new,
already beset with quandaries and cries.

Was I a molten to harden and anneal, the core
of what I was destined to become, or was I

what I seemed, inconsequential, but free?
But if free, why quandaries, why cries?

Danger

Watch out, you might fall, as that one fell,
or fall *ill*, as he or she did, or die,

or worse, not die, be insufficient,
less than what should be your worth.

Be cautious of your body, which isn't you,
though neither are you its precise other;

you're what it feels, and the knowing
what's felt, yet no longer quite either.

Your life is first of all what may be lost,
its ultimate end to not end.

And Fear

Not lurk, not rancor, not rage, nor,
please, trapping and tearing, yet they were *there*,

from the start, impalpable but prodigious,
ever implicit. Even before anything happens,

(how know that this is what happens?)
there was the terror, the wrench and flex,

the being devoured, ingested by terror,
and the hideous inference, that from now

every absence of light would be terror,
every unheard whisper more terror.

The Lesson

One must be *right*, one's truths must
be *true*, most importantly they,

and you, must be irrefutable, otherwise
they'll lead to humiliation and sin.

Your truths will seek you, though you still
must construct and comprehend them,

then unflinchingly give yourself to them.
More than you, implying more even

than themselves, they are the single matter
for which you must be ready to lie.

The Ban

Always my awful eyes, and always
the alluring forbidden, always what I'd see

and the delirious behind or beneath; always
taboo twinned with intrigue, prohibition,

and the secret slits, which my gaze, with my assent
or without it, would slip skittering through.

Though nothing was ever as enchanting
as the anticipation of it, always my eyes

would be seeking again all they imagined,
lewd and low, might be hidden from them.

Pandora

It was clear, now that the story I'd waited
so long for had finally found me,

it was I who englobed the secrets, and the evil,
and the ruined splendor before evil,

for I guessed I'd once been in splendor.
Terrible to have coffered in myself these forebodings,

these atrocious closeds which must never
be opened, but are, ever will be.

Revealed now, though, ratified and released,
at least they were no longer just mine.

Games

The others play at violence, then so do I,
though I'd never have imagined

I'd enact this thing of attack,
of betraying, besting, rearing above,

of hand become fist, become bludgeon,
these similes of cruelty, conquest, extinction.

They, we, play at doing away with,
but also at being annulled, falling dead,

as though it were our choice, this learning
to be done away with, to fall dead.

Devout

I knew this couldn't be me, knew this holy
double of me would be taken from me,

would go out to the ravenous rocks to be dust
beneath rock, glint ashudder in dust,

but I knew I'd miss him, my swimmer in the vast;
without him was only mind-gristle and void.

Disbelief didn't drive him from me, nor the thrash
of austerities I gave him to think might be prayer.

Scorn, rather, for me, for my needing reasons to pray,
for the selves I tried to pray into being to pray.

Self-Love

No sooner had I heard of it, than I knew
I was despicably, inextricably guilty of it.

It wasn't as I'd hoped that kingdom I'd found
in myself where you whispered to yourself

and heard whispers back: that was iniquity too,
but was nothing to this; from this, I could tell,

my inept repentances would never redeem me,
so I must never trust myself again,

not the artifice I showed others, still less
that seething, sinful boil within.

First Love Lost

The gash I inflict on myself in a sludge-slow
brook in a dip in field of hornets and thorns,

I hardly remark, nor the blood spooled out behind
like a carnivore's track; it brings satisfaction,

as though I'd been tested, and prevailed. And the talon
of pain in my palm? I already know pain,

love's pain, which I know is all pain, just as I know
the river will dry, my filthy wound heal

and the wolf be driven to earth, before love,
love everlasting, will relent or release me.

Sensitive

Sensitive on a hillside, sensitive in a dusk,
summer dusk of mown clover exhaling

its opulent languor; sensitive in a gush
of ambient intimation, then inspiration, these forms

not forms bewilderingly weaving towards,
then through me, calling me forth from myself,

from the imperatives which already so drove me:
fused to sense and sensation, to a logic

other than attainment's, unknowns beckoned,
from beyond even the clover and dusk.

My Sadness

Not grounded in suffering, nor even
in death, mine or anyone else's,

it was sufficient unto itself, death and pain
were only portions of its inescapable sway.

Nor in being alone, though loneliness contained
much of the world, and infected the rest.

Sadness was the rest; engrossed in it, rapt,
I thought it must be what was called soul.

Don't souls, rapt in themselves, ravish themselves?
Wasn't I rapt? Wasn't I ravaged?

Tenses

Then seemingly all at once there was a *past*,
of which you were more than incidentally composed.

Opaque, dense, delectable as oil paint,
fauceted from a source it itself generated in you,

you were magnified by it, but it could intrude,
and weigh, like an unfathomable obligation.

Everything ending waited there, which meant
much would never be done with, even yourself,

the memory of the thought of yourself you were now,
that thought seemingly always hardly begun.

III

Elegy for an Artist

for Bruce McGrew
Wichita, Kansas, 1937–Rancho Linda Vista, Arizona, 1999

1. THE REHEARSAL
(*Months before*)

Vivaldi's *Stabat*
Mater, an amateur
ensemble in a church,
the conductor casual
but competent enough,
the strings adequately

earnest so if they thump
a little or go sour,
that igniting passion's
still there. The singer,
waiting, hugs herself,
as though the music

chilled her, then with a fierce
attack, a pure, precise
ecstatic lift above
the weavings of the rest,
she soars, and as I
often do these days,

I think of you, old friend
so far away, so ill,
of how I'd love to have
you listening with me,
though with every
passage you are with

me, always with me,
as music we cherish

is always with us, only
waiting to be ascended
to again, to confirm
again there'll always

be these counterpoints
of memory and love,
unflawed by absence
or sorrow; this music
we hear, this other,
richer still, we are.

2. WEPT
(*The day after*)

Never so *much* absence,
though, and not just absence,
never such a sense
of violated presence,
so much desolation,
so many desperate

last hopes refuted,
never such pure despair.
Surely I know by now
that each death demands
its own procedures
of mourning, but I can't

find those I need even
to begin mourning you:
so much affectionate
accord there was with you,
that to imagine
being without you

is impossibly
diminishing; I relied

on you to ratify
me, to reflect
and sanction with your life
who I might be in mine.

So restorative you were,
so much a response:
untenable that
the part of me you shared
with me shouldn't have you
actively a part of it.

Never so much absence,
so many longings ash,
as you are ash. Never
so cruel the cry within,
Will I never again
be with you? Ash. Ash.

3. WITH YOU
(*Months after*)

One more morning I want
with you, one last dawn
together on your porch,
our families still
sleeping, the night's breezes
barely waned, the foliage

already motionless
in the heat-scorched scrub
across the desert hills,
the wary cactus wrens
and cardinals just
gathering at the feeder;

and one last long walk
out across the ranch,

your paint and brushes
in their beat-up case,
the sheet of *Arches*
paper tacked to its board;

out past your studio,
the wash, the cottonwoods
I helped you plant it seems
months not decades ago,
the sagging barbed-wire fence,
the cow and deer trails

worn through the brush; past
mesquite, paloverde,
saguaro, out to
the boulder-strewn canyon
where I loved to watch
as in that harsh, nearly

mineral glare
you'd labor to transfigure
the world before you
to the luminous
distillations of
yourself your paintings were.

⇐

Then past there, too, past
world and light and art,
past this sadness from which
I speak now, past speech
and the desire to speak,
into that clear place

of effortlessly
welcoming ardor
that being with you

always was, for me
and all who loved you—
(so many loved you);

past everything except
this single moment
of your presence. Not
that anything's missing
from our time together—
we had much together—

and not because I need
anything you haven't
already given me,
or believe the sum
of your life might want
or lack in any way,

nor because I can't bring
myself to let you go,
can't bring myself to offer
a definitive farewell,
but because my sadness
still feels incomplete,

and it's come to me
I need you to help
me grieve for you, as I
needed you to share
all the good and ill
my life has brought me.

❧

But isn't this just what
grief always makes us think?
Isn't this what grief *is*,
this feeling of a final

salutation that might
link a past that's finished

with an affection
and a spiritual
companionship ever
in effect, though no
longer generating
matter for remembrance?

But knowing doesn't
help: so much of
who we are is memory,
and anticipation
of memories to come.
How really believe

there'll be no more strolls
through cities, no museum
afternoons with you
explaining to me
what the painters meant
to do, and what they did,

no stoppings in cafés,
like that evening in
a barrio in Spain
when an old singer
keened an older song
that almost made us cry

with the awful rawness
of its lamentation:
beyond conception then,
to imagine either
of us ever grieving
that way for the other.

4. STILL
(A *year*)

But I do grieve, grieve still;
a continent, an
ocean and a year
removed from you, I still
find it impossible
to think of you as *past*,

and I know too well
by now there'll never
be anything like
a persuasive
reconciliation
for your having gone.

What there is instead
is knowing that at least
we had you for a time,
and that we still have
evidence of you, in
your work and in the love

which eternally
informs the work, that
one love which never ends.
And to be able
to tell oneself that once
one knew a man wholly

unsusceptible
to triviality,
bitterness or rancor,
who'd fashioned himself
with such dedication
and integrity

that he'd been released
from those resentments
and envies that can make
the fullest life seem mean:
your life was never mean,
never not inspiring.

≋

A year, summer again,
warm, my window open
on the courtyard where
for a good half hour
an oboe has been
practicing scales. Above

the tangle of voices,
clanging pans, a plumber's
compressor hectically
intensifying,
it goes on and on,
single-minded, patient

and implacable,
its tempo never
faltering, always
resolutely focused
on the turn above,
the turn below,

goes on as the world
goes on, and beauty,
and the passion for it.
Much of knowing you
was knowing that, knowing
that our consolations,

if there are such things,
dwell in our conviction
that always somewhere
painters will concoct
their colors, poets sing,
and a single oboe

dutifully repeat
its lesson, then repeat
it again, serenely
mounting and descending
the stairway it itself
unfurls before itself.

IV

War

September–October 2001

1.

I keep rereading an article I found recently about how Mayan scribes,
who also were historians, polemicists and probably poets as well,
when their side lost a war, not a rare occurrence apparently,

there having been a number of belligerent kingdoms
struggling for supremacy, would be disgraced and tortured,
their fingers broken and the nails torn out, and then be sacrificed.

Poor things—the reproduction from a mural shows three:
one sprawls in slack despair, gingerly cradling his left hand with his right,
another gazes at his injuries with furious incomprehension,

while the last lifts his mutilated fingers to the conquering warriors
as though to elicit compassion for what's been done to him: they,
elaborately armored, glowering at one another, don't bother to look.

2.

Like bomber pilots in our day, one might think, with their radar
and their infallible infrared, who soar, unheard, unseen, over generalized,
digital targets that mystically ignite, billowing out from vaporized cores.

Or like the Greek and Trojan gods, when they'd tire of their creatures,
"flesh ripped by the ruthless bronze," and wander off, or like the god
we think of as ours, who found mouths to speak for him, then left.

They fought until nothing remained but rock and dust and shattered bone,
Troy's walls a waste, the stupendous Mesoamerican cities abandoned
to devouring jungle, tumbling on themselves like children's blocks.

And we, alone again under an oblivious sky, were quick to learn
how our best construals of divinity, our *Do unto, Love, Don't kill,*
could easily be garbled to canticles of vengeance and battle-prayers.

3.

Fall's first freshness, strange; the seasons' ceaseless wheel,
starlings starting south, the annealed leaves ready to release,
yet still those columns of nothingness rise from their own ruins,

their twisted carcasses of steel and ash still fume, and still,
one by one, tacked up by hopeful lovers, husbands, wives,
the absent faces wait, already tattering, fading, going out.

These things that happen in the particle of time we have to be alive,
these violations which almost more than any ark or altar
embody sanctity by enacting so precisely sanctity's desecration.

These broken voices of bereavement asking of us what isn't to be given.
These suddenly smudged images of consonance and peace.
These fearful burdens to be borne, complicity, contrition, grief.

Fear

September 2001–August 2002

1.

At almost the very moment an exterminator's panel truck,
the blowup of a cockroach airbrushed on its side,
pulls up at a house across from our neighborhood park,
a battalion of transient grackles invades the picnic ground,

and the odd thought comes to me how much in their rich sheen,
their sheer abundance, their hunger without end, if I let them
they can seem akin to roaches; even their curt, coarse cry:
mightn't those subversive voices beneath us sound like that?

Roaches, though . . . Last year, our apartment house was overrun,
insecticides didn't work, there'd be roaches on our toothbrushes and
        combs.
The widower downstairs—this is awful—who'd gone through deporta-
        tion
and the camps and was close to dying now and would sometimes faint,

was found one morning lying wedged between his toilet and a wall,
naked, barely breathing, the entire surface of his skin alive
with the insolent, impervious brutes, who were no longer daunted
by the light, or us—the Samaritan neighbor had to scrape them off.

2.

Vermin, poison, atrocious death: what different resonance they have
in our age of suicide as armament, anthrax, resurrected pox.
Every other week brings new warnings, new false alarms;
it's hard to know how much to be afraid, or even how.

Once I knew, too well; I was of the generation of the bomb—
Hiroshima, the broiling bubble at Bikini, ICBMs.

The second world war was barely over, in annihilated cities
children just my age still foraged for scraps of bread,

and we were being taught that our war would be nuclear,
that if we weren't incinerated, the flesh would rot from our bones.
By the time Kennedy and Khrushchev faced off over Cuba,
rockets primed and aimed, we were sick with it, insane.

And now these bewildering times, when those whose interest is
to consternate us hardly bother to conceal their purposes.
Yes, we have antagonists, and some of their grievances are just,
but is no one blameless, are we all to be combatants, prey?

3.

We have offended very grievously, and been most tyrannous,
wrote Coleridge, invasion imminent from radical France;
the wretched plead against us . . . Then, *Father and God,
spare us,* he begged, as I suppose one day I will as well.

I still want to believe we'll cure the human heart, heal it
of its anxieties, and the mistrust and barbarousness they spawn,
but hasn't that metaphorical heart been slashed, dissected,
cauterized and slashed again, and has the carnage relented, ever?

Night nearly, the exterminator's gone, the park deserted,
the swings and slides my grandsons play on forsaken.
In the windows all around, the flicker of the television news:
more politics of terror; war, threats of war, war without end.

A half-chorus of grackles still ransacks the trash;
in their intricate iridescence they seem eerily otherworldly,
negative celestials, risen from some counter-realm to rescue us.
But now, scattering towards the deepening shadows, they go, too.

Chaos

I saw a spider on a library cornice snatch a plump,
brightly lacquered as-a-yellow-pepper beetle
and dash—that was the word—across its system of webs
until it came to a dark lair where it let itself fall,
settle, and avidly, methodically, with evident delectation,
devour its still so sadly brilliantly hued prey.

All this took place in a dream, but even when I woke,
my revulsion wouldn't abate, nor my dread,
because when I followed the associative tracks
that had brought me to engender such harshness in myself,
I kept being driven further than I wanted to go,
arriving at conclusions I'd never usually entertain.

The beetle, I thought, was the generalized human person,
gullible, malleable, impotent, self-destructive—
gullible, above all, is what kept coming to me;
how the prospect of living without anxiety renders us
ever more anxious, more ready to accede
to interests which clearly contradict ours.

The spider was power, plus limitless greed,
plus an abstraction, not God, but something like God,
which perpetrates something like Babel on us,
within us, though, in our genes; that twist of something
which keeps us with only this many words, and no more,
leaving us all but incoherent to ourselves, thus easily misled.

But why, even in dreams, must I dwell on the dark,
the dire, the *drek*? A foal in a dappling field,
I might have dreamed, a child trailing after with a rope,
but no, the sense, the scent nearly, the dream-scent,
was wild frustration; not pity but some insane collision
with greed, and power, and credulity, above all.

Perhaps I slept then, perhaps I dreamed my muse,
to whom when she appears I too often say,
"You're not as seemly as I believed, nor as pure,"
and my muse forsakes me. But perhaps the spider is muse,
or the beetle, or Babel; no wonder she'd betray me,
no wonder, bending her languorous note, she'd forsake me.

The Future

That was the future I came back from
vomiting the taste of the sulfur of my lowest
intestine on my tongue the taste of active
not theoretical not imagined despair.

It wasn't only the deserts impinging
encroaching devouring nor the fevers
charring the last damp from the rivers
the last lick of sap from the withering wheat.

Nor only the ruins of cities spilled out
on highways like coal like kindling the men
groin to groin bound in their rage and despair
like Siamese twins Siamese hordes.

It wasn't the women cowled like turbines
howling like turbines and the children
sentried on cliffs with nothing to nourish
their genius but shrapnels of scrub.

It was grasping rather that their desires
were like mine without limit like mine
checked only by vile chance not rational
supply and demand as I'd been taught.

That their fear was so fierce they wanted
to no longer be endowed with matter
so when houses were built they were razed
when food was grown it was despoiled.

We were locusts we were scorpions
husks hooked on thorns seeds without soil
wombs of a world without portal
flesh and dream we breathed and we slept.

The Clause

This entity I call my mind, this hive of restlessness,
this wedge of want my mind calls self,
this self which doubts so much and which keeps reaching,
keeps referring, keeps aspiring, longing, towards some state
from which ambiguity would be banished, uncertainty expunged;

this implement my mind and self imagine they might make together,
which would have everything accessible to it,
all our doings and undoings all at once before it,
so it would have at last the right to bless, or blame,
for without everything before you, all at once, how bless, how blame?

this capacity imagination, self and mind conceive might be the "soul,"
which would be able to regard such matters as creation and destruction,
origin and extinction, of species, peoples, even families, even mine,
of equal consequence, and might finally solve the quandary
of this thing of being, and this other thing of not;

these layers, these divisions, these meanings or the lack thereof,
these fissures and abysses beside which I stumble, over which I reel:
is the place, the space, they constitute,
which I never satisfactorily experience but from which the fear
I might be torn away appalls me, me, or what might most be me?

Even mine, I say, as if I might ever believe such a thing;
bless and blame, I say, as though I could ever not.
This ramshackle, this unwieldy, this jerry-built assemblage,
this unfelt always felt disarray: is this the sum of me,
is this where I'm meant to end, exactly where I started out?

Leaves

A pair of red leaves spinning on one another
in such wildly erratic patterns over a frozen field
it's hard to tell one from another and whether
if they were creatures they'd be in combat or courting
or just exalting in the tremendousness of their being.

Humans can be like that, capricious, aswirl,
not often enough in exalting, but courting, yes,
and combat; so often in combat, in rancor, in rage,
we rarely even remember what error or lie
set off this phase of our seeming to have to slaughter.

Not leaves then, which after all in their season
give themselves to the hammer of winter,
become sludge, become muck, become mulch,
while we, still seething, broiling, stay as we are,
vexation and violence, ax, atom, despair.

Night

1.

Somehow a light plane
coming in low at three
in the morning to a local airstrip
hits a complex of tones
in its growl so I hear mingled
with it a peal of church bells,
swelling in and out
of audibility, arrhythmic,
but rich and insistent, then,
though I try to hold them,
they dissolve, fade away;
only that monochrome
drone bores on
alone through the dark.

2.

This is one of our new
winters, dry, windless
and warm, when even
the lightest cover is stifling.
A luxuriant flowering
pear tree used to shelter
the front of our house,
but last August a storm
took it, a bizarrely focused
miniature tornado never
before seen in this climate,
and now the sky outside
the window is raw, the inert
air viscous and sour.

3.

I was ill, and by the merest
chance happened to be
watching as the tree fell,
I saw the branches helplessly
flail, the fork of the trunk
with a great creak split,
and the heavier half start
down, catch on wires,
and hang, lifting and subsiding
in the last barbs of the gale
as though it didn't know yet
it was dead, then it did,
and slipped slowly sideways
onto its own debris in the gutter.

4.

When Ivan Karamazov
is reciting his wracking disquisition
about the evils perpetrated
on children, opining whether
human salvation would be worth
a single child's suffering,
you know he's close to breaking
down, sobbing in shame
and remorse, and I wonder
if he'd imagined our whole planet,
the children with it,
wagered in a mad gamble
of world against wealth,
what would he have done?

5.

What do I do? Fret
mostly, and brood, and lie
awake. Not to sleep
wasn't always so punishing.
Once, in a train, stalled
in mountains, in snow,
I was roused by the clank
of a trainman's crowbar
on the undercarriage of my car.
I lifted the leathery shade
and across a moon-dazzled
pine-fringed slope
a fox cut an arc; everything
else was pure light.

6.

I wanted it to last forever,
but I was twenty, and before
I knew it was back in my dream.
Do I ever sleep that way
now, innocent of everything
beyond my ken? No,
others are always with me,
others I love with my life,
yet I'll leave them scant
evidence of my care, and little
trace of my good intentions,
as little as the solacing shush
the phantom limbs of our slain
tree will leave on the night.

In the Forest

In a book about war, tyranny, oppression, political insanity and corruption,
in a prison camp, in a discussion in which some inmates are trying to
        contend
with a vision of a world devoid of real significance, of existence being no
        more
than brute violence, of the human propensity to destroy itself and every-
        thing else,

someone, an old man, presumably wise, tells of having once gone to live
        in a forest,
far in the North, pristine, populated by no one but poor woodsmen and
        hermits;
he went there, he says, because he thought in that mute, placid domain
        of the trees,
he might find beyond the predations of animals and men something like
        the good.

They'd been speaking of their absurd sentences, of the cruelty of so-
        called civilization,
and the listeners imagine the old man is going to share his innocent rap-
        ture,
but No, he says, No, the trees and their seeds and flowers are at war just
        as we are,
every inch of soil is a battleground, each species of tree relentlessly seeks
        its own ends;

first the insidious grass and shrubs must be conquered, so a billion seeds
        are deployed,
hard as bullets, the victorious shoots drive up through the less adaptable
        weaklings,
the alliances of dominating survivors grow thicker and taller, assembling
        the canopies
beneath which humans love to loll, yet still new enemies are evolving,
        with new weapons . . .

In prison camps, even the worst, in the evening the tormented souls
      come together
to commune and converse, even those utterly sapped by their meaning-
      less toil,
those afflicted by wounds of the spirit more doleful than any we can
      imagine,
even there, in that moral murk that promises nothing but extinction, the
      voices go on.

Does it matter what words are spoken? That the evidence proves one
      thing or another?
Isn't the ultimate hope just that we'll still be addressed, and know others
      are, too,
that meanings will still be devised and evidence offered of lives having
      been lived?
"In the North, the trees . . ." and the wretched page turns, and we listen,
      and listen.

The Hearth

February 2003

1.

Alone after the news on a bitter
evening in the country, sleet slashing
the stubbled fields, the river ice;
I keep stirring up the recalcitrant fire,

but when I throw my plastic coffee cup
in with new kindling it perches intact
on a log for a strangely long time,
as though uncertain what to do,

until, in a somehow reluctant, almost
creaturely way, it dents, collapses
and decomposes to a dark slime
untwining itself on the stone hearth.

I once knew someone who was caught in a fire
and made it sound something like that.
He'd been loading a bomber and a napalm shell
had gone off; flung from the flames,

at first he felt nothing and thought
he'd been spared, but then came the pain,
then the hideous dark—he'd been blinded,
and so badly charred he spent years

in recovery: agonizing debridements,
grafts, learning to speak through a mouth
without lips, to read Braille with fingers
lavaed with scar, to not want to die—

though that never happened. He swore,
even years later, with a family,

that if he were back there, this time allowed
to put himself out of his misery, he would.

2.

There was dying here tonight, after
dusk, by the road; an owl,
eyes fixed and flared, breast
so winter-white he seemed to shine

a searchlight on himself, helicoptered
near a wire fence, then suddenly
banked, plunged and vanished
into the swallowing dark with his prey.

Such an uncomplicated departure;
no detonation, nothing to mourn;
if the creature being torn from its life
made a sound, I didn't hear it.

But in fact I wasn't listening, I was thinking,
as I often do these days, of war;
I was thinking of my children, and their children,
of the more than fear I feel for them,

and then of radar, rockets, shrapnel,
cities razed, soil poisoned
for a thousand generations; of suffering so vast
it nullifies everything else.

I stood in the wind in the raw cold
wondering how those with power over us
can effect such things, and by what
cynical reasoning pardon themselves.

The fire's ablaze now, its glow
on the windows makes the night even darker,
but it barely keeps the room warm.
I stoke it again, and crouch closer.

Low Relief

They hunted lions, they hunted humans, and enslaved them.
One lion, I recall, had been viciously speared; he vomited blood,
his hindquarters dragged behind him like cement in a sack.

Spirits with wings and the heads of eagles flanked them;
the largest sports a rosette on a band on his wrist, like a watch:
a wristwatch measuring blossomings, measuring lives.

They wore skirts, helmets, their beards were permanent-waved.
Carved in stone, enameled in brick, in chariots, on thrones,
always that resolute, unblinking profile of composure.

Did they as they hunted feel sure of themselves,
did they believe they enacted what their cosmos demanded?
Did a god ring through them like a phone going off on a bus?

On each block, each slab, each surface, a slave,
each bound with a cable of what must feel like steel;
their heads loll: hear them cry pitiably into the stone.

Did they have gods who were evil others, like ours?
Even colder than they, indifferent, more given to fury,
vindictive, venomous, stutteringly stupid, like ours?

Their forearms were striated like Blake's ghost of a flea's,
they never savaged themselves in their souls, though;
how lightly they bear the weight of their extinction.

Coherence, things in proper relation, did it fail them?
Was unreason all around, and confusion and depression,
and no coherent, convincing model to explain why?

They move left to right, right to left, like lanes of traffic.
They too, perhaps, found no place to stand still, to judge,
to believe wickedness will never be forgotten nor forgiven.

Also gazelles, beasts of the air, and eyes which contain,
and ears which submit; dew of morn, blaze of noon,
the faces before you wild with the erotics of existence.

And that coming someday to know how foolish,
even confronting the end of one's world, to think
one might spare oneself by doing away with oneself.

Their palace doors were cedar strapped with stout bronze.
The lions, inexhaustibly fierce, never retreat, never give in.
One, off near a column of slaves, glares back at us as she dies.

The Tract

1.

Where is it where is it where is it in what volume what text what treatise
     what tract
is that legend that tale that myth homily parable fable that's haunted me
     since I read it
I thought in Campbell but I can't find it or some scripture some Veda
     not there either
that holy history anyway from those years when I was trying to skull a way
     out of the flat
banal world which so oppressed me I'm sure because it contained me
     wherever it came from
it's haunted me haunted me lurking in everything I've thought or felt or
     had happen to me

2.

The protagonist's not anyone special just a man he's born grows marries
     has children
he's living his life like everyone else pleasure pain pleasure pain then
     one day a flood
a deluge roars through his valley sweeping all before it away his house
     his village the people
only he and his family are left clinging to a tree then his wife's torn from
     his arms
then his children too one by one then the tree is uprooted and he him-
     self is boiled out
into the wild insatiable waves he cries out for his life goes under comes
     up sinks again

3.

and rises to the surface to find himself on an ocean a vast sea and loom-
    ing far above him
is a god a god sleeping it's Vishnu if I remember Vishnu asleep swaying
    serenely like a lotus
and as the person gazes in awe the god wakes sees the man plucks him
    from the waves
and thrusts him into his mouth and there in that eternally empty dark-
    ness the man realizes
that oh all he'd lived the days hours years the emotions thoughts even his
    family oh
were illusion reality was this all along this god huge as a storm cloud the
    horizonless sea

4.

Not only in depression does that tale still come back to attack me not
    only in melancholy
am I infected by its annihilating predications though I've been gloomy
    enough often enough
mostly early on about love then the political bedlam then work absurd
    writing a word
striking it out while all around you as the books of truth say is suffering
    and suffering
at first it would take me yes during desponds but even at moments of pas-
    sion when everything
but what you want and the force of your want is obliterated except at
    mind's reaches

5.

where ancient mills keep heart and brain pumping and some blessèd
        apparatus of emotion
and counter-emotion keeps you from weeping with the desolation that
        lurks in desire
a desolation I don't thank goodness feel anymore not during passion now
        does that story
secrete its acids through me but still it does take me I want to say when
        my vigilance flags
when I don't pay attention then the idea it postulates or the chilling sus-
        picion it confirms
leaves me riven with anxiety for all that exists or has ever existed or
        seemed to

6.

Yet what is there in that no way plausible whatever it is that can still so
        afflict me
philosophically primitive spiritually having nothing to do with any tradi-
        tion even the tragic
to which I feel linked if the wisdom it's meant to impart is that you can't
        countervail misery
with gratification or that to imagine life without suffering is to suffer I've
        learned that
and it doesn't make death more daunting I have death more or less in its
        place now
though the thought still sears of a consciousness not even one's own ex-
        tinguished

7.

Not some rage of mentalism then something simpler though more
    frightening about love
that the man has negated in him not only the world but his most pre-
    cious sentiments
what's dire is that the story denies and so promulgates the notion that one
    can deny
the belief no the conviction that some experiences love most of all can
    must be exempted
from even the most cruelly persuasive skepticism and excluded even
    from implications
of one's own cosmology if they too radically rupture what links real lives
    one to another

8.

To release yourself from attachment so from despair I suppose was the
    point of the text
and I suppose I was looking for it again to release me from *it* and if I
    haven't done that
at least I'm somewhere near the opposite where I'm hanging on not to a
    tree in a dream
but to the hope that someday I'll accept without qualm or question that
    the reality of others
the love of others the miracle of others all that which feels like enough is
    truly enough
no celestial sea no god in his barque of being just life just hanging on for
    dear life

NEW POEMS

The Gaffe

1.

If that someone who's me yet not me yet who judges me is always with
    me,
as he is, shouldn't he have been there when I said so long ago that thing
    I said?

If he who rakes me with such not trivial shame for minor sins now were
    there then,
shouldn't he have warned me he'd even now devastate me for my unpar-
    donable affront?

I'm a child then, yet already I've composed this conscience-beast, who
    harries me:
is there anything else I can say with certainty about who I was, except
    that I, that he,

could already draw from infinitesimal transgressions complex chords of
    remorse,
and orchestrate ever undiminishing retribution from the hapless rest of
    myself?

2.

The son of some friends of my parents has died, and my parents, paying
    their call,
take me along, and I'm sent out with the dead boy's brother and some
    others to play.

We're joking around, and words come to my mind, which to my
    amazement are said.
How do you know when you can laugh when somebody dies, your brother
    dies?

is what's said, and the others go quiet, the backyard goes quiet, everyone
     stares,
and I want to know now why that someone in me who's me yet not me
     let me say it.

Shouldn't he have told me the contrition cycle would from then be ever
     upon me,
it didn't matter that I'd really only wanted to know how grief ends, and
     when?

3.

I could hear the boy's mother sobbing inside, then stopping, sobbing
     then stopping.
Was the end of her grief already there? Had her someone in her told her
     it would end?

Was her someone in her kinder to her, not tearing at her, as mine did,
     still does, me,
for guessing grief someday ends? Is that why her sobbing stopped some-
     times?

She didn't laugh, though, or I never heard her. *How do you know when
     you can laugh?*
Why couldn't someone have been there in me not just to accuse me, but
     to explain?

The kids were playing again, I was playing, I didn't hear anything more
     from inside.
The way now sometimes what's in me is silent, too, and sometimes,
     though never really, forgets.

Thrush

Often in our garden these summer evenings a thrush
and her two nearly grown offspring come to forage.
The chicks are fledged, the mother's teaching them
to find their own food; one learns, the other can't—
its skull is misshapen, there's no eye on one side
and the beak is malformed: whatever it finds, it drops.

It seems to regress then, crouching before the mother,
gullet agape, as though it were back in the nest:
she always finds something else for it to eat,
but her youngster's all but as large as she is,
she's feeding two of herself—she'll abandon it soon,
and migrate; the chick will doubtlessly starve.

Humans don't do that, just leave, though a young woman
I saw rushing through the train station this morning
with a Down's syndrome infant in a stroller
I thought might if she could. The child, a girl,
was giggling so hard at how splendidly fast
they were going that she'd half fallen from her seat,

until the mother braked abruptly, hissed "Shush!"
and yanked her back into place. The baby, alarmed,
subsided but still intrepidly smiled as the mother—
she wasn't eighteen, with smudged eyeliner, scuffed shoes
and a cardboard valise—sped on, wielding carriage
and child as a battering ram through the oncoming crush.

The thrushes have been rapidly crisscrossing the lawn
in and out of the flowerbeds all through the long dusk,
now they leave, the rest of the birds go quiet—
I can hear someone far off calling children to bed—
and it's the turn of the bats, who materialize, vanish,
and appear again, their own after-selves, their own ghosts.

Cows

Face in her hands, bike
thrown down beside her, a girl
on the road from the village
stands brokenheartedly crying.

I assume it's some love-
thing but stop a ways on
to be sure; in a meadow nearby,
ten or so spotted heifers,

each with a numbered tag
in her ear, see me and rush
to the fence and low over,
all of them, all at once,

with so much feeling that not
"Feed me!" do they seem
to be saying but "Save me!"
Save me! Save me! Save me!

Still long-legged,
still svelte, their snug
skin milk-white
and gleaming, obsidian black . . .

I think of Io, transfigured
by treacherous Zeus to a heifer,
whose beauty was still such
men longed to embrace her.

These, by next year, unless
they're taken to slaughter,
will be middle-aged ladies
with udders, indifferently grazing.

When I look in the mirror, the girl —
should I have offered to help her? —
is gone: I'll never know what
happened to her, nor what will.

The cows watch still,
jaws grinding, tails lashing
the squadrons of flies on their flanks.
Save me! Save me!

Marina

As I'm reading Tsvetaeva's essays,
"Art in the Light of Conscience,"
stunning—"*Art, a series of answers
to which there are no questions*"—
a tiny insect I don't recognize
is making its way across my table.
It has lovely transparent wings
but for some reason they drag behind
as it treks the expanse of formica
and descends into a crack.

"*To each answer before it evaporates,
our question*": composed in Paris
during the difficult years of exile.
But which of her years were easy?
This at least was before the husband,
a spy, an assassin, went back,
then she, too, with her son,
to the Soviet madhouse, back . . .
"*This being outgalloped by answers,
is inspiration . . .*" Outgalloped!

Still lugging its filigreed train,
the insect emerges: fragile, distracted,
it can't even trace a straight line,
but it circumnavigates the table.
Does it know it's back where it began?
Still, it perseveres, pushing
courageously on, one inch, another . . .
"*Art . . . a kind of physical world
of the spiritual . . . A spiritual world
of the physical . . . almost flesh.*"

One daughter, dying, at three,
of hunger, the other daughter,
that gift of a sugar-cube
in her mouth, drenched with blood . . .
"A *poet is an answer . . . not to the blow,
but a quivering of the air.*"
The years of wandering,
the weary return, husband betrayed,
arrested, daughter in a camp . . .
"*The soul is our capacity for pain.*"

When I breathe across it,
the bug squats, quakes, finally flies.
And couldn't she have fled again,
again have been flown? Couldn't she,
noose in her hand, have proclaimed,
"I am Tsvetaeva," and then not?
No, no time now for "then not."
But "*Above poet, more than poet . . .*"
she'd already said it, already sung it:
"*Air finished. Firmament now.*"

Blackbird

There was nothing I could have done—
a flurry of blackbirds burst
from the weeds at the edge of a field
and one veered out into my wheel
and went under. I had a moment
to hope he'd emerge as sometimes
they will from beneath the back
of the car and fly off,
but I saw him behind on the roadbed,
the shadowless sail of a wing
lifted vainly from the clumsy
bundle of matter he'd become.

There was nothing I could have done,
though perhaps I was distracted:
I'd been listening to news of the war,
hearing that what we'd suspected
were lies had proved to be lies,
that many were dying for those lies,
but as usual now, it wouldn't matter.
I'd been thinking of Lincoln's
". . . You can't fool all of the people
all of the time . . .," how I once
took comfort from the hope and trust
it implied, but no longer.

I had to slow down now,
a tractor hauling a load of hay
was approaching on the narrow lane.
The farmer and I gave way and waved:
the high-piled bales swayed
menacingly over my head but held.
Out in the harvested fields,
already disked and raw,

more blackbirds, uncountable
clouds of them, rose, held
for an instant, then broke,
scattered as though by a gale.

Wasp

Hammer, hammer, hammer, the wasp
has been banging his head on the window for hours;
you'd think by now he'd be brain-dead, but no,
he flings himself at the pane: hammer, hammer again.

I ease around him to open the sash, hoping
he doesn't sting me because then I'd be sorry
I didn't kill him, but he pays me no mind:
it's still fling, hammer, fling, hammer again.

I'm sure his brain's safe, his bones are outside,
but up there mine are too, so why does it hurt
so much to keep thinking—hammer, hammer—
the same things again and, hammer, again?

That invisible barrier between you and the world,
between you and your truth . . . Stinger blunted,
wings frayed, only the battering, battered brain,
only the hammer, hammer, hammer again.

On the Métro

On the métro, I have to ask a young woman to move the packages beside
    her to make room for me;
she's reading, her foot propped on the seat in front of her, and barely
    looks up as she pulls them to her.
I sit, take out my own book—Cioran, *The Temptation to Exist*—and no-
    tice her glancing up from hers
to take in the title of mine, and then, as Gombrowicz puts it, she "affirms
    herself physically," that is,
she's *present* in a way she hadn't been before; though she hasn't moved
    an inch, she's allowed herself
to come more sharply into focus, be more accessible to my sensual per-
    ception, so I can't help but remark
her strong figure and very tan skin—(how literally golden young women
    can look at the end of summer).
She leans back now, and as the train rocks and her arm brushes mine she
    doesn't pull it away;
she seems to be allowing our surfaces to unite: the fine hairs on both our
    forearms, sensitive, alive,
achingly alive, bring news of someone touched, someone sensed, and
    thus acknowledged, *known*.

I understand that in no way is she offering more than this, and in truth I
    have no desire for more,
but it's still enough for me to be taken by a surge, first of warmth then of
    something like its opposite:
a memory—a lovely girl I'd mooned for from afar, across the table from
    me in the library in school,
our feet I thought touching, touching even again, and then, with all I
    craved that touch to mean,
my having to realize it wasn't her flesh my flesh for that gleaming time
    had pressed, but a table leg.
The young woman today removes her arm now, stands, swaying against
    the lurch of the slowing train,
and crossing before me brushes my knee and does that thing again, as-
    serts her bodily being again,

(Gombrowicz again), then quickly moves to the door of the car and descends, not once looking back,
(to my relief not looking back), and I allow myself the thought that though I must be to her again
as senseless as that table of my youth, as wooden, as unfeeling, perhaps there was a moment I was not.

Peggy

The name of the horse of my friend's friend,
a farmer's son whose place we'd pass
when we rode out that way I remember,
not his name, just his mare's, Peggy,
a gleaming, well-built gray; surprising,
considering her one-stall plank shed.

I even recall where they lived,
Half-Acre Road—it sounds like Frost,
and looked it: unpaved, silos and barns.
I went back not long ago;
it's built up, with rows on both sides
of bloated tract mansions.

One lot was still empty,
so I stopped and went through and found
that behind the wall of garages and hydrants
the woods had stayed somehow intact,
and wild, wilder; the paths overgrown,
the derelict pond a sink of weeds.

We'd gallop by there, up a hill,
our horses' flanks foaming with sweat,
then we'd skirt Peggy's fields
and cross to more woods, then a meadow,
the scent of which once, mown hay,
was so sweet I taste it still.

But now, the false-mullioned windows,
the developer's scrawny maples, the lawns—
I didn't know what to do with it all,
it just ached, like forgetting someone
you love is dead, and wanting to call them,
and then you remember, and they're dead again.

Fish

On the sidewalk in front
of a hairdresser's supply store
lay the head of a fish,
largish, pointy, perhaps a pike's.

It must recently have been left there;
its scales shone and its visible eye
had enough light left in it still
so it looked as they will for awhile

astonished and disconsolate
to have been brought to such a pass:
its incision was clean, brutal, precise;
it had to have come in one blow.

In the showcase window behind,
other heads, women's and men's,
bewigged, painstakingly coiffed,
stared out, as though at the fish,

as though stunned, aghast, too—
though they were hardly surprised:
hadn't they known all along
that life, that frenzy, that folly,

that flesh-thing, would come
sooner or later to this? It hurts,
life, just as much as it might,
and it ends, always, like this.

Better stay here, with eyes of glass,
like people in advertisements,
and without bodies or blood,
like people in poems.

The Blade

November 3, 2004

1.

Usually I don't mind that being out of the city now
means still having to endure the drone of planes,
traffic on the ubiquitous highways, mowers and pumps;
they've become almost a part of the music of nature,

but this morning, the builder's men clearing the woods
facing our house, the roar of their truck hauling away
the old oaks and the screech of the blade of their dozer
scraping the stony soil, seem beyond bearing.

2.

Though I know all too well it's the lost election,
the sense of not only disappointment but betrayal,
of realizing a campaign could succeed by relying
entirely on fearmongering, slander and lies.

And beyond that a foreboding: always before,
whatever party of regression has been in ascendance,
the under-voices of conciliation and reason
were audible somehow: can anyone claim that now?

3.

In Spain, during the reign of Franco, I blundered
into a rally the tyrant had arranged for himself. A butcher,
who'd jailed them for decades in a dark ages of army
and church, the people couldn't cheer him enough.

For a moment, when the swarming mob surged,
I was lifted from my feet and swept towards a line of tanks:
frightening, that mass of bodies heaving against me,
pulling me down, that having to fight not to fall.

4.

So far off on a hill I can't hear him,
a farmer is plowing his fields for the spring wheat.
Just across, though, the excavators hammer
and grunt and whine, unfurling a fog of diesel

that fumes out over the stumps and slashed earth,
and hangs there, as though the ground itself was afire.
It thins when the wind shifts, but still my eyes sting,
and my mouth still tastes of oil and lead.

Miniature Poodle

Her shipboard lover had sent her ahead
to the already full hotel where I was staying
and decamped I heard her sobbing in the lobby
so offered to find her and her poodle a place
to stay and did and she asked me to dinner.

Were we lovers too? Absurd I was nineteen
she fifty at least and alone so alone I'd see her
wherever I went that summer Rome Florence
standing misplacedly on a corner ridiculous dog
in her arms no reason to go one way or another.

She looked more faded each time I saw her
though now the years crumpled behind me
she seems not old at all not gray as I am
not ill as I am my death sniffing at me yes
like a dog jamming its snout in my crotch.

I watched hers that night spoiled thing
as she cut up its meat she wholly absorbed
I scornful as usual never imagining
I'd ever attend with equivalent inappropriateness
to my own obsessions my own mortal disquiet.

Plums

1.

All the beautiful poems
about plum trees in flower,
gold in the moonlight,
silver in the silvery starlight,

and not one of them mentions
that the damned things
if you don't pay attention
will pull themselves apart.

2.

A perfect wall of the hard
green globules of pubescent
plums too late we found
deep in the foliage of ours,

both largest limbs
already fatally fractured
had to be amputated,
the incisions sealed with tar.

3.

None of the poems mentions
either that when the hiding
fruit falls, the same flies
that invade to inhabit

fresh dog shit are all at once
there in the muck of the plums
already rotting their flesh
off as fast as they can.

4.

Abuzz, ablaze, the flies
crouch in the ooze,
like bronze lions it looks like,
drooling it looks like

at the chance to sink up
to their eyes in the rankness,
to suck gorgeously
at the swill.

5.

While our once-lovely tree
waits naked in the naked
day-glare for branches
to bring leaves forth again,

and fruit forth, not for us,
or the flies, but just to be
gold again in the moonlight,
silver in the silvery starlight.

Rats

August 2005

1.

From beneath the bank
of the brook, in the first
searing days
of the drought, water

rats appeared,
two of them,
we'd never known
even were there.

Unlike city
rats skulking
in cellars or sliding
up from a sewer-

mouth—I saw this,
it wasn't dusk—
these, as blithe
as toy tanks,

sallied into the garden
to snitch the crusts
we'd set
out for the birds.

But still, who
knows what filth
and fetor and rot
down in their dark

world they were
before? I shouted
and sent them
hurtling back.

2.

Now the brute
crucible of heat
has been upon us
for weeks,

just breathing is work,
and we're frightened.
The planet all
but afire, glaciers

dissolving, deserts
on the march,
hurricanes without end,
and the president

and his energy-company
cronies still insist
global warming
isn't real. The rats

rove where they will
now, shining and fat,
they've appropriated
the whole lawn.

From this close,
they look just
like their cousins
anywhere else,

devious, ruthless,
rapacious, and every
day I loathe
them more.

Again

1.

On a PBS program, one of my favorites,
a philosopher, or historian of philosophy,
I never quite know the difference,
but whichever she is, in her conviction,
in the passionate cogency with which
she discusses the theme of her new book—evil—
her erudition and dedication are manifest:
evil exists, she says her book says.

2.

Now her interlocutor, earnest as always,
solicitous, gently inquisitive, asks
what is obviously meant to be his last,
most crucial question, the answer to which
will resolve various other critical issues
for which there's no time (her time is up):
"And do you believe," he asks her,
"there is a moral order in the world?"

3.

She hesitates; her lips part to speak,
but she doesn't; they part again,
she's thinking fast, you can tell,
her machine's on high, but still nothing,
until, with his smile of compassionate tact,
the host offers: "If you don't know, who does?"
and she, with relief, "It depends on the day—
sometimes I think so, sometimes I don't."

4.

Well, no great solace there,
one might even be put out a bit.
Isn't this supposedly very wise person saying
that her vision of the human adventure,
her conclusions after years of reflection
and analysis, depend on her *mood*,
on the perceptions and thoughts and emotions
which most recently passed through her?

5.

Isn't she implying that the cosmos
might have some coherence coaxed from it,
but that tomorrow the same evidence
might entail its contrary, or its tragic qualification?
Have all her intellectual efforts come to this?
Has she, and by extension we, not advanced
beyond the most primitive cogitation,
the most conditional, quotidian blurt?

6.

But really, why all the fuss?
What was I expecting? A "moral order"—
does it make any difference if there is
one or not? Does anything change?
Would anyone suffer less, or love more?
Would evil not exist? Whose evil?
Philosophy, ethics, the mind: fuck it all.
And while you're about it, fuck TV.

Frog

Naturally Annie Dillard
knew when she inserts at the outset
of a book a water beetle's
devouring a frog
that the description would shock—

the bug injects enzymes
that dissolve the frog's "organs
and bones . . . all but the skin . . ."
and sucks the poor
liquefied creature out of itself—

but I doubt if she'd have guessed
how often her awful anecdote
could come back, at least
to someone like me, always
with revulsion and terror.

Last night I woke in the dark
with "It burns!" in my mind:
the voice was mine, the tone
a child's anguished cry
to a parent, the image the frog,

and the thought—is that the word?
I hardly knew where I was—
was that this was worse
than nightmare, to regress
awake from the realm of reason.

Dillard is erudite, tender
and wise, and she can be funny—
remember her imagining
literally replicating a tree?—
and she understands always

where our animal nature
ends and our human begins,
but this, slayer and slain,
cruelty and, she says it herself,
"the waste of pain . . ."

When I look down in
the murk of the brook
here, I see only chains
of bubbles rising
sporadically from the slime.

Are there beings there, too,
living their own fear-driven
dream? Is the mud itself
trying to breathe?
If so, must it hurt?

Prisoners

In the preface to a translation of a German writer,
a poet I'd never heard of, I fall on the phrase
"He was a prisoner of war in a camp in the U.S."

and a memory comes to me of a morning
during the second war when my parents,
on a visit to the city they'd grown up in,

took me to what had been their favorite park
and was now a barbed-wire encircled compound,
with unpainted clapboard barracks,

where men, in sandals and shorts,
all light-haired, as I recall, and sunburned,
idled alone or in small groups.

I'm told they're German prisoners, though I know
nothing of the war, or Hitler, or the Jews—
why should I?—I only remember them

gazing back at us with a disconcerting
incuriousness, a lack of evident emotion
I'd associate now with primates in zoos,

and that my mother and father seemed unnerved,
at a loss for what to say, which I found
more disturbing than the prisoners, or the camp,

a reaction my mother must have sensed
because she took my hand and led me away—
the park had a carousel, she took me there.

Are there still merry-go-rounds,
with their unforgettable oom-pah
calliope music, and the brass rings?

If you caught one, you rode again free.
I never did, I was afraid to fall;
I'm not anymore, but it wouldn't matter.

I go back instead to those prisoners,
to the one especially not looking at us,
because he was shaving. Crouched on a step,

face lathered, a galvanized pail at his feet,
he held—I see it, can it be there?—
a long straight-razor, glinting, slicing down.

Wood

That girl I didn't love, then because she was going to leave me, loved,
that girl, that Sunday when I stopped by and she was in bed in her
      nightgown,
(it only came to me later that somebody else had just then been with
      her),

that girl, when my hand touched her stomach under her nightgown,
began turning her stomach to wood—I hadn't known this could be
      done,
that girls, that humans, could do this—then, when her stomach was
      wood,

she began turning the rest of herself to perhaps something harder, steel,
or harder; perhaps she was turning herself, her entire, once so soft self,
to some unknown mineral substance found only on other very far
      planets,

planets with chemical storms and vast, cold ammonia oceans of ice,
and I just had to pretend—I wasn't taking this lightly, I wasn't a kid—
that I wasn't one of those pitted, potato-shaped moons with precarious
      orbits,

and then I was out, in the street—it was still Sunday, though I don't
      recall bells—
and where is she now, dear figment, dear fragment, where are you now,
in your nightgown, in your bed, steel and wood? Dear steel, dear wood.

Fire

An ax-shattered
bedroom window
the wall above
still smutted with
soot the wall
beneath still
soiled with
soak and down

on the black
of the pavement
a mattress its ticking
half eaten away
the end where
the head would
have been with
a nauseous bite

burnt away
and beside it
an all at once
meaningless heap
of soiled sodden
clothing one
shoe a jacket
once white

the vain matters
a life gathers
about it symbols
of having once
cried out to itself
who art thou?
then again who
wouldst thou be?

We

A basset hound with balls
so heavy they hang
a harrowing half
inch from the pavement,

ears cocked, accusingly
watches as his beautiful
mistress croons
to her silver cell phone.

She does, yes, go on,
but my, so slim-
waistedly
does she sway there,

so engrossedly does her dark
gaze drift
towards even
for a moment mine . . .

Though Mister Dog of course
sits down right
then to lick
himself, his groin of course,

till she cuts off, and he,
gathering his folds
and flab, heaves
erect to leave with her . . .

But wait, she's turning to
a great Ducati
cycle gleaming
black and chromy at the curb,

she's mounting it (that long
strong lift of flank!),
snorting it to life,
coaxing it in gear . . .

Why, she's not his at all!
No more than mine!
What was he thinking?
What was I? Like a wing,

a wave, she banks away
now, downshifts,
pops and crackles
round the curve, is gone.

How sleek she was, though,
how scrufty, how
anciently scabby
we, he and I;

how worn, how
self-devoured,
balls and all,
balls, balls and all.

Saddening

Saddening, worse, to read in "Frost at Midnight"
Coleridge's ecstatic hymn to his newborn son, Hartley,
for whom he imagines "all seasons shall be sweet,"
and to find in the biographies how depressingly
their relationship deteriorated when the boy was grown:
the father struggling between his dependence on opiates
and the exertions of his recalcitrant genius, the son trying
to separate from the mostly absent but still intimidating father.

Their final contact has Hartley, a neophyte poet himself—
he'll never attain stature—abandoning his father in the street,
Coleridge in tears, not knowing, as though he were a character
in one of the more than minor tragedies he might have written
if his life had evolved more fortuitously, how to begin
to reconcile his unspoken suffering with his son's,
how to conceive of healing the hurt both had to have felt
before each reeled back to his respective isolation.

The myth was already in effect then—Wordsworth's doing?—
that creativity like Coleridge's thrives best in seclusion.
Even Coleridge, though his poem takes place with his son
beside him and friends sleeping yards away, speaks of
". . . that solitude which suits abstruser musings . . ."
So generations of writers go off to the woods, to find . . .
alcohol—Schwartz, Lowry, too many others to mention—
depression, or even—Lowell, one hates to say it—wife abuse.

Coleridge in fact was rarely out of some intimate situation
for five minutes in his life, sharing his friends' houses
and tables, and there's the scene, saddening, too, worse,
of the poet imploring the captain of the ship ferrying him
home from Malta to administer an enema to unclog
the impacted feces of his laudanum-induced constipation.
Daily stuff for Coleridge—he hardly remarks it, poor man, poor giant—
excruciating for us, spoiled as we are, sanitized, tamed . . .

But what does the life—dope, shit, neurosis, fathers or sons—
have to do with anything anyway? Think of innocent Clare,
twenty-seven years in the madhouse, and isn't there some *fairness*,
you might think, some *justice*, but letting yourself think that,
there's nowhere to go but bitterness, and how regret
that deluge of masterpieces to rejoice in? Coleridge, anyway,
at the end found fulfillment, and Clare, too, if not fulfillment,
then something, perhaps acceptance; even Hartley, too, something.

I was there once, in that cottage, a packet of ill-lit rooms,
at the very spot, beside the hearth, where the poem was made—
(". . . the thin blue flame . . . that film which fluttered on the grate . . .").
You could still sense something in that comfortless cell
resonating with youth and hope, which, almost on his deathbed,
Coleridge wrote, ". . . *embracing, seen as one, were love.*"
Outside, the luminous sea, the hills: easy to understand hoping
to stay in such a world forever, and the qualm to tear yourself away.

Shrapnel

1.

Seven hundred tons per inch, I read, is the force in a bomb or shell in
the microsecond after its detonation,
and two thousand feet per second is the speed at which the shrapnel, the
materials with which the ordnance
is packed, plus its burst steel casing, "stretched, thinned, and sharpened"
by the tremendous heat and energy,
are propelled outwards in an arc until they strike an object and either
ricochet or become embedded in it.

In the case of insufficiently resistant materials, the shards of shrapnel can
cause "significant damage";
in human tissue, for instance, rupturing flesh and blood vessels and shat-
tering and splintering bone.
Should no essential organs be involved, the trauma may be termed "su-
perficial," as by the chief nurse,
a nun, in Ian McEwan's *Atonement*, part of which takes place in a hospi-
tal receiving wounded from Dunkirk.

It's what she says when a soldier cries, *"Fuck!"* as her apprentice, the
heroine, a young writer-to-be,
probes a wound with her forceps to extract one of many jagged fragments
of metal from a soldier's legs.
"Fuck!" was not to be countenanced back then. "How dare you speak
that way?" scolds the imperious sister.
"Your injuries are superficial, so consider yourself lucky and show some
courage worthy of your uniform."

The man stays still after that, though "he sweated and . . . his knuckles
turned white round the iron bedhead."
"Only seven to go," the inexperienced nurse chirps, but the largest
chunk, which she's saved for last, resists;
at one point it catches, protruding from the flesh—("He bucked on the
bed and hissed through his teeth")—

and not until her third resolute tug does the whole "gory, four-inch
    stiletto of irregular steel" come clear.

2.

"Shrapnel throughout the body" is how a ten-year-old killed in a recent
    artillery offensive is described.
"Shrapnel throughout the body": the phrase is repeated along with the
    name of each deceased child
in the bulletin released as propaganda by our adversaries, at whose oper-
    atives the barrage was directed.
There are photos as well—one shows a father rushing through the street,
    his face torn with a last frantic hope,

his son in his arms, rag-limp, chest and abdomen speckled with deep,
    dark gashes and smears of blood.
Propaganda's function, of course, is exaggeration: the facts are there,
    though, the child is there . . . or not there.
. . . As the shrapnel is no longer there in the leg of the soldier: the girl
    holds it up for him to see, the man quips,
"Run him under the tap, Nurse, I'll take him home," then, ". . . he
    turned to the pillow and began to sob."

Technically, I read, what's been called "shrapnel" here would have once
    been defined as "splinters" or "fragments."
"Shrapnel" referred then only to a spherical shell, named after its inven-
    tor, Lieutenant Henry Shrapnel.
First used in 1804, it was ". . . guaranteed to cause heavy casualties . . .
    the best mankiller the army possessed."
Shrapnel was later awarded a generous stipend in recognition of his con-
    tribution "to the state of the art."

Where was I? The nun, the nurse; the nurse leaves the room, throws up;
    the fictional soldier, the real child . . .
The father . . . What becomes of the father? He skids from the screen,
    from the page, from the mind . . .

Shrapnel's device was superseded by higher-powered, more efficient pro-
jectiles, obsolete now in their turn.
One war passes into the next. One wound is the next and the next.
Something howls. Something cries.

Cassandra, Iraq

1.

She's magnificent, as we imagine women must be
who foresee and foretell and are right and disdained.

This is the difference between us who are like her
in having been right and disdained, and us as we are.

Because we, in our foreseeings, our having been right,
are repulsive to ourselves, fat and immobile, like toads.

Not toads in the garden, who after all are what they are,
but toads in the tale of death in the desert of sludge.

2.

In this tale of lies, of treachery, of superfluous dead,
were there ever so many who were right and disdained?

With no notion what to do next? If we were true seers,
as prescient as she, as frenzied, we'd know what to do next.

We'd twitter, as she did, like birds; we'd warble, we'd trill.
But what would it be really, to *twitter*, to *warble*, to *trill*?

Is it *ee-ee-ee*, like having a child? Is it *uh-uh-uh*, like a wound?
Or is it inside, like a blow, silent to everyone but yourself?

3.

Yes, inside, I remember, *oh-oh-oh*: it's where grief
is just about to be spoken, but all at once can't be: *oh*.

When you no longer can "think" of what things like lies,
like superfluous dead, so many, might mean: *oh*.

Cassandra will be abducted at the end of her tale, and die.
Even she can't predict how. Stabbed? Shot? Blown to bits?

Her abductor dies, too, though, in a gush of gore, in a net.
That we know; she foresaw that—in a gush of gore, in a net.

Ponies

When the ponies are let out at dusk, they pound across their pasture,
pitching and bucking like the brutes their genes must dream they still are.

With their shaggy, winter-coarse coats, they seem stubbier than ever,
more diminutive, toy-like, but then they begin their aggression rituals,

ears flattened, stained brown teeth bared, hindquarters humped,
and they're savage again, cruel, all but carnivorous if they could be.

Their shoes have been pulled off for the season, their halters are rope,
so they move without sound, as though on tiptoe, through the rising mist.

They drift apart now, halfheartedly nosing the stiff, sapless remnants
of field hay—sometimes one will lift and gaze back towards the barn.

A tiny stallion lies down, rolling onto his back first, then all the way flat.
A snort, rich, explosive, an answering sigh: silence again, shadows, dark.

INDEX OF TITLES

INDEX OF FIRST LINES

Index of Titles

Index of First Lines

As I'm reading Tsvetaeva's essays, 630
As in a thousand novels but I'll never as long as I live get used to this, 315
As long as they trample the sad smiles of guitars, 11
As one would praise a child or dog, or punish it, 536
As on the rim of a cup crusted with rancid honey a host of hornets sud-, 464
A species of thistle no one had ever seen before appeared almost, 231
A squalid wayside inn, reeking barn-brewed vodka, 554
As she reads, she rolls something around in her mouth, hard candy it, 272
As soon as the old man knew he was actually dying, even before anyone, 305
As the garbage truck is backing up, one of the garbagemen is absorbed, 258
As though it were the very soul of rational human intercourse which had, 232
As though the skin had been stripped and pulled back onto the skull like, 319
A student, a young woman, in a fourth floor hallway of her *lycée*, 555
A summer cold. No rash. No fever. Nothing. But a dozen times during, 144
A tall, handsome black man, bearded, an artist, in nineteen sixty-eight, 526
A tall-masted white sailboat works laboriously across a wave-tossed bay, 509
At almost the very moment an exterminator's panel truck, 601
At last he's being allowed to play in his mother's car the way he always, 281
At the United States Out of Central America rally at a run-down commu-, 243
A whole section of the city I live in has been urban renewed, some of it, 132
A young tourist with a two-thousand-dollar Leica and a nice-looking girl, 239

Because he was always the good-hearted one, the ingenuous one, the, 226
Beds squalling, squealing, muffled in hush; beds pitching, leaping, im-, 465
Beyond anything else, he dwells on what might inhabit his mind at the, 239
Blocks of time fall upon me, adhere for a moment, then move astonish-, 369
Bound with baling wire to the tubular jerry-built bumper of a beat-up, 245
Bulging overnight bags on both shoulders, in one hand a sack with extra, 281
By tucking her chin in toward her chest, she can look up darkly through, 279

Catherine shrieks, 565
chances are we will sink quietly back, 65
Children love gravel, kneeling to play in gravel, 558

Deciphering and encoding, to translate, fabricate, revise; the abstract, 383
Deep asleep, perfect immobility, no apparent evidence of consciousness, 183
Difficult to know whether humans are inordinately anxious, 510
Doesn't, when we touch it, that sheen of infinitesimally pebbled steel, 228
Do you know how much pain is left, 41
do you remember learning to tie your shoes, 59
Do you remember when we dreamed about the owl, 14

Each movement of the Mozart has a soloist and as each appears the con-, 244
Even here, in a forest in the foothills of a range of mountains, lucent air, 312

Not only have the skin and flesh and parts of the skeleton, 564
Not soul, 521
Not to show off, but elaborating some philosophical assertion, "Watch," 422
Not yet a poet, not yet a person perhaps, or a human, or not so far as I'd, 430

Often before have our fingers touched in sleep or half-sleep and enlaced, 490
Often I have thought that after my death, not in death's void as we usu-, 447
Often in our garden these summer evenings a thrush, 627
"Oh, soul," I sometimes—often—still say when I'm trying to convince, 248
Oh my, Harold Brodkey, of all people, after all this time appearing to, 561
On a PBS program, one of my favorites, 647
Once, hearing you behind me, I turned, 567
Once, in Rotterdam, a whore once, in a bar, a sailors' bar, a hooker bar, 263
One more thing to keep, 572
One of those great, garishly emerald flies that always look freshly gener-, 413
One vast segment of the tree, the very topmost, bows ceremoniously, 525
Only heartbreaking was it much later to first hear someone you loved, 571
On the metro, I have to ask a young woman to move the packages beside, 635
On the other hand, in Philadelphia, long ago, at a party on Camac Street, 259
On the sidewalk in front, 638
our poor angel how sick, 68

Perhaps it isn't as we like to think, the last resort, the end of something, 275
Pissing out the door of a cottage, 512
Please try to understand, it was only one small moment, it didn't mean a, 335
Possibly because she's already so striking—tall, well dressed, very clear, 221
probably death fits all right in the world, 90

Rather die than live through dying with it: rather perish absolutely now, 245
Remember me? I was the one, 23
right off we started inflicting history, 76

Saddening, worse, to read in "Frost at Midnight," 657
Seven hundred tons per inch, I read, is the force in a bomb or shell in, 659
Shabby, tweedy, academic, he was old enough to be her father and I, 224
She answers the bothersome telephone, takes the message, forgets the, 227
She began to think that jealousy was only an excuse, a front, for some-, 340
She could tell immediately, she said, that he was Jewish, although he, 248
She keeps taking poses as they eat so that her cool glance goes off at, 278
Shells of fearful insensitivity that I keep having to disadhere from my, 376
She's magnificent, as we imagine women must be, 662
She was fourteen and a half; she'd hanged herself: how had she ever, 274
She would speak of "our relationship" as though it were a thing apart, 232
Slate scraps, split stone, third hand splintering timber; rusted nails and, 412
Snapshots of her grandchildren and great-grandchildren are scattered on, 266

The morning is so gray that the grass is gray and the side of the white, 171
The mummified spider hung in its own web in the rafters striped legs, 475
The name of the horse of my friend's friend, 637
the nations have used up their desire, 60
the not want, 94
The only time, I swear, I ever fell more than abstractly in love with some-, 336
the only way it makes sense, 77
. . . The part where he's telling himself at last the no longer deniable, 254
the pillows are going insane, 72
the president of my country his face flushed, 88
there are people whose sex, 10
There hasn't been any rain, 26
There is a world somewhere else that is unendurable, 19
there's no no like money's, 70
there's no such thing as death everybody, 78
there's somebody who's dying, 83
There was absolutely no reason after the centaur had pawed her and, 415
There was nothing I could have done—, 632
there was this lady once she used to grow, 44
"There were two of them but nobody knew at first because only one hap-, 240
There will always be an issue: doctrine, dogma, differences of con-, 450
The science-fiction movie on the telly in which the world, threatened by, 246
These things that came into my mind, 507
The snow is falling in three directions at once against the sienna brick of, 226
The space within me, within which I partly, or possibly mostly exist, 519
The trouble with me is that whether I get love or not, 24
The way, her father dead a day ago, the child goes in his closet, finds her-, 286
The way, playing an instrument, when you botch a passage you have to, 284
The way boxers postulate a feeling to label that with which they over-, 287
The way it always feels like the early onset of an illness, the viral armies, 285
The way she tells it, they were in the Alps or somewhere, tall, snow-, 246
The way someone stays home, that's all, stays in the house, in the room, 127
The way these days she dresses with more attention to go out to pass the, 337
The way the voice always, always gives it away, even when you weren't, 285
the way we get under cars and in, 40
The way you'd renovate a ruined house, keeping the "shell," as we call it, 511
The whole lower panel of the chain-link fence girdling my old grammar, 192
The whole time I've been walking down the block the public phone at, 274
. . . The word alone sizzles like boiling acid, moans like molten lead, 563
The world's greatest tricycle-rider, 15
They are pounded into the earth, 25
They can be fists punching the water—, 45
They drift unobtrusively into the dream, they linger, then they depart, 367
They hunted lions, they hunted humans, and enslaved them, 616
The young girl jogging in mittens and skimpy gym shorts through a, 242
They're at that stage where so much desire streams between them, so, 276
They're discussing the political situation they've been watching evolve in, 333
They're not quite overdressed, just a bit attentively, flashily for seventy-, 280

When one of my oldest and dearest friends died and another friend, 338
When she's not looking in his eyes, she looks down at his lips, his chin, 277
When she stopped by, just passing, on her way back from picking up the, 238
When the ponies are let out at dusk, they pound across their pasture, 664
When we finally tracked him down, the old man (not really all that very, 261
Where is it where is it where is it in what volume what text what treatise, 618
Where no question possibly remains—someone crying, someone dead—, 262
Wherever Jessie and her friend Maura alight, clouds of young men sud-, 247
which is worse the lieutenant raising his rifle, 62
Why is he wearing a white confirmation suit—he's only about three—on, 280
Why this much fascination with you, little loves, why this what feels like, 544
Willa Selenfriend likes Paul Peterzell better than she likes me and I am, 328
With his shopping cart, his bags of booty and his wine, I'd always found, 311
with huge jowls that wobble with sad o, 16
Without quite knowing it, you sit looking for your past or future in the, 266
Wouldn't it be nice, I think, when the blue-haired lady in the doctor's, 534

You give no hint how shy you really are, so thoroughly your warm and, 247
"You make me sick!" this, with rancor, vehemence, disgust—again, "You, 251
You must never repeat this to him, *but when I started seeing my guru was*, 332
your list of victims dear, 67